CW01020363

Building on Water

To my mother, Greta and Armida

Building on Water

Venice, Holland and the Construction of the European Landscape in Early Modern Times

Salvatore Ciriacono
Translated by Jeremy Scott

Berghahn Books
New York • Oxford

First published in 2006 by

Berghahn Books

www.berghahnbooks.com

© 2006 Salvatore Ciriacono

All rights reserved. Except for the quotation of short passages
for the purposes of criticism and review, no part of this book
may be reproduced in any form or by any means, electronic or
mechanical, including photocopying, recording, or any information
storage and retrieval system now known or to be invented,
without written permission of the publisher.

Library of Congress Cataloging-in-Publication Data

Ciriacono, Salvatore, 1945-
  [Acque e agricoltura English]
  Building on water : Venice, Holland, and the construction of the European
landscape in early modern times / Salvatore Ciriacono.
     p. cm.
  Includes bibliographical reference and index.
  ISBN 1-84545-065-5 (alk. paper)
    1. Reclamation of land--Italy--Venice Region--History. 2. Reclamation
of land--Netherlands--History. 3. Reclamation of land--Europe--History.
4. Hydraulic engineering--Italy--Venice Region--History. 5. Hydraulic
engineering--Netherlands--History. 6. Hydraulic engineering--Europe--History.
I. Title.

S605.2.18C5713 2006
627'.549094531--dc22

                                                          2006042788

British Library Cataloguing in Publication Data

A catalogue record for this book is available from the British Library
Printed in the United States on acid-free paper

ISBN 1-84545-065-5 (hardback)

❧ Contents

❧ List of Maps

❧ Acknowledgements

This work would have been impossible if I had not been able to draw upon the generous research funds of various institutions and the kind collaboration and encouragement of numerous colleagues. Amongst the former I must thank the Italian Consiglio Nazionale delle Ricerche (above all, for the grants for two extended periods of study in Holland and Germany), the Centrum voor Economische Studiën in Louvain, the Max-Planck Institut für Geschichte in Göttingen and the Maison des Sciences de l'Homme in Paris.

As for the method followed here, the comparative approach adopted clearly owes a great deal to the fundamentally-important teachings of Fernand Braudel and the equally fruitful developments upon them by Maurice Aymard. In expressing my personal thanks, my first thoughts go to Luigi De Rosa, Ruggiero Romano and Adriaan Verhulst, recently deceased. Others to whom I am grateful include H. Slicher van Bath, Ad van der Woude, Franz Irsigler, Herman van de Wee, Rudolf Vierhaus, Otto Gerhard Öxle and, especially, Pieter Kriedte of the MPI in Göttingen. Of course, none of them are to be held responsible for the limitations of this book.

For the Dutch section of this book, I also owe special thanks to Beatrijs Augustyn, Cornelis Baars, Greta Devos, Peter W. Klein, Otto Knottnerus, Taeke Stol, and Albert Thurkow, whose advice with regard to bibliography and assistance in the translation of source documents was invaluable.

For the maps and diagrams I am also grateful to Ivano Penzo for his work on the graphics.

List of Official Bodies and Their Functions

Capitanio (or *capitano*)*:* a member of the Venetian nobility serving as military governor of a city of the Republic. The civil and administrative governor was the *podestà*, with the two figures being known as *rettori* (cf.).

College van hoofdingelanden: general assembly of the representatives of various groups (such as property owners and leaseholders) interested in the water management in a Dutch district.

Collegio Solenne alle Acque: formed in 1505, this comprised all the highest officers of the state (the Doge, the Heads of the Council of Ten, the *Savi del Consiglio* and the Procurators of St. Mark's.)

Deputati all'Agricoltura: First elected from within the *Provveditori ai Beni Inculti* in 1768, these two *deputati* were responsible for measures to improve agricultural and herd yields, as well as to introduce scientific/technical innovations.

Dijkgraaf: Dutch chairperson of the water control bodies in managing polders.

Dijkmeester: dike inspector.

Heemraadschap and *Hoogheemraadschap:* Local and regional Water Boards. Water management was and is in the Netherlands in the hands of Water Boards. These are decentralized public authorities with legal responsibilities and are self-supporting financially. They are responsible for flood control, water quantity and water quality. When the *heemraadschappen* extended to embrace larger territories, they became *hoogheemraadschappen*.

Heemraden: together with the *dijkgraaf,* the heemraden were in charge (in the Netherlands) of the day to day management of the local water control body.

Landmeters: land-surveyors.

Maître des digues: official responsible for dike maintainence in France.

Provveditori ai Beni Inculti (or *sopra i Beni Inculti*): Department of Uncultivated Natural Resources. Set up in 1556, this Venetian body was responsible for the irrigation of dry land and the drainage of marshy terrain.

Provveditori all'Adige: first set up to oversee the river Adige in the second half of the sixteenth century and made a permanent body in 1667.

Provveditori alle Biave: from 1365 the *Provveditori alle Biave* (three) controlled the import and distribution of grain inside the Venetian state, fixed prices and had juridical powers.

Provveditori di Comun: this body of three *magistrati* was set up in 1256 to oversee trade and industry, as well as exercise control over the bridges, quaysides, streets and canals within the city. It also regulated the presence of foreigners within Venice.

Provveditori sopra i Beni Comunali: set up in October 1574 to oversee the exploitation of collectively-owned land.

Provveditori sopra i beni inculti del Trevisano e sopra l'adacquatione dei terreni: a special agency set up in 1560 to exploit the uncultivated lands of the Treviso area. Subsequently it would disappear from archive records.

Rason Vecchie (Officiali alle) (and also *alle Rason Nuove*): Venetian *magistratura* (set up as temporary in 1368 and made permanent in 1375) that managed taxes and state assets.

Rettori: city governors in the Venetian Republic. See *capitano*.

Rijkswaterstaat: Dutch department for the maintenance of dikes, roads, canals and bridges; it was set up at the end of eighteenth century during the Napoleonic period (1795).

Savi (three) *ed Esecutori alle Acque* (three): the former were set up in 1501, the latter in 1531. These were not only responsible for the general situation concerning the lagoon but also for work of any complexity involving the rivers that emptied into it – for example, the passing of a new canal bed across an existing river or canal, which could involve the construction of either a 'canal bridge' or of an underground culvert.

Waterschap: Dutch water control body that has the power to enforce water control regulations.

Introduction

Water and Agriculture: Venice, Holland and European Land Reclamation

Water within the Man-Made Environment

This book is the fruit of many years of research, with an initial interest in the agriculture and fluvial system of Venice and its mainland Republic gradually expanding into a study of hydrological management in other areas of Italy and Europe (with particular emphasis on France, Holland and Germany).

In recent years there has been enormous growth in attention to all the various aspects of water as a natural resource, not only with regard to agricultural uses (one of the key concerns behind the irrigation and drainage policies that form a fundamental part of this book), but also with regard to the environment in general. Innumerable publications and conferences have been dedicated to questions as diverse as urban water supplies, water-powered machines, the professions and trades linked with water, water as a source of energy, the science of hydraulics, the role of water in health and personal hygiene, and even the psychological perception of water in the human consciousness. Though the range of contributions to such discussions, at both a European and international level, might give the impression that the area dealt with in this book is excessively restricted, I have maintained the focus within this revised English version on agriculture and economic questions in general, taking the view that the issues of irrigation, land reclamation and the exploitation of water by manufacturing industries are of fundamental importance. True, there is often the tendency to see such manufacturing uses as limited to pre-industrial economies; but to see the dangerous generalisation behind such a notion one simply has to recall the serious environmental threat

1

posed when, in the torrid summer of 2003, the water coolant in French nuclear power stations began to reach temperatures of 40° or 50°C.

As already mentioned, the starting-point – and the constant term of comparison – for this study of water management within Europe is Venice and its mainland territories. As the research of recent years has so clearly demonstrated, Venice provides a particularly rich example of the use of water not only for irrigation but also as a resource for manufacturing industries; in effect, one might say that in both the Veneto itself and the Lombardy areas it was this exploitation of water which laid the basis for the agricultural and economic development of the area over the last few decades of the twentieth century.

A full analysis of this role obviously requires even fuller study of the complex history of the region, so there is a lot more research to do, particularly with regard to comparative studies of irrigation within the Mediterranean basin.

One area that certainly requires fuller study is that of the *regadío* in Spain, where water played a key role in a number of dry regions which were practically forced to opt for extensive land-use since – unlike the fertile Valencia, for example – they were unable to establish *huertas* and citrus fruit orchards. As Macías Hernández's study of the Canary Islands has illustrated, water would also play a key role in the development of the Atlantic economy and modern colonialism: on the Canaries themselves, it was essential to the establishment of a plant that is almost synonymous with early colonialism – sugar cane – and hence became part of a network of international interests (not least amongst which were those of Italian investment capital). In effect, within this very specific habitat water became the key determinant of social and economic hierarchies, a commodity that generated a market which existed parallel to – and independent of – the land market. The distortions in the management of agricultural concerns which resulted from this state of affairs were to have clear social and economic consequences: in various areas of the Mediterranean – in Spain at Alicante, Elche and Novelda; in Sicily at Palermo[1] – the existence of water as a distinct market commodity could lead to the economic value of this natural resource actually outstripping that of land itself. Those who merely owned land but did not control supplies of water were pushed to sidelines of the economic hierarchy and practically excluded from the processes of production, with the inevitable result that they were quickly forced to cede their property to those who could more profitably exploit it.[2]

Be they of Arab creation or dug as part of the reform-driven push towards rapid modernisation in the eighteenth-century,[3] drainage and irrigation canals played no less important a role within Spain itself, even if the full extent of their influence on the social and economic development of the country still requires study in greater depth. In such arid areas as the Iberian peninsula or the southern regions of Italy, irrigation was of dramatic effect; but even within the Venetian Republic its advent served to mark the beginning of an 'agricultural revolution' or – if one considers such terms as 'revolution' to be both misleading and excessively theoretical – made it possible to start tackling previous inadequacies in development. As has been so clearly illustrated by the likes of Kerridge and Morineau (in his *Faux-semblants d'un démarrage économique*, Paris, 1971), this eighteenth-century 'revolution' in agriculture was not as straightforward as it may seem, and still requires careful analysis. However, for all these reservations, it undeniably opened the way to agricultural progress during the course of the century. Not only in Venice but also in France and other areas of Europe, it was only through these changes in technology, social organisation and methods of production that one could break free from an 'under-nourishment trap' within which agricultural productivity was barely sufficient to feed the rural and urban populations, who during the course of the eighteenth century were slowly recovering from the demographic stagnation of the seventeenth.

A comparison with neighbouring Lombardy is an essential benchmark for understanding what was happening in the Venetian Republic, even if in this period – from the sixteenth to eighteenth centuries – Lombardy itself hardly enjoyed the levels of agricultural productivity and crop yields that one sees in the areas of north-eastern Europe. However, whilst such international comparisons help us understand the role of water in the different economies of the continent, they should not be made without due account being taken of the specific characteristics of each individual context, where the differences in national or regional agricultures are to be seen not only in the size and degree of specialisation in peasant farms, but also in the social classes that played a role in the transformation of agriculture (be they *métayers* and *dessicateurs* in France, commoners and undertakers in England, or *Polder-Fürsten* and *Fehntjer* in Germany). Whilst the research in this book is profoundly influenced by the comparative approach championed by Braudel and the French school of historiography, I am also convinced that it is only through detailed study of individual regions that one can bring out the full nature of the transformations that took place within the various states of Europe and the achievements that resulted from them. When faced with water as a threat and peril, or as positive resource to be used in irrigation and the generation of power, the regions of Europe reacted differently; and those differences – the result of a mix of social, institutional and mental factors – can only be understood from the 'inside', by illustrating the distinctive features of each regional or national context.

Water Use within the Venetian Republic

There is no doubt that developments in land drainage and irrigation not only played a key role in the recovery and cultivation of agricultural land, but also represent one of the essential ways in which mankind has exploited water as a resource. Put to such use, water not only increased agricultural productivity, it also contributed to the growth of the urban and rural population as well as to the development of manufacturing processes and, thence, industrialisation proper (even then, its role was not entirely taken over by steam-power). As is well known, the notion of the 'proto-industrial' implies a specific approach to the question of the original accumulation of capital within the agricultural sector and its subsequent transfer to the industrial; it has even been pointed out that some areas developed as centres of proto-industrial or industrial activity precisely because they were poor in agriculture. However, whilst accepting the value of the proto-industrial as an area of research, I am convinced that development within a society and economy – for example, those of Venice in the crucial period from the sixteenth to the eighteenth century – is to be understood in relation to the transformations and improvements being made in its agriculture.

As I have tried to illustrate in the second chapter of this book, the use of water in the Alpine foothills certainly stimulated proto-industrial activities that had a profound effect upon the subsequent industrial development of the Veneto mainland: one need only think of the small- and large-scale industrial concerns located in the various foothill valleys of an area that ranges from Bergamo, through Brescia and Vicenza to Friuli. A study of water concessions, especially from the second half of the seventeenth century onwards, reveals the emergence of not only a proto-industrial Veneto but also one in which there were a number of different sub-regional economies (with the differences being due to pedological and orographical factors that had a direct influence on types of settlement and size of agricultural concerns). On the one hand, one sees the emergence of a river-plain agriculture which used water to extend rice fields, irrigate pastures and cultivate arable land; on the other, one sees within the foothill valleys themselves an almost spontaneous focus on subsistence agriculture and on manufacturing activities that exploited the abundant supplies of timber, wood, coal and hydraulic power.

Even viewed within the context of Europe as a whole, the series of water concessions granted by Venice's *Provveditori ai Beni Inculti* [Office for Uncultivated Natural Resources] provides us with a remarkably rich source of information; the detailed accounts of which areas of land were irrigated provides a very full picture of agricultural conditions within the Veneto and of the wide range of uses to which water resources were being put. This detailed information has made it possible to trace trends which developed over centuries, putting forward possible interpretations and drawing up tables that chart the developments in the use of rice fields, pasture, arable land, market gardening, mills and other machinery powered by water. For all its incompleteness, the picture that emerges from these fiscal documents provides a useful account of a very complex situation.

The scale of water-use by the manufacturing activities within Venice itself confirms not only the city's expansion during the sixteenth century but also underlines the importance of land reclamation, which historians of the Republic have long stressed. Figures reveal the clear existence of a depression of the seventeenth century; but they also show that the crisis which loomed in the second half of that century was largely avoided. This picture bears out the conclusions reached by more recent historians, both in Italy and elsewhere, that the seventeenth century should perhaps be seen as more than simply the 'century of crisis', given its real contribution to the reorganisation of urban, regional and rural economies.

Undoubtedly, the crisis, as noted in the cities of the late sixteenth century, did lead to a focus on extra-urban territory, where the populations of the countryside or of small to medium-sized towns could provide labour at costs lower than those imposed by powerful city guilds. Hence, the crisis of the seventeenth century might be read as the reorganisation/redistribution of an urban economy throughout an entire region. Certainly, one example of this process can be seen in Venice, which, during the sixteenth century, had enjoyed the status of a 'world-economy' but now saw a clear drop in its standing not only within the international economy but also within the more restricted context of its own mainland State.

Still, even if stagnation in the first half of the seventeenth century was followed in the second half by the redistribution of productive activity that accompanied a slight up-turn in the economy, there is no denying that the really extraordinary achievements, in terms both of capital investment and technological innovation, had come in the sixteenth century.

In the case of the Venetian Republic, land reclamation was seen as playing an essential role in the recovery of new terrain; and such schemes would be all the more incisive if they were carried out not by individuals within single estates but envisaged within the framework provided by an articulated network of canals (as had been the case in Lombardy since the Middle Ages). The results achieved are clear in the observations and comments left by travellers and agronomists, especially in the eighteenth century – think, for example, of Arthur Young or Jérôme de la Lande. However, having described the great number of small and large waterways which cut across the plain of the Veneto and complement the economic role of such rivers as the Adige or the Brenta – providing both transportation for goods and irrigation for land and rice fields – these same observers, whose impartiality there is no reason to doubt, then immediately make mention of the denser network of canals and channels within Lombardy, some of which dated from as early as the twelfth century.

An even more striking contrast is with the hydrographical system of Holland, where the system of canals was not only fully exploited along capitalistic lines to provide transport for goods and passengers, but was also closely interwoven with an equally rational and modern network of urban development. In the Veneto, the waterways provided a system of transport that was of nowhere near the same scale or economic significance, for all that numerous watercourses in the region were put to use. More recent studies have explored various aspects of the rivers of the Veneto – the Brenta, the Brentella (which runs off the Piave in the Treviso area), the Battaglia canal in the Padua area, the Sile, and the whole system of rivers linked with the Venetian lagoon (the Adige is the river that has perhaps attracted most attention from historians of the Venetian Republic)[4]. The overall picture which emerges is one of a Veneto where economic practices were much more conservative and limited than in the more dynamic, aggressively capitalistic Holland.

In effect, what Venice was lacking was an agriculture that fully exploited its water resources to boost fodder production, increase herd size and thus achieve higher agricultural yields. For example, comparison with the Waas region of western Flanders – which English travellers of the eighteenth century cited as the most fertile area in Europe – is hardly flattering for the Venetian Republic (even though, to be fair, it should be pointed out that Lombardy itself, the Italian region which enjoyed the highest levels of investment and yield, would not fare much better in such a comparison). Obviously climate played a part here, with the high rainfall of the Waas, as of many other regions in northern Europe, making livestock herds more profitable and increasing levels of agricultural production. What is more, such achievements must also be seen in relation to how the property was run, the level of investment in it, and the types of contract enjoyed by farmers. It would be a mistake to see everything in terms of 'capitalist investment' and ignore those forms of high-intensity labour that were as essential in the *land van Waas* as they were elsewhere. However, having made those caveats, one cannot deny that historical analysis of agricultural development in the Venetian Republic, and its links with projects of irrigation and drainage, reveal how this area lagged behind the standards of agricultural progress being achieved in the heart of Western Europe: in Holland, Flanders, England, and northern France.

The limits that explain and the characteristics that define this 'shortfall' have long been described by a number of historians – most significantly, by Marino Berengo, Daniele Beltrami, and Ruggiero Romano – and their theses are borne out by the detailed research offered in this book. However, the overall picture that emerges is not one of outright catastrophe or of irreversible decline from the sixteenth to the seventeenth century. True, the expansion in irrigation and in the areas of rice cultivation that had continued during the sixteenth century ground to a halt in the first decades of the seventeenth. But it is also true that there was an upturn in the areas of rice fields and irrigated pasture-land in the second half of the century, with this positive trend being further consolidated from the 1730s onwards (something which can also be seen in many other areas of Europe). As has already been pointed out, research seems to confirm this revaluation of the last decades of the seventeenth century, to some extent qualifying all those interpretations that stress solely the expansion of the eighteenth (often more quantitative than qualitative). As in Morineau's analysis (Paris, 1971) of the situation in France, there seems to have been an undoubted increase in production, which went to maintain a concomitant increase in population[5]; but in the Veneto there was also insufficient expansion of irrigated pasture and fodder production, with no development at all in livestock breeding or in agronomic techniques. In effect, entrepreneurial initiative in the countryside seems to have been weak.

Eighteenth-century land reclamation is itself not a story of continual successes. In fact, as one proceeds from the sixteenth to the eighteenth century, the picture becomes less and less encouraging overall. From the point of view of quantity, the data gathered in this book suggests that one should not underestimate the amount of syndicate land reclaimed through drainage from the sixteenth century onwards; such operations never came to a complete stop, and would themselves enjoy an upturn in the seventeenth/eighteenth century. However, the decline of these syndicates – their debts, the conflict within them and the relations of production they implied – meant that the picture for the eighteenth century is far from being one of rapid consolidation: the finances and administration of these consortia were in the hands of a class that was either incapable of or indifferent to meeting the challenges posed by water resources and watercourses which in the Veneto – as in other countries of Europe – were never fully tamed and subjugated.

Reconciling the demands of the lagoon and its port with those of the mainland was an even more delicate affair. It would seem to be the case that perfect balance between these two components of a complex hydro-geological system would not be achieved until after the end of the Republic: in the nineteenth and twentieth centuries, not only had the terms of the problem changed, but so had the relation between Venice and the mainland. The period of Austrian rule is, therefore, very important here, as is the predominance of agricultural – and later, industrial – interests over those commercial considerations that had always been of paramount importance for the Republic[6]; though, of course, one cannot deny the decline that would take place during the course of the nineteenth century, or the grave consequences of industrial development on the mainland areas of the lagoon in the twentieth. With regard to this latter point, however, I would argue that whilst Venetian patricians must, right up to the fall of the Republic, be given full credit for their far-sighted policy concerning the protection of the lagoon, this policy is revealed to be far less laudable when one looks at the problems and environmental instability that continued to exist just beyond the shores of the lagoon throughout the eighteenth century.

Perhaps the champions of Venice's achievements as a *civilisation d'eau* might reply that focus on these failures is excessive; however, whilst archive sources amply document the successes achieved in the arduous task of maintaining a stable relationship between land and water, one should not forget the technological difficulties encountered during the seventeenth and eighteenth centuries. This was the period in which the Dutch would establish their supremacy in the field throughout Europe, whilst Italian hydraulics – which all agree laid the basis for modern hydrostatics – were overtaken by the more advanced research being carried out in France. As in other areas of social or economic life, the absence within Italy of a unifying centre such as Paris or London had a detrimental effect upon the financing and organisation of science. Limited financial resources would have a constrictive effect even on the cultural policies of such States as the Venetian Republic and Tuscany, which had a long-standing tradition of intellectual research (in the Veneto, the continuing openness of cities such as Venice, Padua and Verona to outside influence and input does not seem to have made much difference). The final verdict with regard to the effective place of Italian science within the Europe of the day thus becomes a very delicate one. Though cultural exchange and the reading of scientific papers continued to maintain a link between the old Italian States and the major international centres of research, one cannot deny the diminishing importance of Italian scientists in general; it was the more ambitious cultural policies being pursued outside Italy that were generating dynamic research. However, having said that, it is also true that these centuries saw the continuation of a fascinating historical and scientific tradition, within which eighteenth-century scientists like Giovanni Poleni and Simone Stratico find a place alongside fifteenth/sixteenth-century technicians Marco Cornaro and Cristoforo Sabbadino, and such late-seventeenth/early-eighteenth-century figures as Domenico Guglielmi and Bernardino Zendrini. Figures of some importance, none of whom should be seen as lagging behind the forefront of European research into the 'science of water'.

Holland and Venice: *civilisations d'eau*

The starting-point for this work was my collaboration on the extensive research project behind the *Storia della Cultura Veneta*[7] (indeed, the essays I contributed to it were subsequently incorporated within this book). However, other – no less stimulating – works played a part in the later chapters. I am indebted to Ruggiero Romano for his insistence that one cannot understand the problems of the Venetian lagoon and water management on the terra firma unless one looks at Holland. In effect, it is only by looking at what this relatively small nation achieved in the fields of territorial planning – and the use of water resources therein – that one can understand the original, even if less influential, achievements of the Venetian *civilisation d'eau*.

There can be no doubt that, from the Middle Ages onwards, these were the two regions most intensely involved in the struggle with and regulation of inland and coastal waters. For the Dutch, the raising of *terpen* (mounds on which the population could take refuge during floods) and the building of dikes (initially as river embankments, rather than as a means of reclaiming land for agriculture) were measures predicated on the simple need to survive – just as the fortunes of Venice would have been unthinkable without measures to control the flow of the rivers into the lagoon and protect inhabited islands against the tides of the Adriatic. More than any other European nations, these two States reveal a profound link with water throughout their history, and thus fully merit definition as *civilisations d'eau*.

It seems to have been the case that, from both a technological and institutional point of view, during the Middle Ages it was *civitas Venetiarum* that was more efficient than the Low Countries in dealing with the problems posed by water; this superiority appears particularly marked when one looks at the northern Low Countries, where Amsterdam was far from playing the fundamental role it would have in the seventeenth and eighteenth century. Nevertheless, one must look at the history of this medieval period – as recounted in the works of Fockema Andreae, Korthals Altes, Beekman, van der Linden and Verhulst – if one wants to grasp the original nature of what was happening in the Low Countries from the eleventh century onwards. The first question that comes to mind is why the peoples from the German interior should even have thought of settling in an area of wind-blown marshland which was exposed to frequent flooding by both river and sea (primarily the former). The answer, as offered by van der Linden (1984), starts from considerations of geography to then include questions of social history: in effect, the various populations coalesced into a settled nation precisely because they had to face a common enemy, water. However, another no less influential circumstance was that the feudal lords of the region (the Counts of Holland, above all) were so intent on settling these areas that they granted greater freedom to the settlers, who thus formed closely-bound communities that enjoyed a much higher degree of liberty than the rural populations of Germany. Throughout Dutch history one would see shared community values prevailing over the conflictual tendencies and the urge to domination that would – under a veneer of paternalism – become characteristics of the Venetian Republic.

A second difference between the two States would come in the seventeenth century, when Venice's balance of trade took a downturn and that of the Republic of the Seven United Provinces improved. In such a situation, when Venice was playing a more and more marginal role in the international economy, it was perhaps inevitable – or at least understandable, from a strategic point of view – that the State and its ruling class should fall back upon social and economic conservatism. Here, the existence of an extensive but weakly-organised workforce within the countryside also worked to the advantage of the Venetian patricians, who within the expanding agricultural concerns of their country estates could impose the pay and conditions that suited them.

On the other hand, the international situation of the Low
Countries during the course of the seventeenth century was much
more auspicious. Being able to count on the grain from the Baltic,
Dutch agricultural entrepreneurs could focus on more remunerative
specialist crops and on the raising of dairy herds. This extension of
farmland, together with the exercise of efficient hydro-geological
control of territory, was to play a key role in laying the basis for
Holland's status as a 'world economy'. Dutch historians have spoken
here of a 'mud-based industry' to describe the growing number of
patents and technical improvements involving the various
components of the windmill (waterwheels, Archimedes' screw, sails,
rotating blade mounts, internal mechanisms) which were an
essential feature of the 'Golden Age' enjoyed by seventeenth-century
Holland, when the nation established its superiority not only in
comparison to Venice but also to most other European States.[8]

One can also see a difference between Holland and Venice in the
very approach taken to the infinite problems posed by water: whilst
in the latter – as in the other States of Italy – there was lively interest
in the scientific and theoretical problems posed by hydraulics, the
Dutch approach was much more practical, focusing on the
construction of hydraulic structures and machinery, and the digging
of canals, rather than the publication of learned memoranda or
theoretical studies concerning the movement or nature of water. Not
that Holland was lacking in lively debates of ideas regarding
practical questions – see, for example, the various projects put
forward for the drainage of the famous Harlemmermeer in the first
decades of the seventeenth century – but the broad picture which
emerges is still that of a practical approach to the age-old questions
raised by the relationship between man and water. The inconclusive
theoretical debates that absorbed ever more energy and time within
the Venetian Republic were largely avoided. The end result was the
creation of an agrarian landscape that has become the very symbol
of the country: a geometrical network of canals and dikes, a
constellation of windmills whose power is put to the most varied
uses, and massive sea-walls. These latter can serve as protection
against even the most violent seas – think, for example of the
Deltawerk along the coast of Zeeland – and also help to regulate the
flow of rivers into the seas; through a skilful mix of hydraulic science

and chemistry, they can even play a direct role in agriculture, being used to control the saline content of soil.

During the course of the sixteenth and seventeenth centuries, clashes between vested interests, and differences with regard to the technological solutions to be adopted, did not prevent the *Serenissima* from protecting the key to its own power: the port of Venice and its lagoon. However, by the following century, government indecision, disputes and increasingly limited funds resulted in an inability to completely dominate a unique and highly-delicate hydro-geographical system. Though occurring in different periods, the case of the Brenta at the end of the eighteenth century – when interminable discussions as to the project to be adopted at a key section of the river ultimately came to nothing – and the endless debate within modern-day Venice regarding the use of mobile sea defences, both seem to me to indicate the degree to which Venice has slipped from its former pre-eminence in such fields.

Nevertheless, to some extent the economic and agricultural situation within the two Republics would develop in a similar fashion; and for at least part of the eighteenth century, tendencies within them seemed to have run parallel. In effect, the sharp distinction that historians usually draw between a *rentier* patrician class in Venice and an entrepreneurial class in the Dutch countryside would seem to have become more attenuated in the economic crisis of the eighteenth century. In both cases, there was a fall back on land rents; from the end of the seventeenth century, both the *regenten* and the urban elites in Holland reveal the same tendency to 'live off' rather than 'invest in' the countryside, when – together with the drop in agricultural profits – the fall in the price of grain and, to a lesser extent, that of dairy products led to a reluctance to invest further in undertakings such as land reclamation, which had once been profitable but had now become more risky. As in Venice, the capital that had formerly been invested in agriculture was now channelled into other areas of the economy (though the actual route it took has yet to be fully identified). At the same time, both States were meeting the need to replace their wooden sea defences with stone structures; and here they were helped by the fact that the situation within the agricultural sector towards the end of the eighteenth century seemed much more encouraging.

Political, Socio-Economic and Environmental Factors

Though parallels emerge in a direct comparison of the two Republics, the contrast between them becomes abundantly clear when one looks at them in the wider context of Europe as a whole, where the influence of Dutch technicians was decisive. The role of such figures in water management and land-reclamation projects throughout Europe is a significant complement to achievements within Holland.

The Dutch influence was not only at the level of capital investment and technology (its engineers being much appreciated throughout Europe); it also made itself felt through successful waves of migration and settlement from the Middle Ages onwards. These were a response to population increase (within Flanders or the northern Low Countries), to religious persecution at home, or perhaps explicit invitations from princes or States for settlers to come and farm previously uncultivated land. As an eighteenth-century French source argued, who better than the Dutch to carry out work for which they were renowned: the tough job of reclaiming marshy or swampy terrain?

Such colonisation and settlement went together with the exploitation of peat deposits, which were particularly rich in northern Europe and themselves attracted investment of urban capital. The result there was poor-standard agriculture that went hand-in-hand with peat-digging. This latter activity, both in Holland and in the regions of northern Germany, was controlled by private companies; but behind this capitalist organisation of investment one glimpses a particularly grim social situation, with what is at times outright exploitation of these very special kinds of farmer/labourers.

Another area on which this book aims to throw light is the relation between private capital and the State in the history of European land reclamation. There is no doubt that during the Dutch 'Golden Age' private companies were the main source for channelling capital towards the drainage of marshy areas, both within Holland itself and elsewhere in Europe. However, according to Thurkow (1990), even in Holland the State played no irrelevant role in furthering land-reclamation projects; in fact, when there was a downturn in the economy and speculative capital began to lose interest in drainage projects, the State's role increased in inverse proportion to that of private investors.

And within German principalities, the range of action of the State was no less extensive, even if – especially when economic conditions were favourable – private companies also played a role that can hardly be dismissed as secondary. Obviously, like the nation itself at the time, the history of land reclamation and drainage within Germany presents us with a composite picture. Whilst the rulers and local lords of the North Sea coasts (the *Polder-Fürsten*) appear to have been more open to market forces and to have encouraged the influx of foreign investors and technicians, the Hohenzollerns of Prussia – and the political class that worked under them – intervened much more directly in the processes of settlement and land reclamation. And Bavaria, in the south, seems to have followed a policy that lies halfway between the two. However, this point requires further research; German historians do not seem to be as interested in these questions as they might be.

Historical geographers, on the other hand, have made a great contribution to the study of the questions of land drainage, soil fertility and the reclamation of previously under-used terrain. And it is the questions they raise – together with those that come within the scope of ecology and climatology – which historians should address in their own research. This is no less true with regard to France, where geographers such Vidal de la Blache, Numa Broc and Paul Wagret – together with the more regionally-focused Pierre George, Paul Masson, J.A. Barral – have for some time being producing abundant material for further reflection. However, economic history has not always taken full advantage of this, revealing itself to be rather sketchy in its judgements (and even knowledge) of the numerous inland and coastal marshy areas of France that were the subject of an enormous number of publications during the course of the eighteenth century. It seems that more in-depth archive research focused on individual areas – such as that carried out by Jean-Laurent Rosenthal, Jean-Michel Derex, Patrick Fournier and others – will make a fundamental contribution to our knowledge of the history of French agriculture and the French economy. As for the latter, whilst it may have drawn on Dutch capital and enterprise at the beginning of the seventeenth century, it is also true that by the end of that century it was following an exclusively national course, which was however detrimental to agricultural development as a whole. In effect, France ultimately revealed a regional individualism and levels of local conflict that would hinder many projects involving irrigation, navigable waterways and land reclamation.

The situation in England alone could be taken as the testing-ground for the theoretical premises put forward in this book – that is, the thesis that the reclamation of marshy or under-used land, as well as the irrigation of terrain suitable for improvement, was one of the most important ways in which capitalism penetrated into the countryside (quite as important as the much-discussed question of 'enclosures'). In England, the social problems latent in any speculative process of land reclamation might find violent expression. Popular revolt, the breaking of dikes, a clash of both ideology and agronomy that found an echo in the debates of Parliament – all of these would turn out to be thorns in the side of the various companies concerned (initially made up of Dutch investors, these later brought together the various social classes – City, financiers and merchants, large landowners, courtiers and the monarchy itself – who wanted to put an end to subsistence agriculture managed at a communal level).

Another point to be mentioned is how economic and agricultural progress throughout Europe brought with it a desire for a new equilibrium between man and his environment, first and foremost in terms of health and hygiene. Local authorities were continually pressuring central government to drain swampy marshland that was a source of malaria and other diseases; although such schemes did not always prove as effective as was hoped. This is an aspect of the question of water management that is not dealt with very extensively in this book, so one can understand the criticism that it is rather naive to praise the economic progress brought about by land reclamation whilst ignoring its not always positive environmental results.[9] In effect, a hydro-geological scheme always results in an at least partial modification of a given environment; and technical solutions favoured in one period – for example, the towpaths built along the Loire in the sixteenth century, or the various diversion cuts (*diversivi*) created in the Veneto in the seventeenth and eighteenth centuries – may turn out later to be either inadequate or positively harmful.

Returning to France, there is another question that the authorities had to face in the eighteenth century: land reclamation might led to the recovery of extensive tracts of land, but it also destroyed the livelihood of the hunters and fisherman who lived in those marshy areas, earning more than simple peasants (and thus very reluctant to start working the land). This may be true, but the fact of the matter is that agricultural interests – and policies aimed at eliminating areas that were frequently breeding-grounds of malaria – would over the centuries reveal themselves to have a far from indifferent political and economic influence. Ultimately, their advantages outweighed their drawbacks. And while questions of environmental preservation – the maintenance of the hydro-geological features of a specific natural habitat – have in recent years become a very urgent issue, there is no doubt that in the Early Modern period they were viewed very differently. What is more, whilst the safeguarding of such an environmental equilibrium requires the adoption of ever more advanced techniques and technology, it can also result in a veritable situation of deadlock. It is perhaps significant here that by the end of the eighteenth century Dutch windmills – along with the technology they employed – were revealing their limits in dealing with the increasingly unmanageable hydraulic situations to be found in many areas of Europe. A perfect example of that technological 'impasse' which Braudel (1992) also identifies in contemporary technology.

Notes

1. Glick, *Irrigation and Society in Medieval Valencia*, pp. 12–13; H. Bresc, 'Les jardins de Palerme (1290–1460)', p. 60: water here is private property, alienated 'à perpétuité et dont les propriétaires louent chaque année l'usage' [in perpetuity, with landowners paying annual hire for its use].
2. Macías Hernández, 'Les Îles Canaries, 1480–1525. Irrigation et première colonisation atlantique: le domaine de l'eau', in *Eau et développement*, Ciriacono ed., pp. 37–48.
3. G. Pérez Sarrión, 'Hydraulic Policy and Irrigation Works in Spain in the Second Half of Eighteenth-Century', in *The Journal of European Economic History*, 24 (1995), pp. 131–43.
4. *Il Sile*, A. Bondesan, G. Caniato, D. Gasparini, F. Vallerai and M. Zanetti eds., Verona, 1998; *Il Piave*, A. Bondesan, G. Caniato, F. Vallerai and M. Zanetti eds., Verona, 2000; *Il Brenta*, A. Bondesan, G. Caniato, D. Gasparini, F. Vallerani and M. Zanetti eds., Verona, 2003.
5. Morineau, *Les faux-semblants d'un démarrage économique: agriculture et démographie en France au XVIIIe siécle*.

6. Ciriacono, 'Le bonifiche venete alla caduta della Repubblica e al tempo di Pietro Paleocapa', pp. 317–40.

7. Idem, 'Scrittori d'idraulica e politica delle acque', in *Storia della cultura veneta. Dal primo Quattrocento al concilio di Trento*, Arnaldi and Pastore Stocchi eds., 3/II, 1980, pp. 491–512; idem 'L'idraulica veneta: scienza, agricoltura e difesa del territorio dalla prima alla seconda rivoluzione scientifica', in *Storia della cultura veneta. Dalla controriforma alla fine della Repubblica. Il Settecento*, Arnaldi and Pastore Stocchi eds., 5/II, 1986, pp. 347–78.

8. Israel, *Dutch Primacy in World Trade, 1585–1740*.

9. Cf. for example, Paolo Squatriti's review in *Technology and Culture*, 41 (2004), pp. 368–70.

Chapter 1

Water and Agricultural Production in the Venetian Terra Firma in the Sixteenth and Seventeenth Centuries

Irrigation and Land Reclamation

It is now generally accepted that, in both ancient and modern societies, the mastery of water – as either a resource or a threat – is one of the essential premises for the establishment of state institutions, with work on irrigation canals and protective dikes influencing social hierarchies and stimulating economic development. No less important a factor in productive activity than land or labour, water has always revealed the interplay of social relations and environment, with development obviously being conditioned by access to this finite resource. Adopting the terminology of Fernand Braudel, one might therefore define the environment as a whole as an *ensemble des ensembles* in which the various social agents contend for available resources (water undoubtedly being one of the most important), the degree of their success depending upon the relative power they can exert. Hence, water has long been the object of disputes. These range from its purely agricultural use (in irrigation and drainage); its use as a source of power (for the waterwheels drove mills, fulling machines, jacks, paper mills and the whole range of varied machinery that existed in the era preceding the Industrial Revolution); its use as a domestic urban resource (water supplies for cities).

If one is to focus exclusively upon agricultural uses, one initial methodological consideration emerges immediately: can one really talk about irrigation in isolation from land reclamation? The notion of 'integrated land reclamation' as developed a few decades ago would seem to make it clear that one cannot. For agronomists, drainage does not involve simply digging canals to 'carry off excess water', it also means using that excess for efficient irrigation of the land reclaimed. In effect, irrigation is 'essentially a part – a very important part – of the overall plan of integrated land reclamation'.[1] And within the Venetian Republic itself, the term 'land reclamation' (*bonifica*) covered both the drainage and consolidation of marshy land and the irrigation of dry, gravelly terrain. Given this, it would be arbitrary to analyse irrigation within the Veneto without taking a detailed look at the various land-reclamation consortia which emerged during the sixteenth century – the period of greatest expansion – and then continued to be active through the first decade of the seventeenth.[2] However, one should make some initial comments here. Land reclamation, in the wider sense just used, was a practice that emerged rather late. And if it is true that the 'mandate' of Venetian *Provveditori ai Beni Inculti* [Department of Uncultivated Natural Resources] considered irrigation of dry land and drainage of marshy terrain as two aspects of the same process, it is also true that for a long time agricultural practice kept the two procedures well distinct from each other (depending upon the immediate requirements dictated by the nature of the terrain being dealt with).

Nevertheless by the seventeenth century this process of 'integrated' land reclamation – in the Republic of Venice and elsewhere – was primarily concerned with the recovery of marshy or ill-drained land. 'Reclamation' was intended not so much to boost agricultural productivity as to find some agricultural use for marginal – and frequently malaria-infested – terrain, the authorities' main concern perhaps being to remove the health risks that infested marshy areas posed to the urban centres situated nearby. However, overall I would argue that in the majority of cases the main considerations were agricultural and economic – as one can see from the fact that there was intense work on traditional land reclamation schemes in the river-plain areas of the Veneto, while irrigation work in the foothills and upland areas tended to be ignored.[3]

Nevertheless, even within the areas most affected by land reclamation (primarily the Po valley and delta regions), irrigation work was rather scarce as it clashed with the interests of those whose prime concern was to see excess surface water removed. The same paradoxical insufficiency of irrigation can be seen throughout the lowland areas of the Veneto: in the region of Treviso, for example,

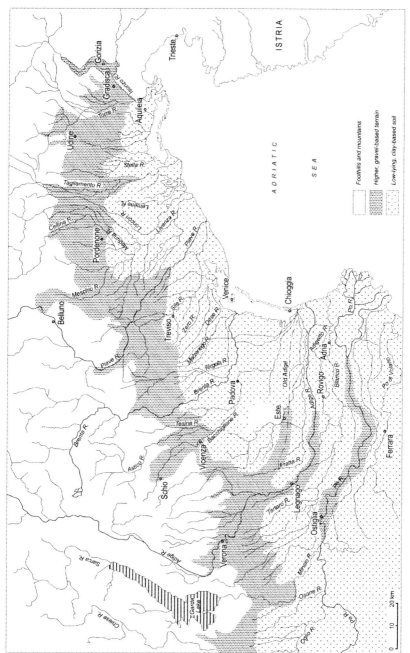

Map 1. Variations of Terrain within the Veneto. Source: C. Grinovero, *Ricerche sull'economia dell'irrigazione. Risultati economici delle irrigazioni nel Veneto*, II, Rome-Milan, 1933, Plate XXXII (simplified).

herd grazing was quite extensive but a 1646 census of the territory of the commune reveals that out of 125,123 *campi* of grazing pasture a total of 53,667 were not irrigated. And even in the Verona and Vicenza areas, although there were irrigation projects, they did not have the direct impact upon livestock farming which they had been intended to. In 1555, for example, Verona declared that it could not supply Venice with the livestock quota that had been imposed in 1529 (1,000 head of cattle) and had to turn to the nearby Mantua region for sizeable supplies of fodder. In 1573, grasslands accounted for little more than 13 per cent of all the terrain recorded in the census of the Verona and Vicenza areas, whilst in the area below Padua that figure fell as low as 6 per cent, and dropped even further in the foothills around Treviso (3.3 per cent). Although by 1618 grasslands and meadows in the Vicenza area accounted for 18.5 per cent, in the Padua area at the beginning of the eighteenth century they still only accounted for 9.9 per cent of the total land dedicated to the production of cereal crops.[4] As Marino Berengo has pointed out, such inadequacies in the production of fodder and the raising of beef are ultimately 'the result of all the defects to be seen in the agriculture of the Veneto under the Republic'.[5] The debate over the reasons for this failure to develop livestock herds has long occupied scholars. Ugo Tucci is, however, probably right when he suggests 'the availability of reasonably cheap livestock supplies from Hungary [...] discouraged farmers within the Veneto from investing in herds, given that this would have meant sacrificing areas that might be used for cereal crops or, in certain zones, laid out with mulberry plantations – both of which were much more profitable'.[6]

So, whilst the focus upon the draining of lowland or marshy areas is perfectly understandable, it did – from an agronomic point of view – lead to a totally mistaken evaluation of the advantages/disadvantages of irrigation. In 1788 the *Deputati all'Agricoltura* were still expressing perplexity – if not outright opposition – with regard to the irrigation of the Padua area, which – they argued – was unsuitable because a large part of the terrain there was clayey, an obviously erroneous judgement which failed to take into account the fact that one can adjust times/duration of irrigation to qualities of soil type. Whilst not denying that irrigation might be useful for other types of crop, the *Deputati* insisted that its result here would be excessive humidity that would have a detrimental effect upon the quantity and quality of grasses and turn meadow-lands into swamps. The rather paradoxical result of all this were still to be seen in the recent past: with the exception of the Rovigo area, in the 1930s all the various zones of the Veneto were still a long way from meeting the needs of modern irrigated agriculture. Important works of drainage had been carried out, but there was no counterpart in irrigation, and hence agriculture had remained largely extensive rather than intensive. With its 266,000 hectares requiring irrigation and only 1,000 hectares requiring drainage, the Padua area in the 1930s is clearly the one which most strikingly demonstrates the long-term contradictions within these attitudes to the two main aspects of land reclamation.[7]

The more perceptive agronomists of the sixteenth and seventeenth centuries were aware that irrigation not only increased the value of land[8] but could also result in an increment in average annual output from some 20 to 500 per cent, depending upon soil quality.[9] Development would have been very different if greater account had been taken of the role water could play in increasing output in a whole range of crops: maize, legumes (sedge, clover, vetch and sainfoin), vines (as long as sparingly irrigated), fruit orchards, rice, vegetables, mulberry, tobacco, beets and wheat.[10] However, it is an almost impossible task to give an even approximate quantification of agricultural 'productivity' during these centuries: documentation is too incomplete and provides no certain information on such fundamental factors as quantities of seed crops, areas cultivated, fertilisers, irrigation. Hence, rather than a measure of productivity what one really has is 'a measure of the echo – and a distant echo, at that – of productivity'.[11]

What is certain is that irrigation marked a break with the traditional cycle of crop rotation. As Pierre Vilar observes with regard to Catalonia, 'irrigation put an end to fallowland (*jachère*) for good. And even outside the *huertas* proper, it made it possible to intermit the usual cereal and legume crops with the much more profitable hemp, or multiple harvest fodder crops such as alfalfa'.[12] The Venetian Republic of the sixteenth and seventeenth century does not always seem to have been aware of these technical possibilities, and this inevitably had important consequences upon policy-making and the economy; the limitations within the agriculture of the terra firma become all the clearer when we compare it not only with the more fortunate and dynamic regions of northern Europe but also with such Italian regions as Piedmont and, above all, Lombardy. The Venetian Republic's most prestigious neighbour, this latter had been developing an integrated system of canals since the twelfth century: work on the Naviglio Grande that carried water from the Ticino to Milan dated from 1179; the Basca canal, from the Sesia, was dug before 1300; the Martesana, which brought water to Milan from the Adda, was completed by 1456, and the Novara and Lomellina areas also had their own networks of canals (the Biraga, the Bolgara and others). As Braudel remarks, the capital of Lombardy had become 'an important water station, which meant that it received wheat, iron and, above all, timber, at lower costs'. The developments within agriculture were no less encouraging, with extensive investment, early introduction of fodder plants in the crop-rotation cycles, the spread of irrigated pasture-land and a resultant increase in livestock herds.[13] It was Lombardy that would first see those structural changes within agriculture that would have such a profound effect on the very appearance of the region (land reclamation work, the introduction of rice-fields, the occupation and cultivation of a large part of church-owned land). As Cipolla underlines, in the second half of the fifteenth century the focus was more on meadow/pasture land than upon putting land to the plough, which meant that 'there was a more expansive trend in livestock production than in the production of vegetable crops; in other words, the areas of Lombardy were undoubtedly tending towards the more developed phases of agriculture';[14] and from the eighteenth to the nineteenth century, irrigation would not only become widespread, it would also achieve the highest technical standards.[15] In fact, as early as the sixteenth century almost half the usable land in the Lodi area – the veritable 'jewel' of the Milanese state – was benefiting from irrigation, with production boosted enormously by the fact that fields could be alternated between cultivation and pasture. Around Cremona, too, a good 20 per cent of cultivated land was irrigated, whilst the figure for the Novara and Como areas was 13 per cent, and that for Pavia and Lomellina was 12.2 per cent. Moving ahead to 1880, the figures paint an even clearer picture, with the percentages for irrigated flatland terrain in Lombardy, Piedmont and the Veneto being 55, 46 and 7 per cent respectively[16].

But agriculture in the Veneto did not just suffer from the lack of a full capillary network of irrigation canals; the very nature of its development was unsound. While in Lombardy and Piedmont there was a clear propensity to invest in agriculture (even in periods of stagnation), with the creation of extended agricultural concerns that were managed along capitalist lines and employed salaried labour, the situation was very different in the Veneto. In the early decades of the sixteenth century the Venetian patricians had shown a clear willingness to invest in the countryside, thus stimulating capitalist development;[17] however, one soon sees the re-emergence of pre-capitalist – and sometimes even feudal – practices: land was rented out in smallholdings and properties were split up as the patrician class showed little interest in running their estates themselves. G. Corazzol's research into the later decades of the sixteenth century reveals that increases in rents and leases were being paid in kind (grain), a phenomenon which provides further proof of the gradual impoverishment and expropriation of the peasant-farmer class by urban capital searching for ways to protect itself against the growing inflation of the period.[18]

Agronomical Literature

The limited resort to irrigation in the Veneto during the sixteenth and seventeenth century contrasts strangely with the abundant quantity of published material on the subject that was circulating within the Venetian Republic. In effect, none of the agronomical treatises or translations that were published in Venice failed to deal with the question, sometimes with original observations, sometimes with an eclecticism that drew heavily on classical and medieval discussions of the subject.

Leading figures in those discussions had been the Bolognese Pietro de Crescenzi (1233–1320) and the Arab scholar Ibn-al-Awwäm (1180–1220). The former's *Opus ruralium commodorum* would initiate a revival in the studies of agronomy that reached its peak in the sixteenth century. Far from being a mere observer of the past, de Crescenzi showed a truly modern spirit in his treatise: not only did he discuss the problems caused by excessive exploitation of plain flatlands as a result of the sharp increase in population during the twelfth/thirteenth century, he also considered remedies for the land erosion watercourses caused in hilly areas.[19]

For his part, Ibn-al-Awwäm marked the high point in Arab studies of agronomy, which after him would begin to go into decline. Whilst it is true that the *Le livre d'agriculture* by the most important Arabic writer in Spain would not be translated into European languages until the eighteenth century, it is undoubtedly the case that his teachings made their mark felt beyond the Arabic-Spanish world.[20] The influence of the Arabic tradition within the Mediterranean area should not be underestimated: inheriting Graeco-Roman teachings and applying them to the Arabic-Spanish world, this tradition would result in medieval Spain becoming one of the earliest and most fascinating examples of a *civilisation d'eau*. The canals of the kingdom of Valencia were justly famous for the fertile *huertas* that they supplied, with the characteristic landscape of the irrigated *regadío* contrasting with that of the *secà* (arid lands).[21] It may be true, as Bolens points out, that treatises in medieval Andalusia dedicated less space to irrigation than to the urban use of water (aqueducts and canals to supply mosques and princely residences), but it cannot be denied that such writings reveal a modern approach to the use of water in agriculture, with clear attention being paid to the need for balanced environments, natural fertilisation and a prudent selection of the land to go under the plough (indeed, a much higher degree of attention than that one sees in the agricultural policies followed nowadays).[22]

The decline of this glorious agricultural achievement would start towards the end of the Middle Ages, when the interests of a more livestock-centred agriculture would focus on the extensive development of terrain and on the so-called *Mesta*, 'ultimately [overwhelming] the great hydraulic civilisation created by the Moors'. The same destructive policy would be followed in Latin America, where the aggressive warriors of Navarra and Castille ... destroyed the hydraulic core of the high American civilisations with the self-same political and economic weapons they had used against the centres of Moorish irrigation in Cordoba, Seville and Granada'.[23]

And even such a figure as Gabriel Alonso de Herrera, considered one of the most important agronomical authors of sixteenth-century Spain, would ignore Arabic achievements in this field to focus solely on the works of Classical Antiquity, which he outlines – often with slavish fidelity – in his *Obra de agricultura, compilada da diversos autores*, a work that enjoyed substantial success throughout Europe (a total of 16 editions were published in Spain, whilst there were eight of the Italian translation – one being published in Venice in 1558).[24] However, I would argue that the Arabs' achievements in hydraulics did have a fundamental effect upon both agricultural practices and agricultural legislation within the Mediterranean area. In fact, when after Cateau-Cambrésis the Spanish took control of Lombardy, the legislation introduced with regard to such matters was inspired by that applying in Spain,[25] with the result that this region became a more advanced model for the neighbouring Venetian Republic, to which it would ultimately export both technology and legislation. Hence the fascinating image emerges of a true circuit of ideas and knowledge embracing the whole of the western Mediterranean and stimulating a constant series of advances and developments.

Alongside this Arabic-Spanish tradition, that of classical antiquity was to be no less influential in a sixteenth century which saw numerous editions of the works of Frontinus, Pliny, Vitruvius and Columella.[26] But soon, both of these traditions together were joined – and to some extent overtaken – by the contributions offered by contemporary authors – people such as Palissy, Olivier de Serres and the above-mentioned Gabriel de Herrera.[27] As recent studies have shown, foremost amongst these contemporaries – both for the number of works published and the range of themes discussed – were Italian writers on agriculture, with treatises originating in Venice offering important theoretical contributions from some of the most innovative agronomists in Italy.[28]

Within the Venetian state a fundamental role was played by the Brescia area, where Giacomo Chizzola would seem to have founded the region's first Academy of Agriculture at Rezzato in around the year 1568; the authors and experimental agronomists active in this zone included figures of European standing – such as Agostino Gallo and Camillo Tarello – as well as significant minor figures like Giacomo Lanteri and Giuseppe Milio Voltolina.[29] Bordering the more developed and better-irrigated Lombardy, the Brescia area was one of the most agriculturally-dynamic in the whole of the Venetian state; numerous accounts mention its abundant crops and its intensive use of irrigation. It was within this context that a very lively theoretical debate developed, with Agostino Gallo and Camillo Tarello being rightly seen as early champions of a capitalistic development of agriculture based on rational crop rotation and the use of fodder crops in alternation with fallow (a policy whose well-known results are increased soil fertility and the provision of stable feed for livestock).[30]

Irrigated pasture and arable land were the linchpin of the theories outlined. In the words of Gallo, 'I would urge that one takes the land with water rather than otherwise. Because, with abundant watering ... it is almost impossible that one does not get double the yield that one gets from all the others'.[31] However, at the same time, he warned against excessive irrigation of land, observing 'that giving each field the water it requires, that field receives it as it would its own good mother; but the longer it holds that water within it, the more it begins to feel it as the worst of stepmothers'.[32] He did nevertheless focus largely on those crops (rice, flax and hemp) that required intensive irrigation. The fact of the matter is that, like many of these writers on agronomy, Gallo paid less attention to the narrow problems of his own farm than to making proposals and suggestions for the owners of large- and medium-sized estates in the fertile valley area below Brescia. His main concerns therefore were how to intensify commercial-based agriculture; how to supply urban markets; and how to improve the income of agricultural landowners.

In his *Ricordo d'agricoltura* (1567), Camillo Tarello too discussed how to increase agricultural productivity in order to meet the demand from a growing population and remedy the downward trend in profits. In effect, the patent that he submitted before the Venetian Senate aimed to achieve these ends thanks to the regenerative influence of fodder grasses as part of the crop cycle – the so-called 'Tarello Revolution', which was based on a good two years of fodder crops within a four-year cycle. There was, however, a clear contradiction in his view that intense irrigation of terrain to increase crop yields of grasses or hay would be detrimental. Clover 'which grows in non-watered land', he observes, 'may grow in smaller quantities than it would in watered land, but it will be better and more tasty'. Hence, the fallow field envisaged by Tarello was a dry one, not the irrigated field to be seen in neighbouring Lombardy (where repeated irrigation made it possible to obtain multiple crops of hay throughout the year, and thus provide the fodder necessary for flourishing livestock herds). What is more, the type of agriculture Tarello aims to develop is still of the subsistence kind, with small-sized holdings and grain crops (the only sort that he believed could guarantee survival and feed the rapidly-increasing population). As Berengo has pointed out, what was actually required was to wean landowners from this obsession with grain and encourage them to make heavy investments in other crops, which would lead to the establishment of another kind of agriculture; but the farmers to whom Tarello was addressing himself – his message being propagated at a local level by parish priests – did not have the sort of capital necessary for such a change. The very property farmed by Tarello himself – the 'Marcina' – covered only 36 *piò* and thus revealed all the theoretical and practical limits of the formula he proposed.[33]

The same sort of approach can be seen in the work of Africo Clementi, a Paduan notary who, from intellectual curiosity and a taste for experimentation rather than any material need, leased a few areas of farmland outside his native city. Produced in a situation of endemic food shortages amongst the peasant population, his *Trattato dell'agricoltura* continued to focus on cereals and vines as the fundamental crops, with only a hasty mention of those crops linked with a capitalistic development of agriculture. The distance between his outlook and a modern approach can be seen in the scarce attention he pays to the subject of livestock herds and fodder: in fact, he argued tree foliage was enough to feed the scant herds in the Padua countryside. And as for soil fertilisers, the key strategy he proposed was the *sovescio*, the digging-in of the plants which grew up there.[34] Clementi did, however, see the importance of fish-farming, which in modern Europe presented an alternative to the raising of livestock herds[35] (this was undoubtedly the case in France at least, given the importance of the Paris market for fish; the situation in Italy and other European countries has been less extensively studied).[36]

In effect, it was the widespread belief that irrigated pasture-land meant less land for precious grain crops which would ultimately hinder its introduction, and that not only within Italy or the Venetian Republic. The size of the population played a key role in the contraposition of the needs of arable crops and livestock – a contrast that was not without its social implications. As Braudel points out, acre for acre, crop cultivation inevitably beat livestock farming, being able to feed ten or twenty times as many people.[37] And even in the Lombardy area around Lodi – where the battle for irrigation had not come to a total end, even if there could now be no doubt as to its ultimate outcome – it was commented that 'it would be better, especially for the poor, that they were sooner without meat and

cheese than without bread. Before the Lodi area had the water
drawn from the Muzza it was always in need of all sorts of forage;
then when most of it was converted for fodder crops, thanks to the
convenient supplies of the water ... primary foodstuffs for its own
inhabitants became correspondingly less abundant'.[38]

The accusation is clear: forage and livestock had become
economic speculations, providing meat and dairy products for the
tables of the wealthy, offering landowners higher returns, and thus
leading to a cutback in the traditional cereal crops that supplied the
stable diet of the poorer classes.[39] However, as Ceredi insists in his
account of this lively and interesting debate, it would have been
wrong to try and put the clock back: far from simply causing a drop
in the production of such a basic crop as grain, irrigation made for
more varied and differentiated agriculture, which was ultimately to
the benefit of the population as a whole.[40]

Agricultural literature paid equal attention to other irrigated crops:
millet, flax, hemp, mulberry, maize, sorghum (sometimes confused
with maize), oats, various types of fruit plants and, above all, rice. [41]
The greater space dedicated to this latter crop was undoubtedly due
to the complexity of the water supply required at the different
phases of growth and the fact that the banks, canals and locks of rice-
fields needed constant attention. If there was one crop whose very
survival depended on abundant supplies of water, it was rice.
Between March and May, water for the rice-fields had to be plentiful:
when the crop was planted, Giuseppe Falcone recommended, 'there
should be about a finger's depth of water over it ... Then it begins to
break the surface and branch upwards. When it begins to turn the
colour of millet, it is mature and the water is drained off ...'[42]

But there was also open hostility to rice, arising primarily from
dietary and sanitary considerations (these latter to be found in the
whole of the Po valley and not just the Veneto). And even when one
looks at very different regions, at different periods of history, the
criticisms of rice as a crop are the same. Again there was the fear that
rice occupied land that could be used for precious cereal crops; and
again 'the cultivation of rice – like the planting of vineyards – was
attacked due to the fear of timid traditionalists that the population
would be left without wheat and the army without straw'.[43]

However, the most violent criticisms were made in the name of
health conditions: doctors and scholars protested against rice-fields,

and even more vociferous were the people who were exposed to those periodic fevers which we now know to have been malaria. But these voices of the weak had little chance of making themselves heard against the powerful interests involved. From Catalonia to the Verona area, the 'lords of water' easily managed to minimise the dangers of rice-fields, insinuating the doubt that it had yet to be shown that 'the poor health conditions in the lowlands depended exclusively on one type of agriculture'.[44]

A high-profit, speculatory crop, rice provided a 'limit case of a specialised eco-system', requiring massive capital investment that only a large landowner or wealthy tenant could afford; given his scarce financial resources, the share-cropper showed very little interest in rice. To have an idea of the expense involved, one need only mention that during the eighteenth century the cost of water (including transport and the regular maintenance of canals and ditches) could amount to 15 per cent of all the monies that the entrepreneurial rice-grower spent in a year (depreciation included). For example, in the Mantua area, the annual upkeep of a rice-field was, acre for acre, four times higher than that for dry-land crops. However, these high initial costs were rewarded with a return that was at least twice as high as that from corn. Given this, one can see how difficult, if not impossible, it was to convince a landowner to destroy a rice-field or sacrifice a harvest (protests against rice generally broke out during the summer, after the crop had been sown). The most that could be obtained was a restriction of rice-fields to certain areas (the low-lying lands or marshy zones), or their removal from the vicinity of cities and villages. The first proclamation in Milan prohibiting the planting of rice within six miles of the city (or within five miles of the other cities of the region) came in 1575, and stirred loud protest from the farmers concerned; in 1662, the restriction was reduced to four miles for Milan and Novara, and three miles for other cities.[45]

The same sort of thing also happened in the Veneto. But such restrictive legislation proved ineffective; and in spite of criticisms that would go on being voiced until well into the nineteenth century, it was rice which emerged triumphant. The crop 'gained ground' throughout the Po valley area – from Piedmont to Mantua, and from Verona to Ferrara – though obviously the rate and timetable of expansion varied from region to region.[46] And in this inexorable advance of rice, the crop's properties as a foodstuff also played their key part: Giuseppe Falcone, for example, commented 'it might make the air of such a site malignant, but the return [on rice] does not take this into account, given that from the crop one can derive soups, loaves, bread (when mixed with other flours) and a lot of strength and energy'.[47]

Legislation and Technology

Within medieval Europe water had long been used both for irrigation and as a source of power; however, the regulation of those uses had largely been at the level of individual communities. With the expansion of agriculture in the sixteenth century, there is no doubt that in most of the countries of the continent there was a corresponding development in the legislation governing such matters. 'Water rights' were defined in legal terms, even if that definition was sometimes inadequate to the complexity of regional and national situations which dated back centuries. Roman Law had, in fact, already drawn a key distinction between rivers and major watercourses on the one hand, which were to be considered as public, and minor watercourses, which could be privately owned and managed. Nor should one overlook those traditional, communal forms of water management which existed at a village or small community level, but whose legal definition was insufficiently clear. The problem was made all the more complex by the fact that the definition of water rights could not but reflect the economic strategies and relations of production that existed within each of the individual 'case studies'. In effect, then as now, the definition of water as a 'public asset' or as a private 'commodity' that answered to the laws of the market was an essential part of a wider political debate.[48]

In the Venetian Republic it was the establishment of the *Provveditori sopra i Beni Inculti* that opened the way to more complete and precise legislation with regard to water concessions. As far as agriculture was concerned, the declared aim was to increase the production of cereal crops by bringing marshy land under the plough and also providing irrigation for arid areas. In proposing this policy, it was pointed out that the area of land dedicated to grain production was insufficient: there were frequent famines and it was not always easy to obtain supplies from other states (who, due to their own internal shortages or open hostility to Venice, might prevent exports).[49] But other factors were to play an equally decisive role here: the slow and extensive transformation of the Venetian patrician class from one of merchants to one of agricultural entrepreneurs (or, at least, landowners); the shift of investment from trade to land, which was seen as safer and more profitable; the various difficulties encountered by Venice's ships at sea; the need to counterbalance trading losses with more remunerative investments on the terra firma; the high price of grain.[50] There is no doubt that in the second half of the sixteenth century, the patrician class of Venice became much more interested in the terra firma, with a resultant stimulus to all the economic activities associated with that area (including those owned by the local nobility): land reclamation and irrigation projects, the spread of new crops, the publication of agricultural treatises and the development of new technologies and machinery are all clear evidence of this shift in interest – as are the institution of such public agencies as the above-mentioned *Provveditori ai Beni Inculti* , or the later instituted *Provveditori sopra i Beni Comunali* (set up in October 1574 to oversee the exploitation of collectively-owned land).[51]

The areas of uncultivated natural resources to be reclaimed by the *Provveditori ai Beni Inculti* (the three-man agency had first been elected in 1545, and became a permanent part of the Venetian administration in 1556[52]) were located around Padua, Vicenza, Verona, Asolo, Rovigo and Istria. The agency's brief did not, however, include the areas around Brescia, Bergamo and Crema, which were the best-irrigated of the mainland Republic[53]; that their superiority was recognised becomes clear when one sees that the 1519 legislation regarding the widening of the old Rosà canal in the Treviso area laid down explicitly that the measures regarding the use of the waters from this new canal were to be based on those applying in the Brescia and Bergamo areas. In effect, when one looks at Venetian legislation concerning water resources it becomes clear that, with some variations, it is modelled on that adopted in Lombardy.[54]

However, one must move forward to the decree of 5 February 1556 to get a full picture of the legalisation at the basis of the work performed by the *Provveditori ai Beni Inculti*. Public ownership of all watercourses – be they large or small – was asserted categorically, with those wishing to exploit such resources having to pay a certain sum for the concession (in effect, once granted, this concession could almost never be revoked). In Lombardy, on the other hand, the individual users of the water enjoyed private property rights, even if there were lease concessions, multi-year rent contracts and – though this was rare – temporary contracts. It is this which, as Mario Romani argued, accounted for 'the absolute perfection which emerged over time in the division and use of water resources, unlike the case in the Mantua area or in the Veneto, where the benefits gained from irrigation were lower than they would have been if a freer hand had been given to private individual interests'.[55]

The legislation in Lombardy, therefore, was similar to that in the more open, dynamic areas of Europe – for example, Valencia or Castillón in Spain.

Another problem that existed was the possible division between the owners of the water and the owners of the land, a situation which guaranteed that the former exerted social and economic dominion over the latter, triggering off a process which in the long run resulted in the re-emergence of backward, feudal relations of production – as would happen in some areas of Spain (Elche, Alicante and Novelda), the Canary Islands, and in part of Sicily (Palermo).[56]

Further evidence of the influence of Lombardy on irrigation within the Venetian Republic can be seen in the fact that Venice had in the early decades of such projects to draw on the services of Lombard, Brescian or even Piedmontese experts to assess the conditions of the terrain through which the irrigation canals were to be created. It was not until 1568 that the Republic appointed three of its own 'permanent experts', expressing the hope that they would prove to be less 'ignorant with regard to the qualities and evaluation of water' than some of their predecessors, who had turned out to be 'very negligent, and not very diligent in perceiving and reporting the true state and value of these waters'.[57]

However, the precise norms governing land drainage that were promulgated in the sixteenth and seventeenth century were not always applied coherently, or perhaps even respected at all. A far from secondary aspect in evaluating a state's administration, this gap between regulations and the observance thereof is all the more important and significant when one is assessing a political entity such as the Venetian Republic, which – with undoubted justification – was celebrated throughout Europe in the political writings of the sixteenth and seventeenth centuries.

Before the establishment of the *Provveditori ai Beni Inculti*, the *Savi alle Acque* [Water Magistracy] was already informing the Senate that there 'were numerous encroachments upon many stretches of the Brenta Nuova and other places'; and – as continuing complaints reveal – even when he held an official concession, the leaseholder might not always respect limitations regarding the quantity of water to be drawn, the way it was to be used, or the number of fields to be irrigated. [58] At a certain point, it was argued that the financial losses suffered were due to the low price at which the water was sold; and though we cannot assess how justified this claim was, it did result in the suggestion that instead of a (substantial) initial payment, leaseholders should pay a yearly fee based on the value of the water. However, the proposal came to nothing.

In effect, precise assessment of the value of this natural resource was considered to be difficult, if not impossible, as it had to take into account such vague and uncertain variables as the quantity and 'quality' of the water drawn and the use to which the concession-holder put it. Given the technical and scientific instruments available at the time, even the mere measurement of the quantity was difficult enough; and as for the 'quality', that was even more difficult to pin down, with water being divided into different broad categories (river, torrent, spring, rain and channel – that is, drained water which had already been put to a use) and experts attempting to assess its other characteristics ('fat' water as opposed to 'cold', 'muddy' as opposed to 'clear'). What is more, the evaluation of price had to take into account the time when the resource was being used, given that in dry periods or in other circumstances it might be in short supply.[59] Similarly, one had to consider the type of soil being irrigated – meadow, plough land, rice-fields, vegetable plots, orchards, gardens – and the type of machinery that might be powered by the water. Nevertheless, in spite of the enormous variety of cases, a basis for quantification can be derived from an analysis of the different concessions. Water drawn off directly from rivers – especially sizeable rivers – was obviously the most costly, whilst the cheapest source of water were muddy, perhaps seasonal, streams and the drainage canals carrying water away from the fields of other users.[60] Water for rice-fields cost the most, given the high profits the crop could yield, whilst personal use (for non-speculative ends) enjoyed some sort of subsidy. Of course, there was a wide variety of uses between these two extremes, from the irrigation of meadow and grassland (the cost of which always took into account the relation between the extent of the terrain and the amount of water available) to that of orchards.[61]

Difficulties in assessing the quantity of water used were due not only to individual fraud but – as has already been mentioned – also to the limited technical knowledge of the day (and the even more limited grasp of it by the appointed technicians and experts). Right up to the end of the eighteenth century, measurement was so rule-of-thumb that accurate quantification was out of the question; technicians frequently admitted their inadequacies, especially when it came to measuring spring or torrent water. In effect, they simply measured the vertical section of the opening of the mouth of the watercourse in square feet – that is *quadretti*[62] – and totally ignored water speed and time in their calculations; not until the scientific revolution of the seventeenth century – and, in particular, the work of Benedetto Castelli (1577–1643) – would a more mathematically-precise approach be taken, with Castelli's *Della misura delle acque correnti* (1628) marking the beginning of water technology based on rational first principles, which would then expand into a whole domain of in-depth scientific enquiry.[63] Perhaps Paolo Frisi exaggerates when he claims that hydraulic science was born in Italy, 'where it was practically perfected, and where written works explored all aspects of hydrometry and hydraulic laws'.[64] Yet there is no denying the contribution made by such authors as Evangelista Torricelli, Domenico Guglielmini, Galileo Galilei and G.B. Barattieri, whose rigorously-exact definition of this area of scientific enquiry resulted in a key contribution to theory. Castelli's own theorem is posited on the idea that the volume of running water is directly proportional not only to the sectional area of the channel in which it flows, but also to its speed.[65] In more exact terms: 'the mass of fluid that in a given moment passes through a given section of a river or a canal is equal to the product of the area of the vertical section and the average velocity of that section'. And given that it was difficult to measure such average velocities, an eighteenth-century source indicates that one took the section to be a rectangular figure and considered the speed as equal to the square root of the depth.[66] From that century onwards, some leases of concession would take this factor into consideration; but when Castelli was writing – that is, in the mid-seventeenth-century – such variable velocities were totally ignored in water-volume calculations (in Lombardy as in the Veneto).[67] And even when during the course of the seventeenth century Venice did issue some regulations concerning the assessment of velocity, they were – as Zendrini points out – so obscure they failed to put an end to the usual abuses of the system:[68] for example, the canal might be widened both upstream and downstream of the evaluation point. What is more, given the irregular shape of many vertical sections and river beds, calculation of the area remained little more than theoretical (even modern hydraulics finds itself faced with similar problems). And while it may be true that the 1764 treaty drawn up between Maria Theresa of Austria and the Venetian Republic – in resolution of a long-running dispute regarding the use of border watercourses[69] – did adopt new and rational terms when fixing the regulations governing the drawing-off of water, it is also true that there is no evidence that these regulations were respected, either in that border area or anywhere else within the mainland Republic. When we look at the more developed irrigation system of the neighbouring Lombardy, one sees the same rule-of-thumb methods being adopted in the eighteenth and even into the nineteenth century.[70]

Throughout the Early Modern period, therefore, one can see only certain constant features in the regulation of water use within Venice's mainland Republic. The experts limited themselves to insisting that at its mouth, the last ten *pertiche* (poles) of the irrigation canal should be faced with hard stone, thus protecting the opening at which the water was drawn off. Sometimes, the water was diverted into the canal by means of a barrier placed across the watercourse from which it was being drawn; necessary when the water in the river was low, such *roste* or traverses could either be made into a permanent feature or else lowered as a temporary obstacle that only hampered navigation for a short period of time. At other times, the diversion barrier might be a simple *pennello* [screen] of canes and stone jutting out part-way from one bank of the watercourse.[71]

Having flowed into the terrain, the water was then fed into a number of small canals, using the system nowadays known as 'flow irrigation'; the most common method then in use, this is to be distinguished from the 'submersion' irrigation of rice-fields or the

much less frequent 'infiltration' method of irrigation (the fact that
this latter was used much less than 'flow' irrigation can be seen from
the numerous drawings and charts in the archives of the *Beni Inculti*,
which clearly show the main canal dividing up into a number of
rivulets).

A certain incline worked to the advantage of the 'flow' technique,
but if it was too sharp – or the field sank towards the middle – then
the water either ran off too quickly or stagnated.[72]

Throughout the sixteenth century various systems were studied for
carrying the irrigation water most effectively to the land to be irrigated;
in many cases, the same machinery might be used to drain and then
irrigate terrain. Taking up a classification proposed in the eighteenth
century by Simone Stratico, one might divided hydraulic machinery
into: first, that which raised water using force, for example, pressure or
aspiration pumps; second, that which raised it smoothly from the
watercourses below – for example, all the various types of wheel used
to lift water up to higher levels, or the Archimedes' Screw.[73]

Although more complicated machinery was developed and
proposed by the relevant authorities, the 'bucket' waterwheel would
remain widely used along the rivers of the Venetian Republic for
years to come.[74] Set up in such a way as not to hinder the movement
of barges or the operations carried on within riverside buildings,
these did however prove costly to run – so much so that they were
only used by noble families or civil and religious bodies with rather
ample means.

The various Venetian bodies responsible for such matters – the
Senate, the *Savi alle Acque*, the *Provveditori ai Beni Inculti* and the
Provveditori di Comun – were frequently presented with designs and
patent applications for machines which their inventors unfailingly
described as exceptional. However, many precious details of these
remain either obscure or have been lost altogether, partly because the
applicants reserved the right to fully illustrate their designs only after
they had obtained their patent (which was not always granted, given
the repetitive nature of a number of proposals) and partly because,
even after receiving their patent, they did not always supply more
specific details.[75] One such inventor, Giovanni Ceredi, did not fail to
note – with a certain satisfaction – that within the secret archives of
the *Provveditori di Comun* there were many designs for hydraulic
machines, but 'being of no greater utility than their predecessors,

they will remain secret'. Obviously, that was not the fate he envisaged for his own invention, presented not to the Republic but to Alessandro Farnese, Duke of Parma and Piacenza, with the hope that the reception of his machine would not be limited to that small state. In effect, what he had produced was just a variation upon the Archimedes' Screw[76]; but he claimed that his machine would profit the whole of the Po Valley, given that he had successfully completed a design that many others – Venetians included – had been striving for in vain.[77] However, his hopes for his brainchild were to be disappointed – at least within the Veneto, where his machine does not seem to have been widely adopted. This one example might be taken as partial confirmation for the claim that many of the machines designed in Italy were merely theoretical, with a sharp divergence emerging between the rich theoretical literature of the day and the practical application of the ideas it put forward.[78] Yet even if this was the case, it is still undeniable that, up to the very end of the sixteenth/beginning of the seventeenth century, Italian hydraulic technology would remain second to none in Europe.

Utopia and Reality: The Canals of the Veneto in the Sixteenth and Seventeenth Centuries

Even if a whole series of canals were dug there during the Middle Ages, it was in the fifteenth century that the Veneto saw an increase in the creation of canals which could bear some sort of comparison with the more technologically-advanced system in Lombardy. The following century would simply develop upon what had been started already, re-adapting or enlarging existing canals. In effect, there was no overall project for the sort of canal system that is essential for an integrated irrigation system.

At the beginning of the sixteenth century there were: the Brentella and Piavesella canals, drawn off the Piave in the first decades of the fifteenth century to provide irrigation in the Treviso area; various medieval channels and canals on the left and right banks of the Brenta (these included the Battaglia and Rosà; the latter, on the left bank, was an important and long-standing source of irrigation and dated from 1370);[79] other canals drawn off the Brenta since the Middle Ages (these numbered at least 14); and the canals of Este and Monselice, another *Brentella* and the Piovego – that linked the Brenta with the

Bacchiglione to the west of Padua[80] (these dated from the twelfth to fourteenth century). All of the above irrigated the Padua, Vicenza and Treviso areas or else served as important routes of transport for merchandise (for example, the Lipsida stone which was carried along the Battaglia canal from the Padua area to Venice). Other less important canals had also been created in the Verona and Friuli areas in the Middle Ages.[81]

Although, over time, the limitations of the way it was used would emerge, the Piave does offer an important example of a rational and well thought-out exploitation of water resources in the Early Modern period. Irrigation in the northern stretches of the Treviso area dated back some time, but it would only become fully consolidated with the 1436 creation of the Brentella canal; drawn off the Piave at Pederobba, this would soon prove to be inadequate and be followed by the creation of the Piavesella in 1447 (drawn off the Piave at Nervesa). Though both canals were destined to serve the same area and exemplified one and the same policy with regard to water resources, their use went beyond meeting irrigation needs and providing water supplies for the fifty-nine towns and villages in the area. Concessions were granted for the use of the water to power mills, saw works and hammers, thus giving rise to a long-lasting conflict between those interested in the water as a source of energy and those more concerned with irrigation and urban supplies.[82]

The local administrators responsible for the distribution of the water were chosen from amongst the wealthiest families in the city of Treviso, and it was the abuses resulting from their vested interests which were subsequently blamed for the gradual deterioration in the maintenance of such hydraulic facilities. But even though the twelve *Provveditori* or *Deputati alle acque di Treviso* were accused by the *rettori* [Venetian City Governors] of favouring relatives and friends, any attempt to eradicate such privileges encountered stiff local opposition, thus hindering the introduction of an integrated irrigation policy for the whole of the mainland Republic. [83]

By 1572 the inefficiency of the *Consorzio Brentella* was clear: the water was insufficient for the four major towns, let alone all fifty-nine; and it came nowhere near its target of providing irrigation for 4,700 *campi*.[84] At this point a solution was put forward by Nicolò Cicogna, who voiced the interests of a Venetian patrician class that was increasingly attracted by the opportunities it saw in the exploitation (and possible expansion) of the Brentella.[85] Thus a Venetian point of view was superimposed upon those local interests that had first led to the creation of the canal. In effect, Cicogna offered to carry out the work required by his project in return for one quarter of the water, the rest remaining to the cities and towns concerned. This meant there would be no resort to *caratade* – taxation or fees upon possible future concession-holders – as would have been the case if the work of renovation and expansion had been undertaken by the *Collegio di Treviso*. However, the city's response was that Cicogna, under the pretence of extending the canal, was actually trying to take control of what was public property. Given that the Venetian Senate's water policy was predicated upon a centralised, publicly-run exploitation of the resource, the Republic turned out to be very receptive to such arguments; as a result, it was the city of Treviso that was given the task of creating a fourth *porta*, with the requirement that work be completed within eighteen months.[86]

The speculative nature of Cicogna's proposal must have been clear to everyone; but it is far from clear that Venice made the right decision in rejecting it. In effect, eighteen months later the work had not been completed; nor was it brought to an end during the various extension periods granted the city of Treviso (though *rettori* continued to stress the urgency of new restoration and refurbishment work, funds continued to be insufficient). At one point, it was proposed to extend the Brentella as far as Treviso itself, and thence use the canal as a waterway for transporting merchandise – above all, the timber that was carried by the Piave down from the Alps to the Venetian lagoon. But again, nothing came of this and the Brentella continued to be inadequate for the purposes it had been intended to serve.[87] All in all, the fact that it was one single city that decided the use of the canal did little to help – indeed, hindered – the implementation of more far-sighted policies.

The picture is no better when one looks at the contribution made by the other Piave canal – the Piavesella, drawn off the river at Nervesa; again, incoherent use resulted in little real improvement in the area. True, a plan was drawn in 1549 to widen and deepen the canal, but this ran up against another fixed point of Venetian water policy – the need to protect the hydraulic equilibrium within the lagoon – because it seemed that increasing the volume of water flowing through the canal would infringe an essential priority:

keeping the waters of the Piave away from Venice. The more respected of the hydraulic technicians pointed out that part of the river's waters already flowed to Treviso along the Piavesella canal, making a contribution to water supplies in the surrounding area; but, they added, the 13-miles canal, whose long tortuous course followed the natural slope of the river, merely released the pressure of water within the Piave and did not present any sort of overflow risk for the lagoon. That risk, they argued, would increase if the volume of water in the Piavesella increased (above all, when the river was running full): in such cases, the Piave would pour down towards Treviso and the lagoon, damaging both. The possible advantages to water transport and irrigation (the latter anyway seen as difficult to achieve) were far less important than the mere possibility of a threat to the delicate environmental balance within the lagoon. In the words of Cristoforo Sabbadino, the technician who could be taken as the champion of this rigorously protective policy, one should think less 'of the profit one might get from wheat [than] of the conservation of the lagoon, which is the fortress of Venice'.[88]

In the Bassano region and the area between the cities of Padua, Venice and Treviso, the numerous irrigation canals drawn off the Brenta were put to no better agricultural use. To increase irrigation resources, the opening of the Rosà was widened in 1519, with the water being sold at the undoubtedly remarkable price of a good 2,900 ducats a *quadretto*.[89] This exceptionally high tariff does not seem to have been matched anywhere else, and it undoubtedly made it difficult to sell the water: in 1556 Zuanne Donà, the official of the *Rason Vecchie* (a *magistratura* that managed state assets) was sent to the area to conclude negotiations of the still uncompleted sales. Nevertheless, the volume of water carried by the Rosà and the other canals drawn off the Brenta can have been in no way inferior to that carried by the Brentella, without in any way diminishing the importance of this latter: the eighteenth century estimate of its water volume as not above eight *quadretti* must have been an all-time 'low'. Then as now, among the other canals it was the Rosà that drew off the most water, with the maximum volume at the end of the seventeenth century being calculated at 60 *quadretti* (for a section 15 feet wide and four high); however, generally not more than 48 *quadretti* were drawn from the river. Then came the Cappello canal – named after the family that held the concession (although part of it seems to have been assigned to the Moccnigo, the Contarini and, above all, the Dolfin): the maximum capacity of its opening was 35 *quadretti*, though usually it only drew 23 (which is still more than the above-mentioned minimum for the Brentella). [90]

The various other canals drawn off the Brenta carried about the same as the Brentella, if the volume of water often did not reach this maximum.[91]

Most of this water was used for irrigation and to power mills, fulling machinery and hammers. From Bassano to Padua a total of 135 *quadretti* was drawn off, 28 *quadretti* to power mills at Dolo alone whilst only 6 served to meet the water needs of Venice. Clearly, at times the Brenta might appear to be exhausted by the demands upon it – so much so that at one point the *rettori* applied for the closure of the *Taglio Novissimo*, the 'new cut' which was a valuable waterway for navigation and carried a further 150 *quadretti* from Mira to the sea.[92]

Thus the needs of agriculture had to be balanced with those of other economic sectors (including manufacturing), even if the use of most of the various canals – above all, those drawn off the Brenta – was primarily agricultural. The Rosà continued to serve the Castelfranco area efficiently, whilst the areas of Bassano and Vicenza were served by such canals as the Grimana, the Cappella, the Morosina, the Isacchina and the Zangiaca, whose names echo those of the powerful aristocratic families who were the concession-holders. Other examples of efficient canals might also be cited in various areas of the Republic.[93]

Numerous projects were put forward in the Verona area; focusing primarily on the Adige, they were however both too ambitious and too abstract, not always taking adequate account of the hydro-geological environment concerned. Although this intense range of publications and writings dealt mainly with irrigation, there was also interest in increasing the volume of river traffic, with the whole series of complex problems involved raising serious doubts as to the actual creation of such canals. In 1587 Antonio Glisenti – known as 'Il Magro' – reproposed a scheme that had already been put forward in 1568 by the Venetian Republic's famous expert on hydraulics, Cristoforo Sorte, who subsequently made an accusation of plagiary. This plan envisaged digging a canal from Lake Garda, with Verona paying for it with half of the *decima* it would subsequently receive from the irrigated land. The city rejected such demands as excessive, pointing out that whilst it financed such work, 5 per cent of the water drawn would go to Glisenti. As happened with the Cicogna project for the Brentella at Treviso, this clash with the interests of the financial elite of the city meant that the scheme ultimately came to nothing.[94]

The irrigation plans put forward by Teodoro da Monte and Benedetto Venier, in 1591 and 1594 respectively, were inspired by the same principles as those behind the schemes of Sorte and Glisenti, even if they did vary in some details (both of the authors, however, insisted on the entire originality of their proposals). The 'regulation' of the Adige was seen as part of an enormous land-reclamation scheme involving some 80,000 *campi* (just under 25,000 hectares) between that river and the Tartaro, with the work also covering a number of minor rivers (in the Vicenza area above all) which posed a threat to both agriculture and navigation due to flooding and overflowing. Da Monte estimated the costs of two canals to be dug from the Adige and Lake Garda at a good 300,000 ducats, but was convinced that the sum could be recouped from the sale of the water and the increased tax revenue resulting from the boost to agricultural and commercial activities.[95] For his part, Benedetto Venier estimated the cost of his project as being much lower. Whatever the truth, neither came to anything.[96]

In the Friuli area the only project of any importance was the canal to be drawn off the Ledra-Tagliamento; but although first proposed as early as the fourteenth century, the implementation of this scheme was put off continually. In effect, there was no real tradition of irrigation in the region, with the main causes of this continuing state of affairs from the Middle Ages onwards probably being the power of the Patriarchate of Aquileia and the low level of urban economic activity: the few channels dug in the twelfth century to draw water off the Tagliamento, the Torre dal Cellina and a few other torrents were decided solely to met domestic and craft industry needs, with irrigation being neglected entirely. When reference was made to agricultural exploitation of water resources, this was within circumscribed areas of sterile and permeable soil, so that even if the Friulan nobleman Nicolò di Maniago declared that the purpose of the Aviano and Colvera canals (1445 and 1453 respectively) was to irrigate the lands of Maniago and Aviano, the canals really served as a means of transporting timber and as a source of water for civil and industrial uses.[97]

However, it would be this same nobleman who in 1457 urged the creation of a canal for the waters of the Ledra and Tagliamento at the point where the two rivers flowed down into the plain, so that the waters might be redirected towards Udine and used to irrigate the dry western area. Here again, however, commercial uses were to go together with irrigation, as it was proposed that river traffic from Germany should use the canal that would ultimately flow into the lagoon of Marano. But once more the *Consiglio Maggiore* of Udine opposed the scheme, perhaps because of insuperable distrust of such ideas amongst the local nobility.

It would be another powerful landowner however – Giulio Savorgnan – who would re-propose the Ledra-Tagliamento irrigation scheme at the end of the century, in 1592. An expert on military questions with a deep knowledge of the entire territory of the mainland state, Savorgnan had been vividly impressed by the areas of Bergamo, Brescia and Verona, where agriculture clearly profited from the presence of irrigation waters: in his own words, 'a field in the Brescia area is worth ten in Friuli'. The consequences of this fact were there for all to see: 'the areas that enjoy irrigation are becoming populated, whilst Friuli has been half deserted now for more than fifty years, because what good there was in the land has been consumed and the peasants are moving away to Germany'. Only by increasing the areas of irrigated pasture land, and thus the size of herds of cattle and horses (the latter an essential requirement in a border region such as Friuli) would there be a recovery in the agriculture and entire economy of the area. However, given that the scheme proposed by Savorgnan was to be financed by the timber merchants, they would be guaranteed three fifths of the water, whilst only two fifths would be used for irrigation. But, again, nothing was done – neither then nor in the following centuries. In spite of the fact that such illustrious scholars as Bernardino Zendrini and Geminiano Montanari championed the Ledra-Tagliamento canal, work on it would not begin until the nineteenth century.[98]

Given their share of property ownership, the influence of the nobility and the Church here proved to be decisive.[99] Largely uninterested in the introduction of new crops – especially those requiring irrigation – they would remain firmly attached to the old system of cereal crop rotations and, above all, the use of land for vineyards. And even the small-scale landowners would, right up to the first decades of the nineteenth century, continue to dedicate only a small amount of land to the cultivation of summer crops (threatened by shortage of water), preferring instead to concentrate on the traditional rotation of wheat, oats and rye. As Antonio Zanon would note in the eighteenth century, even maize was neglected; a foodstuff that might have spared Friuli the 'undernourishment trap', this occupied no more than one quarter or at most two-fifths of total crops sown. The vast expanse of communal land within Friuli (some 41 per cent of the total area[100]) is another reason for the absence of those private landowners who were receptive to ideas of irrigation, drainage and land improvement in general. Nor should one overlook the real difficulties presented by the hydro-geological characteristics of the region: the wide beds of the torrential rivers meant it was almost impossible to construct safe and secure openings for the canals that were to draw water off them.

One eighteenth-century champion of irrigation in Friuli, Cortenovis, did argue that the problems of the area could be resolved by preventing the wastage of what water there was in the dry middle plain of the region, as well as making full use of the spring water available in the lower plain.[101] However, this could only be done if Venice itself drew up a clear plan of action and then imposed it with firmness. Here, the Friulan scholar had come straight to the heart of the problem: not only did Friuli have no independent economic forces interested in such transformations of its rural landscape, but it also came under the rule of an external government that had no unified agricultural policy for its mainland dominions.

Conflicts Over Water: The Mainland and the Venice Lagoon

The complexity of the relations between the *Savi ed Esecutori alle Acque*, responsible for the lagoon itself, and the *Provedditori ai Beni Inculti*, responsible for land reclamation and irrigation on the mainland, was the result of more than a mere overlap of administrative duties; it reflected a more profound problem that influenced the whole definition of Venice's environmental – and, ultimately, economic – policies. The difficulties arose not solely in delimiting areas of responsibility but also in deciding which one of the two authorities was to have final say in policies regarding the region's water resources and its hydro-geological management. Another reason for the long-lasting ambiguity between the two authorities was the fact that before the institution of the *Provveditori ai Beni Inculti*, it had been the *Savi alle Acque* who had overseen 'land reclamation' in the areas bordering on the lagoon (for example, Foresto and Santa Giustina). What is more, even as late as 1560, when the Senate elected the *Provveditori sopra i Beni Inculti* for the Treviso area, it imposed the presence of at least one *Savio alle Acque* to make sure that irrigation 'did not do any harm to our lagoon'. In addition, the *Savi* had to be informed of all the allocations of water from the Brenta and Piave (the two rivers that were the most direct threat to the Venice), because they 'had a say in everything to do with the rivers that emptied into the Lagoon'.[102] This subordination of the *Provveditori* to the *Savi* could still be seen in 1686, when the latter appointed themselves to check the distribution of all the waters drawn off the Brenta, with their own inspectors visiting the river and requiring that all unauthorised openings off it be sealed immediately.[103]

The reconciliation of land reclamation and irrigation also encountered difficulties arising from the multiple uses (military, commercial, agricultural and industrial) to which water was put.[104] Various kinds of machinery and plant were powered by water: mills, paper works, fulling and spinning machinery for the silk industry; hammers and bellows used in working iron; mechanical wood-saws and presses for flax oil. And, of course, given their importance as a source of food, particular attention was dedicated to water-powered flour mills[105]: experts and technicians were constantly being reminded that water drawn off for irrigation should in no way hamper the working of such mills, because 'diverting water from mills is against the law'.[106] There were undoubtedly frequent clashes over this question between private individuals and the communes who were directly responsible for the good working of mills.

Such conflicts over the use of water resources can be found throughout Europe, and inevitably led to a certain impasse. This continued throughout the Early Modern era until, with the advent of the industrial revolution, there came the emergence of water channels and canals 'dedicated' to one specific purpose; thereafter, millers no longer robbed water from farmers, the requirements of manufacturing no longer interfered with river transport, and rural needs no longer undermined urban water supplies (as had been the case with the Brenta and Venice).[107]

Waterways obviously played an important role in the economic life of the Veneto as a whole, with a great deal of attention being focused on the Brenta. As early as 1611 the *Provveditori ai Beni Inculti* were expressing their concern that the quantity of irrigation water being drawn off the river was interfering with the shipping and transportation of goods.[108] This was why legislation was passed which required the widest possible publication of all applications to draw water from the river, even in the stretches beyond Padua and Ponte di Brenta. When for example in 1676 the Venetian nobleman Andrea Capello applied to use five *quadretti* of Brenta water to power his three-wheel mill and irrigate his estate, the *Provveditori* received a flood of protests against such a proposal. The opponents of the scheme included the community of Marostica, the Seven Communes of the Vicenza area, the bargemen of Padua and Limena, and various other private individuals, who all claimed that excessive water concessions were exhausting the river; the boatmen pointed out that drawing off another five *quadretti* would mean that the river only became navigable after heavy rains or the melting of winter snows, whilst such navigation was essential to the livelihood of the foothills populations who relied on the river to transport their timber, coal, meat, etcetera down towards Padua and Venice.[109]

The very opposite fears prevailed where the Adige was concerned, given that the main actions taken by the authorities responsible for the river – the *Provveditori all'Adige* and the *Savi alle Acque* – were concerned to forestall the river breaking its banks.[110] In such a situation, the indiscriminate creation of openings in the embankments of the river and its tributaries could, when the river was running in spate, lead to flooding in the surrounding areas. A decree of 1682 described a situation in which the embankments of the Adige 'are being increasingly undermined ... by the erection of buildings and the opening of waterways to irrigate land and rice-fields'.[111] Certainly, the rivers in the Verona area (and the Adige, in particular) were responsible for very serious flooding – for example, in 1677, 1679 and 1680 (on the first of those occasions, the representatives of the city of Verona estimated the damage caused at some 60,000 ducats, and even though it was in their interests to stress the seriousness of the disaster, their figures cannot be dismissed out of hand). What is more, this was a period when around 21,000 ducats a year was spent on channelling the river, given that for long stretches the Adige has no natural banks as such and flows between man-made embankments. It is therefore perfectly understandable why, throughout the seventeenth and eighteenth century, a great deal of attention was focused on what was considered to be the main river of the Republic, with heavy penalties being inflicted upon anyone who made openings in the river banks or dug wells alongside the Adige or its tributary, the Bussé. Legislation also required that, before granting any concession of water, the *Provveditori* had to inform the *Rettori* [City Governors] of Verona, who would then consider what might be the consequences of the proposed scheme.[110]

Notes

1. A. Serpieri, *La bonifica nella storia e nella dottrina*, Bologna, 1957, pp. 1–2. In Italian the term for land reclamation – *bonifica* – has a more general etymological sense of 'bettering', improving terrain.
2. All the dates taken from Venetian archive documents use the Venetian calendar – that is, with 1 March marking the beginning of the New Year.
3. The upper and middle plain area extends from the base of the alpine foothills to the zone of the various water springs, which obviously have a direct effect upon irrigation and the types of agriculture that could develop here. Of an average width of 3–4 kms, this zone of springs stretches from the Mincio to the Adige (feeding numerous watercourses in the lower Verona area), to then extend beyond Vicenza to the Piave and Tagliamento, and finally curve down to the coast. In the zones upstream from the springs, the terrain is generally permeable, with the water seeping through until it encounters impermeable strata. In the upper plain areas, the soil is coarse and poor; and it is difficult to harness and distribute water supplies; land in the middle and lower plain is much more fertile, even if there are the perennial difficulties of drainage and defence against flooding (F. Marzolo, 'Le irrigazioni nelle Venezie. Aspetti idraulici', in *Atti del convegno delle bonifiche venete* (Padova 27 May 1954), Padua, 1954, pp. 3–4; V. Ronchi, 'Le irrigazioni nelle Venezie. Aspetti agronomici e sociali', in *Atti del convegno delle bonifiche venete*, Padua, 1954, pp. 4 and 14–19).
4. Beltrami, *Saggio di storia dell'agricoltura*, pp. 41–43; idem, *La penetrazione economica dei veneziani in Terraferma*, p. 53 and 156; Ventura, 'Considerazioni sull'agricoltura veneta', p. 535; De Maddalena, *Il mondo rurale italiano nel Cinque e nel Seicento*, p. 389; Gloria, *Della agricoltura nel Padovano*, I, pp. 239–42 and 291. Venetian documents use the term *campo* –

field – as a unit of measurement. The *campo vicentino* measured m² 3,862, like the *campo padovano*; the *campo veronese* was m² 3,003 and the *campo trevigiano* m² 5,204: Martini, *Manuale di metrologia*; idem, *Manuale di ragguaglio fra le misure e pesi veronesi ed il sistema metrico decimale e viceversa*.

5. Berengo, *L'agricoltura veneta dalla caduta della Repubblica all'unità*, pp. 12–15.

6. Tucci, 'L'Ungheria e gli approvvigionamenti veneziani di bovini', p. 159.

7. Areas of land for reclamation in the Tre Venezie (in hectares.):

Province	Terrain for drainage	Terrain for irrigation
Padua	1.000	266.000
Verona	6.000	20.000
Rovigo	8.000	3.000
Treviso	2.000	12.000
Venice	12.000	—
Udine	36.000	59.000

(Caizzi, *Aspetti economici e sociali delle bonifiche nelle Venezie*, p. 103).

8. As has been pointed out, 'systems of irrigation cannot be created overnight; and above all, it takes time to develop the expertise required to implement irrigation' (*Bonifica e programmazione nel Veneto*, pp. 119–20).

9. Vilar, *La Catalogne dans l'Espagne moderne*, II, pp. 278–79.

10. In eighteenth-century Lombardy, it was laid down that in the absence of rain, wheat fields were to be irrigated at least every fifteen days in the period from April to June; for flax and maize fields that interval was reduced to every ten days, and for meadowlands (throughout the summer) to every week. Rice fields had to be entirely covered in water right up to August. (R. Canetta, 'L'irrigazione nella bassa pianura lombarda tra il Sette e l'Ottocento', in *Le campagne lombarde tra Sette e Ottocento*, M. Romani ed., Milan, 1976, pp. 73–74).

11. J. Jacquart, 'La productivité agricole dans la France du Nord aux XVIe et XVIIe siècles', in *Troisième conférence internationale d'histoire économique. Production et productivité agricole, Section II* (Munich 1965), Paris, 1969, pp. 70–74, esp. p.71; B.H. Slicher van Bath, 'La productivité agricole. Les problèmes fondamentaux de la société pre-industrielle en Europe occidentale', ibid., pp. 23–30. Slicher van Bath, however, dedicates much less space to irrigation than he does to land reclamation.

12. Vilar, *La Catalogne dans l'Espagne moderne*, II, p. 279; Braudel, *La Méditerranée et le monde méditerranéen*, I, pp. 65–66.

13. Haussmann, 'Il suolo d'Italia nella storia', in *Storia d'Italia. I caratteri originali*, Romano and Vivanti eds., pp. 90–91; Braudel, *La Méditerranée*, pp. 64–67. The development of irrigation in Emilia was equally limited: R. Tirelli, *Progetto d'estrarre acqua dal Po sopra Piacenza per irrigarne la provincia e quelle di Parma, Reggio, Modena e Bologna*, L.F. Valdrighi ed., Modena 1872, p. 3ff.; C. Broggion and G. Tocci, 'Vie di comunicazione e traffici nella Romagna settecentesca: il canal naviglio Zanelli', in *Studi Romagnoli*, 22 (1971), pp. 1–25.

14. C.M. Cipolla, 'Per la storia delle terre della 'bassa' lombarda', in *Studi in onore di A. Sapori*, Milan, 1957, pp. 667 and 671–72.

15. Romani, *L'agricoltura in Lombardia*, p. 199. Late-eighteenth-century travellers from Britain and Austria – for example, Symonds, Young and Burger – did not fail to celebrate the exceptional results achieved by irrigation in Lombardy (ibid., pp. 23–24).

16. S. Pugliese, 'Condizioni economiche e finanziarie della Lombardia nella prima metà del secolo XVIII', in *Miscellanea di Storia Italiana*, 52 (1924), pp. 31–32; G. De Ricco, *Le irrigazioni dei terreni. Opere e tecnica*, Bologna, 1956, pp. 3–8; for the Lodi area, still the main dairy-product centre within Lombardy, see D. Zanetti, *Problemi alimentari di un'economia preindustriale*, Turin, 1964, pp. 31–34.

17. An enlightening example here is the case of the hemp, which from the mid-fifteenth century onwards was cultivated in the irrigated fields of the Montagnana area to provide the necessary raw materials for the Venice Arsenale shipyards, but then was later abandoned in favour of more profitable cereal crops (it should be pointed out that the hemp for the Arsenale was controlled more by public authorities and *magistrature* than by individual entrepreneurs: F.C. Lane, 'Rope Factory and Hemp Trade in the Fifteenth and Sixteenth Centuries', in *Venice and History*, Baltimore, 1966, pp. 281–84). However, the studies by Ivana Pastori Bassetto and David Celetti reveal that the situation on the Venetian mainland was not that unfavourable to the development of hemp as a crop: cf. I. Pastori Bassetto, 'La canapa nella Repubblica veneta', in *Archivio Veneto*, s.V, 141 (1993), pp. 5–65; D. Celetti, 'Il prezzo della canapa in età moderna. L'interazione del mercato, della moneta e dello stato nella determinazione del valore di una fibra strategica', in *Storia Economica*, 6 (2003), pp. 5–47.

18. Corazzol, *Fitti e livelli a grano*; idem, *Livelli stipulati a Venezia nel 1591*.

19. Pietro de Crescenzi's *Opus ruralium commodorum* published from the sixteenth century onwards: L. Olson, 'Pietro de Crescenzi: the Founder of Modern Agronomy', in *Agricultural History*, 18 (1944), pp. 35–37; P. Toubert, voice 'Pietro de' Crescenzi', in *Dizionario biografico degli italiani*, XXX, Rome, 1984, pp. 649–57.

20. Ibn-al-Awwäm, *Le livre de l'agriculture*, I, pp. 117–34 and 510–36; L. Bonelli-Conenna, *La Divina Villa di Corniolo della Cornia. Lezioni di agricoltura tra XIV e XV secolo*, Siena, 1982.

21. Glick, *Irrigation and Society in Medieval Valencia*, pp. 11–15; M. Aymard, *Irrigations du midi de l'Espagne*, Paris, 1864, p. 18 n.; J. Depassa, *Voyage en Espagne dans les années 1816, 1817, 1818, 1819 ou recherches sur l'arrosage*, I, Paris, 1823, pp. XIII–XVII and 186–208.

22. Bolens, *Les méthodes culturelles au Moyen Age d'après les traités d'agronomie andalous*. In Andalusia, irrigation was not only 'a means of providing moisture for the soil but indispensable in preventing it from being scorched and dried out'. According to the author, one should not draw too sharp a line between the *secano* and *regadío*, as the two types of agriculture overlapped with each other.

23. K.A. Wittfogel, *Irrigation Policy in Spain and Spanish America*, quoted by G.L. Ulmen, 'The Science of Society. Toward an Understanding of the Life

and Work of Karl August Wittfogel', in *Society and History. Essays in Honour of Karl August Wittfogel*, Ulmen ed., p. 481.

24. Herrera, *Libro di agricoltura utilissimo*, pp. 31v.–34v.–167r.–170v.
25. Bruschetti, *Storia dei progetti e delle opere per l'irrigazione del Milanese*.
26. Smith, *Man and Water*, p. 12ff.
27. Serres, *Le théâtre d'agriculture*, II, pp. 223–24, 242, 426 and 527–58; Palissy, *Discours admirables de la nature des eaux et fontaines*, pp. 239–303.
28. Beutler, 'Un chapitre de la sensibilité collective', pp. 1091–1122; Sereni, *Storia del paesaggio agrario italiano*, p. 176; P. Lanaro Sartori, 'Gli scrittori veneti d'agraria del Cinquecento e del primo Seicento tra realtà e utopia', in *Venezia e la Terraferma attraverso le relazioni dei rettori*, A. Tagliaferri ed., Milan, 1981, p. 273ff.
29. G. Lanteri, *Della economica. Trattato di M. Giacomo Lanteri gentilhuomo bresciano*, Venezia, 1560; I. Milius, *De hortorum cultura*, Brescia, 1574. On innovation in the Brescia area, see the useful bibliographical study by F. Grasso Caprioli, 'Camillo Tarello – Agostino Gallo – Giacomo Chizzola e l'Accademia di Rezzato', in *Rivista di storia dell'agricoltura*, 22 (1982), n. 2, pp. 37–122.
30. E. Sereni, 'Spunti della rivoluzione agraria europea nella scuola bresciana cinquecentesca di Agostino Gallo e di Camillo Tarello', in *Miscellanea in onore di R. Cessi*, II, Rome, 1958, pp. 113–28; Berengo, 'Introduzione' to *Camillo Tarello*, pp.VII–XLV; Poni, 'Un privilegio d'agricoltura. Camillo Tarello', pp. 592–610; Ambrosoli, *The Wild and the Sown*, p. 119ff. However, it was only with the agricultural revolution of the eighteenth century that Tarello's teachings would become at all widespread on the Venetian mainland.
31. Gallo, *Le vinti giornate dell'agricoltura*, p. 6.
32. Ibid., pp. 7–8. Similar worries were voiced by the Spaniard Herrera and by the Ravenna agronomist Bussato (Herrera, *Libro di agricoltura*, pp. 31v.–32r. Bussato, *Giardino di agricoltura*, p. 2r.). To counteract the effects that prolonged irrigation might have in carrying away the topsoil, Herrara suggested that manure should also be fed through the irrigation canals, in order to provide soil nutrients and fertilisers.
33. Berengo, 'Introduzione' to Tarello, *Ricordo di agricoltura*, pp. XXVI–XXVII; Finzi, *Monsignore al suo fattore*, pp. 29–34 and 79–113; Tarello, *Ricordo di agricoltura*, p. 100 and n.; Finzi, *Monsignore al suo fattore*, pp. 79–113.
34. Clementi, *Trattato dell'agricoltura*, pp. 26–27.
35. Berengo, *Africo Clementi, agronomo padovano del Cinquecento*, pp. 27–69.
36. Derex, *La gestion de l'eau et des zones humides en Brie*.
37. Braudel, *Civilisation matérielle. Les structures du quotidien: le possible et l'impossible*, I, p. 81.
38. Ceredi, *Tre discorsi sopra il modo d'alzar acque*, pp. 94–95.
39. One can see a similar problem in Northern France in the first decades of the seventeenth century: Jacquart, 'La productivité agricole', cit., p. 73.
40. Ceredi, *Tre discorsi sopra il modo d'alzar acque*, pp. 94–95.
41. Messedaglia, *Per la storia dell'agricoltura e dell'alimentazione*, p. 85. The lengthy list of these agronomists might include such names as Marco

Bussato, Charles Estienne (Carlo Stefano), Africo Clementi, Giovanni Tatti, Costantino Cesare, Bernardo Sacco, Giovanbattista Barpo and Giacomo Agostinetti.

42. Falcone, *La nuova, vaga, et dilettevole villa*, pp. 253–54.

43. Vilar, *La Catalogne dans l'Espagne moderne*, II, pp. 284–89. See also *Istruzione sulla coltura del riso*, in *Giornale d'Italia*, VII, Venezia, 1771, pp. 49–72; D. Mainardi, *Della coltivazione del riso e della coltura dei prati e degli arativi*, Padua, 1792, pp. 5–7; Pugliese, 'Condizioni economiche e finanziarie della Lombardia', cit., pp. 35–38; Zucchini, *L'agricoltura ferrarese attraverso i secoli*, pp. 134–35 and 180–81; Vivanti, *Le campagne del Mantovano*, pp. 17–158; Faccini, *I lavoratori della risaia*, pp. 545–88; idem, *Uomini e lavoro*, pp. 23–28: the other diseases and disturbances were chlorosis (green sickness), neuralgia, nephritis, imbecility, gastroenteritis and dysentery.

44. Vilar, *La Catalogne dans l'Espagne moderne*, II, p. 285; Faccini, *Uomini e lavoro*, p. 120.

45. Pugliese, 'Condizioni economiche e finanziarie della Lombardia', cit., pp. 3 and 38; Faccini, *Uomini e lavoro*, p. 24; P. Lemonnier, 'Acqua', in *Enciclopedia*, R. Romano ed., I, Turin, 1977, p. 184.

46. A valuable export, rice from the Verona and Lombardy areas was often shipped from the port of Venice. (Sella, *Commerci e industrie a Venezia nel secolo XVII*, pp. 87–88).

47. Falcone, *La nuova, vaga, et dilettevole villa*, pp. 253–54; Sereni, *Storia del paesaggio agrario*, p. 240.

48. Some of these questions are dealt with in *Histoire d'une eau partagée. Irrigation et droits d'eau du Moyen Âge à nos jours. Provence Alpes Pyrénées*, O. Aubriot and G. Jolly eds., Aix-en-Provence (Publications de l'Université de Provence), 2002.

49. Mozzi, *I magistrati veneti alle acque e alle bonifiche*, p. 19 n.; Aymard, *Venise, Raguse et le commerce du blé*, p. 7ff.

50. Ventura, 'Considerazioni sull'agricoltura veneta', pp. 519–21; B. Pullan, 'The Occupations and Investments of the Venetian Nobility in the Middle and Late Sixteenth Century', in *Renaissance Venice*, J. Hale ed., London, 1974, pp. 379–408; S.J. Woolf, 'Venice and Terraferma: Problems of the Change from Commercial to Landed Activities', in Pullan ed., *Crisis and Change in the Venetian Economy*, pp. 175–203.

51. G. Ferrari, 'La legislazione veneziana sui beni comunali', in *Archivio Veneto*, n. s., 36 (1918), pp. 29–30.

52. The growing workload meant that in 1589 the three *Provveditori ordinari* were joined by four *Provveditori straordinari*; however, in 1655, the overall number was reduced to five. In 1700 one such *Provveditore* was raised to the rank of *Inquisitore*, to deal with the continual infringements of the law. (Mozzi, *I magistrati veneti alle acque e alle bonifiche*, pp. 5–8; Campos, *I consorzi di bonifica*, pp. 17–22; ASV, S.T., filza 32, Senate decree of 12 October 1560).

53. *Il summario di tutte le leggi et parti ottenute nell'illustrissimo Senato in materia delli beni inculti*, Venezia, 1558; *De' privilegi de veronesi nelle acque*, in *Livellationi fatte per M. Gieronimo Pontara [...] in proposito della regolation*

dell'Adige, Verona, 1596, pp. 64–66. If one wants to know more about the development of irrigation in these provincial areas, one has to consult local archives, given the poverty of extant material in those of the *Beni Inculti*.

54. S.T., reg. 21, 21 July 1519, cc.43v.–45r.; S.T., reg. 40, cc. 156v.–157r., Senate decree 6 February 1556; Bruschetti, *Storia dei progetti e delle opere per l'irrigazione del Milanese*, p. 59).

55. Romani, *L'agricoltura in Lombardia*, pp. 202–3 and n.

56. Glick, *Irrigation and Society in Medieval Valencia*, pp. 12–13; Macías Hernández, 'Les Îles Canaries, 1480–1525. Irrigation et première colonisation atlantique: le domaine de l'eau'; Bresc, ' Les jardins de Palerme (1290–1460)'.

57. Mozzi, *I magistrati veneti alle acque e alle bonifiche*, pp. 6–12; Bruschetti, *Storia dei progetti e delle opere per l'irrigazione del Milanese*, pp. 150–51. On the fame and importance of the Ferrara hydraulic engineers in the fifteenth and sixteenth century, see Zucchini, *L'agricoltura ferrarese attraverso i secoli*, p. 92; now the important edition of Giovanni Battista Aleotti (*Della scienza e dell'arte del ben regolare le acque di Gio. Battista Aleotti detto l'Argenta architetto del papa, et del pubblico ne la città di Ferrara*), M. Rossi ed., Modena, 2000.

58. S.T., reg. 22, cc. 107v.–108r., Senate decreee of 15 July 1522; SEA, *busta* 89, copy of Senate decree of 19 June 1545; S.T., *filza* 64, Senate decree 16 September 1574; S.T., *filza* 342, Document of the Psbi 18 August 1622, attached to the Senate decree of 20 February 1630; Psbi, *busta* 81, Dossier Sagramoso, Secret report to the Psbi, 26 June 1598, accusing the Verona noblemen of usurping for their own use the waters of the Adige and other watercourses. On the theft of water in Spain, see J. Depassa, *Voyage en Espagne dans les années 1816, 1817, 1818, 1819 ou recherches sur l'arrosage*, I, Paris, 1823, p. XVII.

59. The use of the 'wheel' system – with a rotation in the delivery of water over a period of from one to two weeks – was less common in the Veneto than it was in Lombardy, where much greater use was made of water (Canetta, 'L'irrigazione nella bassa pianura lombarda', cit., pp. 74–75).

60. In eighteenth-century Catalonia, too, rainwater cost half as much as river water (see Vilar, *La Catalogne dans l'Espagne moderne*, II, p. 249).

61. The regional variations in the price of water mean that one cannot make any precise deductions on the basis of the data we have regarding such costs. One essential instrument for the Venetian State – both in outlining the general situation of its water resources and in fighting evasion of the dues to be paid for their use – was provided by the cadastral land registers, which listed all the various water concessions. Three such registers are still to be found in the records of the Psbi: one for the Vicenza area, one for the Padua, Treviso and Friuli area, and another for Verona, Cologna, Crema, Cremona, Bergamo and Istria (even if in this latter, the registrations concern Verona alone).

62. The *piede lineare* [foot] (= 0,34 metre) was made up of 12 *oncie* [inches], so that one square foot was made up of 144 square inches, which were also known as *punti*; in practice, however, a *quadretto* was divided into 12 *oncie*, which were again divided into 12 *punti*. The water was also measured in terms of *ruote* [wheels], each one of which was equivalent to one *quadretto*

(Psbi, *busta* 475, Application by Girolamo and Antonio Morosini, 9 March 1557; V. Brunacci, *Memoria sulla dispensa delle acque*, Milan, 1927, pp. 6–25; on the Lombard unit of measurement, the 'Milanese inch', see Canetta, 'L'irrigazione nella bassa pianura lombarda', cit., pp. 75–76).

63. L.E. Harris, 'Land Drainage and Irrigation', in *History of Technology*, III. *From the Renaissance to the Industrial Revolution, c.1500–c.1750*, C. Singer et al. eds., Oxford, 1969, pp. 314–15.

64. P. Frisi, 'Del modo di regolare i fiumi e i torrenti', in *Nuova raccolta d'autori, che trattano del moto delle acque*, Carmignani ed., VI, Parma, 1766, pp. 1–110.

65. B. Castelli, 'Della misura delle acque correnti', in *Nuova raccolta d'autori, che trattano del moto delle acque*, Marsigli ed., III, Bologna, 1822, p. 166. Castelli had been Galileo's pupil in Padua.

66. *Perizia intorno alla misura delle acque erogate dal Brenta [...] estesa dai matematici Ximenes e Stratico [...] nell'anno 1777*, Venice, 1844, pp. 9–10.

67. Ibid., pp. 39–40. Bruschetti, *Storia dei progetti e delle opere per l'irrigazione del Milanese*, pp. 19–20 and 34. Bruschetti's argument appears rather weak when he claims that water speed was taken into account in such calculations within the Milan area during the sixteenth century.

68. *Perizia intorno alla misura delle acque erogate dal Brenta*, cit., pp. 39–40; Zendrini, *Leggi e fenomeni*, pp. 142–43; Brunacci, *Memoria sulla dispensa delle acque*, cit., pp. 57–58.

69. Museo Correr, Mss. P.D., C.975/52, Concordat between the Republic and the Duke of Mantova, 15 March 1548; *Trattato fra [...] l'imperatrice [...] e la Serenissima Repubblica di Venezia sopra l'uso delle acque del Tartaro*, Verona, 1768; *Informazione sopra gli argini, sgoli ed adacquamenti delo stato mantovano*, Mantua 1734, part II, p. 67 and part III, pp. 3–40). On the clashes between Brescia and Cremona over the waters of the Oglio, see C. Cairns, *Domenico Bollani. Devotion to Church and State in the Republic of Venice in the Sixteenth Century*, Nieuwkoop, 1976, pp. 80–117; on disputes over water between Mantua and Ferrara, see Zucchini, *L'agricoltura ferrarese attraverso i secoli*, p. 96).

70. Canetta, 'L'irrigazione nella bassa pianura lombarda', cit., p. 78; Romani, *L'agricoltura in Lombardia*, p. 202.

71. Psbi, reg. 312, cc.19v.–20r., concession granted 23 March 1574; Psbi, *busta* 263, Report of 8 March 1583; Boerio, *Dizionario del dialetto veneziano*, Venezia, 1856, definition of *Penello*; and the entry 'Irrigazione', in *Enciclopedia italiana di scienze, lettere ed arti*, XIX, Rome, 1951, p. 572.

72. Almost all writers of the period agree that the best time for irrigation was the evening or the early hours of the morning (Porta, *Villae libri XII*, pp. 644–45 and 905; Stefano, *Agricoltura nuova*, pp. 120 and 341–46. On these questions see Sinclair, *L'agriculture pratique et raisonnée*, pp. 535–66; Buffon, *Des subversions fertilisantes*, p.109ff.

73. Stratico, *Raccolta di proposizioni d'idrostatica*, pp. XLVI–LII.

74. In effect, these wheels were just a version of the *tympanum* which, together with the *noria*, had been used for this purpose since Classical Antiquity. The literature on this subject is extensive: Bélidor, *Architecture hydraulique*, I,

livre II, cap. IV, pp. 384–87 and *planche* 9; Agricola, *De re metallica*, pp. 131–33; Ewbank, *A Descriptive and Historical Account of Hydraulic*, pp. 109–14; Zonca, *Novo teatro di machine*, pp. 61–63 and 100–15; Besson, *Theatrum instrumentorum*, tavv. 46–52; Veranzio, *Machinae novae*, p. 10ff.

75. There are numerous examples of this to be found amongst the papers of the various Venetian *magistrature*. Galileo Galilei himself obtained a patent in this area from the Republic in 1594 (Berveglieri, *Inventori stranieri a Venezia (1474–1788)*, p. 48).

76. The Archimedes' Screw is a cylinder around which is wrapped a spiralling tube or sloping thread; in Ceredi's model, this spiral and cylinder were contained within a second cylinder. They could be worked by a single man; whilst a horse attached to a wheel could power three. Ceredi also argued that Ferrara had no reason to fear that drawing water from the Po would interfere with navigation, because the river had more than enough water to serve both purposes.

77. Ceredi, *Tre discorsi sopra il modo d'alzar acque*, pp. 1–90.

78. J. Mokyr, *The Lever of Riches: Technological Creativity and Economic Progress*, New York, 1990.

79. S.T., reg. 21, Senate decree July 1519, cit.; Grinovero, *Ricerche sull'economia dell'irrigazione*, p. 173 n.

80. S. Bortolami, 'Il Brenta medievale nella pianura veneta. Note per una storia politico-territoriale', in *Il Brenta*, A. Bondesan et al. eds., Verona, 2003, pp. 211–33.

81. M.C. Billanovich, *Attività estrattiva negli Euganei. Le cave di Lispida e del Pignaro tra Medioevo ed età moderna*, Venezia, 1997; Marzolo, 'L'idraulica veneta e l'apporto dell'Università di Padova nelle discipline idrauliche', p. 96.

82. Vergani, *Brentella. Problemi d'acque nell'alta pianura trevigiana*, pp. 37–43 and 61ff.; Serena, *Il canale della Brentella*, pp. 9–22 and 43–48. The first pressure to open a canal at Pederobba had come from the citizens of Castelfranco in 1425 (*Rellation scripta intorno la Brentella se ha da trasar per adacquare le campagne*, in R. Brenzoni, *Fra Giovanni Giocondo veronese*, Firenze, 1960, p. 152).

83. 'The poor die of *dexaxio* [dehydration] and haven't enough water to drink, whilst the grand not only have water left over for their meadows and fields, but even enough to wash out their stables' (*Relazioni dei rettori veneti in Terraferma. Podestaria e Capitanato di Treviso*, Tagliaferri ed., Report by Marco Zantani, 1 October 1525; see also L. Doglioni, *Ragionamento epistolare sopra le irrigazioni del territorio trevigiano*, Bassano, 1799, pp. 10 and 21).

84. Psbi, *Capitolare secondo*, cc. 138r.–139v., Application from the ambassadors of Treviso to the Collegio, 27 July 1572; ibid., cc. 133v.–140r., Written document by Nicolò Cicogna 22 June, 21 and 29 July, 1 August 1572.

85. Cicogna must have had a vested interest in such extensions of irrigation, given that in 1475 a certain Francesco Cicogna had bought land at Montebelluna (Serena, *Il canale della Brentella*, p. 135 n.).

86. In June 1572 Cicogna applied for half the water, but by 1 August he was willing to settle for one quarter (S.T., *filza* 59, Senate decree 2 August 1572;

cfr. also *filza* 60, Senate decree 3 December 1572 and attached document by Cicogna, 22 November 1572; 'Relazione Francesco Bragadin', 9 September 1537, in *Relazioni dei rettori veneti in Terraferma. Podestaria e Capitanato di Treviso*, Tagliaferri ed., p. 12; 'Relazione Francesco Diedo', 12 October 1569, ibid., pp. 52–53; Psbi, *busta* 263, *Report by the expert Feliciano Perona*, 13 November 1595. This latter document provides detailed information on the development of rice-fields and their irrigation in the Friuli, Po delta and the Treviso areas).

87. In 1595 irrigation had only covered some 4–5 per cent of the consortium's agricultural land, which ammounted at the time to around 23,000 hectares (Vergani, *Brentella. Problemi d'acque nell'alta pianura trevigiana*, p. 318).

88. SEA, *filza* 85, 11 January 1550; C. Sabbadino, 'Per adacquar il Trevisan da Nervesa in zoso', in ASV, *Archivio Proprio Zendrini*, reg. 24, cc.56–59, between 1550 and 1558; Serena, *Il canale della Brentella*, pp. 132–33.

89. S.T., reg. 21, Senate decree 21 July 1519, cit. The areas irrigated were Bassano, Rosà, Cassola, Rossano Veneto, Castello di Codego, Castelfranco (cfr. *Carta delle irrigazioni* cit., p. 44).

90. S.T., reg. 40, cc.128r.–128v., Senate decree 29 August 1556.; S.T., *filza* 1074, Report by the *rettori* of Padua, 14 September 1686 attached to Senate decree 26 September 1686. In fact, nowadays the canal is known as the Dolfina canal; it carries some 5,058 cubic metres, as opposed to the 6,744 of the Rosà (for this data, and that concerning the volume of other canals, see Grinovero, *Ricerche sull'economia dell'irrigazione*, p. 175).

91. According to the *rettori* of Padua, there were at least 14 large and small canals drawing water off the Brenta (S.T., *filza* 1074, Senate decree 26 September 1686 and attached document; S.T., *filza* 1049, Report by Marchio Moretti, 14 August 1683, deputy expert on rivers, attached to Senate decree 19 August 1684; *Carta delle irrigazioni venete*, cit., pp. 44–49).

92. Report by the *rettori* and Senate decree of 6 September 1686, cit.

93. A. Keller, *Prosciugamenti ed irrigazioni nel Padovano*, Padua, 1878, pp. 58–59 and 60–64; C. Bionda, *L'irrigazione dei prati di Bacchiglione in provincia di Vicenza e di Padova*, Vicenza, 1896.

94. *Modo d'irrigare la campagna di Verona, e d'introdur più navigationi per lo [...] stato di Venezia, trovato fino dal 1565 da M. Christoforo Sorte [...] e anco di Antonio Magro, e del Sig. Theodoro da Monte*, Verona, 1593, pp. 16–24 and 44–48. According to Sorte's calculations, the work would have reclaimed some 7,500 hectares, increasing its value and boosting fodder production (Petition of C. Sorte, ibid., pp. 5–10; see also ASV, SEA, *busta* 529, Report by A. Glisenti, 20 November 1587). Like the other parts of the Veneto mainland, the Verona area imported beef from Mantua, Ferrara, the Trento region and even the distant Hungary because of the insufficiency of local fodder (M. Lecce, 'Le condizioni zootecnico-agricole del territorio veronese nella prima metà del '500', in *Ricerche di storia economica medievale e moderna*, Verona, 1975, pp. 85–116).

95. Teodoro da Monte, 'Breve discorso sopra l'irrigazione delle campagne veronesi e scollation sua', 21 December and 10 June 1593, in *Modo*

d'irrigare, cit., pp. 105-11. Teodoro da Monte took up C. Sorte's idea of drawing an irrigation canal off Lake Garda; he intended to supplement this with a further irrigation canal drawn off the Adige. He also suggested the creation of a special shipping canal between the river and lake; but the course he plotted for this was rather bizarre (see the *Compendio di tutti li raccordi et suppliche presentate da diversi [...] in proposito d'irrigar la campagna di Verona*, Verona, 1594, p. 87ff.; *Aggionta al compendio di tutti gli raccordi et suppliche [...] in proposito d'irrigar la campagna di Verona*, Verona, 1594, pp.119-33; *Livellazioni fatte per M. Gieronimo Pontara, et per M. Bartolameo Montino [...] ad istantia del Sig. Theodoro da Monte*, Verona, 1595, pp. 5-9; 'Supplica di Teodoro da Monte al senato veneziano', in *Modo d'irrigare*, cit., pp. 98-104; ibid., 'Breve discorso sopra l'irrigazione', pp. 111-21, document submitted to the *rettori* of Verona, s. d., in *Aggionta al compendio*, cit., pp. 31-51. Da Monte planned to irrigate around 25,000 *campi*; even if in another passage he does speak of 150,000 *campi*. Similarly, his estimates of fodder production vary from 60,000 to 300,000 cartloads. Clearly he wasn't above a little exaggeration when promoting his scheme.

96. Benedetto Venier, *L'unica maniera d'irrigare le campagne veronesi da due parti dell'Adige, principalmente con l'escrescenze sue facendo navigazioni, et essicationi*, Verona, 1594, pp. 5-28 and 39-40.

97. G. Valente, 'Cenni storici sull'irrigazione in Friuli', in *Atti dell'Accademia di Scienze Lettere e Arti di Udine*, Udine, XXI (1942), pp. 1-9 and 17. The city governors in their reports often stress how agriculturally backward this scarcely-populated area was, in spite of the fact that it was of great military importance as a border zone between the Venetian Republic and the Holy Roman Empire (*Relazioni dei rettori veneti. La Patria del Friuli (Luogotenenza di Udine)*, Tagliaferri ed., pp. XVII, XXXI-XXXIV). The Aviano canal (after 1486 known as the 'Brentella') has been rhetorically defined as 'a monument to the hydraulics of the fifteenth century' (see *Documenti del terzo scavo del canale di San Marco o Brentella da Montereale al Musile* (Nozze Brusasco-Cossettini), Pordenone, 1884 and G.B. Bassi, *Sulla irrigazione colle acque del Cellina nella provincia del Friuli*, Udine, 1875; idem, *Memoria sull'antico divisamento di costruire un canale navigabile da Udine al mare*, Udine, 1829; G. Occioni Bonaffons, *Bibliografia storica friulana*, I, Udine, 1883, p. 180 and II, p. 135.

98. C. Cattaneo, 'Delle irrigazioni del Friuli in paragone al canale Cavour e ai nuovi progetti dell'Alto Milanese', in *Scritti economici*, A. Bertolino ed., III, Florence, 1956, pp. 440-42; *Scrittura di Giulio Savorgnan nel 1592 sull'incanalamento del Ledra* (Nozze Occioni Bonaffons-Crisicopulo), Udine, 1876. The governors themselves commented upon the abundance of water that was practically unused (see, for example, Giovanni Moro in 1527: *Relazioni dei rettori veneti, La Patria del Friuli*, cit., p. 10). On Giulio Savorgnan, of the Osoppo branch of the family, see F. Bonati Savorgnan d'Osoppo, 'I Savorgnan d'Osoppo', in *Archivio Veneto*, s. V, 100 (1973), pp. 10-11; P. Quaglia, 'Della irrigazione di un vasto territorio alla destra del Tagliamento colle acque del Cellina', in *Bolletttino dell'Associazione agraria friulana*, II, Udine, 1874, p. 1.

99. According to the cadastral register of 1661, the nobility of the 'Patria del Friuli' owned 18,131 hectares, as against the 8,003 owned by commoners, that is 66.5 per cent as against 29.5 per cent (cf. Beltrami, *La penetrazione economica*, p. 94; C. Grinovero, *L'evoluzione dcll'agricoltura friulana. Monografia economico agraria*, Udine, 1966, pp. 14–16).

100. Berengo, *L'agricoltura veneta*, pp. 129–30.

101. Valente, *Cenni storici sull'irrigazione in Friuli*, cit., pp. 15–16; Biblioteca comunale di Udine, Mss. 585, Angelo Maria Cortenovis, *Sull'irrigazione del Friuli. Dissertazione accademica letta nell'Accademia di Udine*, 1772.

102. Mozzi, *I magistrati veneti alle acque e alle bonifiche*, pp. 13–16. The *Savi* were generally responsible for work of any complexity involving the rivers that emptied into the Lagoon – for example, the passing of a new canal bed across an existing river or canal, which could involve the construction of either a 'canal bridge' or of an underground culvert. See the Senate decrees of 12 October and 6 February 1560 (S.T., *filza* 32) and D. Guglielmini, 'Trattato sulla natura dei fiumi', in *Nuova raccolta d'autori, che trattano del moto delle acque*, Carmignani ed., II, Parma, 1766, pp. 255–58.

103. G.A. Pedrinelli Pissina, *Compendio dei decreti e terminazioni [...] circa gl'affari del Magistrato ecc.mo delle acque*, Venezia, 1706, p. 23. It was the *Savi* and not the *Provveditori* who, in 1681, gave permission for the community of Gambarare outside Padua to draw a *quadretto* of water from the Brenta *nuovissimo*; they even contributed 250 ducats to the cost of the scheme (ibid., p. 21). On other occasions they made changes in the status quo; for example, in 1559 a Ducal decree by Girolamo Priuli put an end to a concession granting three *quadretti* of water from the Brenta for irrigation because, after use, that water flowed into the Lagoon (Psbi, reg. 300, c.19r., Ducal decree by Girolamo Priuli to Psbi (copy), 21 November 1559).

104. As is well known, throughout the sixteenth and seventeenth century, 'before the time of Newcomen' the only natural sources of energy were men, animals, wind and water: cfr. A. Ruppert Hall, 'Scientific method and the progress of techniques', in *The Cambridge economic history. The economy of expanding Europe in the sixteenth and seventeenth centuries*, E.E. Rich and C.H. Wilson eds., IV, Cambridge, 1967, p. 103; D. Sella, *Contributo alla storia delle fonti di energia*, in *Studi in onore di A. Fanfani*, V, Milan, 1962, pp. 619–31.

105. On the paper industry and its location in the foothills area, see I. Mattozzi, *Produzione e commercio della carta nello stato veneziano settecentesco. Lineamenti e problemi*, Bologna, 1975, pp. 67–70; on the silk industry, C. Poni, 'Archéologie de la fabrique: la diffusion des moulins à soie 'alla bolognese' dans les Etats vénitiens du XVIᵉ au XVIIᵉ siècle', in *Annales E.S.C.*, 27 (1972), pp. 1475–96. Hammers and bellows do not seem to have used much water (Psbi, *busta* 94, Report by the expert Tommaso Fiorini, 4 July 1695). By the second half of the seventeenth century, metal furnaces might be ventilated by bellows (driven by water wheels) or by hydraulic air pumps, which were introduced into Italy around the middle of the previous century (C.S. Smith-R.J. Forbes, 'Metallurgy and assaying' in *History of Technology*,

III. *From the Renaissance to the Industrial Revolution, c1500–c1750*, cit., pp. 51–53). On Italian fulling-mills or *gualchiere*, see Malanima, *I piedi di legno. Una macchina alle origini dell'industria medievale.* On mills in general and their increase from the Middle Ages onwards, see M. Bloch, *Lavoro e tecnica nel medioevo* (Introduction of G. Luzzatto), Bari, 1974, pp.73–110; Cipolla, *Before the Industrial Revolution*, pp. 137–59; U. Forti, *Storia della tecnica. Dalla rinascita dopo il Mille alla fine del Rinascimento*, II, Turin, 1974, pp. 139–42.

106. Psbi, reg. 550, c.81r., Document by Michele Priuli, 24 September 1535; Psbi, reg. 307, cc.58v.–59r., Document by Psbi 16 March 1569.

107. On canals and rivers, see J. Day, 'Strade e vie di comunicazione', in *Storia d'Italia. I documenti*, pp. 101–2; ibid. U. Tucci, 'Credenze geografiche e cartografia', pp. 62–66; P. Laven, 'The Venetian rivers in the Sixteenth Century', in *Montagnes, fleuves, forêts dans l'histoire*, J-F. Bergier ed., St. Katharinen, 1989, pp. 198–217. On these issues, see also F.C. Lane, *Navires et constructeurs à Venise pendant la Renaissance*, Paris, 1965, pp. 206–7 and 213–16; *Relazioni dei rettori veneti in Terraferma, Podestaria e Capitanato di Belluno – Podestaria e Capitanato di Feltre*, Tagliaferri ed., pp. 291, 313, 318, 371, 407, 411 and 418; Sereni, *Storia del paesaggio agrario*, pp. 198–204; Cipolla (*Before the Industrial Revolution*, pp. 92–93 and 112) argues that Italy had already started to compromise its woodlands and forests very early, leading to the creation of marshland and terrain subject to flooding. From another perspective, that of mentality and sensibility, see Schama, *Landscape and Memory*, p. 75ff.

108. Psbi, *Capitolare secondo*, c.98r., 22 February 1611. Similar concerns to reconcile the needs of shipping and irrigation can often be seen in Lombardy: G. Cesare Zimolo, 'Canali e navigazione interna nell'età moderna', in *Storia di Milano. Sotto l'Austria (1815–1859)*, XIV, Milan, 1960, pp. 835–38.

109. M.C.V., Mss. P.D., C.827/37, Applications 16 September 1678, 24 March 1679, 9 September 1679. See also ASV, SEA, *busta* 89, Application by F. and G.B. Garzadori, 9 August 1565, regarding an opening off the Bacchiglione, opposed by Simone Da Porto of Vicenza.

110. On the responsibilities of the *Provveditori all'Adige*, first set up to supervise that river in the second half of the sixteenth century and made a permanent body in 1667, see Da Mosto, *L'archivio di Stato di Venezia*, I, p. 158. With regard to the Adige, see the numerous essays in *Una città e il suo fiume. Verona e l'Adige*, Borelli ed.

111. S.T., *filza* 1021, Senate decree 11 april 1687. On the course of the Bussé see the 'Carta idrografica del Veronese, Polesine e Padovano' attached to Giovanni Coi, *Ragionamento intorno ai fiumi del Veronese, Polesine e Padovano* (Padua 1777); and ASV, P. all'A., Disegni n. 28, *Corso generale delle acque da sette miglia inferiormente a Verona fino al mare*, 30 July 1784. A tributary on the right bank of the Adige, the Bussé cuts diagonally across the ample curve of the river and all the channels drawn off the upper part of the river flow into it.

112. Application by the City of Verona, 10 April 1681 and Report by the *Presidenti del Collegio dell'Adige*, 11 March 1682, enclosed with Senate decree of 11 April 1682.

Irrigation and Land Drainage in the Venetian Republic during the Sixteenth and Eighteenth Centuries

Agricultural Development of the Venetian Terra Firma during the Sixteenth Century: The Lombard Provinces

Various recent studies have cast new light on that process of 're-feudalisation' which occurred during the sixteenth and seventeenth century in Italy and elsewhere when, faced with sluggish trade and manufacturing sectors that were losing in profitability, urban capital 'fell back' upon investment in agriculture. Though an undoubted reality, this phenomenon is not to be seen in purely negative terms, especially when one looks at the general picture of the European – and, particularly, the Venetian – economy around the middle of the sixteenth century. In fact, this re-direction of urban capital was due less to a slackening-off in Venetian trade than to the steady upward trend in cereal and agricultural prices that had begun around 1520 in concomitance with the undoubted demographic growth of the second and third quarter of the century.[1] As Braudel comments 'it was the increase in prices and agricultural profits that drove Venetian capital onto the mainland'; though he also underlines that 'land ownership was not a step towards social elevation; it was only a question of investments and revenues'.[2] The same general point is made with regard to sixteenth- and seventeenth-century Milan by De Maddelena, when he rejects 'the widespread accusations that the countryside of the region had a 'narcotic' effect upon enterprise and capital, drawing them away from profitable investment within the city and thus initiating the socio-economic decline of the Milanese state'. In effect, in sixteenth-century Lombardy, as in the Venetian Republic of the day, this shift towards the countryside reflected a clearly chosen strategy of the industrial and mercantile 'establishment'.

In Lombardy, the stimulus thus given to agriculture and the organisation of agricultural activity was unique within Europe, while the effects within the Venetian Republic were less remarkable.[3] It is, therefore, important to look at the significance of land reclamation and irrigation projects within the Venetian Republic, asking why the Venetian nobility focused more on the former (land reclamation) than on a modern system for the use of water, which would have resulted in an increase in agricultural productivity. In Lombardy, on the other hand, land reclamation had a much less significant effect upon boosting productivity and earnings than did the spread of irrigated meadows and rice as a crop: as Aymard and Basini comment 'water use in Lombardy was much more productive than it was elsewhere, due both to the level of technology used and, perhaps, to the level of investment'.[4]

In effect, throughout the world, modern agricultural development rests on an increase in irrigated meadow-land and herd size (to supply urban meat markets and provide fertilisation for the soil) and on crop diversity and rotation (to break out of what has been called the 'blocage céréalier'). Of course, higher wheat production would long remain the number-one priority of European agriculture, and there was great reluctance to adopt a revolutionary 'field grass system' such as that which began to be fully operative in England in the sixteenth century; in Lombardy itself – and even more so in Tarello's Brescia – the introduction of fodder into the crop cycle was predicated primarily on the need to increase cereal crop production. Nevertheless, whilst in sixteenth-century France the demand for corn would effectively paralyse the development of livestock herds, in other areas of Europe – fifteenth and sixteenth-century Holland, late-sixteenth-century England, or the Lombardy plain areas of the fifteenth/sixteenth century – there was a marked trend towards an increase in meadow-land and irrigation. For example, from the middle of the sixteenth century to the beginning of the eighteenth, fodder crops in Lombardy increased by 320 per cent, and whilst there was a decrease in areas of permanently-irrigated meadow-land, there was a sizeable increase in cereal/fodder rotation and a clear improvement in the agricultural techniques used in growing crops.[5] Even the spread of maize as a crop did not undermine the central role of fallow-land in rotation cycles as it occurred at the expense of the less important cereal crops.

In the Venetian Republic development was not so clear-cut. In 1573 the agricultural land owned by the city's nobility in the various areas of the mainland comprised relatively low percentages of meadow-land: 13.2 per cent in the Vicenza area, 6 per cent around Padua and only 3.3 per cent in the Treviso area. Such figures do go up when one looks at the land owned by the actual inhabitants of the terra firma, but even there the maximum is 18.5 per cent in the Vicenza area. The limited quantity of permanent or rotation-cycle meadow-land – whether irrigated or not – meant that the modest-sized herds of the Veneto had to rely for fodder on the neighbouring markets of Ferrara, Mantua and Trento; reference has already been made to the dispute that arose between Verona and Venice in the period 1529–1557 when the former claimed it was incapable of meeting the beef quotas set by the Venetian government. What is more, the fact that share-croppers in the Veneto were not obliged to provide themselves with the necessary livestock (as they were in the Bologna region, for example, where they were granted the right to all the fodder produced on the land they farmed) might well provide another explanation for the scarce interest in expanding fodder crops.[6] Nor should one overlook here the influence of the fact that for a long time Venice was happy to meet part of its beef needs from the well-stocked herds of Hungary, with the result that meat was never in abundant supply and was expensive (both in Venice and on the mainland). According to Vera Zimányi, meat consumption in Venice over the period 1624–1647 never went above an annual average of 21 kilograms per head (in the mainland cities it was even lower); admitting the exceptional circumstances of Hungary, she points out that over the same period, average annual consumption figures for every single inhabitant of that country were 60 kilograms of meat, 50 kilograms of animal fat, 50 kilograms of pork and around 600 to 700 litres of milk.[7]

However there were partial success stories in water use within the Venetian state, above all in the areas 'beyond the Mincio': around Brescia, Cremona and, to a lesser extent, Bergamo. Thanks to the irrigation canals drawn off the Oglio, the Garza and the Mella, the mediocre soil of the Brescia area was made 'most fertile in grasses, hemp, vines and all sorts of fodder'. It was commonly said that the Oglio was like the Nile, making fields fertile, fattening the land of meadows and olive groves, and producing fine wines.[8] According to a report of 1563, the Cremona area was no less fertile: three-quarters of the zone enjoyed the benefits of irrigation, producing hemp (in 1599 it is calculated there were some 500 linen looms), corn, millet and hay. In the seventeenth and eighteenth century, these crops would be joined by rice and mulberry, both of which flourished in the area. Irrigated crops undermined the emphasis on cereals and vines that would long continue to be dominant in the countryside of the Veneto as a whole; it is no coincidence that in 1597 stress was laid on how the area dedicated to vineyards in this province was rather low owing to the prevalence of irrigation.[9]

In the Bergamo area, the Brembo and the Serio provided power for mills, hammers, saw-works and fulling machinery, but the reports of the *rettori* [City Governors] make it clear that not all the available water sources were put to full use: the province was, for example, not entirely self-sufficient in grain and often had to import from the neighbouring Cremona area. Furthermore, proposals to channel the waters of the Brembo and Serio – or use the Lake of Spinone as a reservoir of irrigation water – fell on deaf ears.[10]

The Verona Area

In the lands 'on this side of the Mincio' – that is, in the Venetian Mainland proper – the shortcomings noted in the Bergamo area become even clearer: for example, the failure of numerous irrigation projects in the upper and middle plain areas around Verona at the end of the sixteenth century, or the poor performance of the Brentella canal near Treviso. Comparison of irrigation investment with that in projects for the draining of low-lying areas – particularly around Padua and in the Po delta – reveals a sharp bias towards the latter. It has been estimated (with some approximation) that two million ducats was spent on land drainage during the sixteenth century alone,[11] whilst the records of concessions by the *Provveditori ai Beni Inculti* (from 1556 onwards) suggest only 50,000 to 55,000 ducats was spent on the actual use of water. Of course, one must also add to this figure the costs of creating canals, digging irrigation ditches, building embankments and other preparation of terrain. As we shall see in the case of rice-fields, water accounted for about one-sixth of total costs, and therefore perhaps the above sum of 50,000 to 55,000 ducats for concessions should be multiplied by six (though for irrigated pasture land the factor should certainly be lower). Overall, therefore, the revenue of the *Beni Inculti* suggests that the amount spent on irrigation work might be put at around 100,000 to 200,000 ducats.

It is beyond question that there was some significant increase in the areas of irrigated pasture land, arable land, vegetable plots and, above all, rice-fields during the sixteenth century. This is particularly clear in the Verona area, located between the well-irrigated western part of the Venetian state and that central-eastern area which was less irrigated and more in need of constant drainage. Here, the local – and to a lesser extent – the Venetian nobility managed to take advantage of the numerous rivers and springs of the area to increase the value of their sizeable estates. There was a profound change in the landscape due to the massive reduction of waste land, woodland and marsh, with a large part of the Verona plain being irrigated and land being turned over to the cultivation of rice. This transformation began as early as the second half of the fifteenth century, when the local feudal aristocracy – as well as the mercantile and financial aristocracy of the city – began the conquest of this 'agrarian frontier' which would turn the province of Verona into the most original example of agricultural development in the Venetian terra firma. As Giovanni Zalin makes plain, investment in the agriculture of the area by Venetian patricians amounted to almost 70,000 ducats during the fifteenth century, even if – as Beltrami points out – their presence here was not destined to grow as it did in other mainland areas (such as Padua and the Po delta).[12] This latter point would explain why so few of the water-concession holders in the sixteenth century were Venetians, whilst a much larger number came from the powerful families of Verona itself, whose role within this province should not be underestimated. The entrepreneurial dynamism of the Veronese nobility is clear from the second half of the fifteenth century onwards, and by the second half of the following century their awareness of the chances offered by the growing markets for agricultural produce in Venice and throughout Europe was leading them to increase output of rice, mulberry, fodder, fruit and garden vegetables, as well as invest in ways of improving the fertility of their lands.[13]

In the Verona area alone, sales of water for agricultural and manufacturing use (but primarily the former) in the period 1558 to 1604 accounted for some 29,452 ducats out of a mainland total of 54,837 ducats – that is, more than half – even if, according to one source, the water purchases in the area made by the Venetian aristocracy over this period amount to little more than 1,000 ducats (in 1586 and 1595 the Boldù family paid to irrigate 440 *campi*, whilst in 1589 the Cavalli family bought water to create some 60 rice-*campi*).[14] And even if this source does not include all Venetian water purchases – for example, the water used by the Donà from 1563 onwards for 50 rice-*campi* at Albaro; the 150 rice-*campi* created in the Colognese area by the Querini in 1560; or the water that the Gritti must certainly have used to irrigate their estate at Villabella – it does seem that the lion's share of the water was being put to use by the local aristocracy. At the end of the fifteenth century such great Verona families as the Giusti, the Serego, the Cipolla and the Sagramoso had already started land reclamation on the left bank of the Adige – along the Bussé and the Tartaro – and would subsequently invest substantial sums of money in the creation of rice-fields and the irrigation of their vines, pastures and arable land.[15] For example, extensive stretches of the Serego estate in the Cologna area benefited from irrigation that drew on the waters of the Fibbio and the drainage from other aristocratic estates [16]: at Cucca and Becciacivetta alone the irrigated land was said to total 765 hectares, including 500 rice-*campi* (between 1570 and 1579 the Serego paid some 1,350 ducats to the *Provveditori ai Beni Inculti*).

For their part, some time between 1520 and 1530 the Sagramoso had followed the example of Teodoro Trivulzio – said to have been the first to introduce rice as a crop in this area – by investing in land reclamation, irrigation and the creation of paddy-fields (the Maffei, another powerful Verona family, probably began to do so shortly afterwards). However, in this period it was technically almost impossible to reconcile the needs of rice-fields, land drainage and irrigation, as one can see in 1599 when the sizeable land-reclamation consortium in the area between Palù and Isola Porcarizza – headed since 1561 by the Sagramoso – came under savage criticism from the Presidents of the Ronca and Tomba consortia located in the area where the Bussé flowed into the Adige. It was argued that the Sagramoso rice-fields were causing serious damage to the drained land by drawing excessive quantities of water from the Adige – perhaps as much as 50 *quadretti* – which then overflowed embankments and flooded the terrain that had been reclaimed with such difficulty.[17]

The Sagramoso were not the only ones to be accused of exceeding the water quotas fixed by the *Provveditori* experts. The Boldieri, for example, obtained a concession for some 6 *quadretti* from the Menago but actually drew off more than 50; true, this latter figure was calculated in times of heavy rain, but it certainly meant that the concession-holders had much more water at their disposal (the Boldieri were also accused of cultivating some 800 of their 2,000 *campi* with rice, whilst the original concession had authorised only 500). The *Provveditori*, always seeking to protect their revenues, clearly took these charges very seriously, but Orazio Boldieri – who personally oversaw 'the rice-workers and the other seasonal and permanent labour' – replied that the agreed area for rice-fields had been exceeded because an attempt had been made to use not only the purchased waters of the Menago but also other spring water, in an experiment that had turned out to be a costly failure. What is more, his brother, Francesco, who had herds of cows and horses, had leased some 300 *campi* of pasture land which he had then discovered sloped downwards at the centre; hence he had made them over for the cultivation of rice.[18]

Further confirmation that aristocrats personally ran their own estates comes from the development of different types of contract during the sixteenth century, resulting in 'hands-on' estate-management by property owners, with a resultant reduction in the number of long-lease tenants and the traditional access to open fields and natural resources. The Bonetti, for example, totally abandoned trade for farming – as their 'neighbours' pointed out with some acrimony[19] – and the list of those who became more active in agriculture would include some of the greatest names of the Verona aristocracy (owners of the largest and most profitable rice-fields) as well as recently-wealthy bourgeois.[20]

The 'race for water' that emerged so clearly in the second half of the sixteenth century involved not only the digging of water channels but also the harnessing of spring water. Although far from easy to raise to the surface, this latter was exploited precisely because river water was an expensive resource contested by so many.[21] And just how expensive water might be can be seen from the fact that, in optimum conditions, experts estimated it at 200 to 250 ducats per *quadretto*, with the smaller landholders – for example, the Cermisoni brothers who purchased 500 ducats worth of water in 1559 – paying in instalments. However, the very existence of such staggered payments reveals that the profitable exploitation of this valuable resource was not limited to the city's aristocracy.[22]

Rice

Amongst all the irrigated crops, rice occupied the largest areas and drew the largest amount of speculative capital in the Verona area. The middle and lower Po valley regions – together with the dry and gravelly upper plain area above the zone of the water springs – underwent irrigation on some scale, with benefits for pasture land, arable crops, vineyards, mulberry plantations and *broli* (fruit and vegetable gardens), all of which often resorted to water concessions.[23] However, it was rice – particularly in the middle and lower Po valley areas – which spread most extensively as a crop. Nevertheless, comparison of the Verona area with Piedmont and Lombardy reveals that in the former rice had nowhere near the same role as a stimulus of agricultural development. Between 1558 and 1604, 1,448 hectares were given over to rice-fields in the Verona region[24], some 0.46 per cent of the entire surface area of the city's province (3.096 km^2). This compares very well with the percentage that emerges from a similar comparison made with regard to Lombardy at the end of the sixteenth century by Pugliese and De Maddalena (0.5 per cent). However, by the beginning of the eighteenth century, the percentage of total area given over to the cultivation of rice in the latter region had increased almost sevenfold to 3.4 per cent.[25] In effect, a more flattering term of comparison for the Verona province would be others in the lower Po valley area – for example, Ferrara and Mantua. At the end of the eighteenth century, in fact, the total area of rice-fields in Mantua (4,216 hectares) was still lower than that in the Verona province at the end of the seventeenth (4,965).[26]

When considering why, in spite of the high initial costs, rice was preferred to other crops, one has to bear in mind its persistently high returns (up to two to four times more than corn or maize) as well as the fact that rice could figure as part of a crop-rotation cycle. What is more, the agricultural entrepreneur required only a limited permanent workforce, being able to employ seasonal labour for the harvesting, husking and threshing, thus restricting his wage bills to certain periods of the year. However, the role of many variables is yet to be fully clarified. How high a part of initial costs was accounted for by water? In discussing a later period – the end of the eighteenth century – Luigi Faccini says that the costs of water and its delivery/transport amounted to some 15 per cent (allowing for depreciation) of all the expenses a rice-grower had to meet during the course of a year.[27] Venetian government experts calculated in 1655 that about 10 ducats were needed to set up a rice-*campo* (the actual figure given being 1,000 ducats for 100 *campi*). This would include the costs of digging channels, raising embankments, connecting them with the irrigation canal and actually purchasing the water (to this were to be added another 600 ducats per year for running costs: the wages for the *risaro* [rice farmer] and for the occasional labour and so on).[28] In another case – the rice-fields set up by Pietro Zenobi in 1655 – the government experts assessed total costs at 220 ducats – a good 200 of which went for the water concession (that is, 90 per cent of the total). One gets therefore the clear impression that the 15 per cent estimate for eighteenth-century Lombardy could rise sharply in other contexts, above all in the years when there was a high demand for water (the period of agricultural growth when the rice-fields were being set up).[29]

The high yields associated with rice are to be seen in conjunction with the growing demand for cereals within the Venetian Republic and abroad. But whilst wheat was a crop largely grown for local consumption (and subject to restrictive legislation), rice was much more of a market crop, providing aristocratic land-owners with a high return on their initial investment, particularly after the sharp increases in prices at the end of the sixteenth century. Although there has been no comprehensive study of rice consumption, it does seem reasonably certain that it was seen as a luxury replacement for wheat. Even if in times of shortage, rice might also be used to make loaves that were sent to the Levant to feed galley slaves – and was therefore subject to the same norms regarding commerce and consumption as other cereal crops – it was some time before it become part of the popular diet (for example, in the pea risotto known as *risi e bisi*). Proof of just how long it maintained its status as the chosen food of the urban classes is to be found in the fact that a substantial part of the crop found its way to market: most of the rice from the Verona province (in 1584, some 100,000 *minali* = 2,860,100 kilograms) was shipped to the port of Venice, where it was joined by the (perhaps even larger) amounts imported from Lombardy.[30] This 'boom', however, very soon drew attention to other aspects of rice that were far from positive: the unhealthy air in the neighbourhood of the rice-fields; the destruction of pasture land; the shortage of other cereals and fruit; the detrimental effect on the diet of the poor (although the number of rice-fields continued to increase, so did the price of the crop, and thus consumption at the lower levels of society dropped).

All of this led to the decree of 17 September 1594[31], which undoubtedly slowed development of rice production in the Verona area (and throughout the Venetian terra firma) for some decades to come, its effects being aggravated by the stagnation of the early decades of the seventeenth century. The same train of events can also be seen in Lombardy, where restrictive legislation was introduced some twenty or so years before – the result of the same sharp clash of socio-economic interests between the large land-owners and the local population, which had stimulated a lively debate as to the health risks posed by rice-fields.[32] As for the Venetian Republic, the legislation meant that, from 1594 onwards, rice-fields could only be created in low-lying marshy areas and certainly not on reclaimed land along rivers – a restriction that led to a sharp inversion in the growth trend of the previous decades.[33] The 'destruction' of rice-fields in the Verona area was, however, less extensive than in other areas of the mainland Republic – for example, around Vicenza. Perhaps one reason for this was that the local aristocracy had always been viewed as forming an intimidating political group, and great prudence was required before making any moves that might clash with their economic interests.[34]

Other Provinces of the Venetian Mainland

Both irrigation and rice plantation became features of agriculture in the other provinces of the terra firma during the course of the sixteenth and seventeenth centuries, even if they affected more limited areas. In the zone around Vicenza, irrigation was present from the upper plain lands of the north-west to the Brenta in the east. However rice-fields tended to be concentrated in the *bassa* [lowland areas], with some exceptions to the north of the city and along the banks of the Brenta itself.[35] Up to 1595 a total of 774 hectares (2,000 *campi*) were sown with rice, around one-half of the figure for the Verona area (1,448 hectares).[36] As a result of the 1594 decree, however, the number dropped substantially – by about 40 per cent (320 hectares) – due to enforced closures.[37] Thus, as elsewhere in the Venetian state, rice in the Vicenza province over the coming decades would make only a limited contribution to meeting food needs. By 1794 Vicenza was nevertheless producing 36,206 bushels of rice, which put it in second place – but a long way behind – the province that continued to be the main rice-growing area of the Republic: Verona (88,621 bushels).[38]

In Vicenza, too, the Venetian landowners – whose estates here in 1661 actually totalled 1,000 hectares more than in the Verona area (10,079 hectares as against 9,141) – had less resort to the *Provveditori ai Beni Inculti* than did the local aristocracy: in 1594–5 only nine of the rice plantations in the Vicenza area were owned by Venetian noblemen and five of those would be destroyed after the 1594 decree. The only ones that remained in production were those owned by the Grimani at Carmignano (100 *campi*); by the Pisani at Bagnolo (300 *campi*); by the Priuli at Villa del Ferro (Sossano), where rice alternated with wheat in 343 *campi* shared with the Dolfin; and by the Balbi at Saianega (100 *campi*, laid out as a rice plantation around 1580).[39]

Expenditure on water tells the same story, with the Venetians falling far behind the local Veronese nobility; although there were exceptions, for example the 600 ducats paid by Zuanne Mocenigo to irrigate his fields near Marostica.[40]

In the province of Padua the major concession-holders for the use of water were Venetian patricians, as might be expected given their extensive presence in this area as land-owners (with estates totalling some 66,236 hectares in 1661). However, even here the purchase of surface water was not widespread and concerned some few hundred *campi* (arable, pasture land, rice-fields) as against the approximately 100,000 *campi* that were drained for agricultural use here during the sixteenth century. There were attempts to introduce rice-plantations, but they did not meet with much success. For example, Girolamo Grimani stirred up the protests of the Gorzon land-reclamation consortium because of the damage caused by his plantation;[41] and though we do not know the response to the applications made by Piero Marcello, Bartolomeo Querini and Piero Morosini to develop rice plantations at Masi, Piacenza and Castelbaldo – using the drainage from the Grimani plantation as well as water drawn from the Gorzon and Adige – they were probably as unsuccessful as those made by Girolamo Barbarigo and Antonio Cavalli. All in all, water sales in the Padua area between 1558 and 1604 did not go above one thousand ducats, a more than modest sum.[42]

Numbers alone would suggest that irrigation was pursued no more actively in the Treviso area; but this is a case where the official concessions granted are a poor illustration of the actual historical situation. In fact, irrigation was much more extensively practised than was indicated by the approximately 1,500 ducats received in payment for concessions in the second half of the sixteenth century. This was largely due to the fact that, thanks to the Brentella canal, the Treviso province comprised a sizeable area of irrigation (in the north-west), within which water distribution had taken place in the fifteenth and sixteenth centuries. According to figures for 1572, the Brentella consortium covered some 2,446 hectares[83] (Raffaello Vergani argues that in 1595 only 4–5 per cent of the area of agrarian land, at that date around 23,000 hectares, was being irrigated).[43] Certainly, this fell far short of what had been expected of the project. And if one bears in mind Bruno Caizzi's estimates that, as late as 1937, the land in the Treviso area requiring intense irrigation amounted to 12,000 hectares, one can see that the thirst of this terrain had only been partially satisfied.[44]

This problem is linked with that of herd size in the Treviso province. Even if some scholars (for example, Jean Georgelin) argue that it was large enough to supply meat needs during the course of the eighteenth century, one should not forget that a large part of the livestock was 'in transit' (from Austria and Hungary), feeding here before passing on to slaughterhouses in Venice.[45] If the pasture lands of the province were sufficient, it was probably due to the transitional nature of the livestock grazing.

As far as rice is concerned, the few attempts to create plantations in Treviso (at Oderzo, Castelfranco, San Donà) were faced with the limits imposed by the Venetian Senate.[46]

As in Bassano, it was market-gardening that was more prevalent here, occupying part of the grounds of the numerous villas owned by the Venetian aristocracy; there were numerous *broli* of even 20 to 30 hectares within the larger estates that were extensively irrigated. Nevertheless, it is probable that artistic considerations prevailed over agricultural in the laying-out of the grounds of Venetian villas.

Water concession-holders also included small land-owners, who however rarely irrigated pastures and vegetable gardens of more than 2 to 3 hectares.

In Friuli and the Po delta there was an almost total absence in this period of irrigation and rice plantations; these would only expand in the latter area during the course of the eighteenth century (in the sixteenth, Feliciano Perona wrote, 'In the Polesina, it is universally said that there are no rice plantations or irrigation – and for all I have ridden over and seen [a lot] of the area, I have encountered none'). As shown by the extensive literature on the subject, land reclamation here would have required greater financial investment than elsewhere. As for Friuli – where the area of the *bassa*, with its ample supplies of water, would have been particularly suitable for the crop – there were only two attempts to set up rice plantations, both of which came to nothing (in 1595 the 60–*campi* plantation created seven years earlier some two miles from San Vito al Tagliamento was made into pasture land, whilst the 120–*campi* plantation at Prata di Pordenone, owned by the nobleman Giovanbattista Bernardo, proved to be insufficiently supplied by the 3 *quadretti* of water drawn off the Cellina[47]).

The Crisis of the Seventeenth Century

Investments in water purchases within the Republic dropped in both number and size during the first decade of the seventeenth century, signalling what is generally regarded as a slow-down – if not a reversal – of the expansive trend of the sixteenth. Wallerstein, however, sees the seventeenth century as marking only a temporary pause in the growth of the capitalistic world-economy that had reached maturity over the previous one hundred years;[48] and this idea of an essential continuity between the two centuries is undoubtedly proved by the fact that a new phase of expansion would begin very quickly. Given the different dates for this slow-down and subsequent new growth within the various states of Europe and Italy, it is perhaps legitimate to wonder whether this variegated crisis formed a single whole. What is certain is that agriculture within the Venetian Republic did not enter its period of stasis until the decades 1600–1610, when the difficulties caused by weather conditions and food shortages that had occurred around 1590 had been overcome. This was only partly due to a drop in population; the plague of 1575 had had a dramatic effect upon numbers, without however significantly depressing demand and, therefore, prices (the Republic differed from the other states of north-western Europe – and even southern Italy – in having managed to contain the situation up to the end of the century).[49] However, the drop in investment in the next few decades is shown from the irrigation revenues of the *Beni Inculti*[50]: 29,047 ducats for the period 1605–1645, as against 54,837 ducats for the period 1558–1602.[51] The fact that numerically there was an increase in concessions during the first half of the seventeenth century (428, as against 384 in the second half of the sixteenth) is misleading as they involved much small areas, especially in the province of Vicenza. Concessions there actually doubled – from 142 to 280 – but only 109 rice-*campi* were added to the 1,176 still in production at the end of the sixteenth century: the total area planted with rice in 1645 amounted to just 496 hectares.[52] The situation in the Verona (and Cologna) areas seems to have been better, where the Venetian Senate ratified the conversion of a further 944 *campi* (283 hectares) for rice production as they were judged low-lying and marshy; the total area of rice plantation here in 1645 was 1,731 hectares.[53]

There was no increase at all in rice plantation in the Treviso, Friuli or Padua areas, where the slump in irrigation itself is clear from the fact that water purchases totalled only a few hundred ducats. In the Padua province, such irrigation as there was remained the preserve of the Venetian nobility – the Barbarigo, the Contarini, the Pesaro, the Corner and other families – whereas in the Verona and Vicenza areas there were few exceptions to the rule that it was the local nobility that played the leading role in rice production and irrigation.[54] Overall, what emerges in this period is the consolidation of large landed concerns, with a static focus on extensive rather than intensive agriculture and a tendency to live off the status quo until market conditions improved. Small-scale concessions did not, however, disappear altogether: in fact, it is no coincidence that, with the modest capital they required, they form the majority of concessions in the first half of the seventeenth century. Nevertheless, in the case of rice, the difficulties of withstanding a situation of falling demand and prices were all too clear:[55] attracted to this crop by the favourable agricultural/economic circumstances of the second half of the sixteenth century, the small- and medium-sized agricultural concerns were now in no condition to meet the high costs involved in cultivating rice '[given that they rested] on the traditional principles of mixed agriculture and estate self-sufficiency. The way for large-scale agricultural enterprises thus opened up automatically'.[56]

The low point of the seventeenth-century crisis as far as the Venetian Republic is concerned comes around 1630, coinciding with a serious plague outbreak of that year. However, if it is legitimate to take irrigation as an index of agricultural activity as a whole (especially given the weakness of other such indices – for example, tithes – and the absence of sufficiently wide-ranging regional studies of fluctuations in wheat prices[57]), it seems that the 1640s saw a new influx of capital and entrepreneurial energy into the countryside of the terra firma. In this period, the average of one to two concessions per year would increase slowly but surely; and this is further borne out by the taxation calculated for each irrigated *campo* (which passed from the 3 ducats per *campo* which had been maintained right up to 1631, to 4–5 ducats and then, as early as 1641, to 10 ducats). The solidity of this upward trend remained uncertain until the 1650s; but it seems clear that the years 1645–46 marked a turning-point. Very probably it was the supplies required for the War of Candia (1645–1669) that pushed agricultural production levels up to what they had been before the crisis. Another factor in this new influx of capital into agriculture may have been the up-turn in population figures following the plague.[57]

If the above conclusions are correct, then the Venetian Republic was one of the first states in Europe to move beyond the agricultural stagnation of the first part of the seventeenth century, which Le Roy Ladurie describes as 'the bitter fruit of war, taxation, weather conditions and perhaps the breakdown in the monetary system'. Another comparably early recoverer was Spain, where there was an improvement in agricultural production from 1645 onwards; at the other end of the scale comes somewhere like Southern Italy, where the crisis in the sector lasted up to 1690.[59]

In the Venetian Republic there were encouraging signs in land reclamation, with a return to projects of a certain scale (even if it is true that throughout the early decades of the century there was no excessive slump in agricultural activity but only a sharp drop in the capital invested). As mentioned above, the War of Candia had a significant influence, coming as it did in conjunction with the sale of common lands (above all, in the Po valley area).[60]

The increase in the number of water concessions led to a concomitant increase in total revenues for the *Beni Inculti* during the period 1646–1700. Though in many cases these were confirmations of old use rights, one has the clear impression of increased activity and expansion. Even taking into account inflation, it seems that the overall sum of 66,732 ducats collected in the period marks a return to – if not an improvement on – the sum collected during the second half of the sixteenth century (54,837).[61] All the various provinces were affected by this phase of expansion; however, once again, it was more modest in the areas of Padua, Treviso and Friuli. In the province of Vicenza, *Beni Inculti* revenue totalled 15,394 ducats, which may not have been exceptional but is noteworthy for other reasons: a growing amount of the water purchased was in fact destined to power paperworks, sawmills, hammers, spinning mills and, above all, flour mills. It would seem that in this period of fundamental importance for the history of the Republic a sharp division of roles was appearing within the economy of the state, with the province of Vicenza becoming predominantly proto-industrial[62] and that of Verona predominantly agricultural. The latter, in fact, invested a good 44,582 ducats in water purchases (66 per cent of the total for the Republic), thus confirming and continuing the brilliant performance of the sixteenth century.

191 (40 per cent) of the 486 concessions granted in the Verona area were for rice plantations (as opposed to 47 in the Vicenza area, 8 in the Padua and 3 in Friuli); and by the end of the century a further 3,234 hectares (10,772 rice-*campi*) had been added to the 1,731 already dedicated to rice production in the Verona area in 1645. Assuming that there were no substantial reductions or changes of use in the land covered by the 1645 figure, this means that the total rice-growing area within the province was 4,965 hectares (triple the 1,448 hectares in use at the end of the sixteenth century). And though the increase in the Vicenza area was on a lesser scale, the figure for the end of the seventeenth century (1,000 hectares) is still more than double the 454 hectares at the end of the sixteenth.[63]

The expansion of rice as a crop led to important improvements in agricultural practice, especially within the Verona area, with rice being part of a two- three- or four-year rotation cycle involving wheat, maize, fallow land and pasture.[64] It seems, in fact, that this increase in the use of rice as part of a crop cycle represented a technical advance on permanent rice-fields; however, even these latter – with rationalised periods of 'fallow' and re-fertilisation – could be just as productive.[65]

Similarly, how can one not see a sign of progress in both technology and productivity in the applications to the Venetian authorities for permission to dedicate ever larger expanses of land to profitable crop-rotation? Or in the growing demand for water from rice plantations that had not increased in surface area? And when on looks at the concessions granted, one gets the clear impression that the Venetian Senate and the *Provveditori* fully approved of the way things were developing. The old decree of 1594, which limited rice fields to low-lying terrain, was no longer respected: rice plantations now expanded into 'pasture land' and 'non-productive (sic) raised land', whilst old applications were granted or else permission was generously given to 'irrigate and create rice plantations freely'.[66]

Once again, such plantations were highly profitable.[67] In 1651 the state's experts estimated the average income per *campo* for a rice plantation as 7 ducats, double that from normal arable land; in 1682, Giammaria Sagramoso declared an income of a good 300 ducats from just 30 rice-*campi* at Palù.[68]

Given that circumstances were improving, the numerous families of the Verona nobility once more turned their financial resources and speculative acumen towards the countryside. Whilst one does not intend here to make any revolutionary claims, exaggerating the contribution that the aristocracy of seventeenth-century Italy made to stimulating entrepreneurial activity, it is important to underline the error of those interpretations which see the nobility's role in the countryside as being merely parasitic. On the contrary, the case of the Venetian terra firma – and of the province of Verona in particular – reveals the existence of a patrician class that was ready to venture beyond the safety of the land-rents in which it had taken refuge during the stagnation of the early part of the seventeenth century, once market conditions made a more active presence in the countryside potentially profitable. Just as in the neighbouring

Lombardy at around the same time[69], one sees a return to the direct management of agricultural estates that had proved so successful in the past.[70]

This period also saw the aristocracy of Venice and Vicenza becoming more active in the countryside. Slowly but surely, the patricians of the capital became a more capillary presence within the terra firma (as one can see from the growing number of water concessions held by such families as the Duodo, the Grimani and the Balbi).[71] And in the Vicenza area greater dynamism is to be seen not only in the activities of the important families – such as the Trissino and the Da Porto, etc. – but also in those of the wealthy religious institutions of the city.[72]

Irrigation and the 'Agricultural Revolution' of the Eighteenth Century

The eighteenth century saw continuing use of those surface water supplies which, regulated by the *Provveditori ai Beni Inculti*, had enabled the Republic to increase the area of its irrigated pasture land and establish rice plantations. However, exploitation of this water was yet to lead to the establishment of modern and capitalist-based agricultural enterprises similar to those which were emerging in the regions of northern Europe. In effect, the seventeenth century had been the watershed that marked the clear separation between a northern Europe that was agriculturally, politically and economically advanced, and a southern Europe that had failed to break free entirely of the late-sixteenth/early-seventeenth-century recession (not that one should slip back into an interpretation of this latter century as a period of 're-feudalisation', 'bourgeois betrayal' and the 'decline of urban elites' – all concepts which prevent a proper understanding of that slow transfer of energy and economic initiative from the cities to the countryside and the smaller towns).

Even in this 'century of crisis' things were happening in the countryside of Italy, and of the Venetian Republic in particular, making it clear that the division between a rich and fertile northern Europe and an arid and backward southern Europe is far too schematic. The north of the continent too had its less fortunate regions as well as those where agriculture was more developed and crop yields higher (for example, Flanders, Brabant, Zeeland and

Friesland, all of which were being highly praised by English travellers by the middle of the seventeenth century, some time before efforts were made to introduce into England what has been misleading defined as 'new agriculture').

It is no coincidence that from the Middle Ages onwards the more advanced regions had seen the need for irrigated pasture land, the cultivation of fodder crops and for more differentiated cycles of rotation. For a long time one of the most agriculturally-advanced regions in Europe had been the Po valley, a status revealed by the 'revolutionary' teachings of such figures as Camillo Tarello and Agostino Gallo, which made such a mark upon the agriculture of Lombardy and the Veneto. The problem was that, in the Venetian Republic as in other regions of Europe, such teachings were very slow in becoming widespread; even eighteenth-century England, in the analyses of Slicher van Bath, emerges as home to a gradual evolution rather than a sudden revolution in agriculture, with knowledge gleaned from the writers of Classical Antiquity continuing to play a role. However, the fact is that in eighteenth-century England such measures as the introduction of rape and other leguminous plants into the rotation cycle; the increase in area of irrigated pasture land and herd size; the upturn in agricultural yields and the spread in the use of fertilisers – in effect, all of that which comes under the umbrella term of 'the agricultural revolution' – benefited from a highly-favourable socio-economic situation: more modern relations of production (enclosures, a very 'hands-on' presence of landowners); heavy investment; and government policies that were very attentive to the needs of agriculture. Nevertheless, some English historians have been at pains to argue that this process of development was not as straightforward as some accounts make it appear. For example, it has been pointed out that the progress achieved within particular estates cannot be automatically extrapolated to cover the country as a whole (accurate estimates of overall production are not available) and that in spite of significant internal migration there would not be a decisive drop in the size of the rural population living on agriculture until around 1850.[73]

This more nuanced picture has to be borne in mind when attempting to draw conclusions regarding the Venetian Republic and its failure to implement its own 'agricultural revolution'.[74] However, one thing is undeniable: the role of water in increasing agricultural production. By providing essential fodder for livestock and being the *sine qua non* of more complex crop-rotation cycles, this resource was indispensable to the undoubted development in agriculture within eighteenth-century Europe.

And yet even if in 1768 the *Provveditori ai Beni Inculti* was joined by another agency – the *Deputati all'Agricultura* – which was specifically intended to study ways of increasing yields and herd size and of introducing new agricultural techniques, the government's measures to manage water-use and promote agriculture do not always seem to have been adequate to the situation. Proposals, theoretical dissertations and memoranda of a strictly-local focus far outnumber the genuine steps taken towards agricultural progress; even if it would be unfair to argue that the Venetian state did not have an agricultural policy worthy of the name, there was undoubtedly much greater dynamism in the cultivation and exploitation of new agricultural land elsewhere in Europe. In England, for example, Parliament had long played a key role in the drainage of the Fens, and from the sixteenth century onwards had permitted those enclosures which stimulated the development of a market-focused agriculture on privately-owned farmland.[75] Of course, the English model is not always an adequate term of comparison for the developments everywhere in Europe – for instance, France[76] – but one only has to look at an area such as northern Germany to see more openness to experimentation and a shrewder level of agricultural management than one finds in the Venetian Republic. This is partly explained by the fact that after the accession to the English throne of the House of Hanover, numerous agricultural treatises were translated into German and made their influence felt in the north of the country.[77]

This does not mean that there were no longer contacts between Venetian agronomists and those elsewhere in Europe: the works of Duhamel du Monceau, Johann Beckmann, Albrecht Thaer and Arthur Young were well known in Venice, where they became the object of detailed commentary. But, given the absence of figures who could actually implement innovation, discussion and description rarely got beyond wishful thinking. Certainly, there were those in Venice who experimented with new crops, and land-owners who were directly involved in the running of their estates[78], but this was not enough to guarantee a real turn-around in the productivity levels and range of the region's agriculture. And the fact that the members of the Venetian aristocracy also controlled the government and the land-reclamation consortia – dealing with land in which they had powerful vested interests – inevitably means that an interpretation of the course of agricultural development here must take into consideration the political context – and the very Constitution – of the Venetian Republic.

The Eighteenth Century and the Development of Rice Plantations

Obviously in discussing the flow of capital investment towards agriculture in the Venetian Republic – or anywhere else in eighteenth-century Europe – one also has to take into account the prevailing international situation. The improvement in this sector of the Venetian economy from the 1730s onwards should be seen in a wider context, with the agricultural sector of Europe as a whole benefiting from increasing population numbers and a consequent growth in cereal prices. Moreover, in the case of Venice, the end of the seventeenth and the beginning of the eighteenth century also saw the conquest of the Peloponnese and the peace treaties of Carlowitz and Passarowitz (1699 and 1717 respectively), all of which gave a boost to the Venetian economy as a whole. It is no coincidence that this was a period of more intense agricultural activity and a higher number of water concessions. As has been pointed out, the second half of the seventeenth century had already seen a certain recovery from the stagnation of the first half, with the so-called 'crisis of the seventeenth century' being more circumscribed than the traditional label leads one to assume (even if the above-mentioned recovery was, overall, a very slow one).

Of course, the expansion of rice plantations within the Veneto was nowhere near comparable to that of the agriculturally stronger areas of the Po valley, such as Lombardy and Piedmont (to cite just one example, between 1710 and 1803 the Vercelli province of Piedmont saw rice plantations pass from an already noteworthy 8 per cent of total agricultural land to 33 per cent).[79]

Once again, within the Veneto it was the Verona and Vicenza areas that took the lead, with the late-sixteenth-century reservations regarding this type of crop appearing to be abandoned. Even if every single document still makes formal reference to the health dangers posed by the miasmas raised by rice-fields near residential areas, and even if there were still anxieties that expanding rice plantations were taking away arable and pasture land, there is no denying the growth within this particular area of agriculture. In the Verona area a further 1,975 hectares (6,578 *campi*) were given over to rice production during the eighteenth century, theoretically making a total of 6,940 hectares by the end of the century (an increase of about 40 per cent on the 4,965 hectares at the end of the seventeenth).[80] Rice also spread socially, even if Berengo does point out that in the nineteenth century domestic consumption of the crop was still 'concentrated in urban centres, and largely restricted to the more affluent classes'.[81]

The wealthier families of Vicenza – the Thiene, the Monza, the Barbarano, the Capra, the Piovene and the Garzadori – showed no less an interest in this typically speculative crop: a further 630 hectares (1,634 *campi*) were given over to rice, marking an approximately 60 per cent increase on the previous 1,000 hectares (though still only making a modest 0.60 per cent of the total agricultural land of the Vicenza province).[82]

Other areas of the mainland state followed the same trend: Padua, Treviso and, above all, the Po delta areas (where the first rice plantations of the eighteenth century were the beginning of the extensive growth of this sector here in the nineteenth). In effect, as a result of the diversion of a branch of the Po – the so-called Portoviro Cut (1599–1604) – the very ground area of the delta would increase continually due to the greater amount of silt deposited by the river; and this new terrain presented new opportunities of profitable investment for the area's landowners (most of whom were Venetian patricians).[83]

In 1766 the Soranzo family were granted a water concession for a 22–*campi* rice plantation at Lendinaro di Rovigo, whilst the Mocenigo would flood a further 30 *campi* in 1778 at Gnocca 'on the branches of the Po'. Two years later, Giovanni Battista Mora exploited the waters of the river to make rich rice-fields of 60 'marshy and low-lying' *campi* at Donzella (again in the Rovigo area).

Favourable economic circumstances meant that even far from wealthy landowners could invest in rice, as had already happened in the second half of the sixteenth century, when the better-off amongst the smallholders had been caught up in the interest in land reclamation and irrigation.

The sharpest peaks in the curve that I have tried to chart on the basis of water-concessions for irrigation and rice plantations come in the decades 1760–1790. In the first two decades of the century there was a clear increase in the number of rice plantations; this was followed by a certain loss of momentum, explained by some as due to strong competition from the rice-growers of Lombardy and Piedmont.[84] Thereafter improving economic conditions would lead to Veneto rice recovering some ground on the international market; hence, this partial but significant indicator illustrates and confirms a chronology in which European – and not just regional – factors come into play.

Over this period this was also a concomitant improvement in methods of cultivation: many landowners did not just increase the areas of their rice plantations, they made rice a key part of complex rotation cycles that were intended to boost yields.

The Trend in Irrigation and Land Reclamation: Limits of Agricultural Growth

The general trend in the curve of the graph plotting the number of irrigation projects is the same as that for rice plantations, even if it is rather more even and less inclined to brusque variations (rice was more subject to market fluctuations). In both cases one can see a definite improvement from the 1730s onwards, with difficulties becoming apparent in the last decade or so of the century.

It is clear that in these favourable conditions both the small- and medium-sized holdings had greater access to water, with numerous small plots of just a few hectares (and sometimes even smaller) being irrigated to improve the fertility of land intended for pasture or (more rarely) arable crops. Nevertheless, it was still the large landowners who made the most considerable investments in the irrigation of pasture and arable land. For example, Alvise and Filippo Balbi, two brothers of the Venetian nobility, would in 1763 extend irrigation from 100 to 900 *campi* in the San Floriano area outside Treviso (paying the *Beni Inculti* some 646 ducats), whilst another important Venetian aristocrat, Nicolò Tron, would have an irrigation channel dug that added a further 60 irrigated *campi* to the main body of his 545–*campi* property.[85]

Analysis of the concessions reveals the continuing dependence upon the rivers of the regions – and the Adige in particular (the canals drawn off this watercourse were much more numerous than those off other comparable rivers such as the Brenta, the Piave, the Sile). And given that most irrigation canals depended upon river water there was less resort to spring or underground sources, with increasing use of mechanical instruments – bucket wheels, pumps and so on – to raise water (especially from the Adige); even those of limited financial resources applied for authorisation to install such machinery.[86]

Nevertheless, the revenue from water concessions for irrigation remained relatively limited, as can be seen from the fact that

Water Concession Revenues over Five-year Periods (in ducats, allowing for depreciation)

For Rice Cultivation			Irrigations
1701–1705	duc.	1,725	2,180
1706–1710	"	1,667	1,345
1711–1715	"	3,226	2,180
1716–1720	"	1,318	2,215
1721–1725	"	558	555
1726–1730	"	931	410
1731–1735	"	1,206	385
1736–1740	"	1,606	890
1741–1745	"	998	450
1746–1750	"	2,505	1,375
1751–1755	"	1,448	615
1756–1760	"	1,673	2,805
1761–1765	"	2,891	3,090
1766–1770	"	5,411	1,910
1771–1775	"	3,107	2,230
1776–1780	"	3,316	2,250
1781–1785	"	5,814	1,455
1786–1790	"	5,722	4,380
1791–1795	"	2,342	2,265
1796	"	112	—-
1797	"	—-	—-
Total	"	47,576	22,375
General Total	"	69,951[87]	

throughout the century they totalled 22,375 ducats (whilst the revenue from rice plantations reached 47,576 ducats).

A comparison with the figures for the previous century immediately reveals the limits of the expansion that took place during the eighteenth; for if, in the second half of the seventeenth century, around 66,000 ducats was invested in water concessions, over the entire eighteenth the figure does not top 70,000 (taking into account inflation). True, this latter figure does not include manufacturing uses of water, but even so one would have expected the total to be rather higher during what is considered to have been a growth period in Venetian – and European – agriculture. However, in the second half of the seventeenth century alone, the rice-plantations in the Verona area increased by 86 per cent, whilst the figure for the entire eighteenth century is around 40 per cent (the same figures for the Vicenza area are around 100 per cent and 60 per cent). Hence, once again, there is a need to review the prevailing opinions with regard to the two centuries. Morineau has, in fact, already defined the eighteenth century as a false start, a 'démarrage économique manqué', highlighting the discrepancy between demographic growth, calls for agronomic development and the actual investment of technical resources and funds in order to bring it about (although his argument deals with France, his conclusions are equally valid with regard to Venice).[88]

The picture is just as nuanced when one looks at land drainage, which continued to be an important part of the Republic's agricultural policy. The extrapolated data regarding the areas of land drained by consortia show that one should not underestimate the importance of this activity; and even though it is clear that some areas were subject to periodic re-flooding, the overall situation is not as grim as it at first appears. Whilst it had previously been estimated that within the Venetian Republic a total of around 150,000 hectares were drained and reclaimed over the period 1500 to 1800 – with the figure for Holland over the same time-span being about 280,000 hectares[89] – more extensive study of the documentation[90] suggests that the total area of reclaimed land within the various consortia active in the terra firma at the end of the eighteenth century amounted to some 188,000 hectares, so the gap between the two countries must be re-assessed (we shall see below further evidence in support of this claim).

Still, in spite of the openness to innovation that can be seen in published writings, in government policy and in the concession of patents[91], the limits and contradictions in the agriculture of the Veneto emerged clearly. The impact of agricultural land-use upon the environment was worrying, and the action of the various land-reclamation consortia – and even the *Provveditori ai Beni Inculti* themselves – were not always adequate. One gets the clear impression of a gradual breakdown in organisational structure, with a certain irreconcilable conflict between the various social agents involved in the maintenance of reclaimed land. The result of this is clear from the description of the Verona area given in 1738 by the *Provveditore* Andrea Longo: many fields that had been reclaimed as arable land had subsequently become pasture land or even marshland. Similarly, the land of the Lower Gorzon consortium was described in 1787 as in 'a terrible state', as was the reclaimed land alongside the Brancaglia. The former, where the consortia members were from Padua and Venice, had become little more than a drainage basin for the water run off from the rice-fields and irrigation canals of the Verona area, whilst the second – where the drainage dams had been designed as early as 1521 – was suffering as a result of miscalculations in the creation of a new drainage canal.[92] And things were little better[93] at the other consortia of the Padua area: the Fratta, the Middle Gorzon, the Upper Gorzon and the 'Seven Channels (*Prese*) of the Brenta'. In the latter area, due to the level of the last cut off the Brenta, the river actually ran higher than the surrounding countryside, so the water in the drainage channels flowed backwards. Throughout the eighteenth century various attempts were made to remedy the problem – imposition of a new *campatico* tax on land-owners and investment in such schemes as canal-bridges, culverts and moving gates to shut off the channels – but the hydro-geological imbalance remained.[94]

Overall, a general state of neglect made it inevitable that canal-bridges collapsed, drainage channels became blocked and watercourses overflowed onto land that had taken years to reclaim. Obviously crops suffered, in particular the hemp that was an essential raw material for the Venice Arsenale shipyards and was intensively cultivated in the low-lying Padua area that was criss-crossed by such watercourses as the Gorzone, the Frassine and the Brenta.[95]

As far as energy sources are concerned, peat may have been the subject of various state projects and studies, and have been championed by various 'enlightened' writers and journals of the period, but it never achieved the same economic importance as it did in the Netherlands (in part due to the poor deposits of this fuel within the Veneto). And in spite of all Simone Stratico's efforts in championing what was the key technological innovation of the late-eighteenth century, the steam-driven drainage pump made little impact here, owing to restricted finances and the consequent unwillingness of the Venetian patricians to invest in it. In effect, this failure to innovate could be seen as symptomatic of their ultimate decline.[96]

At an administrative level, there was an equal degree of uncertainty: in 1728 the consortia members responsible for the reclaimed land along the Brancaglia failed to achieve a quorum to vote on the most urgent work required, and thus it was the *Beni Inculti* themselves who took on responsibility for measures which were outlined in a precise Senate decree. In 1790 it was not even possible to elect Presidents for the Frassine consortium; the *Capitano* [Military Governor] had undoubtedly been correct when, a few years earlier, he had commented that land-owners were more interested in running their own estates than in carrying out the work necessary for the consortium as a whole.

If this was the case, it was inevitable that whenever they got the chance, consortium members would try to get out of paying their dues to consortium funds. The result of such 'disobedience' was the increasing debt of the consortia themselves, a phenomenon that was clear from the early decades of the seventeenth century. The remedies sought for this situation were half-hearted improvisations: the imposition of special field taxes (*campatici*), which often the communities could not pay, or the seizure of goods from the land-owners who had failed to pay their dues.[97] To pay for the more urgent work, the consortium often borrowed money by mortgaging land. However, if one looks at the records of those providing such loans, one finds the names of all the best-known Venetian families; in other words, those same Venetians who were unwilling to pay their dues to their particular consortium, granted mortgages which financed minimal maintenance of the hydro-geological equilibrium within the consortia areas themselves.[98]

The scarce political will to undertake thorough-going territorial measures throughout the plain area of the Veneto – see, for example, the numerous unsuccessful attempts to reclaim the land of the *Valli veronesi* – went together with a clear impasse in the very technology of land drainage (which, as we shall see, also became apparent in other areas of Europe, in spite of the fundamental developments that had occurred in seventeenth-century Holland). As Simone Stratico perceptively observed, Venetian technicians knew 'no other way of reclaiming land than through the use of embankments and internal drainage channels'.[99]

There is, of course, no doubt as to the historic role and importance of the Venetian nobility in the management of land-reclamation consortia: they provided the most investment; they controlled the largest expanses of land; and they acted as the representatives of the consortia in relations with the *Beni Inculti*. In fact, throughout the seventeenth and eighteenth century, the very structure of consortium management perpetuated patrician control over land reclamation and exploitation; even as late as the middle of the eighteenth century peasant farmers were not only required to dig the drainage and irrigation channels, but they were also 'afflicted and further impoverished ... by severe special contributions in money'.[100] (For a long time, the payment of rent 'in kind' – wheat, maize, and so on – had been far from an uncommon practice). Clearly capitalism was having difficulty emerging in the countryside of the terra firma if an eighteenth-century account still mentions that, in the management of their estates, the Venetian landowners limited themselves to renting out one or two *campi* to a poor peasant-farmer who lived there in a miserable hut. At the same time, the tenants had to provide labour for the safeguard of hydraulic installations (one man for every twenty *campi*). In this very burdensome situation, ripe with potential conflict, it is no surprise if smallholders tried in every way possible to get out of the maintenance work required by the consortium – so much so that the magistrates themselves had to force the holders of large *boaria*-contract estates to undertake the urgent work on the drainage and irrigation systems.[101]

However, it would be historically inaccurate to describe the situation on the terra firma as one of mere backwardness. First of all, small-scale landowners continued to exist, even within consortia dominated by the aristocracy. And secondly, in the seventeenth – and even more so, the eighteenth – century, the maintenance of reclaimed land relied not only on the labour of smallholders and tenant farmers but also involved outside contractors, who not only provided 'fair pay for the workmen',[102] but were also required to create the necessary infrastructures ('huts, barriers, strengthening for dams and river walls, and other reinforcement') and supply the necessary materials (wheelbarrows, shovels, ropes, nails).[103] Hence, the situation was more nuanced than it at first appears.

Those in power also took measures which relieved – or were designed to relieve – the harsh conditions of life that the hydrogeological imbalance caused the rural population.[104] Nevertheless, those living on land level with – or even below – the rim of rivers and canals often had to flee their miserable housing to take refuge on embankments or migrate to safer land.[105] This happened most frequently in that key area stretching from the Verona and Padua Po valley areas to the river delta and the neighbouring Ferrara; the fact that this was a border region simply added to the difficulties of taking any decisive measures to counteract the continual flooding that occurred, for example, during the latter part of the eighteenth century. And that general conditions had not improved by the turn of the nineteenth century is clear when one sees that the 18,000 *campi* of fertile land within the old Lower Gorzon consortium had gradually decayed into unhealthy marsh areas that served solely as fish farms.[106]

The rural population of the Padua area was not the only one to suffer in this way. In proposing reclamation schemes, mention was often made of the contribution they would make to improving health conditions – for example, as early as 1589 it was observed how the dredging and embankment of the Vallio near Treviso would not only help trade but also make the area more salubrious[107] – but when such schemes started to become run-down and neglected, they had the very opposite effect: by 1634 the decay of the Lugugnana reclamation near Portogruaro was said to have resulted in the creation of a swamp that was a threat to the lives of all who lived there. A century later – in 1763 – the district doctor of this latter area, Carlo Giuseppe Patrini, would note how such places as Fossalta, Villanova, Grado, Gussago and Lugugnana had a ghostly air due to the fact that the local population were gradually abandoning them. Infant mortality was high; and those who reached old age were described as 'sickly, cachectical and scurvy-ridden [...] Subject to terrible verminosis, very few of them have the strength to survive it'.[108]

Notes

1. Ventura, 'Considerazioni sull'agricoltura veneta', p. 528; Pullan, 'Wage-Earners and the Venetian Economy', in *Crisis and Change in the Venetian Economy,* Pullan ed., p. 148.
2. Braudel, *Civilisation matérielle. Les jeux de l'échange,* II, p. 247.
3. A. De Maddalena, 'A Milano nei secoli XVI e XVII: da ricchezza 'reale' a ricchezza 'nominale'?, in *Rivista Storica Italiana,* 89 (1977), pp. 558–59. On the early development of capitalism in the Po valley, M. Aymard, 'La transizione dal feudalesimo al capitalismo', in *Storia d'Italia. Annali 1,* Romano amd Vivanti eds. pp. 1133–34. On the relation between feudalism and the Venetian patrician class, G. Gullino, 'I patrizi veneziani di fronte alla proprietà feudale (secoli XVI–XVIII). Materiale per una ricerca', in *Quaderni Storici,* 15 (1980), n. 43, pp. 162–93. On agriculture in Lombardy, Chittolini, 'Alle origini delle 'grandi aziende' della bassa lombarda', pp. 828–37.
4. M. Aymard and G.L. Basini, 'Production et productivité agricoles en Italie (XVIe–XVIIIe siècle)', in *Proceedings of the Seventh International Economic History Congress,* Flinn ed., I, p. 144.
5. On this question, see the comments in B. Bennassar, 'L'Europe des campagnes', in *Histoire économique et sociale du monde,* Bennassar and P. Chaunu eds. (P. Léon General editor), I, pp. 470–71. On the spread of Tarello's ideas, see G. Schröder-Lembke, *Studien zur Agrargeschichte,* Stuttgart, 1978, pp. 139 and 168. On the limits of the development of an 'agrarian capitalism' in Languedoc, E. Le Roy Ladurie, *Les paysans de Languedoc,* I, pp. 291–313; idem, 'Les paysans français du XVIe siècle', in *Conjoncture économique, structures sociales. Hommage à Ernest Labrousse,* Paris, 1974, p. 341. Similarly, many of the new fodder crops developed in France from 1630 onwards in the area around Paris did not become part of crop-rotation cycles. The increase in beef and dairy produce in Normandy was more a case of regional specialisation than a step towards an authentic 'agricultural revolution' (J. Jacquart, 'Traditionalismes agricoles et tentatives d'adaptation', in *Histoire économique et sociale du monde,* Jacquart and P. Deyon eds. (P. Léon General editor), II, pp. 446–47). See also Ambrosoli, *The Wild and the Sown,* pp. 163–222; J. Thirsk, 'Farming Techniques', in *The Agrarian History of England and Wales, 1500–1640,* Thirsk ed., IV, Cambridge, 1967, pp. 180–81; De Vries, *The Dutch Rural Economy,* pp. 32–33.
6. Coppola, *Il mais nell'economia agricola lombarda,* p. 44; Beltrami, *La penetrazione economica,* pp. 52–53; Poni, *Gli aratri e l'economia agraria nel Bolognese,* p. 46.
7. Tucci, 'L'Ungheria e gli approvvigionamenti veneziani di bovini', pp. 153–59; V. Zimányi, 'Venedigs Rinderimport in den Jahren 1624–1647', in *Agrartörteneti Szemle,* 14 (1972), pp. 387–97.
8. *Relazioni dei rettori veneti. Podestaria e Capitanato di Brescia,* Tagliaferri ed., XI, 1978, pp. 3–4, 10 and 97.
9. *Relazioni dei rettori veneti. Podestaria e Capitanato di Crema – Provveditorati di Orzinuovi e Asola,* Tagliaferri ed., XIII, 1979, p.75, 90 and 320. On flax/linen

production in Lombardy, see D. Sella, 'Per la storia della cultura e della lavorazione del lino nello stato di Milano durante il secolo XVII', in *Felix olim Lombardia,* Milan, 1978, pp. 781–803.

10. In the area 'beyond the Mincio' agriculture was already more comparable to that in Lombardy than in the the Venetian Terrafirma. A fundamental work on the hydro-geographical situation in the Bergamo area is *Descrizione di Bergamo e suo territorio, 1596,* edited by Giovanni da Lezze, Bergamo, 1988. See also *Relazioni dei rettori veneti. Podestaria e Capitanato di Bergamo,* Tagliaferri ed., pp. 144–45, 274–75, 450–51 and 475; *Relazioni dei rettori veneti. Podestaria e Capitanato di Crema,* Tagliaferri ed., p. 43.

11. Ventura, 'Considerazioni sull'agricoltura veneta', p. 539.

12. *Relazioni dei rettori veneti. Podestaria e Capitanato di Verona,* Tagliaferri ed., 22 April 1575, p. 96; Zalin, 'Economia agraria e insediamento di villa', p. 55; Beltrami, *La penetrazione economica dei veneziani,* pp. 94 e 141.

13. E. Le Roy Ladurie and J. Goy, 'Peasant Dues, Tithes and Trends in Agricultural Production in Pre-industrial Societies', in *Proceedings of the Seventh International Economic History Congress,* Flinn ed., I, Edinburgh, 1978, pp. 118–20; Zalin, 'Economia agraria e insediamento di villa', pp. 62–64.

14. Psbi (henceforth, unless otherwise specified, all archive references are to this series), *busta* 264, Concession 23 September 1586; *busta* 378, Concession 22 September 1595; reg. 316, cc. 28v.–29r., Concession 12 August 1589. An individual concession could envisage various different uses for the water. Such figures should, however, be treated with a certain caution because it was not uncommon for payments not to be made in full (or at all), and for concessions (once granted) not be taken advantage of. What is more, numerous unlicensed irrigation canals were opened.

15. With regard to the rice plantation of Leonardo Donà, see Davis, *A Venetian Family and its Fortune,* p. 81; Girolamo Querini's right to run the family rice plantation was confirmed by a Senate decree of 1684: S.T., *filza* 1053, 16 December 1684. The Venetian families of the Malipiero, Corner, Loredan and Mocenigo owned particularly extensive property in the Cologna area (Borelli, 'Per una tipologia della proprietà fondiaria della villa', pp.143–44; Zalin, 'Economia agraria e insediamento di villa', pp. 74–76).

16. *Busta* 44, 23 April 1570 and 25 May 1570; *busta* 89, 3 July 1570 and 27 June 1579; *busta* 262, 15 July 1574.

17. *Busta* 81, Applications 13 January 1561, 16 May 1572 and 19 June 1599.

18. *Busta* 11, Application 23 May 1570 (the concession was granted on 20 March 1568); ibid., 29 November 1591, 9 March 1592 and 29 April 1592.

19. Zalin, 'Economia agraria e insediamento di villa', pp. 70–75; *busta* 13, Lawsuit against the Bonetti by Leone Aleardi, 8 July 1561.

20. Psbi, *Catastico of Verona,* c.36v., 29 March 1572; ibid., cc. 37, 94v. and 100v., 26 May 1570, 26 February 1589, 22 April 1592; reg. 310, cc. 68r.–v., 27 March 1572; reg. 264, cc. 139r.–140v., 27 March 1572.

21. *Busta* 9, Application 19 November 1569; *busta* 377, 5 June 1589; reg. 300, cc. 24v.–26v., 10 January 1558.

22. Borelli, 'Città e campagna in rapporto all'Adige', p. 311; *Catastico of Verona*, cit., c. 8r., 5 October 1559; c. 14v., 13 June 1562; reg. 309, cc. 111v.–112r., 22 June 1571; *busta* 376, 12 June 1584; ibid., 14 May 1586; S.T., *filza* 465, Senate decree 2 January 1642. The *conferme di possesso* (recognition of ancient use rights) did not usually require payment.

23. The *brolo* was a 'field laid out for the cultivation of vegetables and perhaps with some fruit plants'; but the term might also be used to refer to a garden or park. On the *broli* in the Verona area, see V. Bonuzzi, 'Il brolo', in *La villa nel Veronese*, Viviani ed., p. 173.

24. *Catastico of Verona*, cit., cc. 4r.–133v.; *buste* 376–79.

25. Pugliese, 'Condizioni economiche e finanziarie della Lombardia', p. 30 e n.; De Maddalena, 'Il mondo rurale italiano', pp. 380–85, espec. p. 381; Faccini, *Uomini e lavoro in risaia*, pp. 36–41 and *L'economia risicola lombarda*, pp. 75–104.

26. De Maddalena, 'Il mondo rurale italiano', p. 385; C. Vivanti, *Le campagne del Mantovano nell'età delle Riforme*, Milan, 1959, p. 158.

27. Faccini, *Uomini e lavoro in risaia*, pp. 18–20; De Maddalena, 'Il mondo rurale italiano', pp. 382–83; see also the item *Acqua*, by P. Lemonnier, in *Enciclopedia*, R. Romano ed., I, Turin, 1977, pp. 181–97. Rice-farming might also use a fixed labour force.

28 *Busta* 78, Report of 20 August 1655 concerning the rice plantation of Vincenzo Righi.

29. Reg. 603, Report by the Psbi, 9 September 1655. Generally, the *Provveditori* established the costs of the water by looking at average values for quantity, at the provenance of the water (river water was always the most expensive) and the area of land involved. On average, a *quadretto* was valued at 100 ducats if used for irrigation, and 150 if used for a rice planation (at least in the 16th cent). The cost was in direct proportion to the area of the ground involved, with account also being taken of the increased productivity due to the use of the water. A *quadretto* was considered enough for between 50–100 rice-fields (*busta* 262, Report by the expert Panfilo Piazzola, 15 July 1574; *busta* 11, Report by Antonio Glisenti il Magro, 17 April 1592).

30. Sella, *Commerci e industrie a Venezia*, p. 87; De Maddalena, 'Il mondo rurale italiano', p. 383; Falcone, *La nuova, vaga, et dilettevole villa*, pp. 253–54; *Provveditori alle biave, busta* 34, 5 January 1672.

31. S.T., *filza* 133, Senate decree 17 September 1594.

32. Pugliese, 'Condizioni economiche e finanziarie', pp. 33–38; V. Mazzucchelli, 'Catasti e storia dell'agricoltura', in *Critica Storica*, 16 (1979), p. 325.

33. *Catastico of Verona*, cit., c. 114ff.; *busta* 378, 9 June 1595 and 37 April 1602).

34. Cf. on this point the comments in J.E. Law, 'Verona and the Venetian State in the Fifteenth Century', in *Bulletin of the Institut of Historical Research*, 52 (1979), p. 22.

35. See the Map 1, 'Variations of Terrain within the Veneto' at p. 21; *busta* 264, 'Report by the expert Bartolomeo Galese', 12 August 1595.

36. The area given over to rice was thus only 0.2–0.3 per cent of the total area of the province (Km.² 2.722) (Georgelin, *Venise au siècle des lumières*, p. 222).

37. 'Report by the expert Bartolomeo Galese', 1595, cit.

38. Georgelin, *Venise au siècle des lumières*, p. 222.

39. Beltrami, *La penetrazione economica dei veneziani*, p. 94. In effect, the *quadretto vicentino* cost in monetary terms about one-third as much as the *quadretto veronese* or *bresciano* (cf. Psbi, *Catastico of Vicenza*, c. 23v., Concession 28 June 1584 and *Report by the experts*, 12 January 1580).
The list of these local patrician families is as long in the Vicenza area as it is in that around Verona. The investments could be quite sizeable: 1.300 ducats invested by Girolamo Schio and the Valmarana family in 1589 for 270 fields (pastureland and rice); 480 ducats by Conte Muzio Muzani for 100 fields (irrigated arable land and rice); 800 ducats by conte Girolamo Capra for 3 *quadretti* from the Zugliano canal for his 200 fields (see Psbi, *buste* 376, 377 and 378, Concessions 23 February 1589; 9 June and 18 July 1593; 13 April 1594; *Catastico of Vicenza*, cit., c. 33v., 24 May 1593 and c. 34r., 9 June 1593; reg. 306, cc. 2v.–3r., 22 March 1567). Other rich families that irrigated land included the Da Porto, Trissino, Garzadori, Franceschini, Thiene and Ghellini; whilst the Traversi, Caldogno, Godi and Loschi bought water for their rice plantations.

40. Reg. 300, cc. 7v.–8v., 8 April 1557; *Catastico of Vicenza*, cit., c. 1ff..

41. Ventura, 'Considerazioni sull'agricoltura veneta', p.537; *busta 377*, 2 August 1590; Psbi, reg. 532, c. 17r., 15 March 1589. Grimani had paid 420 ducats for one-and-a-half *quadretti* from the river Fratta, to irrigate 400 *campi* at Castelbaldo as a rice plantation. Compared to wheat, rice would long be a negligible crop in the Padua area.

42. M.C.V., Mss. P.D., C. 519/6, Applications 28 March 1590, 29 April 1589, 30 March 1590 and 4 June 1590; ASV, SEA, *busta* 89, 14 and 23 January 1573; Psbi, *Catastico of Padova, Treviso and Friuli*, cc. 3v.–4r. Between 1571 and 1604 I have found only 6 water concessions and 2 *conferme di possesso*.

43. Vergani, *Brentella. Problemi d'acque nell'alta pianura trevigiana*, pp.224–25; Psbi, *Capitolare secondo*, cc. 138r.–139v., 27 July 1572; ibid., cc. 133v.–140r., 22 June, 21 and 29 July, 1 August 1572; *busta 263, Report by the expert Feliciano Perona*, 13 November 1595. Written in response to the Senate decree of 17 September 1594, the report by Perona provides a detailed picture of irrigation within the Treviso area.

44. Caizzi, *Aspetti economici e sociali*, p. 103.

45. Georgelin, *Venise au siècle des lumières*, p. 210; A. Pozzan, *Zosagna. Paesaggio agrario, proprietà e conduzione di un territorio tra Piave e Sile nella prima metà del secolo XVI*, Treviso, 1997.

46. S.T., *filza* 182, Senate decree 2 August 1597 and Report enclosed by the Psbi, 26 February 1597; *Report by the expert Feliciano Perona*, cit., cc. 2r.–29v.; *busta 388*, 8 May 1679.

47. *Report by the expert Feliciano Perona*, cc. 34r.–35r.; *busta 377*, Concession 20 September 1593 to G.B. Bernardo.

48. I. Wallerstein, 'Y a-t-il une crise du XVIIe siècle?', in *Annales. E.S.C.*, 34 (1979), p. 133. The need to re-assess the seventeenth century has often been reiterated in the last few years: see E. Le Roy Ladurie, 'The seventeenth

century: general crisis or stabilization ?', in *Tithe and Agrarian History from the Fourteenth to the Nineteenth Centuries*, Le Roy Ladurie and Goy eds., Cambridge, 1982, pp. 120–53; G. Koenigsberger, 'The Crisis of the 17th Century: a Farewell ?', in *Politicians and Virtuosi. Essays in Early Modern History*, London, 1986, pp. 149–68; H. Lehmann, 'Die Krisen des 17. Jahrhunderts als Problem der Forschung', in *Krisen des 17. Jahrhunderts*, M. Jakubowski-Tiessen ed., Göttingen, 1999, pp. 13–24; E. Stumpo, 'La crisi del Seicento', in *La Storia. L'età moderna. Stati e società*, 3, N. Tranfaglia and M. Firpo eds., Torino, 1986, pp. 313–37.

49. Braudel, *La Méditerranée*, II, pp. 950–51; B. Pullan, *Wage-earners and the Venetian Economy, 1550–1630*, in *Crisis and Change in the Venetian Economy*, Pullan ed., p. 153; Jacquart, 'Les inerties terriennes', in *Histoire économique et sociale du monde*, Jacquart and Deyon eds. (P. Léon General editor), II, pp. 351 and 356; Le Roy Ladurie and Goy, 'Peasant Dues, Tithes and Trends', in *Proceedings of the Seventh International Economic History*, Flinn ed., cit., p. 122.

50. At the same time, there was a drop in the number of excavation projects to raise water.

51. Psbi, *Catastico of Verona, Cologna, Vicenza, Padova, Treviso and Friuli*, cit.; *buste* 376–379.

52. *Catastico of Vicenza*, cit., c. 79r. and 115r.; S.T., *filza* 241, Senate decree 17 August 1620 and *filza* 270, Senate decree 15 October 1624.

53. Psbi, *Catastico of Verona and Vicenza*, cit.; *buste* 379–382.

54. Among many others, conti Enza and Adriano Thiene – together with G.B.Valmarana – at Thiene and Schio; Girolamo and Vincenzo Garzadori; Antonio Maria Da Porto; Marc'Antonio Capra (*buste* 379–380, 28 March 1608, 28 February 1611, 26 September 1612, 14 December 1613). In the Verona area, there were the rice plantations of the Pompei (150 *campi*), the Emilei (120 *campi*), the Spolverini (99 *campi*), and the Sanbonifacio, Pellegrini, Morando, Maffei and Lisca (*Catastico of Verona*, c. 173v., 12 December 1624; S.T., *filza* 252, Senate decree 20 May 1622; *filza* 273, 17 April 1625; *Catastico of Verona*, c. 174r., 3 July 1625; ibid., c. 154v., 4 April 1620; S.T., *filza* 192, 7 November 1609; *Catastico of Verona*, c. 176v., 29 November 1635; *busta* 382, 29 July 1645; *busta* 379, 19 September 1606; S.T., *filza* 182, 29 May 1607). The Donà received a concession of 40 rice-fields in Legnago in 1642, with two *quadretti* to be drawn off the Adige and then drained into the Tartaro. In 1613, the Grimani and Tomaselli paid 1,360 ducats to irrigate their properties at Spessa, S. Pietro in Gù and Ancignano, in the Vicenza area, with 4 *quadretti* from the Brenta (S.T., *filza* 465, Senate decree 2 January 1642; *Catastico of Vicenza*, cit., c. 74r.).

55. On the vulnerability of the smaller as opposed to the larger agricultural concerns, see the fundamental study by Abel, *Agrarkrisen und Agrarkonjunktur*; on rural pauperisation, Jacquart, 'Des sociétés en crise', in *Histoire économique et sociale du monde*, Jacquart and Deyon eds. (P. Léon General editor), II, pp. 462–67.

56. M. Berengo, 'Patriziato e nobiltà: il caso veronese', in *Rivista Storica Italiana*, 87 (1975), pp. 502–3.

57. The pioneering work by G. Lombardini *(Pane e denaro a Bassano tra il 1501 e il 1799)* has been followed by few similar studies. See, however, the bibliography collected by G. Cozzi, M. Knapton and G. Scarabello in *La Repubblica di Venezia nell'età moderna. Dal 1517 alla fine della Repubblica*, Turin, 1992, pp. 527–28.

58. The cadastre in the Verona area has only eleven water concessions for the period 1627–1635, whilst there are seven for the year 1646 alone.

59. Le Roy Ladurie, 'Peasant Dues, Tithes and Trends', cit., pp. 120–22.

60. Hydraulic maintenance and safeguard work was undertaken by the comune of Cavarzere in 1650; nel *retratto* [reclaimed area] of the Gorzon, in 1663; and in the S. Giustina area in 1665 (Georgelin, *Venise au siècle des lumières*, p.370); G. Ferrari, 'La legislazione veneziana sui beni comunali', in *Archivio Veneto*, n.s., 36 (1918), pp. 39–62.

61. The concession payment is always expressed in *ducati buona valuta*, not *ducati valuta corrente*, the other form in which these public payments were given with increasing frequency during the seventeenth century. (U. Tucci, 'Convertibilità e copertura metallica della moneta del Banco giro veneziano', in *Studi Veneziani*, 15 (1973), pp. 349–51; on depreciation, see also J.G. Da Silva, *La politique monetaire à Venise*, ibid., 11 (1969), p. 67).

62. For a general account, cf. H. Medick, P. Kriedte, J. Schlumbohm, *Industrialisierung vor der Industrialisierung*, Göttingen, 1977; Ciriacono, 'Venise et la Vénétie dans la transition vers l'industrialisation. A propos des théories de Franklin Mendels', in *Etudes en mémoire de Franklin Mendels*, R. Leboutte ed., Ginevra, 1996, pp. 291–318; idem, 'Protoindustria, lavoro a domicilio e sviluppo economico nelle campagne venete in epoca moderna', in *Quaderni Storici*, 18 (1983), pp. 57–80.

63. *Catastico of Verona and Vicenza*, cit.; *buste* 382–92.

64. S.T., *filza* 676, Senate decree 19 May1670; *busta* 385, 28 April 1667; ibid., 16 July 1667. On the basis of nineteenth-century figures regarding the Verona and Vicenza areas, Berengo argues that the best rice-fields rotated the crop yearly with clover (Berengo, *L'agricoltura veneta*, pp. 280–81).

65. Faccini, *L'economia risicola lombarda*, p.120; Mazzucchelli, 'Catasti e storia dell'agricoltura', cit., p. 330).

66. *Busta* 385, 1 April 1664; ibid., 28 April 1667; *busta* 383, copy of the Senate decree 21 July 1656; S.T., *filza* 699, Senate decree 18 March 1662.

67. Average yield per hectare was around 848 kilos, rarely reaching 1,300. It was certainly lower than the 1,600 per hectares achieved in the Milan area in the period 1750–1800; though still double the 342–513 kilos achieved in the Verona area in the sixteenth century (cfr. M. Lecce, 'Un'azienda risiera veronese nel XVII e XVIII secolo', in Lecce, *Ricerche di storia economica medievale e moderna*, cit., pp. 125–27; Aymard and Basini, 'Production et productivité agricoles', cit., p. 143; Borelli, 'Introduzione storica' to *Relazioni dei rettori veneti. Podestaria e Capitanato di Verona*, Tagliaferri ed., p.XXVII). The richest part of the exports went northwards, spec. England

and Holland: *Provveditori alle biave, busta* 34, 29 April 1670, 27 December 1670 and 5 January 1672; *busta* 35, 22 December 1693, 11 June 1695; Sella, *Commerci e industrie,* p. 88).

68. Psbi, *buste* 388–392; Borelli, *Un patriziato della Terraferma,* p. 313.

69. Faccini, *La Lombardia fra '600 e '700,* pp. 236–46.

70. For example, after 1653 the Bevilacqua ceased to rent out their land and ran it themselves (Borelli, *Un patriziato della Terraferma,* p. 76). In 1650 Francesco and G.B. Bevilacqua Lazise had already invested 400 ducats in some rice plantations at Nogarole; twelve years later, they would invest another 1,000 ducats in water and the construction of two power hammers (*Catastico of Verona,* c. 199v., 29 May 1650; Psbi, *busta* 384, 18 March 1662). In 1687 Ottaviano Spolverini added to the 20–*campi* rice plantation set up by his father Girolamo in 1678, spending 1,050 ducats to extend it to 270 *campi*. A good investment, as under the equally skilful management of G.B. Spolverini, the plantation would be yielding 3,000 ducats by 1745. (S.T., *filza* 1091, Senate decree 12 February 1687; Berengo, 'Patriziato e nobiltà', cit., pp. 505–6).

71. *Busta* 383, 21 July 1656; *busta* 385, 15 September 1665 and 26 April 1668; *busta* 43, 16 September 1660, 29 March 1661, 20 November 1663, 26 February 1664; S.T., *filza* 967, Senate decree 26 March 1678; *busta* 43, 15 July 1689; *busta* 389, 5 September 1682; *busta* 391, 10 May 1691; *Catastico of Verona,* cit., c. 315r., 24 March 1685.

72. S.T., *filza* 628, 9 August 1656; *filza* 899, 3 November 1674; *filza* 1024, 24 June 1682; ; *filza* 1024, 25 July 1682; *Catastico of Vicenza,* c. 243v., 23 February 1673; Psbi, *busta* 383, 9 May 1654; *busta* 384, 5 February 1657.

73. B.H. Slicher van Bath, 'Eighteenth-century Agriculture on the Continent of Europe: Evolution or Revolution?', in *Agricultural History,* 43 (1969), pp. 169–70. This line of interpretation is also taken by Kerridge, *The Agricultural Revolution,* pp. 15–40; idem 'The Agricultural Revolution Reconsidered', in *Agricultural History* 43 (1969), cit., pp. 463–75. See also ibid., pp. 181–83, F. Dovring, 'Eighteenth-century Changes in European Agriculture: a Comment'.

74. Clark re-assesses the role of manual labour in English agriculture during the first part of the nineteenth century, reducing the role of that mechanisation which theoretically should be one of the linchpins in any industrial or agricultural revolution ('Productivity growth without change in European agriculture before 1850', pp. 419–32).

75. J. Thirsk, 'Agricultural Policy: Public Debate and Legislation', in *The Agrarian History,* Thirsk ed., V/2, p. 298f.; Kerridge, *The Agricultural Revolution,* pp. 326–48; G. Garavaglia, 'Una questione mal posta ? Il ruolo delle recinzioni in Inghilterra dalla crisi del Trecento alla Rivoluzione industriale', in *Società e Storia,* 9 (1986), n.34, pp. 903–45.

76. E. Le Roy Ladurie, 'De la crise ultime à la vraie croissance, 1660–1789', in *Histoire de la France rurale,* G. Duby and A. Wallon eds., II, Paris, 1975, p. 580.

77. O. Ulbricht, *Englische Landwirtschaft in Kurhannover in der zweiten Hälfte des 18. Jahrhunderts. Ansätze zu historischer Diffusionsforschung,* Berlin, 1980, p.

52ff.; G. Schröder-Lembke, 'Englische Einflüße auf die deutsche Gutswirtschaft im 18. Jahrhundert', in *Studien zur Agrargeschichte*, Stuttgart, 1978, pp. 103–10; Ciriacono, 'Agricoltura e agronomia a Venezia e nella Germania del nord (fine Settecento-inizi Ottocento): un approccio comparativo', in *Fra studio, politica ed economia: la Società Agraria dalle origini all'età giolittiana*, R. Finzi ed., Bologna, 1992, pp. 15–41.

78. Gullino, 'Le dottrine degli agronomi', pp. 400–7.

79. G. Bracco, 'Acque e risaie del Vercellese nel XVIII secolo', in *Agricoltura e trasformazione dell'ambiente, secoli XIII–XVIII* (11th Settimana di studio, Prato), Guarducci ed., p. 757.

80. Psbi, *buste* 393–409. This made for 2.25 per cent of the area of the province, a respectable figure. The assumption that the previous rice plantations had not been abandoned is based on the fact that authorisation usually had to be obtained from Venice when the water was no longer being put to this use. Of course, due account must be taken of the continuing fraud in such matters (on this point, see Berengo, 'Patriziato e nobiltà', cit., pp. 501–4).

81. Berengo, *L'agricoltura veneta*, p. 283.

82. Psbi, *buste* 393–409.

83. Lazzarini, *Fra terra e acqua. L'azienda risicola di una famiglia veneziana*, p. 117ff.; G. Scarpa, *L'agricoltura del Veneto nella prima metà del XIX secolo. L'utilizzazione del suolo*, Turin,1963, specially Appendix IV, Zona XV, Basso Polesine; E. Bevilacqua, 'L'influenza dell'uomo nella costruzione del delta del Po', in *Les deltas méditerranéens*, J. Bethemont and C. Villain-Gandossi eds., Doubrovnik, 1987, pp. 271–75; M. Zunica, 'Sul filo della piena', in *Il delta del Po. Terra e gente al di là dei monti di sabbia*, Zunica ed., pp. 50–51; P. Preto, 'Dagli interessi ferraresi e veneziani allo sciopero de *la boje*', ibid., pp. 101–10; D. Kelletat, *Deltaforschung. Verbreitung, Morphologie, Entstehung und Ökologie von Deltas*, Darmstadt, 1984, p. 114.

84. *Busta* 404 (1760–1767); *busta* 405 (1768–1775); *busta* 406 (1776–1782); *busta* 407 (1783–1788) and 408 (1789–1793); Lecce, *La coltura del riso in territorio veronese (secoli XVI–XVIII)*, Verona, 1958, pp. 36–46

85. *Busta* 404 (1760–1767).

86. *Busta* 402 (1748–1752); *busta* 406 (1776–1782).

87. *Buste* 393–409.

88. Morineau, *Les faux-semblants d'un démarrage économique*.

89   Romano, *Tra due crisi*, pp. 56–57; Cools, *Strijd om den grond*, p. 131; Smith, *An Historical Geography of Western Europe*, p. 507. Neither Romano nor the other authors cite their historical sources.

90. Psbi, *buste* 736, 741, 767, 779, 781–82, 785–86, 789, 791–92, 796, 799, 806, 809–14, 817, 819, 827 bis, 828–29, 831–32, 917; P. all'A., *buste* 259, 261, 262; S.T. 2701.

91. Berveglieri, *Inventori stranieri a Venezia (1474–1788)*; idem and A. Rossetto, *Tre secoli di privilegi veneziani (1474–1788). I casi polesani*, Verona, 1988.

92. P. all'A., *busta* 258, 3 February 1738; Psbi, *busta* 750, Report of 18 September 1787 and 11 April 1788.

93. In the nineteenth century, all this area would be described by Pietro Paleocapa as the *maremma veneta* because of the vast areas of low-lying land that it was difficult to drain (he does distinguish it from the Tuscan *maremma* for its absence of marshes, scrubland and woods): P. Paleocapa, *Parere sulla bonifica dei due consorzi padovani Gorzon medio e Gorzon inferiore*, Rovigo, 1868, p. 11; idem, *Su la condizione idrografica della maremma veneta e le bonificazioni di cui è suscettibile*, Venezia, 1848, p. 22.

94. The 'Sette Prese' consortium – covering a vast area that ran from Padua and Treviso to Asolo and Mestre – had been set up at the beginning of the sixteenth century, when the Brenta *nova* was being dug (Caporali, *Brenta vecchia*, pp. 68–74; SEA, reg. 320, 10 June 1795 and 15 March 1796; reg. 307, 2 May 1757).

95. Psbi, *busta* 735, 18 May 1735; *busta* 812, 31 May and 2 June 1772; *busta* 790, Report by the Podestà and Vicecapitano of Montagnana, 2 November 1778; S.T., *filza* 1637, Document from the Podestà and Capitanio of Este, 2 April 1725.

96. P. Preto, 'La torba: un esempio del rapporto 'lumi'-territorio nel Veneto del '700', in *La Nuova Olanda. Fabio Asquini tra accademia e sperimentazione*, L. Morassi (ed.), Udine, 1992, pp. 69–74; L. Morassi, 'Un nobile imprenditore nel Friuli del Settecento. Mattoni e calcina alla 'Nuova Olanda''', in *Quaderni Storici*, 52 (1983), pp. 81–103; V. Giormani, 'La mancata introduzione della macchina a vapore nelle bonifiche dello stato veneto nell'ultimo decennio del '700', in *Studi Veneziani*, 17 (1989), pp. 157–224. It is no coincidence that many of the marshy areas would not be fully drained until after the end of the Republic, when modern steam pumps would make a decisive difference (Ciriacono, 'Le bonifiche venete alla caduta della Repubblica e al tempo di Pietro Paleocapa', pp. 317–40).

97. Psbi, *busta* 736, 20 March 1728; *busta* 781, 21 May 1699 (Consortium of Brancaglia); *busta* 790, 4 July 1778 and 8 August 1790; *busta* 794, Information on the reclaimed land of the Gorzon – undated, this is undoubtedly from the second half of the eighteenth century; *busta* 795, 2 August 1677, Appeal by the community of Monselice; *busta* 801, 4 July 1633 (Consortium of Lozzo); *busta* 804, 8 June 1696.

98. In 1749 the Frassinella consortium, in the Rovigo area, had an outstanding debt of 20.000 ducats, owed to the Venetian nobleman Bernardo Michiel since 1639: S.T., *filza* 2098, Senate Senate decree of 9 August 1749.

99. E. Bevilacqua, 'Le grandi linee di evoluzione del paesaggio agrario in territorio veronese', in *Uomini e civiltà agraria in territorio veronese*, Borelli ed., I, p. 28; S. Stratico, *Osservazione sulla necessità che ha la Repubblica di Venezia di rivolgere le applicazioni del suo governo a riordinare alcuni fiumi principali del suo stato*, place of publication unknown, 1771.

100. SEA, reg. 305, Document of the Savi, 1749.

101. Psbi, *busta* 798, Note of how much collected by Giacinto Corradin, agent of the *President of the ritratto of Lozzo*, 1687. Contractual relations of this kind are mentioned in the Gastaldia consortium at Livenza, which covered 2686 *campi* (cf. Psbi, *busta* 819, 26 August 1778). See also *busta* 745, 31 December

1657; *busta* 736, Report 6 May 1789 (Consortium Brancaglia); *busta* 745, 28 November 1713 (Consortium Frassinella).

102. *Busta* 794, Copy of Senate decree, 7 October 1679.
103. *Busta* 812, Auction of the Consorzio del Piavon, 27 March 1748; P. all'A., *busta* 260, Note by the Presidency of the consortium of Castagnaro, Rovigo, 18 April 1794.
104. Expression of this view by the Venetian Senate: cf. P. all'A., *busta* 260, Copy of the Senate decree 1 June 1774.
105. Psbi, *busta* 812, Report by the *Inquisitore alla sanità* Giacomo Nani, 3 June 1772; *busta* 741, Report by the Psbi, 19 September 1764.
106. P. all'A., *busta* 263, 10 March 1691; Psbi, *busta* 741, Report by the Psbi, 19 September 1764; *busta* 812, Report by the *Inquisitore straordinario alla sanità* Giacomo Nani, 3 June 1772. On Nani, see P. Del Negro, 'Giacomo Nani. Appunti biografici', in *Bollettino del Museo civico di Padova*, 60 (1971), pp. 115–22; idem, 'Giacomo Nani e l'Università di Padova nel 1781', in *Quaderni per la storia dell'Università di Padova*, 13 (1980), pp. 101–9; S.T., *filza* 2701, Senate decree 26 August 1779 and attached Document of the *Provveditori all'Adige*, 17 August 1779.
107. Psbi, *busta* 827, Copy of Senate decree 16 November 1589.
108. Psbi, *busta* 804, 3 January 1634 and 17 April 1763.

Chapter 3

Hydraulics in the Venetian Republic:
Technicians and Scientists from the Early Fifteenth Century to the Second Scientific Revolution

A History of the Lagoon

The problems posed by the agriculture and hydrology of the mainland inevitably overlapped with those of the Venetian lagoon itself, to which the state – primarily a maritime power – had always been most sensitive. Throughout the Republic's history, the lagoon and the five entrances[1] which gave access to it from the sea, had been a special focus of Venetian legislation. Over this lengthy period of time, a number of technical-scientific works were dedicated to the subject, their celebratory tone often tinged with regret for that legendary period when the glorious state of Venice had first been founded. As each century looked back nostalgically to its predecessors, in a sort of perennial search for the origin that defined the very archetype of 'Venice', the length, width and depth of the lagoon were measured, with the – sometimes doctored – results being used in a comparison of the past and the present that aimed to underline the gradual reduction of the 'maternal lake' that had given birth to the city. Of course, there were cases where this 'nostalgia' produced work of real rigour. For example, Cristoforo Sabbadino, perhaps the most talented hydraulic scientist of the sixteenth century, would write a series of stinging attacks upon those who had altered this very special environment, backing up his argument with accurate analyses of the impact of the manufacturers located within it.

In effect, the long-term history of the lagoon is a tale of defeats and successes, of glum pessimism and level-headed realism, of renewed dangers and carefully-laid plans of defence. Ultimately, the long-running debates of the fifteenth and sixteenth centuries would result in the work that saved the lagoon from the rivers which were causing it to silt up. However, as is well known, this expanse of water would then fall victim to an industrial civilisation that paid little attention to matters of ecological equilibrium.

Canals and Lagoons: Two Different Policies?

It is generally assumed that those writing upon hydrology within the Republic were automatically writing about the lagoon (an assumption given further weight by the massive and invaluable work edited by Roberto Cessi). Certainly there can be no doubt that the most decisive hydrological projects were those concerned with the re-routing of the rivers which flowed into the lagoon, an issue that generated numerous original works during the course of the fifteenth and sixteenth century. However, as I have repeatedly underlined, the need to increase agricultural output also made it necessary to extend the network of existing watercourses and undertake drainage and land reclamation (operations which were far from risk-free, especially in the areas around the lagoon). This was a period in which a new political and economic balance had to be struck between the commercial and maritime interests of Venice itself and the requirements of the agricultural and manufacturing industries that were developing upon the terra firma. But if the major projects concerning the redirection of rivers were carried out successfully, the same success cannot be seen in this balancing of conflicting interests:[2] works of drainage, irrigation or other economic activities associated with a canal or watercourse were automatically sacrificed if they were seen as posing any sort of threat to the lagoon. Further signs of the priority given to the lagoon are the fact that the *Savi alle Acque*, responsible for the protection of the lagoon, was set up as early as 1501, some decades before the *Provveditori ai Beni Inculti*, responsible for the agricultural resources of the terra firma; or again, the fact that the *Savi* had as early as 1505 been supplemented by another body, the *Collegio Solenne alle Acque*, which comprised all the highest officers of the state.[3]

Scientific Theory and Rule of Thumb

Throughout the fifteenth and most of the sixteenth century, hydraulic know-how in the Veneto was not as advanced as that one finds in Lombardy; and this technological short-fall meant that numerous people not only from Lombardy but also other regions of Northern Italy worked on projects involving the lagoon and the creation of water channels and irrigation canals. In 1436 Maestro Ravanello da Brescia and Domenico Carabello da Bergamo were appointed to direct the work upon the Brentella at Treviso, where they were soon joined by another native of Lombardy, Michele da Caravaggio. The fifty workmen Ravanello wanted on his squad were also from his native city, as were the two experts working with him, Amedeo degli Orti and Cristoforo de Travagliato. At the beginning of the sixteenth century it was the Bergamo-born Alessio di Aleardi – a hydraulic engineer much appreciated by the Republic – who would work on the first re-routing of the Brenta. Amongst the other examples of such 'outsiders' one might list: Antonio da Piacenza, who is mentioned as inspecting the embankments of San Giuliano in 1458; Alvise de Marchi from Crema, whom Marco Cornaro describes as a 'perfect engineer'; Pinzino da Bergamo, who would oppose that same Cornaro's project for the re-routing of the Brenta; Gabriele da Crema, who a few decades later – in 1535 – would submit his own report on this question; and a whole series of fifteenth-century hydraulic engineers whose work served as a necessary point of reference – Aristotile da Bologna, Bertola da Novate, Aguzio da Cremona and even Leonardo da Vinci himself (author of a *Treatise on the Motion and Measurement of Water*).[4]

Thanks to this input, Venice was able to achieve high levels of success both in the protection of the lagoon and in its projects of land reclamation, in spite of a narrow range of technical means which Braudel lists as 'ditches, water channels, canals and weak pumps. Dutch engineers in the following century [the seventeenth] would develop more efficient methods. But they were yet to make their mark in this period'.[5] One might take up this observation to make a geographical comparison of the material and intellectual instruments available within hydraulics in the fifteenth and sixteenth century. What were the differences between the drainage techniques which the Dutch had, since the eleventh century,[6] developed in their on-going battle with the sea, and those used by the Venetians in the drained areas of Gorzon, Foresto or Santa Giustina? What contacts – and what differences – existed between hydraulics as practised in Lombardy and in Provence (where a whole school of engineers followed in the footsteps of Adam de Craponne, who in 1558 had drawn off from the river Durance the canal that would be named after him)?[7] The very fact that one cannot always give complete answers to such questions reveals the continuing scope for study within the history of 'the science of water'.

What is beyond doubt is that the limits encountered in Venice were specific to a historical period rather than a geographical area. In the absence of a rigorous mathematical method, the Republic drew on oral traditions, especially when it came to knowledge of the lagoon. Boatmen, fisherman and sailors were continually urged to take soundings of canals and to report changes within them or the emergence of sandbars and so on (in Lombardy itself, Fra Giovanni Giocondo commented that 'levelling [that is, measuring the exact location of the various points of terrain through which one intended to dig an irrigation canal] is something that is based on information from numerous peasant farmers').[8] This pre-scientific period was one in which practical knowledge continually supplemented the 'mathematical' knowledge of hydraulic phenomena produced by experts and *proti*; official science had yet to establish itself as an entirely distinct body and methodology of knowledge. This meant there were innumerable instances of small-scale intervention on the large rivers or around the shores of the lagoon; individuals would, on their own initiative, open up artificial canals, widen openings off rivers and otherwise interfere with the flow of fluvial waters – all in spite of numerous laws passed during the fifteenth and sixteenth century to regulate such work.

However, at the same time, an interdisciplinary scientific community was emerging within the Republic, integrating hydraulics, geography, cartography and architecture. For example, the important fifteenth-century geographer Fra Mauro often tackled problems raised by the nascent science of hydraulics; in 1444 he would make his contribution to a lively debate of that period by giving a favourable opinion on the project for the diversion of the Brenta at Fusina. For his part, the great sixteenth-century military engineer and architect Michele da Sanmicheli would comment upon how the difficulties encountered at the lagoon opening of Malamocco were due not only to the silt carried by rivers but also to the action of the sea, thus introducing a scientific observation of fundamental importance to modern hydraulics (he also recommended narrowing the Malamocco opening).[9] And whilst the famous humanist and physician Girolamo Fracastoro may have admitted that the subject of water 'lay far outside his profession', he argued (with excessive pessimism) that it was inevitable that the lagoon silt up and the river areas turn to marshland (his rather exotic remedy was to raise hills using the marshy silt deposited).[10]

Amongst the geographers-cartographers who held important positions was the Piedmont-born Giacomo Gastaldi, 'Cosmographer to the Republic' and probably the greatest cartographer of the sixteenth century. Remarkable documentation of the problems associated with water, the maps of the lagoon and terra firma areas that he produced for the *Provveditori ai Beni Inculti* and the *Savi alle Acque* would then be supplemented by the conscientious contributions made by functionaries and water experts, some of whom – for example, Nicolò dal Cortivo and Cristoforo Sabbadino – became justly famous in their own right, others remaining obscure. But all are equally noteworthy for the precision of their fascinating depictions of the lagoon and the region's rivers.[11]

Another important Veneto-born humanist with an interest in science was Fra Giocondo da Verona (1433–1515).[12] A scholar of Graeco-Roman texts and inscriptions – he would, for example, produce an edition of Frontinus' *De aquae ductibus* – Fra Giocondo was also an architect and military engineer who specialised in the digging of canals and the creation of embankments and sea defences. It was in hydraulics that the full range of his Renaissance versatility found best expression, as one can see from the only two projects that are known to us in any detail: the re-routing of the Brenta and the repair work on the Brentella.

As we have already seen, by the beginning of the sixteenth century it was already clear that this latter canal was not living up to expectations. In 1503 Venice sent one of its most capable hydraulic engineers, Alessio di Aleardi, to try and remedy the chronic water shortage in the area; but even he failed to make much impression on the poorly-managed water resources. And by 1506 the pressure of the waters of the Piave would lead to the Pederobba outlet being completely blocked, with some even suggesting that it be filled in permanently. It was at this point that Fra Giovanni was sent to report on the situation, having been called from Paris to draw up projects for the re-routing of the Brenta and the laying-out of a new bed for the Brentella canal. His proposal was to divide the Piavesella into two branches, one for irrigation, the other to meet the usual water and energy needs of Treviso. However, his solicitude in drawing up the scheme was not matched by that with which this urgent work was carried out: in 1518 it had still to be started, and – as we know – the performance of the Brentella did not improve very much.[13]

His proposals for the re-routing of the Brenta were no more successful, being set aside in favour of the official project carried out by Aleardi. However, as Sabbadino would note, Fra Giocondo had been right to suggest a deviation starting further upstream (at Strà) rather than at Conche (where the actual re-routing was cut in 1507), expressing doubts that the gradient of the Brenta *Nova* created by this latter scheme would be insufficient to carry the water down to Chioggia.

In his debate on these questions with Aleardi, Fra Giocondo expressed his opinions forcefully but without sinking into personal diatribe. As has often been commented, he emerges as a true hydraulic engineer, applying a scientific method to the solution of problems, making no *a priori* claims and continually subjecting his data and measurements to on-site verification.[14] While it would be no exaggeration to claim that he is one of the most significant forerunners of the mathematical method that would be championed by Galileo, one should however recognise the fact that nearly all these late-fifteenth/early-sixteenth-century writers on hydraulics seem to have eschewed rhetorical flourishes in their discussions. In effect, their work reveals such limited literary – as opposed to scientific – ambitions that they entirely side-step the heated debate within Venetian scientific circles regarding the suitability of Italian as a replacement for Latin.[15]

Fifteenth-Century Writers on Hydraulics

The best work on hydraulics inevitably came in providing a response to the pressing problems posed by the silt carried down into the lagoon by numerous watercourses. Marco Cornaro (1412–1464) is rightly credited with being the first to think out a series of projects designed to halt a process that would have marked the end of Venice as a commercial port; and, even more importantly for us, he was a very precise observer of what was happening in the lagoon, leaving an invaluable record of 'that long and industrious period – from 1424 to 1459 – which began and ended with the reign of doge Francesco Foscari'. By then, Venice had asserted its dominion over Padua and thus had the whole course of the Brenta under its control. This necessarily meant that the problems posed by defences against river flooding could be approached in a way that had been impossible before (the Brenta had only flowed into the Venetian lagoon since 1142, when the Paduans – concerned to protect their own land against its floodwaters – had re-directed the river, leaving the Venetians to handle the problems it posed). Even though Cornaro was not the first to propose re-directing the river at Strà – the idea had already been put forward by the Treviso-born engineer Antonio Carraro da Silvelle – some of his insights into questions of water dynamics were of great value. He saw that it was due to the pressure exerted by the denser salt water that the rivers tended to deposit silt when they flowed into the lagoon; that the sea tide might have a noteworthy role in 'sweeping' the bed of the lagoon clean but a minimal effect upon displacing silt; that the less water flowed into the lagoon, the narrower and shallower a lagoon opening became; that the wind and the sea together were two essential factors in determining the environmental balance of the lagoon and the maintenance of the lagoon's sea openings. Such observations were to be of clear importance in the future development of Venetian hydraulics, and show that it is Cornaro – not Cristoforo Sabbadino – who is to be credited with the axiom 'good sea openings make for a good lagoon'.

Essentially, Cornaro's work is known to us through two texts. The first was produced after a 1442 inspection of the Sile and Tagliamento, providing 'a copious quantity of hydrographical and topographical information' regarding the places, internal canals and rivers of this area. However, it is in the second text that his qualities as both a theorist and writer emerged most clearly. This contains not only a long account of the various re-routings of the Brenta – from that of 1142 up to the most recent, in 1452 – but also Cornaro's own proposed remedies for the ills he observes. Even before Fra Giocondo, he suggests re-routing the Brenta at Strà so that it would run down to the Brondolo sea-opening into the lagoon of Chioggia, thus by-passing the Venetian lagoon altogether. Cornaro then continues with a description of the painstaking levelling and site-inspection undertaken, as well as charting the tense – sometimes dramatic – debate between technicians, experts and the *Savi alle Acque* as to which proposal best met Venice's needs (at one point, the authorities even considered the possibility of drawing off some of the waters of the Brenta as far upstream as Bassano). However, the end result was that Cornaro's proposal was set aside (just as Fra Giocondo's would be) in favour of a less demanding scheme: in 1452 it was decided to channel the Brenta into a series of canals which reached the coast opposite Malamocco on the Lido. This meant that the river continued to flow into the Venetian lagoon and thus continued to pose a threat, with Cornaro commenting glumly: 'But I, Marco, wanted to turn the river at Strada ... but these gentlemen decided that I wouldn't have been able to'.[16]

Once again, scope for action was determined by the old idea that one should intervene at the mouth of the Brenta, rejecting the possibility of taking more radical action outside the context of the lagoon itself. And, once again, it was feared that such a proposal as Cornaro's could provoke a complete interruption of river traffic along the Brenta; possibly interfere with Venice's fresh water supply; and clash with numerous vested interests due to the closure of mills and other water-powered facilities along the river.[17] Given the weight of such economic and psychological factors in determining Venetian policy with regard to fluvial waters, it was inevitable that the other innovative schemes put forward by Cornaro again met with no success, even if he clearly anticipated the great sixteenth-century debate upon the re-direction of the lagoon rivers – when he proposed that the Sile should be re-routed to run into the sea to the north of Venice – and made (an admittedly vague) suggestion that the equally-dangerous Piave should be channelled out to sea elsewhere. In effect, Cornaro was already pushing for an overall plan of lagoon management – 'all the waters from Lio Maggiore to the Brondolo lagoon opening' – and voicing sharp criticism of the deterioration in the lagoon environment caused by *la desobendientia* which resulted in 'some filling in canals here, some there, without any consideration for how they are interrupting the flow of the lagoon waters, as one can see everywhere but most clearly in the area around the Grand

Canal, that is at Rialto'.[18] However, for all the urgency with which Cornaro and others pushed for measures to be taken, there would be repeated procrastination in the implementation of the proposed modifications to the lagoon environment.

More extensive and co-ordinated work upon the lagoon would begin to emerge towards the end of the fifteenth century, thanks to the work of Paolo Sabbadino and Paolo Sambo. Father of the more famous Cristoforo, the former could stand as a clear demonstration of how the solution to the problems of the lagoon did not emerge fully-fledged but was the culmination of a process of reflection and small-scale achievements. It is, in fact, clear that many of the projects put forward by the son take up the illuminating suggestions to be found in the father's work: for example, the request made by Paolo Sabbadino that the entire Brenta be diverted towards Fosson (that is, beyond the lagoon of Chioggia) and that the Sile (after having been channelled together with the Marzenego, the Dese and the Zero) should be linked up with the mouth of the Piave at Lio Maggiore in the northern section of the lagoon. But the real originality in Sabbadino Senior's reflections upon the lagoon concerned his insistence on the need for a flow of sea water to flush clean canals and drainage channels, as well as to counterbalance the silting produced by the fresh water that flowed into the lagoon. This notion would be reiterated repeatedly by Cristoforo Sabbadino and others – for example, Alvise Barbaro, when he argued that as much sea-water as possible should be allowed to flow into the lagoon 'because then the outgoing tide of this water guarantees better flow through the openings into the lagoon'.[19]

Although he too would insist upon the need to redirect the rivers, Paolo Sambo's approach to the protection of the lagoon had a slightly different focus, being predicated upon the creation of an embankment to enclose the whole. However, whilst this would undoubtedly have prevented the flow of drainage water into the lagoon, it would also have hindered the action of the sea water in counterbalancing the effects of alluvial deposits. That the dangers posed by such deposits were far from over is clear from the fact that the risks of silting at the crucial San Nicolò opening into the lagoon had increased alarmingly (due, it was said, to the re-routing of the Brenta to Malamocco).

Some of the other technicians and experts appointed together with Sambo and Fra Giovanni to report upon the re-directing of the Brenta do not seem to have had as clear an overall vision of the issues concerned. There were even those who questioned that the flow of rivers into the lagoon posed any threat at all. Nicolò Trevisan, for example, argued that fluvial waters did not silt up the lagoon openings because 'their effect was counterbalanced by the action of the incoming and outgoing tide'. The sandbars at the openings were, he said, produced when opposing marine currents ran into each other. For his part, Alvise Zuccarin said that the fluvial waters posed a threat only in two or three periods of the year, when they carried large quantities of mud and silt. [20] And Piero Ziani argued that it would actually be a mistake to re-direct the Sile, because its lighter waters had a beneficial effect upon the environmental balance of the lagoon[21]. As far as the Brenta was concerned, however, Ziani agreed with such figures as Fra Giovanni, Pietro Sambo, Raffacan di Raffacani, Giovanni Carrara, Piero de Fanti and Bartolomeo Bozato that the Malamocco solution had clear drawbacks.

The final decision was that, work having begun on the Brenta *Nova* to draw off part of the waters of the Brenta, two minor relief canals – the Tresse and the Toro – should be created in the stretch of this new canal before it met up with another Padua river (the Bacchiglione) and then flowed into the lagoon of Chioggia.[22] Other palliative measures included: the creation of a channel running along the coast to take the Dese and the Marzenego away from Venice towards Malamocco (with the waters running in the opposite direction to that they would flow naturally); the raising of the San Marco embankment in 1534; and the subsidiary canals of Cava Zuccarina (1531) and Taglio di Re (1535), to protect the north-eastern area of the lagoon from the pressure of the inflowing waters of the Piave.[23] However, the authorities failed to see the need for radical intervention in this section of the lagoon, just as they failed to see that the joint action of the Brenta-Bacchiglione in the south and the Piave-Sile in the north was the cause of an overall environmental imbalance.[24]

An Extraordinary *Proto alle Acque*: Cristoforo Sabbadino

Even more so than Alvise Cornaro, a Paduan aristocrat whose role will be discussed in more detail below, it was Cristoforo Sabbadino who first presented a solidly-based overall project for tackling the problems he identified in the lagoon. A profoundly Venetian personality who maintained close links with the fisherman and sailors of Chioggia, Sabbadino was appointed *Proto alle Acque* in 1542. However, he was much more than a mere public official;[25] his *Discorsi de il Sabbattino per la laguna di Venetia* and his *Istruzioni [...] circa questa laguna, et come l'era anticamente, et come la si trova al presente* are some of the finest things ever written on this vital aspect of Venetian life. Worthy of comparison with the *Memorie storiche della Laguna di Venezia*, written by the great eighteenth-century historian and hydraulic 'mathematician' Zendrini, they are a perfect example of scientific literature that sees a concrete approach to questions as the indispensable complement to theoretical considerations.

It is true that subsequent writers criticised parts of Sabbadino's historical account of the alterations the lagoon and its rivers had undergone over time; and there is no doubt that – like Marco Cornaro – the writer depicts an almost legendary lagoon, which may never have existed and is (perhaps deliberately) in powerful contrast to the marshy, neglected environment he sees around him.[26] Zendrini himself, for example, shows that there is no serious basis for Sabbadino's claim that the lagoon once extended from the river Isonzo in Friuli down to the river Savio in the Ravenna area, making up seven basins of water that could be compared to the 'Seven Seas' of the Antiquity. However, given the range of the man's merits and talents, one can perhaps forgive such rhetorical flourishes in his passionate advocacy of his cause.[27]

In his rigorous and closely-argued account of how the lagoon had been damaged by things done and things left undone, Sabbadino focuses on three main problems: the sea, the rivers and human action.[28] This latter is seen as the main culprit of the hydrological imbalance within the lagoon, with the *proto* saying that 'three classes of men have ruined the lagoon: nobles, engineers and private individuals, with the nobles being most responsible of all'.[29] How? By opening up water channels, erecting water-driven mills, carrying out ill-planned projects of land reclamation, and extending the areas for vines and wheat fields beyond reasonable measure.[30] Men had caused more damage than rivers, not because of their sloth but because of their determination to modify the lagoon at all costs. Sabbadino notes paradoxically that when the Carraresi of Padua re-

routed the Brenta into the lagoon of Venice and the Bacchiglione
into that of Chioggia, their aim was to silt up the lagoon in those two
points alone, whilst subsequent engineers 'in shifting the course of
the Brenta this way and that, have in a short time so undermined the
well-being of this lagoon that it will take a most skilled physician to
restore it to health'. The 'engineers' of whom he is most critical are
those from Lombardy and Bergamo, and even such famous
technicians as Aleardi and Fra Giocondo, by whom the Venetians let
themselves be taken in. Sabbadino admits that such figures were
qualified to 'level rivers, dig irrigation channels from one point to
another, and to set up mills and fountains'; but work on the lagoon
was a very different matter 'as it should draw on long experience of
both the sea and the lagoon'.[31]

The *proto's* view on land speculation was no less firm: a total halt
should be imposed on land-reclamation project bordering on the
lagoon; and it should be forbidden to raise embankments or lay out
pasture-land – both of which accelerated the process of silting.[32]
However, the main focus of Sabbadino's proposal concerned the re-
routing of the rivers flowing into the lagoon. Of course, such
schemes obviously concerned not only the areas through which the
Brenta *Nova* ran, but also the very delicate environment where their
waters finally emerged, with fundamental errors having been
committed – for example, the re-routing of the Brenta and
Bacchiglione to Chioggia, which was silting up that lagoon without
saving the port of Venice.[33]

With regard to the left-hand branch of the fluvial system running
into the central and eastern part of the lagoon, as early as 1540
Sabbadino was suggesting the creation of a new canal that, starting
from Mirano, would then carry the waters of the Musone, the
Marzenego, the Dese, the Zero and the Sile to the northern side of
the lagoon (between Jesolo and Lio Maggiore). By 1552 the details of
the proposal had been worked out in full, and the following year he
received broad government approval for the scheme. However, a
committee of *proti e ingegneri* – Giovanni Carrara, Piero de Guberni,
Domenico dall'Abbaco and Paolo da Castello – whom the *Collegio alle
Acque* appointed to write up a report on the possible effects of the
plan were very critical, describing it as both costly and risky. The
truth was that the local nobility saw the new canal as threatening
their agricultural interests and depriving them of a profitable source

of energy. Alvise Cornaro, the effective spokesman for these threatened interests, argued vehemently that the Musone and the other rivers of the Padua area could be channelled towards Chioggia, whilst the Marzenego, Sile, Dese and Zero might well continue to flow into the lagoon (being karst spring rivers, they did not pose the threat that Sabbadino claimed).[34]

Given this conflict of evaluations, no rapid decision as to the implementation of Sabbadino's scheme was taken, but that in no way diminishes the importance or originality of his writings on hydraulics.

Alvise Cornaro: Hydraulic Engineer or Land Speculator?

Whether one looks at his role in questions relating to the sea openings or to the regulation of the lagoon environment as a whole, the figure of Alvise Cornaro is much more controversial, and ultimately open to real suspicion; Sabbadino, for example, had little difficulty in demonstrating that a number of his proposals were based on totally unfounded premises. As far as the re-direction of the rivers is concerned, Cornaro in fact seems to represent a retreat from – and threat to – what had already been achieved, with his request that the Bacchiglione, the Brenta *Nova*, the Musone and all the small streams running between these latter two watercourses should be allowed to empty into the lagoon of Chioggia. As Sabbadino correctly pointed out, if that were done, the 'lagoon of Chioggia will not have a drop of salt water through its sea opening'. Cornaro even went to so far as to concede that his scheme might lead to the silting-up of the latter port, but that was far preferable to the risk of silting in the Venetian lagoon.[35] A cavalier attitude that was bound to incense the Chioggia-born Sabbadino.

A nobleman who had fallen on hard times (although Menegazzo even doubts the truth of that aristocratic origin[36]), Alvise Cornaro was prone to great simplifications in his presentation of matters of hydraulics – for example, when he compared the flow of water in the lagoon to the passage of people through the *calli* of Venice – and one could cite numerous occasions when Sabbadino's solidly-based arguments had him floundering. Overall, what one gets is not the impression of an original mind but of someone who was good at

eavesdropping on the ideas and projects that must have been widely
discussed at the time amongst the city's enginecrs, *proti* and *Savi alle
Acque*. Look, for example, at his *Trattato alle Acque*. Opening with a
declaration that it was written at the venerable age of ninety-six, this
was intended to be the crowning achievement of a seventy-year
career dedicated to the study of hydraulics. The twenty-odd years of
disputes with Sabbadino are amply represented; but there is little to
support the author's modest claim that he had put pen to paper
because 'there is no one else who has written upon such an
important subject'.[37] However, although prone to self-delusion as to
his own worth – he even believed himself to have been the
inspiration for the establishment of the *Provveditori ai Beni Inculti* –
Cornaro was undoubtedly a determined polemicist and revealed a
certain talent for tackling a variety of subjects (architecture, theatre,
literature, agriculture). But with what degree of originality?

The main bone of contention with Sabbadino concerned the
problems posed by lagoon embankments and land reclamation, of
both of which he was an indefatigable champion. He himself argued
(in good faith?) that the main function of the embankments he
proposed should run across the lagoon from Brondolo to Torcello
was to stop the further flow of alluvial material that would otherwise
be deposited there. Making a rather tenuous distinction between
'raised' and 'low' marshland, he argued that the former only went
underwater three to four times a year and was an integral part of the
lagoon terrain. Therefore, he claimed, such areas should be made the
object of land-reclamation projects that could be used to provide
more wheat for the Republic's granaries.[38] The truth was that
extensive embankments would inevitably have reduced the area of
the water basin[39], preventing the essential flow of the tides into the
further canals and channels of the lagoon. As Sabbadino insisted, it
was only the deep penetration of the tidal waters into the lagoon that
made it possible for them to carry away the reeds and soil waste
which, in the long term, would produce silting.[40]

Faced with this argument, Cornaro could do nothing better than
sing the praises of land reclamation *tout court*, mentioning the 1,000
campi he had already reclaimed, those at his Fogolana estate (Santa
Margherita di Calcinara) that he intended to put under the plough,
and the 12,000 ducats he had already invested in this promotion of
agriculture. In effect, these perorations in favour of the land-

reclamation schemes carried out since 1530 actually give the game away, revealing his interests and concerns to be 'more those of a Padua landowner than of a citizen of the lagoon'.[41] It was Sabbadino's determined opposition that would by 1541 lead to a reversal in the fortunes of this speculative investor in land-reclamation, whose property included 40 *campi* in Chioggia and a further 1,600 at his Fogolana estate (which he describes as being in the area of the Padua, though in fact it was perilously close to the lagoon). Thereafter, Cornaro would, with querulous insistence, keep on repeating that he was not the only one to have undertaken intensive land-reclamation in the area bordering on the lagoon, providing a detailed list of other, ecclesiastical and aristocratic, offenders (a document that merits further study, this mentions, for example, a total of 100,000 *campi* cultivated by the monks of Santa Giustina[42]). For his part, Sabbadino continued to emphasise that he was not opposed to all land reclamation but only that which posed a threat to the lagoon. In conclusion, one could cite the portrait of Cornaro that emerges from Emilio Menegazzo's work, which suggests that not only should extreme caution be used when quoting the data given by the author of *Discorsi intorno alla vita sobria* and *Scritti d'idraulica*[43], but also that the man enjoys a far higher reputation than he deserves.

Large-Scale Hydraulic Projects: Rivers and the Lagoon in the Seventeenth Century

If the main guidelines for lagoon policy were in place by about 1550, it is in later centuries that one sees the success or failure of the approach taken. The channelling and re-direction of rivers would continue within an unchanging general framework, predicated on the need to distance river waters from the lagoon and divide the fluvial system of the mainland into two distinct systems: the Brenta-Bacchiglione to the south, and the Piave-Sile to the north of the lagoon. All of this reveals the unflagging determination to safeguard the interests of the port of Venice, even if in the long-term that policy clashed with the agricultural and manufacturing interests of the Venetian and mainland aristocracy, as well as undermining the hydro-geological balance of vast areas that bordered on the lagoon (Dogado, Padua, Treviso).

What we see is an approach that should have posed itself two general objectives: the defence of the lagoon and the management of surface water within the terra firma. The failure to tackle this second issue coherently means that, whilst the lagoon represents a hydraulic achievement which is not only one of the oldest and most glorious but also one of the best documented in Europe (the documentation it produced would have a significant influence on the development of cartography itself), [44] alongside it one finds a situation of serious hydro-geological imbalance. On the terra firma, Venice – a European leader in hydraulic science – ultimately fell behind developments being made elsewhere in drainage technology.

When one looks at the writings on the lagoon published in the Republic from the middle of the sixteenth to the end of the seventeenth century, it is clear Sabbadino remained a dominant presence. The three main threats continued to be identified as the sea, the rivers and mankind, with the latter the most dangerous of all. It was man who was responsible for the shrinkage in the area of the lagoon, thanks to the cultivation of hill terrain (resulting in the creation of streams), the reclamation of areas bordering on the lagoon itself and the creation of drainage channels that ran into it. [45]

With regard to the northern area of the lagoon, the policy followed took up one very precise point made in Sabbadino's writings. Given that the creation of the Brenta *Nova* in 1507 had, in part, resolved the problem posed by the Brenta, by 1555 the *proto* was arguing that the mouth of the Piave should be shifted northwards – from Jesolo to Cortellazzo – and that the abandoned bed of this river should be used to carry the waters of the Sile and other smaller watercourses (the Musone, the Marzenego, the Dese and the Zero), which may have been less sizeable but nevertheless posed a constant threat of silting and swamping in the central-northern area of the lagoon.

By 1561 the idea had been accepted; but it would take another century for the plan to be put into effect (and even then with results that fell short of the original expectations). [46] Only in 1685 was Sabbadino's insight – supported in the Senate by the authoritative voice of Geminiano Montanari – put into practice, with the Piave flowing out to the sea at Cortellazzo. Into the old riverbed was diverted the Sile, following a project drawn up by the technician Cumano, even if in 1683 Montanari had presented clearly-argued objections to the principles on which that scheme was based[47]. In its new course, he argued, the Sile would flow too slowly, thus causing more alluvial deposits, raising the level of the river bed and creating a hydraulic imbalance within the entire area (the drainage canals would no longer empty into the river, but flow backwards). However, such grim forecasts were ignored; nor did the Senate accept Montanari's 'compromise' suggestion that only a part of the waters of the Sile should be diverted into the old Piave riverbed (in order to reduce the volume of alluvial deposits).

Similarly, it was against the advice of the Moderna-born engineer that the so-called Businello *diversivo* was created in 1695 to relieve pressure within the river (the areas around Treviso had become increasingly subject to flooding since the diversion of the Sile). The question of how effective such *diversivi* were would long be debated throughout the eighteenth and nineteenth century; with regard to this one, Zendrini would comment: 'the effect in no way corresponded to those promised by the proposal'. As the Businello flowed into the lagoon, it brought with it damaging alluvial deposits; what is more, with less water in it, the Sile flowed even slower, thus increasing the rate of alluvial deposits. Part of these difficulties were only obviated much later, in 1769, when the Businello was closed; though, even here, the results were disappointing.

But if no definite solution was reached for the other rivers (the Dese, the Zero and the Marzenego), with the matter continuing to be a centre of debate right up to the fall of the Republic, one must recognise two clear achievements in Venetian hydraulic policy. The first is the completion in 1610 of the Brenta *Novissima*, dug at Mira (the 1507 Brenta *Nova* ran off the river at Dolo) to relieve the threat posed to the lagoon around Chioggia and Brondolo by the waters of the two rivers (Brenta and Bacchiglione). The second achievement is the 1655 completion of the Mirano canal, which diverted the Musone (the lower reaches of which were known as the Bottenigo) from the lagoon into the fluvial system of the Brenta.[48]

Defining the Perimeter of the Lagoon

The idea of defining the perimeter of the lagoon was inspired by two main needs: to protect it from the influx of fluvial water and to mark a clear limit for the expansion of the tides within it. A decisive moment in the defence of the lagoon, it involved the construction of embankments running from the Chioggia to the river estuary in the north, and thus naturally touched upon the perennial conflict of interests between the requirements of agriculture and the various activities that exploited the lagoon proper (fishing and the harvesting of reeds and aquatic grasses). There is perhaps no need to point out yet again that every single project of hydraulic engineering in this area aroused a series of complaints from the landowners and/or waterfolk who claimed that their economic interests were being damaged. However, whether one accepts the myth of Venetian government action as being *super partes* or argues that its territorial policies were ultimately determined by the interests of the ruling aristocracy, there appears to be no doubt that such individual voices of opposition had little effect upon state projects (the Republic's awareness that undue pressure might be exerted by vested interests is clear from the decision made by the Council of Ten in 1505 to exclude from the *Collegio alle Acque* anyone owning land that bordered upon the lagoon).[49]

The creation of the Brenta *Novissima* in 1610 marked a clear step towards precise definition of the uncertain boundaries between land and water, fixing the perimeter of the lagoon at the left embankment of that canal and banning any sort of agricultural activity within its limits; even temporary cultivation was totally outlawed on the *barene* (those earthbanks that emerged periodically at low tides). Part of a more coherent strategy to prevent the deleterious alterations to the lagoon environment resulting, for example, from land reclamation, the erection of mills and the creation of salt-works,[50] these measures went together with a total ban on any sort of fishing or fish-farming activity that might undermine that environmental equilibrium (with some exceptions being made for communities with long-established rights).[51]

Made up of both man-made embankments and natural riverbeds, the 'Small Wall of Venice' – and the Brenta's *Taglio Novissimo*, in particular – inevitably affected agricultural interests : not only did it result in agriculture being banned on previously cultivated land, it also meant that many of the drainage canals feeding into the lagoon were shut off and, as a result of the drop in the presence of fresh water, meant that the terrain itself became more saline.[52] Nor does the creation of culverts under the Brenta (*bottisifoni*) seem to have obviated the risk of overflowing in the drained fields. The difficulties faced by local populations and farmers is well illustrated by the history of the *Sette Prese del Brenta* consortium, which was set up in the early sixteenth century, comprised territory spread over some eighty communities in the Padua area and had a total of almost 3,000 farms for land reclamation.[53] The problems created for such consortia obviously resulted in difficulties for the Venetian government itself; the complexity of the issues involved being clear from the fact that the definition of the lagoon perimeter may have began in 1610 but would only be properly completed in 1783. Even then 'private sabotage' might result in breaches of the embankments or the discharge of drainage water into the lagoon (in 1788 it was estimated that repairs to the damage caused the lagoon embankments would cost some 8,000 ducats).[54]

The Scientific Revolution: Hydraulic Knowledge in Venice and in Europe

The Venetian authorities were active in promoting hydraulics as an empirical science that made it possible to judge and predict the effects of river re-routing, canal-building and dredging at the lagoon openings; extant archive material reveals that regular tests and soundings were carried out in the lagoon for centuries.[55]

In effect, boatmen, fishermen and water folk in general were expected to keep the *Savi alle Acque* informed with regard to water depth, the emergence of *barene* and the shifting of sandbars and banks of seaweed (the so-called *bari*) within the lagoon. However, the opinions on these matters expressed by official technicians and those based on popular traditions were very different: the 1578–79 inquiry, for example, shows the two experts Guglielmo De Grandi and Battista Lurano voicing optimism about the state of the lagoon (lowering of the *barene* and *velme*, increased water depth in the sea outside, and a hydro-geological improvement in various key areas of the city), whilst those who had daily experience of the canals and bed of the lagoon were much more pessimistic.[56]

Both popular wisdom and official experts in hydraulics agreed that the flowing of watercourses into the lagoon was a real source of problems – an interesting example of the relation between science and empirical observation. However, in hydraulics – more than in any other scientific discipline – one sees a growing gap between empirical praxis and theory from the late seventeenth century onwards.

Long-seen as a perfect testing-ground for practical and theoretical ideas in this field, the Venetian lagoon would thus prove indispensable to the man who is considered to be the founder of the science of hydraulics, Benedetto Castelli. A Benedictine monk, Castelli was, significantly, a native of Brescia: it was in the fertile provinces of that city and Bergamo – together with the equally advanced agricultural region of Lombardy – that the questions of water distribution and the measurement of fluid volume had first become pressing problems. As Castelli would point out in his treatise *Della misura dell'acque correnti*, up to this point the distribution of water had been based on a measurement that totally ignored one essential factor: flow speed.[57] In effect, all that was measured was the section of the opening or canal through which water was drawn off, the quantity thence being considered equivalent to that area.

Even though one cannot deny that Leonardo da Vinci's thoughts on hydraulics would make their mark in the Venetian state through the work of two men who were his pupils – the Venetian Giovanbattista Benedetti (1530–1590)[58] and the Paduan Bernardino Baldi (1533–1617)[59] – it was Castelli who defined the concept of fluid flow in modern terms, even if with some inaccuracies: Torricelli, Mariotte and Domenico Guglielmini would show water speed is not proportional to depth, as Castelli argued, but rather to the square root of that depth.[60] The gap between scientific theory and actual practice within Italy is clear from the fact that, in Venice and elsewhere, the calculation of the quantities of water used for agriculture or to power manufactories would continue to ignore Castelli's notion of water velocity. Nevertheless, the fertile period of the seventeenth century did produce ever more precise scientific laws in the field of hydraulics, beginning with the Flemish scientist Simon Stevin's observations regarding pressures in liquids and culminating with Evangelista Torricelli's laws on atmospheric pressure and pressures in fluids. The 'corpuscular' concept of fluids also meant there was fruitful mutual interchange between mechanics, physics and hydraulics, with the latter area of study straddling a number of disciplines (mathematics, geometry, geography, meteorology, geology, engineering)[61].

In effect, developments within the science were stimulated not only by economic, social and political interests, but also by the emergence within Europe of a new scientific culture predicated on experimental postulates and laws.[62] Within that broader context, seventeenth-century Italy is generally held to have been at the forefront in theoretical studies of hydraulics – something which is hardly surprising given the importance of irrigation, fluvial re-routing and the problems posed by river spates in many regions of the country.[63] However, by the middle of that century, other European countries were catching up. The foundation of the Royal Academy in London (1662), the Académie Royale des Sciences in Paris (1666) and other similar institutions in other capitals (in Berlin in 1700, in St. Petersburg in 1724)[64] would allow these new centres to achieve a level of focus in research and efficiency in the interchange of information that were quite beyond the old regional states of Italy.

Nevertheless, the fact that Castelli was quickly translated into French reveals the importance Italian studies had for this area of study: Marin Mersenne, for example, corresponded with various scientists in Italy (and throughout Europe) and from 1644 onwards would play a key role in broadcasting the results achieved in this field by Galileo and Torricelli, thus making an essential contribution to the writing of Pascal's *Traitez de l'équilibre des liqueurs*.[65]

French scientists would also break new ground in the study of the transfer of water through the atmosphere. Whilst some scientists of the stature of Descartes, Gugliemini and Kircher[66] continued to repeat age-old errors, Jean François, Bernard Palissy and Pierre Perrault would provide figures and estimates to show that rain and snowfall were the origin of fluvial waters (Perrault's 1674 *De l'origine des fontaines* was fundamental here). This important step towards the notion of a catchment basin[67] marked a clear break with the traditional idea that rivers were produced by sea water seeping into the earth and then evaporating upwards within mountains due to underground temperatures.

Even more substantial advances would come in the study of the laws of impact between fluids and solid bodies, which became increasingly important during the course of the eighteenth century. However, Edme Mariotte's 1673 *Traité de la percussion ou choc des corps* followed on from a series of experiments carried out at the Royal Society in 1666[68], so the eighteenth-century Milanese mathematician and hydraulic scientist Paolo Frisi was clearly exaggerating[69] when he claimed: 'Mariotte, Picard, Genneté and other famous writers in France added only a little to what had been achieved by our own authors.' By that point, in fact, the main centres of scientific centre had moved elsewhere in Europe; and whilst some Italian cities – Venice, in particular – remained active in this field, their role clearly does not bear comparison with that of the more centralised academies of research.

The Bologna School of Hydraulics: Geminiano Montanari and Domenico Gugliemini

The significant theoretical advances in hydraulics within seventeenth-century Venice were not made in total isolation from any sort of empirical trial; each new postulate required testing within the circumscribed geographical area of the lagoon and its fluvial system. However, that did not mean there were not temporary set-backs – if not reversals – in both theory and practise: Castelli, for example, when commissioned by the Venetian government to present proposals regarding the lagoon, actually advised that the rivers should once more be allowed to empty into it.[70] Some authors have argued this shows the limits of Castelli's theoretical work, with the application to the lagoon of concepts – such as water volume and flow speed – which had been developed solely through a study of rivers.[71]

In fairness to Castelli, one should point out that acceptance of the damage caused by rivers was still not as universal as one might believe: as late as 1717 Bernardo Trevisan's treatise on the lagoon expressed doubts on the efficacy of re-routing rivers, and the same reservations were expressed by Giacomo Filiasi. As Zendrini would comment, there was no lack of quixotic proposals: in 1641, for example, a certain Pusterla flew in the face of decades of careful research and evaluation when he suggested that the Livenza, the Piave, the Sile and all the other watercourses in the northern area of the lagoon should be re-routed into the Brenta, and thence flow out to Chioggia.[72]

A more balanced proposal regarding the age-old problem posed by the rivers came in 1673 from Alfonso Borelli, another product of the Galileo school of hydraulics and a pupil of Benedetto Castelli. Consulted by a Venetian Senate which was open to suggestions from 'the Galileo school of hydraulic scientists, who came equipped with theories applicable in the management of tides and lagoon locks', he recognised the value of the previous re-routing and also proposed a new method for protecting this complex environment: a wide-ranging programme of dredging, with 740 boatmen using long rakes to remove the slime that had been deposited on the lagoon bed.[73]

Knowledge regarding the behaviour and management of water would take an important step forward at the end of the seventeenth century with the arrival in the lagoon of Geminiano Montanari, an expert in all the mathematical disciplines, especially 'those known as composite'. It is no surprise that he – together with his pupil Domenico Gugliemini, 'one of the most illustrious professors of the century, and a great expert on water' – was a product of Bologna University, given that at this particular time that city was playing a leading role in scientific research.[74] And just as Venice had turned to the renowned experts of Lombardy in the late fifteenth and early sixteenth century, now it turned to those of Bologna in an attempt to obtain the best solutions for the urgent problems posed by its complex environment.

The reflections and ideas put forward by both Montanari and Guglielmini would have a positive influence not only upon the management of the lagoon but also upon the course of research at Padua University: in 1678 a special chair of 'Astronomy and Meteors' was set up for Montanari at that University – in Bologna he had held the chair of Mathematical Sciences – and the Republic would thereafter consult him on problems relating not only to hydraulics, but also mining, artillery and coin mintage.[75]

In his work as a hydraulics expert, Montanari was very attentive to what might be learnt from popular traditions and know-how, producing projects for the creation of new canals (for example, in Friuli) and, most significantly, for sea defences and the management of river estuaries.[76] He had no doubt that the key to maintaining the lagoon as a viable environment was the prevention of fluvial silting; however, he also saw that equal vigilance had to be exercised with regard to the sea openings, where *speroni* (breakwaters) should be constructed to defend against the sand and seaweed that were carried there by the action of the rivers (no matter how far away they emptied into the sea). Perhaps Montanari's main contribution was in seeing that the direction of flow at river estuaries depended upon the force exerted by the sea water itself. A comparison of the rivers of the Veneto with other rivers in Italy revealed that the former flowed to the right, leaving sandy deposits to the left, as a result of the circular motion of Adriatic (a characteristic that had already been observed by Sabbadino), whilst other rivers of any volume turned left at their mouth, depositing silt to the right.[77]

Domenico Guglielmini, too, saw the close interdependence between the sea openings into the lagoon and the network of canals within it:[78] his observation that variations in the beds of the channels running through the former regulated the entire system of the latter marked a fundamental step forward in Venetian hydraulics. Like Montanari, he was consulted on questions regarding the hydrography of the terra firma, but it was the lagoon and its problems that remained the focus of his concerns. And although he had no illusions as to the real efficacy of what had already been done with regard to the rivers, he certainly did not share the general pessimism about the future of the lagoon that he noted amongst Venetian technicians and experts (even if he did complain that the lack of standardised and consistent series of soundings within the lagoon made it impossible to offer coherent comparison of its past and present state).

One particular area of concern was retreating tide waters: as Guglielmini noted, whilst they might appear to be able to carry away the silt and alluvial material brought in with the tides, unless special measures were taken *velme* [sandbars] might form near the sea openings, with the bed of the channels nearest those openings becoming dangerously shallow.[79]

The Eighteenth Century: The Beginning of the Second Scientific Revolution

The teaching posts held at Padua University by Montanari and Guglielmini would leave a lasting mark on a series of Venetian scientists, including Bernardino Zendrini (who was Guglielmini's pupil) and Giovanni Poleni (who would occupy Montanari's former chair of Mathematics and Meteorology).[80] However, Bologna was not the only influence on the science of the Venetian Republic during this Age of Enlightenment; Europe as a whole made its effect felt on a scientific community that was far from reduced to sterile provincialism.

Introduced in the first decades of the century, the reforms in scientific teaching at the Republic's University have been described as 'grafting the experimental approach of Bologna upon the old trunk of Padua'. By 1710 this new graft would already be bearing fruit: Padua was by then 'the more productive centre of scientific research', maintaining important links with scientists throughout Europe. This new status is demonstrated by the appointment of such top-ranking mathematicians as Jacob Herman and Nikolaus I Bernoulli (the latter succeeding to the former's Chair of Mathematics in 1716) and by the foundation of the *Giornale de' letterati d'Italia* in 1710. Published up until 1740, this important innovation in the world of Italian scientific research had an influence that extended well beyond the Veneto and was co-founded by such figures as Zendrini, Vallisneri and Poleni. The former published within it his *Modo di ritrovare ne' fiumi la linea di corrosione* (1715), the latter various works on physics and astronomy, and the free-thinker Vallisneri produced for the journal a number of papers which reveal the full range of his scientific interests.[81] All three men would take part in the various competitions organised by the main academies of Europe, as well as contributing to such prestigious publications as the *Philosophical Transactions* of the Royal Society and the *Acta Eruditorum* of Leipzig (founded in 1682, this latter publication would make a fundamental contribution to the spread of scientific ideas throughout Europe).[82]

It is undeniable that, more than with any other area of study, the history of science clearly contradicts traditional notions of this period as one of Italian 'decline'. Investigation of individual scientific disciplines – such as hydraulics – reveals that the situation was much more nuanced than that suggested by a clear split between the Renaissance Age of Galileo and a subsequent period of decrepitude. What is more, recent research has shown that the usual emphasis on the baneful role played by the Church of the Counter-Reformation has been exaggerated: not only is it impossible to 'identify a constant or even dominant policy of opposition to scientific research in the strict sense of the term', but there is now ample evidence of the existence of 'Jesuit science', with high numbers of monks and priests being involved in the most varied areas of scientific research.[83]

A more disputable question is the long-term influence of Italian scientific institutions when compared to those to be found elsewhere in Europe. Although it is clear that the former kept up with developments – it would be wrong to see Italian scientists as merely passive recipients of notions imported from abroad – there can be no question that in the long run scientific enquiry in other European countries emerged as better-structured and more generously financed. Whilst research within Italy suffered from the fragmentation between the numerous states of the peninsula, European academies could be more incisive precisely because they were more centralised.[84] This explains why the collaboration and competition between French and Italian scientists working in the field of hydraulics would reach a turning-point in the early decades of the eighteenth century.[85] Obviously, these were not the only two countries to make a contribution to this area of study: in England there was Isaac Newton (whose 1687 *Principia* contained numerous formulae applicable to fluids), Colin MacLaurin, Edmond Halley and Christopher Wren; in Holland, Willem Jacob 's-Gravesande, Johan Lulofs and Christiaan Brunings, who carried on in the great tradition of such figures as Simon Stevin and Christiaan Huygens; and in Germany, there were such eighteenth-century scientists as Albert Brahms and Reinhard Woltman. However, for the scientists of half of Europe the main point of reference in both experimentation and the development of theory was Paris, home to the Académie des Sciences, to important schools of military and naval engineering, and to the Ministère des Ponts et Chaussées [Bridges and Roads]. As Biswas observes with some justification, the Italian focus on the examination and re-examination of the same group of questions posed by running water would lead to that country's scientists falling behind their rivals to the north, where original new ground was being broken in the areas of phoronomy, fluid resistances and the calculation of the power generated by water.[86] The central position of France is demonstrated by the fact that Bernard de Bélidor's 1737 *L'Architecture hydraulique* would now take over from Guglielmini's late-seventeenth-century *Trattato dei fiumi* as the comprehensive summary of contemporary hydraulics.[87] Just one year later, Daniel Bernoulli would publish the *Hydrodinamique* which has been seen as laying the foundations for 'hydrostatics, the science of the equilibrium between fluids, and hydraulics, the science of the movement of fluids', thence opening the way to a whole series of studies that would culminate in 1755 with Euler's laws of fluid motion.[88]

Hydraulics held a central place in eighteenth-century science. Drawing as it did on the expertise of mathematicians, astronomers, physicists, chemists and agronomists, it stimulated such things as the development of infinitesimal and differential calculus, and the study of the spherical nature of the globe, of fluid resistances, mineral chemistry and the evaporation/transpiration of liquids in plants. Only at the end of the eighteenth/beginning of the nineteenth century would water cede its place to steam and gas, with the emergence of new theories of thermodynamics, electro-magnetism, radiation and statics – a change that marked the end of the first scientific revolution and the beginning of the second (which would then continue into the twentieth century).[89] However, these eighteenth-century studies of hydrodynamics would not have captured the attention of central governments if water had not had key economic uses as a means of transport, an agricultural resource, a source of energy and as a medium whose qualities had to be studied to improve the hydrodynamic design of ships.[90] It is no accident that in the Venetian Republic, too, nautical engineering would remain closely linked with studies of mathematics and hydraulics, the main European treatises of these subjects being quickly translated and discussed.[91]

The Theory of Fluids and Hydraulic Engineering: Bernardino Zendrini, Giovanni Poleni, Antonio Vallisneri and Simone Stratico

That the Venetian Republic remained firmly linked with the main scientific circuits within Europe is demonstrated by the fact that Daniel Bernoulli, the founder of hydrodynamics, spent some time studying in Venice under the doctor Pietro Antonio Michelotti, whose studies of the flow of blood through the body would first stimulate his interest in the subject. The same medical background emerges in the case of Zendrini (1679–1747) from Saviore (Brescia), who after passing from medicine through the necessary theoretical mathematics would became a European authority on hydraulics. Deeply-versed in the main theories being put forward in those years, he was in close contact with numerous important scientists (Huygens, Leibnitz, Herman, Francesco Domenico Michelotti and Scipione Maffei) and would make an original contribution to developments upon the principles laid down by Newton and Bernoulli, as well as tackling the complex problems posed by the 'flow of water through the base of vessels' (phoronomy).[92]

His lively interest in the theoretical questions raised by the study of 'running water' is clear in his support for infinitesimal calculus, which was already widespread in France, Germany and England but was encountering stiff resistance in Italy. He also took part in the debate regarding 'living forces', in which the followers of Newton and Descartes clashed with those of Leibnitz.[93] However, just like Poleni and Vallisneri, Zendrini is yet to be the subject of a full scientific biography, even if he made important contributions to the study of rivers and the influence of wind upon flowing water[94] (the main achievement of his original work as a scientist is his *Leggi e fenomeni della acque correnti*).[95]

As was inevitable in anyone who had to deal with the very special environment of Venice, Zendrini was keenly aware of the practical questions raised by hydraulics, and his *Memorie Storiche* reveal him to be a faithful historian of the lagoon and a passionate chronicler of this fundamental aspect of Venice's very idea of itself.[96] Covering four centuries – from 1300 to 1700 – these *Memorie* are essential material for anyone who wants to understand the historical evolution of the lagoon and its immediate hinterland; and whilst Bernardo Trevisan's *La Laguna di Venezia* and Giacomo Filiasi's *Memorie storiche dei veneti primi e secondi* are important supplements to the more chronological account given by Zendrini, they still strike one as compilations when compared to his passionate and well-argued work. The final achievement of the man's many-faceted career as a scientist and hydraulic engineer would be the erection of the *murazzi*, of which more will be said below.

An equally exceptional figure was the Marquis Giovanni Poleni (1683–1761), who would leave his mark upon both theory and practise for the whole of the eighteenth century, especially as he never tired of pointing out that theory should not limit itself merely to abstractions. What sense did a purely abstract theory of fluids make anyway?[97] Poleni would practise what he preached by setting up a well-equipped physics laboratory at the University of Padua in order to tackle the difficult problems raised by practical experimentation. That this dedication to modern experimental technique did not cover a poverty of theoretical thought is clear from modern hydraulics' continuing use of an equation that bears Poleni's name[98]. It was he who introduced such concepts as *aqua mortua*, *aqua viva* and *motus mixtus*. A perfect area for the study of this latter was provided by the sea openings into the Venetian lagoon and the currents within them, the investigation of which enabled Poleni to make a fundamental contribution to the development of hydraulic theory.

It is no accident that the marchese's influence would be felt in Dutch hydraulics, particularly by Christiaan Brunings (1736–1805), who in 1769 took over from Johan Lulofs 'as general superintendent to the rivers of Holland and West Friesland [... and] is considered one of the fathers of the modern Dutch organisation devoted to water control'.[99]

De castellis per quae derivantur fluviorum aquae, habentibus latera convergentia liber[100] was Poleni's contribution to the very new science of phoronomy, containing a study 'of the flow of fluids from a constantly full vessel, and in particular the quantity of water flowing out though openings in the form of upright or inverted cones'. The work was also a contribution to the debate concerning 'living forces', offering non-traditional arguments that enabled the author to go beyond the impasse in which so many of the scientists of the day were caught (the notion Poleni hints at here is not that of 'force' but the subsequently developed concept of 'energy').[101]

Like Zendrini before him and Stratico after him, Poleni would not fail to put his technical and theoretical expertise at the service of the Venetian state, which consulted him frequently on matters concerning the lagoon, mainland rivers and borders.[102] A multi-talented scientist, he also made an important series of temperature measurements and meteorological observations (which he then compared with the Réaumur scale); these were subsequently used by Giuseppe Toaldo, the promoter in Padua of the fledgling science of meteorology.[103] The fact that the Paris Academy of Sciences would grant Poleni an award for a paper concerning 'the best way for a ship to measure distances at sea without resort to astronomical observations' is further proof that in the area of navigation too, science in the Veneto equalled what was being achieved elsewhere in Europe.[104]

Another with close links to the French scientific community – particularly with regard to the questions of underground water and atmospheric cycles – was Antonio Vallisneri (1661–1730). A doctor, naturalist and geologist, it was he would be responsible for the circulation within the Veneto of the theories regarding the origin of wells and springs put forward by Perrault, Mariotte and De La Hire. His own research covered artesian wells – providing a better explanation of them than had Bernardino Ramazzini – and the thermal waters of the Euganean Hills.[105] As well as being supported by solid argument, the subsequent *Lezione accademica intorno all'origine della fontane* which Vallisneri produced as a result of this work 'was illustrated by six geological sections, ... drawn by the naturalist Scheuchzer ... and among the earliest geological sections ever drawn'.[106]

Zendrini and – even more so – Poleni were a powerful influence on not only those who studied under them (for example, Giordano Riccati, Antonio Belloni, Tommaso Temanza, Simone Stratico and Anton Maria Lorgna) but also upon a number of hydraulic engineers and technicians who worked in Venice and the other cities of the Republic. Once again, these experts prove to be multi-talented figures, including architects (Andrea Tirali, Tommaso Temanza), geographers (Vincenzo Coronelli), 'enlightened' aristocrats with a wide range of interests and simple technicians from a modest cultural background.[107]

Amongst the aristocrats, one might mention Count Iacopo Riccati of Treviso, his son Giordano and such leading figures in the Venetian 'Enlightenment' as Girolamo Ascanio Giustinian and Angelo Querini.[108] However, with regard to the latter, neither his vast amount of writings – including the famously vitriolic debate with Angelo Artico over the umpteenth proposal to regulate the flow of the Brenta in the stretch beyond Padua – nor the extent of his civic commitment were matched by the sort of scientific knowledge required in such discussions by the end of the eighteenth century.[109]

Is this to be taken as indicating that the study and practice of hydraulics within the Veneto did not meet the full requirements of scientific rigour? What is true is that, elsewhere, this science was the domain of strict specialisation rather than interdisciplinary study (however brilliant), as one can see from Turgot's institution of a Chair of Hydrodynamics in 1775.[110] Padua University itself would not have a Chair in Hydrometry until after the fall of the Republic, whilst Bologna had appointed Guglielmini to a similar position as early as 1694.[111] Having said that, one cannot deny that in his courses Simone Stratico (1733–1824), professor of mathematics and nautical theory at the University of Padua, kept apace with the innovations in hydraulic science being made at a European level.[112] What is more, he – together with other progressive professors – would play a key role in the foundation of the Padua *Accademia delle Scienze* in 1779[113]. This institution was particularly important because the overlap between its own activities and the university – together with the Venetian government's reliance on its own body of *proti*, engineers, mathematicians and other experts – might well provide an explanation of how hydraulics within the Veneto could continue to develop in tandem with an oral tradition that reflected the very special needs of the lagoon and its river system.

The Rivers of the Veneto: A Threat or a Source of Wealth?

As far as the main laws of physics and hydrodynamics were concerned, rivers and lagoon formed distinct but not conflicting entities. However, the continuing focus on the end-stretch of rivers – because of their impact upon the lagoon – meant that government failed to develop those overall policies for the management of the region's rivers which, the more perceptive authors of the eighteenth century argued, were so important. What is more, given that a number of these waterways passed through areas that came under different political authorities (think, for example, of the Po and Adige), there was often local intervention in one stretch that took no account of the possible consequences elsewhere along the river.

By the end of the seventeenth century, rivers were breaking their banks with increasing regularity, and a wide range of solutions were put forward for this problem. From the Verona area, through Vicenza and Padua to Treviso and the Po delta region, there was repeated – often doom-laden – lamentation of new problems and of the errors of the past. Some even argued that the Po, Adige and Brenta 'have come to the end of their life within their present beds, so that one may advance the hardy suggestion that soon there will be a catastrophic shift in their course'.[114]

This apocalyptic vision of rivers was not limited to the Venetian Republic. In various European countries – France, for example – such opinions were being advanced as developments upon the claims made by Guglielmini and Bélidor that 'river flooding is the

result of the continual gullying away of surface water! Given that
rivers were losing their ability to carve out their own bed, within the
course of just a few centuries they would overflow irreparably.
'Reduced to a terrifying level, land in the future will be nothing but
a vast, uninhabitable marsh.'[115]

But if, as in France, deforestation, the cultivation of hill slopes and
the resulting amount of detritus carried by rivers were given as the
main causes of this continual flooding, treatises in the Veneto also
began to highlight other aspects of the problem. The enormous
number of canals drawn off the main rivers without any overall plan
were seen as undermining the equilibrium of the hydro-geological
environment. Similarly, it was argued that the embankment of the
upper stretches of the rivers channelled water too rapidly into the
plain area, its effects conflicting with the mistaken projects
implemented along the end-stretches of those same rivers – for
example, the *diversivi*.[116] Originally intended as overflows for rivers
in spate that threatened to break their banks, these channels criss-
crossed the entire plain area of the Veneto, from the Verona to the Po
delta; and whilst originally some of them may have been formed
naturally, they had since the Middle Ages been increasingly nurtured
by human intervention, practically becoming new riverbeds in their
own right (for example, the Sabbadina, the Castegnaro, the
Malopera, the Adigetto and the Loreo canal, running off the Adige).
Very soon, however, it had become clear that these *diversivi* caused as
many problems as they resolved, slowing down the flow of the
rivers, increasing silting and causing the gradual raising of the
riverbeds. In fact, as early as 1504 writers had seen the desirability
of cutting out some of the meanders that slowed down the flow of
the Adige (something that would be done ever more frequently
during the course of the eighteenth century). But the real solution to
the problem was the closure of the *diversivi*, something called for not
only by the more perceptive hydraulic engineers but also by the
populations living in the areas most subject to flooding. People
became ever more convinced that the raising of embankments to
counteract the effects of the raising of the riverbed was not a
permanent solution; in fact, it had the effect of simply adding to the
'hydrostatic load when the rivers was in spate or even partially high.'
What is more, land reclamation in the lowlands may have created
more terrain for agriculture, but it cut into the overspill area for

river flooding, making the effects of a river breaking its banks all the more dramatic. And just how frequent that occurrence was can be seen from the fact that between 1650 and 1750 embankments along the Adige were breached a total of fifty times (the picture is no less grim when one looks at the other rivers of the Republic: the Agno-Guà-Frassine, the Fratta-Gorzone, the Bacchiglione, the Brenta, the Piave and the Sile).[117]

During the eighteenth century, it was the Adige and the Verona area that inspired the greatest number of treatises, not only because of the crucial importance to the Republic of this river and the fertile land around it but also because of the relative autonomy Verona enjoyed within the Venetian state. Amongst the local experts called upon to resolve the problems posed by the river were Scipione Maffei, Zaccaria Betti, Antonio Belloni and, above all, Anton Maria Lorgna. Like Belloni, this latter had been a pupil of Poleni's at Padua and would apply his noteworthy theoretical knowledge of hydraulics in a very practical, experimental approach to the question of fluvial waters. Some of the themes he tackled included pressure within fluids, the resistance of solids within a current, the changes of speed within different parts of a river, viscosity, and the transfer of momentum (with specific reference to the hydrodynamics of Bernoulli).

Lorgna's decisive contribution to the debates concerning the Adige was his insistence on intervening not only at the river's mouth but also upstream, underlining the importance of regulating embankments, *diversivi* and the innumerable channels drawn haphazardly off the river. What is more, he saw the numerous meanders of the river – and the large number of artificial barriers jutting out into it as it flowed through the city itself – as further causes of the frequent floods, arguing for the elimination of all obstacles to the free running of the water, the straightening of the more tortuous twists and turns and the closure of the main *diversivi*. Naturally, he was also aware of the damage caused by deforestation even if, given the extent of the political and economic interests involved, he did not explore the question to the point where certain conclusions would have become inevitable. As far as the mouth of the Adige was concerned, he proposed the closure of two of the three branches of the estuary and the building of a breakwater which would prevent the coastal current from depositing silt. Such precise proposals were not received with any eagerness by the authorities in

Verona or Venice, who were more concerned in shifting onto each other the responsibility for taking a definite decision. It would only be in the nineteenth century that many stretches of the river were straightened, many of the urban obstacles to the flow of its waters removed, and a number of the canals and *diversivi* drawn off it closed (the much-debated Castagnaro would not be closed finally until 1838).

Like almost all the hydraulic engineers working in the Republic in the last decades of the eighteenth century, Lorgna would be involved in drawing up plans for the re-organisation of the Brenta, which – just like the Adige – was the object of a lively (and ultimately unproductive) debate.[118] From 1777 to the end of the Venetian Republic, a constant steam of detailed proposals and counter-proposals were made, all fuelling a relentless discussion. However, all more or less agreed that – along with the other factors already mentioned – one cause of the continual flooding of the Brenta was the collapse of a regulator (*colmellone*) – at Limena (upstream from Padua) in 1649. This installation had never been repaired, even though the urgency of the matter had been stressed by such hydraulic engineers as Montanari, Guglielmini, Zendrini and Poleni. A first consequence of this damage to the *colmellone* was a greater flow of water from the river into the Brentella canal, due to the widening of the openings at Limena. This meant that the Brenta itself began to carry more water, affecting the whole river system (the Battaglia canal, the Piovego, the Brenta *Nova* and Brenta *Novissima*, as well as the final stretch running into the lagoon). In 1779, for example, it was calculated that the sizeable sum of 520,000 ducats had been spent solely on repairing damage to the river's embankments.[119]

The debate also covered the state of the beds of the Brenta, and of the new channels of the Brenta *Nova* and the *Novissima*. Lorgna focused not only on the importance of repairing the *colmellone*, but also of correcting the gradual loss of gradient along the river's course and the resulting meanders that led to the creation of marshland. In the meanwhile, the Venetian government had consulted various of the leading experts of the day – Paolo Frisi of Milan, Leonardo Ximenes of Florence and Simone Stratico of Padua – and this multiplicity of 'chefs' led to a debate that it was not easy to resolve. Ultimately the Venetian Senate rejected Lorgna's plan in 1779, but then of course found itself having to deal with a situation of hydro-geological imbalance that simply got worse and worse.

The years 1786–87 again saw the most renowned hydraulic engineers and mathematicians of the Venetian state apparatus attempting unsuccessfully to find some answer to the problem. The scientific debate would then attract the senator of the Venetian Republic Angelo Querini, who weighed in against the plans put forward by Angelo Artico (whom he dismissively referred to as 'the taxman') and by Girolamo Ascanio Giustinian (ironically labelled 'the citizen'[120]). In such a situation, one can understand why the Venetian government found it difficult to take decisive action, however urgent the need. In the meantime, something had been done in 1774 to repair the *colmellone* regulator at Limena (though only one opening of it); but it is easy to see why the debate surrounding the Brenta would continue long after the fall of the Republic, involving such nineteenth-century figures as Piero Paleocapa and Vittorio Fossombroni.[121]

All in all, in spite of the numerous treatises dedicated to the question during the eighteenth century, little had been done to resolve the urgent problems posed by the region's rivers. And this incapacity of government to take decisive action meant that rather than enhancing productivity and contributing to wealth, the rivers – even when re-directed away from the areas of reclaimed land – still remained a menace and a liability.

Rivers, Lagoons and Sea Defences: The Venetian *Murazzi*

The situation in the eastern area of the lagoon was no less alarming. As figures such as Montanari had repeatedly pointed out, the Sile was already too full to receive the other small rivers and streams of the area, and was meandering dangerously in the twisting bed once occupied by the Piave. As has already been mentioned, the 1769 closure of the Businello *diversivo* (opened in 1695 to draw off part of the waters of the Sile) had had very disappointing results: not only did it damage the financial interests of the Treviso landowners by depriving them of an important drainage canal, it did not even save the area from the repeated overflowing of the Sile itself (due to the landowners' own poor maintenance of the network of drainage canals). Further damage was also being caused by the Dese, the Zero and Marzenego, which continued to flow into the lagoon even though it was generally held that they should be re-directed elsewhere. In effect, in spite of being lower in water volume than the Piave and the Sile, they carried more silt and thus posed a greater threat to the area where they emptied (the *Palada di Dese*).[122]

Within the lagoon as a whole, the necessary dredging work in the internal canals and the channels leading off the sea openings employed much less efficient machinery than that which could be found in Northern Europe. Venetian documents of the time however frequently referred to the new methods of dredging that had been developed in Denmark, England and Holland. The latter was probably the source of the horse-drawn barge used at the Arsenale from around the middle of the eighteenth century, whilst the 'wheel device, powered by two to four men and set on small mud-dredging barges',[123] was given as being of Danish origin but was also used in the Low Countries.[124] We do not know whether the patent to use this was taken up, just as we know nothing of the decision taken regarding a system of bellows to be mounted on barges to disperse the sand brought up from the lagoon bed by a series of cog-driven drills, or of the proposal to use two horses (instead of the previous manpower) to move a winch linked to a large harrow that would scoop up sand and tip it into a container. Some projects were clearly unrealistic – for example, that put forward by Giovanni Cattaneo, which envisaged blasting the lagoon bed clear by using water jets fed by a horizontal pipe mounted on a barge – and yet there is no denying that this imaginative array of winches, barges and machinery reveal a determined effort to keep apace with the latest developments in dredging technology.[125]

At times, the quite genuine increases in productivity and efficiency – for example, in the horse-powered dredging machines – were actually redundant, given that needs could be met using hand-powered scoops mounted on barges. In fact, such machinery was considered of real use in tackling resistant, clayey soil, and so was little used in clearing the muddy beds of the internal canals; it was ultimately reserved for the deeper, more difficult, channels out in the lagoon. The high point of such technology in Venice, the horse-powered dredger, was built and managed directly by the Arsenale but might be leased out to other government authorities – the

Provveditori alle Adige, Provveditori alle Biave, and so on – or to private contractors; the more day-to-day equipment – shovels, scoops, barges and rafts – was either be owned by the contractors themselves or rented from the *Savi alle Acque.*[126] Labour – largely from the Treviso or Friuli areas – was hired directly by those undertaking the work, who even in the eighteenth century still enjoyed total independence as to the conditions they offered.[127]

So, whilst not exemplifying great dynamism and progress, the maintenance of the lagoon cannot be seen as demonstrating total technological stagnation. Undoubtedly, as Giacomo Maria Figari observed, the key to the survival of Venice was not – as it had been in Holland – the development of mechanical means for removing alluvial silt, but rather the deviation of the region's rivers.[128]

Whilst those rivers – and the serious imbalances within them – were a threat that lay in wait behind Venice, the city looked out towards another danger: the increasing number of rough seas that risked undermining the centuries-old defences of the Lido, the *palade*. These single – but sometimes double and triple – rows of piles set upright or at an angle in the sea bed were reinforced with iron bands and larch-wood, forming large *casse di colmata* (rubble-filled buttresses) which shored up the sea boundaries of the lagoon. However, the *palade* were subject not only to wear and tear but also to the 'rapacity' of the people living on the Lido (to quote a Venetian magistrate); and with the arrival at the beginning of the seventeenth century of the sea worms that devoured the wood, the need for constant repairs became ever more pressing at the same time as there was a growing shortage of timber.[129]

It was probably this shortage that convinced the Venetian technicians of the need to look for a replacement material: *pietra viva* (rough stone). This need had already become clear in the first decades of the sixteenth century, when the Republic set itself to resolve the problem of how to corner supplies of *pozzolana*; a new mortar of volcanic origin to be found in the regions of central-southern Italy (Lazio, Abruzzo), this had the very important advantage of cementing stone below sea water. Up to the eighteenth century, the main material used to fill the *palade* had been stone from Lipsida near Padua, and this continued to be the case right up to 1754, even if the Venetian authorities were then looking with interest at the possibility of using Istrian stone. The latter ultimately won out, due not only to its hard-wearing qualities but to the increased costs of quarrying and transporting stone from Lipsida.[130]

According to tradition – which has been borne out by the most recent research – it was Zendrini who designed and built the first stretch of the solid stone defences (*murazzi*), which replaced the mixed-material *palade* with an imposing vertical wall rising above two stepped horizontal levels jutting out into the sea. However, the series of projects produced in the seventeenth and eighteenth century by such figures as the geographer Vincenzo Coronelli, the architect Andrea Tirali, the *proto ai fiumi* Angelo Minorelli and the state technician Lorenzo Boschetti all undoubtedly made a significant contribution to the fine solution proposed by Zendrini. From 1744 to 1755, about 4,000 metres of the Pellestrina littoral were furnished with these sea walls, a further 1,200 then being erected to protect Chioggia. Work would in fact continue right up to 1782 (after the death of Zendrini, under the *Proto alle Acque* Tommaso Temanza, who however encountered difficulties of financing and of supplies).[131]

The *murazzi* can therefore be taken as the emblematic culmination of the sea defences to which Venice had dedicated centuries of care and attention. A commercial port well aware of the essential role the lagoon played in its existence, Venice would here show itself at its best. On the mainland things were rather different; there one sees a Republic whose contradictory and ineffectual policies reveal it to have been incapable of combining the complex needs of the *Stato da mar* and the *Stato da terra*.

Notes

1. The openings were: S. Erasmo, Treporti, S. Nicolò (directly opposite Venice), Malamocco and Chioggia.
2. The redirection of the Brenta through the Bassano area for irrigation purposes was, Marco Cornaro commented, 'useful for the countryside, but not for Venice': Cornaro, *Antichi scrittori d'idraulica veneta. Scritture sulla laguna*, p. 99. This focus on the concerns of Venice emerges continually in many writings on hydraulics produced in the Veneto. Significantly, C. Sabbadino would oppose a deepening and widening of the Piavesella, because of the risk of overflow into the lagoon (ibid., p. 121).
3. Almost certainly it was the worrying state of the lagoon which led the Council of Ten to set up a permanent body and abandon the previous policy of work carried out by *ad hoc* agencies. In 1531, the three *Savi* were joined

by three *Esecutori alle Acque*; and in 1542 a 'mathematician' was appointed to oversee the state of all the waters of the State (the previous corps of technicians had comprised three *proti* – for lagoon and sea-openings, rivers and littorals – three *vice-proti* and three assistant technicians). See Mozzi, *I magistrati veneti alle acque*; P. Selmi, 'Politica lagunare della veneta Repubblica dal secolo XIV al secolo XVIII', in *Mostra storica della laguna veneta*, Venice, 1970, pp. 109–14; on the *magistrature* in the 13th–15th centuries, Crouzet-Pavan, *'Sopra le acque salse'*, I, p. 267ff.

4. Cornaro, *Antichi scrittori d'idraulica veneta. Scritture sulla laguna*, pp. 9, 96 and 98; Cessi, 'Prefazione' to *Antichi scrittori d'idraulica veneta. La difesa idraulica della laguna*, Cessi and Spada eds., 1952, pp. VII–XXII. Aristotile Fioravante is credited with the work on the first shipping basins created in Italy (in Milan, 1438–39): L. Beltrami, *Vita di Aristotile da Bologna*, Milan, 1912, p. 13; Marzolo, 'L'idraulica veneta e l'apporto dell' Università di Padova nelle discipline idrauliche', p. 100.

5. Braudel, *La Méditerranée*, I, p. 60. Bernardino Zendrini mentions, however, that as early as 1536, the German 'Antonio Colb' had made proposals for two new machines: one to dredge up mud, the other to drive in the piles used in creating the city's waterfronts (cf. Zendrini, *Memorie storiche*, I, p. 197).

6. Slicher van Bath, *The agrarian history of Western Europe*, p. 151ff.; De Vries, *The Dutch rural economy*, pp. 28–32.

7. Bennassar, *L'Europe des campagnes*, pp. 470–71.

8. 'Rellazion scripta', in R. Brenzoni, *Fra Giovanni Giocondo veronese*, Florence, 1960, p. 151.

9. *Scrittura di Michele Santo Michele*, in Zendrini, *Memorie storiche*, II, pp. 291–93; cf. also *Scrittura letta il 25 gennaio 1534 more veneto*, quoted by Selmi, *Politica lagunare*, cit., p. 106.

10. *Lettera di Girolamo Fracastoro sulle lagune di Venezia ora per la prima volta pubblicata ed illustrata*, Simone Stratico ed., Venice, 1814, pp. 5–10.

11. Think of the famous 1534 map by Nicolò dal Cortivo, or the equally relevant works produced by Cristoforo Sabbadino in 1546, 1556, 1557, 1558. It has been observed that cartographical skill was 'not merely an accessory accomplishment for a professional hydraulic technician; it is an indispensable ability' (Zendrini, *Memorie storiche*, I, p. XXV). See also E. Bevilacqua, 'Geografi e cosmografi', in *Storia della cultura veneta. Dal primo Quattrocento al Concilio di Trento*, Arnaldi and Pastore Stocchi eds., 3/II, 1980, p. 360; R. Almagià, 'Cristoforo Sorte, il primo grande cartografo e topografo della Repubblica di Venezia' (1957), in *Scritti geografici (1905–1957)*, Roma, 1961, p. 613. A noteworthy print of the Padua area attributed to Gastaldi can be seen in in R. Almagià, *Carte geografiche a stampa di particolare pregio o rarità dei secoli XVI e XVII esistenti nella Biblioteca Apostolica Vaticana*, Vatican City, 1948, plate IX. On the superiority – or greater reputation and distribution – of the topographical maps produced in fifteenth-century Lombardy when compared to their Veneto counterparts, see F. De Dainville, 'Cartes et contestations au XVe siècle', in *Imago Mundi*, 24 (1970), p. 99.

12. Cf. V. Branca, 'L'Umanesimo veneziano alla fine del Quattrocento', in *Storia della cultura veneta. Dal primo Quattrocento al Concilio di Trento*, Arnaldi and Pastore Stocchi eds., 3/I, 1980, espec. p. 149ff.
13. Serena, *Il canale della Brentella*, p.111ff.; idem, *Fra Giocondo*, pp. 11-12 and 28; Brenzoni, *Fra Giovanni Giocondo*, cit., pp. 13, 67-90 and 153-55. He would come to regret his period in France, as his ideas would not be received with all due attention by the Venetian government.
14. 'Scritture sul regolamento della Brenta' (1506), in Brenzoni, *Fra Giovanni Giocondo*, cit., pp. 127 and 129-41; Piero Ziani, 'Dela Brenta et altre acque, che offendono la laguna' and Raffacan di Raffacani *inzegner*, 'Che la Brenta Nova sii separata dal Bachion', 7 and 16 June 1505, in *Antichi scrittori d'idraulica veneta. La difesa idraulica della laguna*, Cessi and Spada eds., 1952, pp. 16-18 and 22-24; Alessio di Aleardi, 'Del separar le acque dolci dalle salse', 15 June 1505, ibid., pp. 20-21; the defence of Aleardi and his work is to be found in Zendrini, *Memorie storiche*, II, pp. 275-90.
15. C. Dionisotti, 'La lingua italiana da Venezia all'Europa', in *Rinascimento europeo e Rinascimento veneziano*, V. Branca ed., Florence, 1967, pp. 1-10; P.L. Rose, 'The Accademia Veneziana. Science and Culture in Renaissance Venice', in *Studi Veneziani*, 11 (1969), pp. 201-3 .
16. Cornaro, *Antichi scrittori d'idraulica veneta. Scritture sulla laguna*, pp. 7-9, 25-47 and 75-157. There are omissions in Cornaro's account: for example, the fact that in 1324 the Brenta was re-directed from Lizzafusina (or Fusina) – opposite Venice – leftwards to S. Marco in Lama, but then brought back to Fusina in 1336. A further re-direction would come in 1340, with the river again emptying into the lagoon at Fusina in 1359; due to pressure from Foscari, it would be re-directed again in 1395, but would be back at Fusina in 1437. See also Cessi, 'Prefazione' to Sabbadino, *Antichi scrittori d'idraulica veneta. Discorsi sopra la laguna*, pp. XIII-XIV; ibid., 'Discorsi de il Sabbattino per la laguna di Venetia', p. 27.
17. These supplies came by means of barges, loaded with water from the Brenta. Primarily for military reasons, the Republic would consistently rule out the possibility of building an aqueduct. (G. Bianco, *Sui modi più acconci di provvedere Venezia d'acqua potabile*, Venezia 1862, p. 10; Costantini, *L'acqua di Venezia. L'approvvigionamento idrico della Serenissima*).
18. Cornaro, *Antichi scrittori d'idraulica veneta. Scritture sulla laguna*, p.150; A. Averone, *Sull'antica idrografia veneziana*, Mantova, 1911, p. 12. Any such decision resulted in damages being paid to the Venetian noblemen affected: for example, the Valier were to receive 200 ducats a year for the closure of their mills due to the construction of the Corbola canal. To prevent these vested interests weighing too heavily, it was in 1488 decided to exclude from the councils debating the problems relating to the Brenta all of the families whose interests might be involved.
19. Cessi, 'Prefazione' to *Antichi scrittori d'idraulica veneta. La difesa idraulica della laguna*, Cessi and Spada eds., 1952, pp. X-XIII; 'Opinion del Q. Mistro Paulo Sabbadin da Chioza trovata sotto uno desegno messa a stampa già anni cinquanta in 52', ibid., pp. 3-4.

20. Piero Sambo, *Circa il levar le acque dolci della laguna, che la dannificano,* 1505, ibid., p. 7; Nicolò Trivisan, *Circa il mandar le acque del Bottenigo a Mestre,* 1505, ibid., pp. 12–15.
21. Alvise Zuccarin, *Che le acque salse siino agiutate per farne intrar più che si può nella laguna, et raccorda il modo,* 1505, ibid., pp. 28–30.
22. Piero Ziani, 'Dela Brenta et altre acque, che offendono la laguna', cit.; Piero di Fanti's *Che le acque bianche vadino per li suoi torrenti et non atterreranno la laguna,* 1505, ibid., pp. 25–27, which illustrates his plan for re-directing the rivers away from the lagoon.
23. Zendrini, *Memorie storiche,* I, pp. 174 and 185; Vacani, *Della laguna,* p. 113.
24. See on this issue 'Discorso sopra l'aere di Venezia' and the 'Discorso sopra la laguna di Venezia' of Andrea Marini, in Marini, *Antichi scrittori d'idraulica veneta. Discorsi,* spec. pp. 4–8 and 21–22. Written at almost the same time – between 1559 and 1566 – Marini's *Discorsi* give the opinion of a physician who was only an 'amateur' in hydraulics. Analysing the causes of the unhealthy air in Venice, he cites the 'weakness of the incoming and outgoing tides. Many years ago, when the lagoon was big, they were swift and large; but now that it has shrunk, they have become puny and sluggish.' In fact, given that the incoming was now larger than the outgoing tide – and that the capacity of the lagoon had shrunk – flooding was common. In his account of the former area of the lagoon, and of the damage caused by man, river and sea, Marini was very clearly influenced by the hydraulic technicians of the day – especially Cristoforo Sabbadino.
25. 'Discorsi de il Sabbattino per la laguna di Venetia', in Sabbadino, *Antichi scrittori d'idraulica veneta. Discorsi sopra la laguna,* p. 33.
26. '... This lagoon of ours ran from Aquileia to Ravenna and from Ravenna to Aquileia. It was all salt water; and from the littorals to the mainland, in some places it was 30 miles, in some 25, some 20 and some 15'. On the boundaries of the lagoon stood the – as yet unsilted – sites of Aquileia, Concordia, Altino, Oderzo, Ravenna (that these included Padua, however, is open to reasonable doubt): Cornaro, *Antichi scrittori d'idraulica veneta. Scritture sulla laguna,* p. 109.
27. 'Discorsi de il Sabbattino', cit., p. 19; Zendrini, *Memorie storiche,* I, p. 5. See also Bernardo Trevisan, *Della laguna di Venezia* (Venezia 1718), p. 4 and (with regard to Marco Cornaro) Filiasi, *Memorie storiche de' veneti,* I, p. 235.
28. Undoubtedly, Sabbadino 'is not a theoretician, and even less a theoretician who is creating a science [...] His approach is empirical, and he is just as empirical in evaluating phenomena'. One significant example is his interpretation of the tides, which he discussed at length – especially in a Dialogue between two functionaries of the Magistrato alle Acque. However, he never moves away from the currently-held theories, and in particular that of Iacopo Dondi, who offered the best explanation of the phenomenon. (Sabbadino, *Antichi scrittori d'idraulica veneta. Discorsi sopra la laguna,* pp. 149–65, esp. p. 151; R. Almagià, 'La dottrina della marea nell'antichità classica e nel Medio Evo' (1905), in *Scritti geografici, 1905–57,* Roma, 1961 pp. 108–9); on the tides see the ample discussion in P. Ventrice,

La discussione sulle maree tra astronomia, meccanica e filosofia nella cultura veneto-padovana del Cinquecento, Venice, 1989.

29. For its part, the sea damaged the lagoon in three ways: 1) due to the sand carried by the south-east winds; 2) due to the resistance created in its encounter with fluvial waters, thus causing the deposit of alluvial material; 3) due to the fact that in places it became mixed with, rather than overwhelming, fresh water ('Discorsi de il Sabbattino', cit., p. 29).

30. 'Such men prefer to see wheatfields and vineyards where now you catch clams, shrimp and oysters', he commented colourfully (ibid., p. 34). It was, however, true that the wickerwork grilles used in fishing throughout the lagoon did themselves contribute to silting (ibid., pp. 31–32; 'Opinion di M.A. Cornari e di C. Sabbadini circa il conservare la laguna', in Sabbadino, *Antichi scrittori d'idraulica veneta. Discorsi sopra la laguna*, p. 115).

31. 'Discorsi de il Sabbatino', cit., p. 36.

32. Ibid., p. 33. As one example of a serious concession to mainland interests of certain Venetians, he cited the permission to carry part of the waters of the Sile to Mestre to power mills. As if , he said, the waters of the Bottenigo, Marzenego, Dese and Zero were not enough! (Sabbadino, 'Stato della laguna e rimedii per conservare la sua integrità', 1541, in Cornaro and Sabbadino, *Antichi scrittori d'idraulica veneta. Scritture sopra la laguna*, pp. 88–89).

33. The alluvial material in the water had increased with the increasing cultivation of hillside and valley terrain. Once upon a time, the Musone, Sile, Piave, Livenza, Tagliamento and Isonzo were not so baneful in effect as now 'because they flowed down from uncultivated hillsides and through also uninhabited valleys' (Sabbadino, *Antichi scrittori d'idraulica veneta. Discorsi sopra la laguna*, 1540, p. 5).

34. In line with the best line of thought in these matters (from Marco Cornaro to Fra Giovanni), Sabbadino thought that only an 'upstream' re-routing of the Brenta (at Strà at least) would provide a solution for the root of the problem ('Discorsi de il Sabbattino', cit., pp. 65–67 and 214–24; Cessi, 'Prefazione' to Sabbadino, *Antichi scrittori d'idraulica veneta. Discorsi sopra la laguna*, Cessi and Spada eds., 1952, pp. XVII–XXIII); Sabbadino, 'Circa le acque del Muson', 1552, in Cornaro and Sabbadino, *Antichi scrittori d'idraulica veneta. Scritture sopra la laguna*, pp. 129–31.

35. Cornaro and Sabbadino, *Scritture sopra la laguna*, pp. 155–71; 'Terza scrittura del Mag.co Messer Alvise Corsaro', 1556, in Sabbadino, *Antichi scrittori d'idraulica veneta. Discorsi sopra la laguna*, p. 228; 'Ultima scrittura et aricordo datto per il Magn. Messer Alvise Cornaro apresentada all'officio', 1556, ibid., p. 231. However, it should be remembered that in 1540 Cornaro had proposed re-directing the Sile, Dese and Bottenigo towards Torcello and (due to the influence of Sabbadino?) the Brenta, Bacchiglione and part of the Adige so that they emerged beyond the Brondolo sea-opening, making a new opening in the littoral. Later he obviously changed his mind (Cornaro, 'Discorso [...] della cavation della laguna, et accrescer l'intrada pubblica et della vittuaglia' (1540), in Cornaro and Sabbadino, *Antichi scrittori d'idraulica veneta. Scritture sopra la laguna*, pp. 3–10).

36. See the essay by Menegazzo, 'Alvise Cornaro: un veneziano del Cinquecento nella Terraferma padovana'.
37. To support his plan of a re-routing of the Musone, Brenta and Bacchiglione towards the Brondolo opening, he comments that all waters turn rightwards when they flow into another mass of water – for example, the Mediterranean as it flows out past Gibraltar into the Atlantic, and the Atlantic as it flows into the Mediterranean ('Opinion di M.A. Cornaro e di C. Sabbadino circa il conservare la laguna', in Sabbadino, *Discorsi sopra la laguna*, pp. 86–87); Cessi, 'Preface' to Cornaro and Sabbadino, *Antichi scrittori d'idraulica veneta. Scritture sopra la laguna*, Cessi and Spada eds., 1952, p. XII; 'Trattato di acque del Magnifico Meser Luigi Cornaro', 1566, ibid., p. 61.
38. 'Scrittura del Messer Alvise Cornaro circa li arzeri di Fogolana', ibid., pp. 11–15. On the increasing need for grain resulting from demographic growth, 'Discorso [...] della cavation della laguna', cit., and 'Scrittura in difesa del piano di banca', 1565, ibid., p. 53. The collection of Cornaro's writings is in G. Fiocco, *Alvise Cornaro, il suo tempo e le sue opere*, Vicenza, 1965.
39. By a third, said Sabbadino ('Deposizione circa gli argini Corner e Molin', 1541, in Cornaro and Sabbadino, *Antichi scrittori d'idraulica veneta. Scritture sopra la laguna*, pp. 83–87).
40. 'Deposition de C. Sabbadin circa il coltivar, arzerar, e pascolar de sotto li arzeri maestri de Brenta noua', 1541, in Cornaro and Sabbadino, *Antichi scrittori d'idraulica veneta. Scritture sopra la laguna*, pp. 81–82).
41. E. Menegazzo and P. Sambin, 'Nuove esplorazioni archivistiche per Angelo Beolco e Alvise Cornaro', in *Italia Medioevale e Umanistica*, 7 (1964), p. 211. His estimate of some 500,000 *campi* of uncultivated or marshy land ready for reclamation on the banks of the lagoon and throughout the terra firma is to be given the benefit of the doubt. Clearly he was very interested in the massive state investment in land-reclamation consortia, for which the State received fifty percent of the reclaimed land. Above all, those whose founding consortium members were from Padua and Venice (Agostino Coletti, Francesco Forzatè and the *procuratore* Marco Molin) ('Discorso [...] della cavation della laguna', cit., pp. 7–8).
42. Another exaggerated figure, even if like all church properties in general, this monastery played an important role in land reclamation (see on this question A. Stella, 'La crisi economica veneziana della seconda metà del secolo XVI', in *Archivio Veneto*, 86 (1956), p. 23 n.; idem, 'La proprietà ecclesiastica della Repubblica di Venezia del secolo XV al XVII', in *Nuova Rivista Storica*, 42 (1958), pp. 67–70).
43. Menegazzo ('Alvise Cornaro',) concludes that the improvements in his lagoon properties were nowhere near as sizeable as Cornaro claimed.
44. Bevilacqua, 'Geografi e cosmografi', cit., pp. 368–71.
45. C.A. Bertelli, *Discorso sopra opinione probabile che la veneta laguna durerà tanto quanto duri il mare Adriatico*, Venice, 1674, p. 5; Trevisan, *Della laguna di Venezia*, pp. 17–44.

46. By 1620 the indecisiveness must have become intolerable if, faced with the increasing complaints from the inhabtiants of Torcello, Mazzorbo and Burano about the deterioration of their 'air' as a result of the formation of silt marshes, the Senate finally set up a 12-man *Collegio* to take concrete action. However, once again, there were delays (cf. the decree of 24 July 1620 quoted in Vacani, *Della laguna*, pp. 146-73).

47. G. Montanari, 'Scrittura circa la diversione del Sile', 12 February 1683, in an appendix to Zendrini, *Memorie storiche*, II, pp. 359-62. According to the Modena hydraulic engineer, the drop in the Sile was less: given that the previous bed – from the point of the re-routing to the lagoon – was 5 and a half miles, and the new bed was 16 and a half. But given a threefold drop in the speed of the water, there would also have been a three-fold increase in volume – creating far from negligible risks of repeated flooding. Montanari was, however, convinced of the need to divert the Sile into the old bed of the Piave: its current would serve to prevent the flow of silt towards Venice, which had increased drastically after the re-routing of the Piave into the northern estuary.

48. Zendrini, *Memorie storiche*, II, p. 231; Vacani, *Della laguna*, pp. 178-79.

49. See the decision of the Council of Ten, 19 May 1505, cit. in *Laguna, lidi, fiumi*, Tiepolo ed., p. 28; Zendrini, *Memorie storiche*, II, pp. 329-39.

50. The Paduans were, for example, forbidden to use the water of the lagoon for their own saltworks. But whilst closing mills might be decided to protect the lagoon, it could create other problems on the mainland, especially when (as at Mestre in 1552) the water channels were not totally closed off, or when there was no adequate drainage of the water which otherwise stagnated (Bertelli, *Discorso sopra l'origine delle atterrazioni della laguna*, p.10; Zendrini, *Memorie storiche*, I, p. 236).

51. Piero Bevilacqua tends to support the myth of Venice as a champion of the environment *ante litteram* (Bevilacqua, *Venezia e le acque*, pp. 46-53 and esp. p. 49).Whilst one cannot deny that the State took measures regarding the environment, the logic behind them is hardly to be interpreted as a modern one.

52. ASV, SEA, *busta* 128, Decree of the Senate (copy) 23 November 1672. The Savi pointed out that one of the limitations of Sabbadino's approach was the excessive focus on the effects of the sea and too little on the role of fresh water in the agriculture. On some occasions the land created as a result of the deposits left by river flooding was sold off: in 1657, 1800 *campi* at the mouths of the Brenta and Bacchiglione, along with others at the Po delta, were sold for cultivation (Vacani, *Della laguna*, p. 159).

53. Caporali et al., *Brenta vecchia, nova, novissima*, pp. 69-74. By 1637 the definition of the perimeter extended as far as Marghera-Fusina; between 1670 and 1750 it would be extended to the Cona lagoon and Cavallino (*Laguna, lidi, fiumi*, Tiepolo ed., pp. 40 and 107).

54. SEA, reg. 317, cc. 134r.-135v., 10 April 1788.

55. Comment made by E. Bevilacqua in 'Il territorio veneto attraverso la cartografia', in *Laguna, lidi, fiumi*, Tiepolo ed., pp. 12-14.

56. Whilst fisherman thought the deposit of the *bari* on the lagoon bed helped to make it more solid and to lower it, technicians thought the exact opposite. In effect, the survey of the lagoon in 1633 showed that they led to the break-down of the *barene*, with the deposit on the lagoon bed of particles of sand as the result of the action of the predominantly salt water (Cessi, 'Prefazione' to *Antichi scrittori d'idraulica veneta. La difesa idraulica della laguna*, Cessi and Spada eds., 1952, p. XVIII; cf. also the 'Depositioni di ser Paulo Dal Ponte, Gieronimo Righetti e Battista Lurano' (26 March 1579, 23 June 1578 and 26 March 1579), ibid., pp. 34, 46, 54).

57. Even fifteen centuries after Frontinus, the quantity of water flowing through an opening was calculated solely on the basis of its area (Biswas, *History of hydrology*, p. 160).

58. G.B. Benedetti would draw on the hydrostatics of Archimedes rather than that of Aristotle (C. Maccagni, 'Mechanics and hydrostatic in the late Renaissance: relations between Italy and the Low Countries', in *Italian scientists in the Low Countries*, Maffioli and Palm eds., pp. 81-82). On G.B. Benedetti see also the Acts of the International Conference *Giovanbattista Benedetti e il suo tempo. Cultura, scienze e tecniche nella Venezia del Cinquecento*, Venice, 1987.

59. In a perhaps undervalued work, Lombardini, underlines the influence on Castelli's theory of Leonardo's work, which he says he was able to consult in the Biblioteca Barberini in Rome: Lombardini, *Dell'origine e del progresso della scienza idraulica nel Milanese ed in altre parti d 'Italia*, pp. 35-40 and 56-58. A fundamental work is H. Rouse and S. Ince, *History of hydraulics*, p. 60. An important influence on Castelli was Galileo, who is to be credited with having studied fluids as made up of particles 'round, oblong or of an inifinte variety of shapes' (cit. in S. Rotta, 'Scienza e "pubblica felicità" in Geminiano Montanari', in *Miscellanea Seicento*, II, Firenze, 1971, p. 100). Studying the fall of weights, he applied the same laws to the flow of rivers. However, his studies are held to have made a contribution to hydrostatics rather than hydrodynamics, which would be developed in later years (on this point, see Bernard, *Nouveaux principes d'hydraulique appliqués à tous les objets, particulièrement aux rivières*, p. 111).

60. It was Castelli who more fully developed the kernel of the idea of 'continuity' in Galileo's work. His First Proposition states 'the sections of the same river pass equal amounts of water in equal periods of time, even if the cross-sectional areas vary' (B. Castelli, *Della misura dell'acque correnti*, Roma 1628, re-published in the fourth edition of *Nuova raccolta d'autori italiani, che trattano del moto delle acque*, Marsigli ed., III, Bologna, 1822, p. 166; see also now the edition edited by Altieri Biagi and Basile in *Gli scienziati del Seicento*, II, pp. 180-212, and 'Nota introduttiva' of Altieri Biagi and Basile, pp. 141-45).

61. Torricelli's physics was deeply influenced by its applications in hydraulics (ibid., 'Nota introduttiva' to E. Torricelli, p. 277; J. Tixeront, 'L'hydrologie en France au XVII siècle', in *Three centuries of scientific hydrology (1674-1974)*, Paris, 1974, pp. 11 and 24).

62. The debate as to whether the greatest influence was internal changes within individual disciplines or mutual interaction remains open. On this question, see A. Herlea, 'Deux histoires des techniques', in *Revue d'Histoire des Sciences*, 35 (1982), pp. 57-63. For a picture of national scientific cultures as part of an overall European culture – in spite of occasional advances or delays in individual countries – see G. Micheli, 'Scienza e filosofia da Vico ad oggi', in *Storia d'Italia. Annali 3*, Micheli ed., p. 551.

63. Biswas, *History of Hydrology*, p. 202. The first instrument for measuring the current of a river was probably that devised by Santorio Santorio (1561-1630), around 1610 (ibid., p. 199). On Santorio, see A.H. Frazier, 'Dr. Santorio's Water Current Meter, Circa 1610', in *Journal of the Hydraulic Division*, 95 (1969), pp. 249-54.

64. R.S. Westfall, *The Construction of Modern Science. Mechanism and Mechanics*, Cambridge, 1980; A. Quondam, 'La scienza e l'accademia', in *Università, accademie e società scientifiche in Italia e in Germania dal Cinquecento al Settecento*, L. Boehm and E. Raimondi eds., Bologna, 1980, p. 45. Leibnitz considered universities solely as places for politicking not for real research (N. Hammerstein, 'Accademie, società scientifiche in Leibnitz', ibid., pp. 395-419). Indeed historians agree that during the course of the seventeenth century, the academies became more important than the universities. However, one should point out that the terms 'research' and 'science' have to be used with caution here, belonging more properly to the nineteenth and twentieth centuries (ibid., p. 398 n.); though in the centralised France, where the State tried to form a scientific élite, one can see some institutionalised figures that bear comparison with their later counterparts. In England, the Royal Society was less centralised and more open to the publication of results and the admission of new members. A fundamental work on the Académie des Sciences is Roger Hahn, *The Anatomy of a Scientific Institution. The Paris Academy of Sciences, 1666-1803*. On the role played by the academies in research during this century, see J. Voss, 'Die Akademien als Organisationsträger der Wissenschaften im 18. Jahrhundert', in *Historische Zeitschrift*, 230 (1980), pp. 43-74, spec. p. 45, with ample bibliography. On French academies and their increasing openness to science (21 out of the 30 founded before 1760 would focus on such matters), see D. Roche, *Le siècle des lumières en province. Académies et académiciens provinciaux, 1680-1789*, I, Den Haag-Paris, 1978, pp. 50-51.On universities and academies in Padua and Italy, see *Accademie scientifiche del '600*, P. Galluzzi, C. Poni and M. Torrini eds., Special Issue of *Quaderni Storici*, 16 (1981), n. 48, p. 757ff.; M.L. Nichetti Spanio, 'Accademie padovane nel Sei e Settecento', in *Accademie e cultura. Aspetti storici tra Sei e Settecento*, Florence, 1979, pp. 211-21; Dooley, 'Social control and the Italian Universities, from Renaissance to Illuminismo', pp. 205-39; P. Del Negro, 'L'Università', in *Storia della cultura veneta. Il Settecento*, Arnaldi and Pastore Stocchi eds., I, 1985, pp. 47-76. On the decline of Padua University in the seventeenth century, see S. De Bernardin, 'La politica culturale della Repubblica di Venezia e l'Università di Padova nel XVII secolo', in 'Studi

Veneziani', 16 (1974), pp. 443-502 (whose conclusions are a little too pessimistic).

65. B. Castelli, *Traité de la mesure les eaux courantes*, Paris, 1645; B. Pascal, *Traitez de l'équilibre des liqueurs, et de la pesanteur de la masse de l'air*, Paris, 1663, espec. the *Préface*, s.p. Pascal established that in a fluid the pressure is transmitted equally in all directions (Rouse-Ince, *History of hydraulics*, pp. 77-79) – a far from obvious conclusion if you consider that Vincenzo Viviani and Alfonso Borelli, leading figures of the 'Scuola Galileiana', 'had not yet accepted the idea of lateral and upward pressure in fluids' (Rotta, 'Scienza e "pubblica felicità" à' in Geminiano Montanari', cit., p. 99). On Pascal, see *L'oeuvre scientifique de Pascal*, P. Costabel ed. ('Introduction' of R. Taton), Paris, 1964, spec. pp. 264-70. On Marin Mersenne (1588-1648), see the entry by A.C. Crombie, in Gillispie, *Dictionary of scientific biography*, IX, pp. 316-22. His 'Hydraulica pneumatica arsque navigandi' (in *Cogitata physico mathematica*, Paris, 1644, pp. 122-34) not only illustrates the main terms of contemporary hydraulics but also deals with the debate concerning the significance of fluid speed; however, his conclusions are less original than those of Edme Mariotte, whose *Traité du mouvement des eaux et des autres corps fluides divisé en V parties, mis en lumière par les soins de Mr. De La Hire* (Paris 1686) is considered as laying the basis for the emergence in France of the experimental/empirical method – as well as being the first complete work of hydraulics not produced by an Italian (Rouse-Ince, *History of hydraulics*, pp. 63-68). On Mariotte see also the entry by M.S. Mahoney, in Gillispie, *Dictionary of scientific biography*, IX, pp. 114-22.

66. Guillerme, *Les temps de l'eau*, pp. 190-91. On Guglielmini, see Bernard, *Nouveaux principes d'hydraulique appliqués*, p. XI; Soppelsa, 'Le scienze teoriche e sperimentali', p.302ff. Athanasius Kircher, it has been argued, was excessively influenced by the animist and hermetic-alchemical traditions (Baldini, 'L'attività scientifica nel primo Settecento', p. 524 n.).

67. Mariotte would make an especially important contribution to ground hydrology by demonstrating that 'the annual volume of rainfall in the Seine basin is higher than the volume of water carried by this river over the same period of time' (A. Guillerme, 'La prospection de l'eau souterraine', in *Milieux*, 10 (June-September 1982), p. 33).

68. R. Dugas, *La mécanique au XVIIe siècle*, Neuchâtel, 1954, pp. 287-88 and 532-36. In discussing the impact between bodies, the Society aimed to elucidate the laws of movement, opening a competition to which it invited entries from Christiaan Huygens, Cristopher Wren and John Wallis. This latter is to be credited with distinguishing between the laws for elastic bodies and those he defined as 'hard', whilst Huygens carried out his experiments on the force of and resistance to water, calculating (around the same time that Mariotte was at work) the impact of water on the paddles of a millwheel. Wren provided algebraic equations for the impact of equal and unequal bodies.

69. P. Frisi, 'Dei fiumi e dei torrenti libri tre', in *Nuova raccolta d'autori italiani, che trattano del moto delle acque*, Marsigli ed., VI, Bologna, 1823, p. 163. On

L. De Genneté, author of *Expérience sur le cours des fleuves* (Paris, 1760), cf. Doorman, *Patents for inventions in the Netherlands*, p. 194, who underlines the theoretical limits of the work. Jean Picard (1620–82) was essentially an astronomer.

70. B. Castelli, *Considerazioni intorno alla laguna di Venezia*, 20 December 1641; idem, 'Modo di esaminare le torbide, che entrano e rimangono nella laguna di Venezia' and 'Discorso sopra la laguna di Venezia al signor Giovanni Basadonna', in *Raccolta d'autori italiani che trattano del moto delle acque*, Marsigli ed., III, Bologna, 1822, pp. 185–204 and pp. 213–19). Bernardino Zendrini would react indignantly to what he read in Castelli: that, due to the re-directing of the rivers away from the lagoon, an important counterweight within the environmental equilibrium had been removed, resulting in a gradual emergence of the *barene* and a dangerous lowering of level of the sea (Castelli, 'Della misura dell'acque correnti', in *Gli scienziati del Seicento*, Altieri Biagi and Basile eds., II, p. 184 n.).

71. Lombardini, *Dell'origine e del progresso della scienza idraulica*, pp. 50 and 53.

72. Trevisan, *Della laguna di Venezia*, pp. 45–46; G. Filiasi, *Osservazioni sopra la lettera diretta all'autore delle riflessioni sopra la laguna e i fiumi*, Venezia, 1819, p. 3ff. Trevisan would be judged 'superficial in hydraulic theory and superficial in his compilation of data' (G.A. Giustinian, *Pensieri di un cittadino sul fiume Brenta*, Padova, 1786, pp. 14–15 and now P. Ulvioni, *Atene sulle lagune. Bernardo Trevisan e la cultura veneziana tra Sei e Settecento*, Venezia, 2000, p.162). On Giacomo Filiasi see the biography by G.J. Fontana, in Tipaldo, *Biografia degli Italiani illustri*, VII, 1840, pp. 391–404, spec. pp. 397–98. On Pusterla's project, Vacani, *Della laguna*, pp. 153 and 183.

73. G.A. Borelli, 'Discorso sopra la laguna di Venezia. All'emin.mo e rev.mo cardinale Pietro Basadonna', in *Nuova Raccolta d'autori italiani, che trattano del moto delle acque*, Marsigli ed., III, Bologna, 1822, pp. 289–325; now also in *Gli scienziati del Seicento*, Altieri Biagi and Basile eds., II, pp. 447–83. In proposing a new system of dredging in 1725, Ortensio Zaghi would claim that 'the rakes and harrows used previously to remove the sands' had not been adequate to the task (SEA, *filza* 565, document of 8 May 1725).

74. Zendrini, *Memorie storiche*, II, pp. 175, 219, 236–40; Baldini, 'L'attività scientifica', pp. 473–79.

75. Fabroni, *Vitae italorum doctrina excellentium qui saeculi XVII et XVIII floruerunt*, III, pp. 69–119; Altieri Biagi and Basile, 'Nota introduttiva' to *Gli scienziati del Seicento*, Altieri Biagi and Basile eds., pp. 487–92; Soppelsa, 'Le scienze teoriche e sperimentali', spec. § 5.

76. Montanari, 'Scrittura circa la diversione del Sile', cit.; SEA, reg. 115, *Scritture circa porti, laguna e fiumi*, 1683–86; *Archivio Proprio B. Zendrini*, reg. 21, *Scritture in materia di acque*, 1679–87; 'Il mare Adriatico e sua corrente esaminata e la naturalezza de' fiumi scoperta, e con nuove forme di ripari corretta', 22 September 1684, in reg. 115, cit., edition published in Venice in 1715 and then included in *Nuova raccolta d'autori italiani, che trattano del moto delle acque*, Marsigli ed., IV, Bologna, 1822, pp. 461–93, spec. 476–77.

For further discussion of the ideas in Montanari's hydraulics (corpuscular theory and the definition of velocity – taken from Castelli, with the above-mentioned inaccuracies), see Rotta, 'Scienza e pubblica felicità in Geminiano Montanari', cit., spec. pp. 96–112. But the cited archive material requires more in-depth study.

77. Cf. 'Il mare Adriatico e sua corrente esaminata', cit. The principle of 'moto radente' – that marine currents run left-right, not flowing into the sea-openings of the lagoon but continuing on their natural course – would influence the proposals put forward by both Zendrini and Poleni for remedies to the silting of the lagoon openings. This notion led them to see little purpose in deviations of rivers, because the sea waters passing in front of the lagoon openings would carry away with the silt they deposited (SEA, *filza* 566, 'Scrittura di G. Poleni', 3 March 1727; *filza* 567, 'Scrittura di B. Zendrini', 2 December 1741).

78. On Guglielmini, see V. Pallotti, 'Domenico Guglielmini sopraintendente alle acque', in *Problemi d'acque a Bologna,* pp. 9–62; Soppelsa, 'Le scienze teoriche e sperimentali', spec. § 6. Bolognese mathematician and hydraulic scientist of European stature, soon known in France (thanks to Daniel Bernoulli; Fontenelle would also write an essay in praise of his work), his writings were quickly translated. The *Aquarum fluentium mensura novo methodo inquisita* (1690–91) and *Della natura dei fiumi. Trattato fisico matematico* (1697) would mark the fusion of the theoretical ideas of seventeenth-century hydraulics with a practical-didactic approach. Guglielmini is also credited with outlining the notion of 'stability' as applicable to rivers, and with defining numerous laws regarding velocity, resistance and pressure in fluids (Guillerme, *Les temps de l'eau,* p. 205; L. Dubuat, *Principes d'hydraulique, vérifiés par un grand nombre d'expériences faites par ordre du gouvernement,* Paris, 1786, pp. XII–XIII; S. Escobar, 'Il controllo delle acque: problemi tecnici e interessi economici', in *Storia d'Italia. Annali 3,* Micheli ed., p. 93; 'Eloge de D. Guglielmini', in *Oeuvres de Monsieur De Fontenelle,* V, Paris, 1742, pp. 274–301; the biography in Fabroni, *Vitae italorum doctrina excellentium,* IV, pp. 330–59).

79. ASV, *Archivio Proprio G. Poleni, filza* 8, 'Scrittura di D. Guglielmtni per la diversione della Brentella', 14 April 1707; 'Relazione di D. Guglielmini, matematico di Padova, sopra la laguna di Venezia', 17 February 1699, in appendix to Zendrini, *Memorie storiche,* pp. 373–83. The original is in reg. 22, ASV, *Archivio Proprio B. Zendrini,* cc. 193–210. Cf. ibid., cc. 213–438, for numerous other writings on the problems tackled by Guglielmini in the years 1699–1709. For a record of his teaching in Venice cf. SEA, *filza* 565, *Scritture di scandagli e ricordi,* Ortensio Zaghi, 22 March 1725. The result was that no less attention should be paid to the situation in secondary canals, in which the sand brought by the sea could be deposited. Guglielmini also makes an interesting comparison of the *velme* and the *marezane* (the banks rising to contain torrents-rivers) – an example of the knowledge derived from a study of rivers being applied to the lagoon.

80. The fundamental biographies on B. Zendrini and G. Poleni are by G. Riche de Prony and J. Bernardi, respectively, in Tipaldo, *Biografia degli Italiani*, II, 1835, pp. 152-63, and X, 1845, pp. 336-46. Poleni has been the subject of even more biographies and studies: P. Cossali *Elogio di Giovanni Poleni*, Padua, 1813, spec. p. 11; G. Gennari, *Elogio del marchese Giovanni Poleni*, Padua, 1839; Fabroni, *Vitae italorum doctrina excellentium*, XII, pp. 66-110 (an elogy would also be delivered at the Académie des sciences by Grandjean de Fouchy in 1763); the entry by B.A. Boley, in Gillispie, *Dictionary of Scientific Biography*, XI, pp. 65-66; the small volume of essays, *Giovanni Poleni (1683-1761) nel bicentenario della morte*, Padova 1963.

81. Baldini, 'L'attività scientifica', p. 476; Ferrone, *Scienza, natura, religione*, pp. 244-45; on the 'Giornale' see B. Dooley 'The 'Giornale de' letterati d'Italia'Modern Culture in the Early Eighteenth Century Veneto', in *Studi Veneziani*, n.s., 6 (1982), pp. 229-90.

82. In the 'Philosophical Transactions' Poleni would publish the results of the meteorological observations he had undertaken since he had been appointed to the Chair of Astronomy and Meteorolgy in Padua in 1709 (Ferrone, *Scienza, natura, religione*, p. 247 n.).

83. M. Torrini, *Dopo Galileo. Una polemica scientifica (1684-1711)*, Florence, 1979, p. 41ff.

84. Baldini, 'L' attività scientifica', pp. 513-15. Just some examples of clerics within the Veneto interested in science and hydraulics, were Giovanni Coi, Cristoforo Tentori, Antonio Rocchi, Giovambattista Nicolai, Giuseppe Gennari, representing some times the offical science of Padua University. Coi was Rector of the Padua Seminary and would publish a *Ragionamento intorno ai fiumi*, which was not however very well received by the official world of hydraulics (G. Vedova, *Biografia degli scrittori padovani*, I, Padova, 1832, pp. 270-71). A wide-ranging compilation on the lagoon's legislation was written by the abbot Tentori, who rather slavishly follows in the footsteps of Rompiasio (*Metodo in pratica di sommario*): C. Tentori, *Della legislazione veneziana sulla preservazione della laguna* (Venice 1792). See also G. Gennari, *Notizie giornaliere di quanto avvenne specialmente in Padova dall'anno 1739 all'anno 1800*, L. Olivato ed., Padua 1982.

85. On these aspects, see the unpublished papers by M.B. Hall and Roger Hahn, 'La scienza italiana vista dalla Royal Society' and 'Scienziati italiani in Francia', delivered at the Colloquium on 'Scienza e letteratura nella cultura italiana del Settecento, Bologna 31 March to 3 April 1982.

86. Biswas, *History of Hydrology*, pp. 279, 221-28; Dugas, *La mécanique au XVIIe siècle*, p. 296; Rouse-Ince, *History of Hydraulics*, p. 114; Maffioli, 'Italian Hydraulics and Experimental Physics in Eighteenth-century Holland. From Poleni to Volta', in *Italian Scientists in the Low Countries*, Maffioli and Palm eds., pp. 252-58.

87. Rouse-Ince, *History of Hydraulics*, p. 95; Pallotti, 'Domenico Guglielmini', p. 47; Dugas, *Histoire de la mécanique*, p. 275.

88. C.A. Truesdell, 'Rational Fluid Mechanics, 1687-1765. Introduction' to *Leonhardi Euleri Opera omnia*, s. II, XII, Lausanne, 1954, pp. X-XI and

XXIX–XXX; Biswas, *History of Hydrology*, pp. 279–80; Rouse-Ince, *History of Hydraulics*, p. 139ff: the French also made an essential contribution to the development of instruments.

89. Bellone, *Il mondo di carta. Ricerche sulla seconda rivoluzione scientifica*, p. 11; Guillerme, *Les temps de l'eau*, p. 208: 'unlike air, water is a visible and homogeneous fluid of measurable viscosity; it can be stored and is divisible into as many parts as one likes'.

90. It was a precise economic end – the creation of a network of canals around Paris – which led to the drawing-up of a collective work that is considered to be a fundamental contribution to the theory of fluids: Guillerme, *Le temps de l'eau*, pp. 208–17; R. Hahn, 'L'hydrodynamique au XVIII siècle. Aspects scientifiques et sociologiques', Conférence donnée au Palais de la Découverte de Paris, 7 November 1964, Paris, 1965, p. 22. In 1714 Jean Bernoulli would publish his *Essai d'une nouvelle théorie de la manoeuvre*, whilst in 1732 would come Henri Pitot's *Théorie de la manoeuvre réduite en pratique*, developing upon some ideas already put forward in the seventeenth century, when trigometry began to be applied to the calculation of the movement and manoeuvring of vessels in water.

91. Dedicating ample space to the mathematical study of the movement of ships, Simone Stratico would also translate and produce a commentary to the work of Euler (see his *Teoria compiuta della costruzione e del maneggio dei bastimenti*, Padua, 1776: the first Latin edition was published in 1749).

92. Hahn, 'L'hydrodynamique au XVIII siècle ', cit., p. 16. On the links between D. Bernoulli and Iacopo Riccati, Brusatin, *Venezia nel Settecento*, p. 147; Angelo Zendrini, 'Elogio', in Zendrini, *Memorie storiche*, I, p. XXXVI; C. Truesdell, 'The rational mechanics of flexible or elastic bodies, 1638–1788. Introduction' to *Leonhardi Euleri Opera omnia*, cit., X–XI, 1960, pp. 126–29.

93. A. Zendrini, 'Elogio', cit., pp. IX–XVI. The controversy was over the determination of the 'force of bodies in movement', or, as it was called then, *vis viva*. Not taking acceleration into consideration, the Cartesians and Newtonians defined this as 'momentum' (mv); for the Leibnitzians it was equal to mv2, thus including the notion of the 'ascensional force' conserved by a body in movement. See S. Bergia – P. Fantazzini, 'Dalla regolamentazione delle acque alle leggi dell'urto centrale elastico. Una rivalutazione del ruolo di Giovanni Poleni nella disputa delle forze vive', in *Giornale di Fisica*, 21 (1980), pp. 46–60; G.B. Gori, *Scienza e sperimentalismo in 's-Gravesande. La fondazione dell'esperienza in 's-Gravesande*, Firenze, 1972, p. 101. Bernoulli's application of the concept of *vis viva* to liquids (the theorem that bears his name states 'the work performed by the forces applied to a liquid in movement in a set time is, if there are no losses of energy, equivalent to its kinetic energy') would mark an important step forward in both physics and hydraulic engineering (D. Bernoulli, *Hydrodynamica, sive de viribus et motibus fluidorum commentarii*, Argentorati, 1738). The application of the principle of *vis viva* to machines would open up a key new sector of research (C.C. Gillispie and A.P. Youschkevitch, *Lazare Carnot savant et sa contribution à la theorie de l'infini mathématique*, Paris, 1979, pp. 46–47 and 130).

94. Truesdell, 'The rational mechanics', cit., p. 129. Zendrini's theories on vibrating bodies – the subject of a rich exchange of letters with Huygens and Leibnitz – would offer insights that remained fundamental until the more precise formulations offered by Bernoulli and Euler.

95. He did essential work with regard to the equilibrium of fluids and the calculation of velocity in sections of a river. He also carried out original studies of wind and its effects upon the flow and height of waters in the sea and rivers (see 'Modo di ritrovare ne' fiumi la linea della corrosione', in *Giornale de' letterati d'Italia*, XXI, 1715, pp. 105–36; *Leggi e fenomeni delle acque correnti* (Venezia, 1741); 'Appendice intorno agli effetti delle macchie per rapporto alla alterazione dell'aria', ibid., X, 1826, pp. 68–83; the biography by G. Riche de Prony, in Tipaldo, *Biografia degli Italiani illustri*, II, 1835, pp. 158–59).

96. In 1720 Zendrini was appointed 'Matematico e Magistrato alle acque' as well as 'Sopraintendente ai fiumi, alle lagune e ai porti' (an office created specifically for him). Well-known beyond the borders of the Republic, he was called to defend the position of several Italian towns over the threatened re-routing of the rivers as (Ferrara, Bologna, Lucca, Viareggio). He was also consultant to the courts of the Duke of Modena and the Emperor of Austria. In Ferrara he was nominated 'Matematico', in Modena 'Primo Ingegnere' and in Vienna he received an offer of a permanent position (*Alcune considerazioni [...] sopra la storia naturale del Po per servire di lume nella controversia che verte fra le città di Ferrara e di Bologna*, Ferrara, 1717). As yet inadequately studied, material regarding Zendrini's reports on the rivers, littorals and lagoon is to be found in the *Archivio Proprio B. Zendrini* and the SEA. The *Memorie* were published posthumously with an 'Elogio' by Zendrini's nephew, himself a hydraulic engineer. The material gathered by Bernardo Trevisan is now in the *Archivio Proprio di Bernardo e Francesco Trevisan* at the ASV.

97. R. Hahn would comment 'Les savants let a gulf be created between theory and experiment. Their own comments reveal they were aware of this'. A new turn towards the experimental approach would emerge in the mid 18th century. In his *Essai d'une nouvelle théorie de la résistance des fluides* (1752), D'Alembert would bemoan the existence of two terms – *hydrodynamique* for scientific theory and *hydraulique* for practice – but would underline how the number of independent variables present in fluids made it difficult to adopt an axiomatic approach (Hahn, 'L'hydrodynamique au XVIII siècle', cit., pp. 18–20).

98. A. Ghetti, 'Giovanni Poleni idraulico teorico', in *Giovanni Poleni (1683–1761) nel bicentenario della morte*, cit., p. 20; F. Marzolo, 'Giovanni Poleni nell'idraulica applicata', ibid., pp. 43–54; Biswas, *History of Hydrology*, p. 256.

99. Maffioli, 'Italian Hydraulics and Experimental Physics in Eighteenth-century Holland', cit., pp. 247–53, spec. p. 252. See. ibid., pp. 253–59, for the influence on Dutch hydraulic science on Italian scientists such as Paolo Frisi and Domenico Guglielmini.

100. Published in Padua in 1718, the treatise was subsequently translated and included in all the editions of the *Raccolta d'autori italiani, che trattano del moto delle acque.*; Cossali, *Elogio di Giovanni Poleni,* cit., pp. 31–32.

101. This is the conclusion drawn in Bergia-Fantazzini, 'Dalla regolamentazione delle acque', cit., pp. 55–60.

102. The correspondence developed by Poleni included exchanges with such European scientists as Euler, the Bernoulli, and P.L. de Maupertuis.

103. Cossali, *Elogio di Giovanni Poleni,* cit., pp. 18–20; the biography by B. A. Boley in Gillispie, *Dictionary of Scientific Biography,* XI, p. 65. Toaldo, professor of astronomy, geography and meteorology at the University of Padua, pushed for the establishment of an astronomical observatory that would become 'a modern and up-to-date centre of research' He recognised the pioneering work carried out by Poleni in the field of meteorological observations (cf. Gennari, *Notizie giornaliere,* cit., pp. 11–12; G. Toaldo, *La meteorologia applicata all'agricoltura,* Fortezza, 1775, pp. X and 40; idem, 'Delle osservazioni del sig marchese Poleni e del sig Temanza', in *Della vera influenza degli astri sulle stagioni e mutazioni di tempo. Saggio meteorologico di D. Giuseppe Toaldo vicentino,* Padova, 1781, pp. 73–88).

104. Ghetti, 'Giovanni Poleni', cit., pp. 32–33. Poleni used French units of measure, thus demonstrating the supremacy the French had by now gained in this field.

105. A. Vallisneri, *Lezione accademica intorno all'origine delle fontane,* Venice, 1726, espec. pp. 10–16; the biographies by G. Montalenti, in Gillispie, *Dictionary of Scientific Biography,* XIII, pp. 562–65, and by Fabroni, *Vitae italorum doctrina* excellentium, VII, pp. 9–90. Ramazzini suggested using the waters that emerged in the Modena area to feed shipping canals to Venice (Bisaws, *History of Hydrology,* pp. 193–96).

106. Biswas, *History of Hydrology,* p. 254.

107. Andrea Tirali was appointed *vice-proto* and then *proto* of the *Magistrato alle acque* (E. Bassi, *Architettura del Sei e Settecento a Venezia,* Napoli, 1962, pp. 281 and 292). The Venetian Tommaso Temanza (1705–89) was an architect of some renown (the biography by Tipaldo himself, *Biografia degli Italiani illustri,* V, 1837, pp. 196–202). Pupil of Zendrini and Poleni, he would take over from Zendrini as *proto ai lidi,* continuing the work on the *murazzi* from 1751 onwards. Vincenzo Coronelli was well-known geographer: *Epitome [...] o introduttione all'astronomia, geografia e idrografia per l'uso [...] delle sfere, globi, planisferi...,* Venice, 1693; *Effetti naturali delle acque [...] sopra la moderazione del Danubio in Vienna nel 1717,* Venice, 1718. See also the collection of essays, *Terzo centenario della nascita di Vincenzo Coronelli,* Venice, 1950.

108. Iacopo Riccati (1676–1754), a multifaceted scientist of the first half of the eighteenth century, studied physics under Poleni and with him carried out work for the *Savi alle acque,* inspecting the lagoon openings and the course of the Adige (see his *Della forza, colla quale i corpi fluidi s'oppongono al moto dei solidi;* the *Osservazioni sopra il moto de' corpi solidi nei mezzi fluidi;* two *Scritture circa l'affare di Reno,* signed by I. Riccati, G. Poleni and B. Zendrini

in SEA, reg. 300, 15 settembre 1731. Also Girolamo Ascanio Giustinian, reformer of Padua University, *Prefetto* of the Biblioteca Marciana and *Savio del Consiglio*, took an interest in scientific and hydrological problems as it has been in the Venetian tradition.

109. On Senator Angelo Querini (1721–1796), a man of the European Enlightenment, see Georgelin, *Venise au siècle des lumières*, pp. 764–70; Del Negro, 'Giacomo Nani', cit., pp. 94–96. For a list of his numerous works and treatises, Marzolo and Ghetti, *Fiumi, lagune e bonifiche venete*, p. 23. Even one of the best-known chroniclers of the seventeenth-century Venetian State, Nicolò Contarini, has re-emerged as a careful observer of such phenomena, as well as appointee to oversee a number of important projects – for example, the *Taglio del Po* at Porto Viro (1598): cf. *Storici, politici e moralisti*, II, *Storici e politici veneti del Cinquecento e del Seicento*, G. Benzoni and T. Zanato eds., Milan-Naples, 1984, pp. 185–86 and 196–97.

110. R. Hahn, 'The chair of Hydrodynamics in Paris, 1775–1791: a creation of Turgot', in *Actes du Xe Congrès international d'histoire des sciences*, II, Paris, 1964, pp. 751–54.

111. As it had been in the Middle Ages, hydrostatics was basically seen as falling within the area of mathematics (Baldini, 'L'attività scientifica', pp. 518–19). On the establishment in Ferrara in 1675 of 'a readership in Geometry for the training of hydraulic engineers' – the first university recognition of the importance of this subject in the Po valley – see ibid., p. 478. On Guglielmini's teaching at Bologna, financed by a fund left by the Venetian nobleman Alvise Venier, Pallotti, 'Domenico Guglielmini', p. 46; Marzolo, 'L'idraulica veneta e l'apporto dell'Università di Padova nelle discipline idrauliche', p. 96.

112. Stratico, *Raccolta di proposizioni d'idrostatica*, which devouts ample space to the laws of pressure and equilibrium in fluids (hydrostatics) and those of velocity and momentum (hydraulics proper). A pupil of Poleni's, he spent a short period in England, where he noted how behind Venetian ship-building had fallen. In Padua he was appointed to the Chair of Mathematics and Nautical Science in 1764, with his teaching covering hydrometry and civic architecture. Like Poleni, he was involved in many actual projects of hydraulics: regarding the Adige (1773), the Valli Grandi Veronesi (1780–1782) and the digging of the Gorzone (1787–1794). For this latter work, he championed the use of steam-driven machinery (F. Rossetti, 'Della vita e delle opere di Simone Stratico', in *Atti del R. Istituto Veneto di Scienze, Lettere ed Arti*, 19 (1876), pp. 21 and 53–56).

113. Gennari, *Notizie giornaliere*, cit., pp. 158–59 and 357 n.: a man of great academic reputation, Stratico was also politically open-minded – so much so that he showed some sympathy for the Veneto 'jacobins'. See also Del Negro, 'Giacomo Nani', cit., p.93 n.

114. M. Zunica, *Le spiagge del Veneto*, Padua, 1971, p. 15; G. Marchi, *Vicenza inondata dal Bacchiglione e suo vero rimedio umiliato alla medesima*, Bassano, 1731; C. Scarabello, *Discorso del pubblico ingegnere e perito intorno la possibilità di sistemare il tronco attuale del fiume Brenta*, place of publication unknown, 1790; G. Fantuzzi, *Dei fiumi*, Venice, 1795, p. 56.

115. Dubuat, *Principes d'hydraulique*, cit., p. 105 and Guillerme, *Les temps de l'eau*, p. 205.

116. Stratico would observe: 'Hydrostatic laws mean that extending the bed of the river leads to a raising of the water level in its upper stretches blocking the chance for the drainage channels to empty into them; it also decreases the gradient, slowing it down and thus causing possible flooding' (S. Stratico, *Osservazione sulla necessità che ha la Repubblica di Venezia di rivolgere le applicazioni del suo governo a riordinare alcuni fiumi principali del suo stato*, place of publication unknown., 1771, p. VIII).

117. L. Miliani, *Le piene dei fiumi veneti e i provvedimenti di difesa. L'Agno-Guà-Frassine-Fratta-Gorzone, il Bacchiglione ed il Brenta*, Florence, 1939, p. 15ff.; G. Franco, *Dissertazione intorno alla regolazione de' fiumi, e degli scoli del Polesine di Rovigo*, Rovigo, 1775, p. 111ff.

118. Lorgna is to be credited with having given the exact measure of a *quadretto veneto*, establishing it as 140 l./s. (the *quadretto veronese* was generally given as 145 l./s.): v. F. Marzolo, 'Le opere di A.M. Lorgna nel campo idraulico', in *Anton Maria Lorgna. Memorie pubblicate nel secondo centenario della nascita*, published by the Accademia di agricoltura di Verona, Verona, 1937, p. 50. Lorgna's reputation is clear from his appointment as 'correspondent member' of the Paris Academy of Science – to which however there was much opposition: F. Piva, 'L'elezione di A.M. Lorgna a socio corrispondente dell'Accademia delle scienze di Parigi', in *Atti e Memorie dell'Accademia di agricoltura di Verona*, 152 (1976–77), pp. 123–40.

119. SEA, reg. 314, cc. 85–111, 19 April 1779.

120. A. Querini, *Cogitata et visa ossia osservazioni e riflessioni posteriori alle considerazioni pubblicate intorno la migliore sistemazione di Brenta*, place of publication unknown, 1790, pp. V–XIV; idem, *Brevi annotazioni [...] per la più pronta [...] regolazione di Brenta*, Treviso, 1790, pp. 6–12; D. Munaretto, *Osservazioni locali sopra l'acqua della Brenta*, Padua, 1777, pp. XII and 24–25; Giustinian, *Pensieri di un cittadino*, pp. 49–56. Some said that the threat that Artico's plan posed to Querini's Villa at Altichiero – famous for its park and art works – was the real reason for his own opposition (cf. the biography by E. Cicogna, in Tipaldo, *Biografia degli Italiani illustri*, I, 1834, p. 321). What is certainly true is that one should consider vested economic interests when examining conflicts of this kind.

121. Some suggestions made by Artico were taken up in 1842–1858, when a new bed was dug for the Brenta, shortening it by some 29 km. (Vacani, *Della laguna*, p. 195; Caporali, *Brenta vecchia*, pp. 77–78). Development in the opposition direction would take place in the Brenta delta, where expanses of water would during the course of the nineteenth century be reclaimed for agricultural land. Agriculture thus won out against the more complex demands of the lagoon which had prevailed up to then (see M. Zunica, ''La bonifica Delta Brenta'. Un esempio di trasformazione del paesaggio nella laguna di Venezia', in *Rivista Geografica Italiana*, 81 (1974), pp. 5–60; idem, 'Une zone de bonification dans la lagune de Venise: le delta de la Brenta', in *I paesaggi rurali europei*, Perugia, 1975, pp. 531–44.

122. SEA, reg. 319, 26 aprile 1793. The *Savi* noted that if in 1762 the lagoon bed at Palada di Dese had been three feet under the *comune* (the usual water level), in 1787 it was only one foot below, so that in fifty years that entire area of the lagoon would have become silted up (Vacani, *Della laguna*, pp. 195 and 203; P. Lucchesi, *Il Businello del Sile e suoi effetti*, Venezia, pp. 13–15 and 23.

123. SEA, *filza* 565, 'Scrittura di Ortensio Zaghi', 8 May 1725. Zaghi proposed the Dutch solution of spreading sheets of canvas on the sea/lagoon bed near the littorals to prevent the shifting of sand. Other admirers of the hydraulic techniques used in Northern Europe were Giuseppe Iseppi *(Esposizione di una nuova macchina per escavare il fango di sottacqua*, Venice, 1776, p. VI) and Bernardo Trevisan *(Della laguna di Venezia*, p. 109), even if they did not discuss the matter at any length.

124. Van Veen, *Dredge, Drain, Reclaim*, pp. 78–79; see also Doorman, *Patents for inventions*: the entries *Drainage mills, Dredging, Hydraulic architecture.*

125. SEA, *filza* 565, 'Report and drawings by Gaetano Folega', 12 June 1725; ibid., 'Report and drawing by Antonio Benussi', 2 August 1725; ibid., 'Report and drawing by Giovanni Cattaneo' 11 June 1725. Other projects are in SEA, reg. 303, 3 November 1743; reg. 305, 9 December 1752; reg. 306, 3 September 1754. For other designs and applications, see *Laguna, lidi, fiumi*, Tiepolo ed., pp. 67–69.

126. SEA, reg. 315, 9 January 1782; reg. 317, 18 January 1787; ibid., 7 May 1787; reg. 301, 26 April 1735; reg. 303, 16 June 1742; reg. 304, 5 December 1747 and 20 April 1748; reg. 320, 19 August 1795. Usually the barges were set on one side of the canal, from where the entire width of the canal was dredged; sometimes it was necessary to work from both sides. Complex calculations were used, especially with regard to determining how much mud should be removed.

127. In the sixteenth century it was even proposed that the *villici* – the labourers who carried out the dredging work – should be billeted with Venetian families (who would receive no payment); the idea was then dropped (cf. Tentori, *Della legislazione veneziana*, p. 207). 500 men were brought from the Po delta, Bassano and Padua areas for the overall lagoon dredging of 1546. Such general projects were repeated in 1565 and 1677. Thereafter more local projects were favoured. Up to the sixteenth century, the dredged mud was used to extend and consolidate the islands in the lagoon; thereafter – except in rigidly-controlled cases – it was carried beyond the boundary of the lagoon (see ibid., pp. 199–206 and 212; Zendrini, *Memorie storiche*, I, pp. 256–57; see also SEA, *filza* 129, documents 17 March and 13 July 1677; *busta* 155, 31 March 1760).

128. Cf. G.M. Figari, *Trattato massimo delle venete lagune*, Venice, 1714, pp. 16 and 27.

129. Cf. M.F. Tiepolo, 'Difese a mare'*della laguna veneta*

⟨Ⱥ⟩ Chapter 4
___

Venice and Holland: Amphibious States

'Hydraulic Societies' and 'World Economies': The Dutch in Italy

In his discussion of 'hydraulic societies'(1957), Karl Wittfogel describes a model of oriental despotism in which the state exerts authoritarian control over the major water resources – and, hence, all the main works of hydraulic engineering – within a nation. At the same time, he argues that the environmental conditions for such despotism – including the need to irrigate arid land – existed in western Europe as well.[1] However, T. Glick's studies of Spain, and particularly the situation in Valencia, brought out how 'political centralisation in irrigation is an independent variable', with some very efficient irrigation systems being independently organised by decentralised authorities. In the above-mentioned case of Valencia, for example, social control of water resources traditionally remained under the control of local institutions and was in the hands of those directly involved in irrigation schemes. The autonomy of these communities, it is said, was recognised at all levels of power and was consolidated by consuetudinary law.[2]

Although criticised as merely schematic, Wittfogel's interpretations have a fundamental merit: they do not solely focus on one particular historical case-study – for example, Asia or Spain[3]– but invite one to investigate the way other (particularly European) countries set about controlling and managing water resources.

An investigation of this kind obviously brings one to consider such states as Venice and Holland, in which water played an essential role not only in the political and economic fortunes of the nation but also in its very survival. Comparison of the two can be extended to cover various aspects of water management, given the multiple links that

were often seen to exist between the two Republics. For example, the
two attracted the joint attention of numerous political theorists and
commentators during the course of the sixteenth century. Ludovico
Guicciardini, for instance, is a very precious source of historical
information regarding the sixteenth-century Netherlands as a whole;
as early as 1567 he was drawing an explicit parallel between Venice
and Amsterdam.[4] What is more, there can be no doubt that the two
states stand out amongst other European countries both for the
degree of tolerance enjoyed within them, and the fact that power in
each was largely held by the same social class – that is, an urban
patrician class whose wealth was based on trade.

When at the height of their power – Venice in the late fifteen/early
sixteenth century and Holland throughout most of the seventeenth –
these two states ranked as 'world economies' (whether we accept the
definition of the term given by Braudel and Wallerstein,[5] or apply
subsequent, more nuanced, uses of that expression).[6] However, any
sort of commercial or economic expansion still had to rest on a solid
agricultural basis, given the key importance of agriculture in all pre-
industrial economies: even in the eighteenth century – that is, the
period which comes after the great Dutch expansion of the
seventeenth – Faber calculates that half the population of the
Netherlands was still employed in agriculture, with the proportion in
some regions, such as Veluwe, reaching two-thirds (for the south of
the country, Vandenbroeke puts the figure as high as 80 per cent).[7] In
the Venetian Republic the agricultural population would remain
similarly numerous right up to the fall of the *Serenissima*,[8] even if the
notion of any sort of agricultural revolution would postulate that this
population should have dropped, with greater percentages of the
work-force gradually being absorbed by other sectors of the
economy.

Other similarities between the two states can be seen in the fact
that – admittedly, at different periods – both were obliged to exercise
control over the most far-flung sources of supplies (Venice in the
Mediterranean, Holland in the Baltic) at the same time as they had
to make substantial efforts to develop their own hinterlands. With
regard to this latter point, Braudel contrasts Amsterdam with the
other cities and territories of the United Provinces and wonders if
one might not say that the city stood in 'a position comparable with
that Venice held in relation to the cities of the mainland'.[9]

The presence of large expanses of inland water, as well as the threat posed by rivers and seas, furthermore required the Dutch and Venetians to invest in the most efficient means of defending themselves against these natural forces; and their centuries-old struggle against water certainly makes them describable as *civilisations de l'eau* (in the full sense of the term *civilisation* as used by Braudel).

There can be no doubt that from the seventeenth century onwards Holland was recognised throughout Europe as offering the most advanced examples of hydraulic engineering. But many historians – and particularly, northern European historians – have tended to overlook the fact that up to that point the two states were following parallel paths in the development of their hydraulic expertise – developments which reflected specific characteristics of the technology, geography and relations of production obtaining within these city-states, as well as the forms of political dominion they exercised over their subject territories. With regard to this point, it is significant here that Dutch and Venetian hydraulic engineers demonstrate almost total ignorance of each other's work and achievements. For example, Vierlingh says absolutely nothing about Italian hydraulic technology in his *Tractaat van Dijckagie* (1570), the most representative of sixteenth-century works on the construction of dikes;[10] and among all the various European countries mentioned in Leeghwater's 'autobiography', Italy – which the writer had never visited – is conspicuous by its total absence.[11] As for Venetians authors, the fifteenth-century Marco Cornaro and the sixteenth-century Alvise Cornaro, Cristoforo Sabbadino, Fra Giovanni Giocondo – plus a whole host of other hydraulic engineers – are similarly silent about their Dutch counterparts, seen as having to tackle problems very different to those faced by the Venetians, who in the fifteenth and sixteenth centuries were primarily concerned solely with stopping rivers from silting up the lagoon. In effect, if Venice during this period did draw on hydraulic know-how from outside, it looked to its neighbours rather than to Holland – and even such borrowings were much less important than the technological and empirical knowledge developed *in situ* within the lagoon itself.

This point is worth stressing because the trend in other Italian regions would seem to have been different. The Papal States, for example, were already calling upon the services of Dutch engineers towards the end of the sixteenth century in order to continue the land-drainage projects in the area around Ferrara which had begun under the rule of the D'Este dynasty (think, for example, of the important land-reclamation projects of the sixteenth century and the Bentivoglio scheme of land reclamation undertaken in the 1620s).[12] In 1601 Duke Alessandro Farnese appointed Gillis van den Houte to improve the management of water resources in the area around Parma; that same Van den Houte would subsequently present Pope Clement VIII with a land-reclamation scheme for the marshy terrain around Ferrara. A few decades later, another Dutchman, Nicolaes van der Pellen, would become the associate of Paolo Marucelli, who had since 1648 been tackling the chronic problem posed by the Pontine Marshes; Van der Pellen invested some 30,000 *scudi* in the project, without however achieving any great results.

Another hydraulic engineer who travelled from Holland to Italy was the Zeeland-born Egidio Vandenhoute, who in 1599 was appointed to work on the re-direction of the river Reno into the Po. On 16 November of the same year, Everardo Corceine – Everardus van Cortgene – was paid some 500 *scudi* for 'his work as an engineer in the drainage of the marshes around Bologna, Ferrara and Ravenna'.[13]

As research by Korthals Altes and Hoogewerff so clearly shows, the presence of Dutch hydraulic engineers was noteworthy in both the sixteenth and seventeenth century, especially in the lands of the Papal States[14] (as yet there has been insufficient follow-up to the scholars' work, even if one has the clear impression that there is a lot still to learn about the presence of Dutch engineers in other regions of Italy).

There can, however, be no doubt of a sizeable Dutch presence in Tuscany, largely due to the mercantile links between the two states (as is well known, there was a large community of Dutch merchants in Livorno, especially during the seventeenth century). The Flemish Willem de Raet, for example, an engineer from Bois-le-Duc ('s-Hertogenbosch), worked between Wolfenbüttel and Italy and was an expert in both drainage and building technology (be it Dutch, German or Italian). In 1557 he was in Lucca, called there by a local merchant, Landi, who had business interests in Antwerp. De Raet was appointed to drain 1,600 hectares of terrain around Massaciuccoli. To this end he had a dike built at Burlamacca, between the mountain and the main drainage channel, which became known locally as 'the Flemish dike' (some time afterwards the Lucchesi themselves demolished the dike in order to avoid clashes with the Florentines and Pisans).[15] On some rare occasions it was the Tuscans themselves who travelled north – for example, Grand Duke Cosimo de' Medici, who at the beginning of the seventeenth century was present at the start of the important drainage schemes involving the Schermeer, which he commented upon most admiringly.[16]

Even if the direct involvement of Dutch technicians in land-reclamation projects within the Venetian Republic is yet to be shown, there is clearer documentary evidence regarding the licences and patents the Venetian authorities granted for dredging work in the lagoon itself (by the end of the sixteenth and beginning of the seventeenth century, northern supremacy in this field was already beginning to make itself felt). One unanswered question is whether it was merely a coincidence that Nicolaes Corneliszoon de Wit, known as Scapecaes, was in the Venetian Republic when he died in 1639. We know that in 1629 Scapecaes, who had also worked at La Rochelle in France, collaborated in Rome with Gillis van den Houte on the Pontine Marshes reclamation project, within which he was responsible for the digging of canals, the building of mills and the introduction of Dutch-style working of linen and flax. Later he would be appointed by the Republic of Genoa to turn the wooded terrain of Corsica into agricultural land; his payment was to be a tenth of the reclaimed land, but the project ultimately came to nothing because of the sudden death of the engineer whilst he was in Padua.[17]

Dutch Windmills and Canals

There was a long process of development behind the emergence of those technologies for agricultural land reclamation and maintenance that resulted in the Netherlands becoming the home of a veritable 'mud-based industry', whose greatest period of expansion came during the seventeenth century. Although the first use of a windmill in a Dutch drainage project dates from the beginning of the fifteenth century (marking the emergence of a type of technical knowledge that would be of enormous importance to the Netherlands), one should also point out that towards the end of that same century Benedictine monks near Padua introduced the no less revolutionary technology of the *colmata*. Based on a long tradition of practices, whose origin can be dated back to the previous century in Tuscany, this technique involved using the alluvial detritus borne by rivers themselves to create raised, drained terrain (the time necessary for the completion of such a process was very long, up to fifty or sixty years).[18] However, whilst there was continuity in the application and development of the Dutch technology, the Italian technique of the *colmata* was characterised by a mixture of advances, stalemates and reversals – due not only to the changes in the Italian states and their institutions but also to the role which imported sciences and technologies began to play.

There is no doubt that drainage windmills gave the Netherlands a superiority that would become ever more marked with the passage of time. As already mentioned, windmills were first used for this purpose at the beginning of the fifteenth century; and once the first rudimentary drainage pumps – initially man-powered, then driven using horses or oxen – had been replaced, the perfected model of the *wipmolen* was gradually developed as a definitive replacement for the traditional octagonal windmill. It seems that the first windmill of the *wipmolen* type was built in 1408 (at Alkmaar, by Floris van Alcmade). It would be used for an entire century (the first, experimental, attempts to harness wind power in order to drain water date from a few decades earlier, with the technology itself having been developed during the course of the fourteenth century).[19] As proof of just how efficient and profitable these *wipmolen* were, one might cite the fact that by the end of the fifteenth century a good seventeen of them were at work in the region of Vliest alone. These machines would undergo slow but continuous improvement, not least with the introduction of the oblique-angled waterwheel (which had already been known to Vitruvius). That wheel was first re-introduced in 1629, during the drainage of the Naardermeer, and after successive modifications which De Jong developed in two different windmills would also play a part in the draining of the Watergraafsmeer in 1744.[20] The gradual replacement of the traditional waterwheel (*scheprad*) with the Archimedes' screw during the course of the sixteenth century was another important advance in drainage technology, making it possible to raise water through greater differences in level. Work efficiency and output was further increased by a whole series of innovations; this series of small steps which totally transformed processes of production included Cornelis

Dirckszoon Muys's 1589 design for a windmill with an angled shaft, and the development of the rotating-head windmill (which meant it was no longer necessary to rotate the entire body of the windmill to harness wind power efficiently).[21] No less attention was dedicated to the design of the actual blades of the windmills. This tradition of studies started with Simon Stevin and resulted in more obliquely-angled and flexible blades which, again, better harnessed wind power. Such improvements ultimately led to the introduction of a windmill designed by the famous *waterbouwkundige* Jan Blanken (1755–1838) and equipped with multiple waterwheels at different heights, which meant the machine could adapt to the changing depth of water.[22] This is just one fascinating episode in the gradual transformation and perfection of the drainage windmill – a series of developments that is amply illustrated by the numerous patents granted during the seventeenth and eighteenth century and recounted in great detail by the extensive literature dedicated to this glorious national achievement.[23]

From the point of view of hydraulic engineering, an equally decisive role was played by the polders' efficient networks of canals to carry away the drained waters. A truly original and unique feature of these projects was the use of strategically-placed windmills (very often in groups of up to four) to raise the water from one level to another; in the Beemster, for example, there were forty-two windmills organised in fifteen teams (generally of three each).[24] The water from these individual canals would then run into a main spillway – known in Dutch as a *boezem* (or *slotring* if circular) – which flowed around the entire polder; sometimes part of it might coincide with a river tributary or the shores of a lake.[25] The level of water in these *boezem* was therefore the official level of water within the polder as a whole – the so-called *boezemgebied* – which measured in proportion to a national standard level, that found in the region of Amsterdam.[26]

Dutch Technology in Venice

In terms of hydraulic engineering, right up to the seventeenth century Venice could not be said to have lagged behind the Low Countries in either the policies it followed or the administrative structures that existed to implement those policies. However, from

that century onwards, the situation undoubtedly changed. As has
already been noted, Venetian government and scientific circles had
always been remarkably receptive to input of outside know-how
(even if rather less prompt to adopt the patented processes taken into
consideration). In the fifteenth and sixteenth century, the main
source of this external input had been Lombardy, but in the
seventeenth century, when the weaknesses in Venetian hydraulic
policy became all too clear, resort was made to Dutch expertise,
particularly with regard to the ever-present problem of the dredging
and clearing of the lagoon.

Up to the sixteenth century it cannot be said that Italian – and,
above all, Venetian – technology in this field fell behind any that was
available elsewhere in Europe; a parity that is confirmed by the fact
that it was Italian engineers who were gaining patents not only in the
states of the peninsula but also to the north of the Alps. For example,
in 1561 the Venetian Pietro Venturino obtained a patent for his new
form of dredger (often incorrectly described as a type of the modern
bucket dredger),[27] whilst in 1566 Paolo Pergolato and Battista Varro
of Vicenza obtained a patent for 'supplying sweet water to cities and
garrisons' both in the Republic of the United Provinces (for example,
Brabant) and in the territories on the other side of the Meuse.[28] And
wasn't it the great Galileo Galilei himself who in 1593 presented
before the Venetian Senate his new suction pump for drawing
water?[29] But this historic trend was inverted from the beginning of
the seventeenth century onwards, with more and more Dutchmen
arriving in Venice with procedures that had been successfully
developed in their home country. One of these newcomers was
Cornelius Meijer, who arrived in Venice in 1675; contrary to the
claims traditionally made by historians, this was before he went to
work in the Papal States, where he would work on the most
interesting drainage projects in Italy. A technician of great experience
and practical flair, Meijer was a native of Amsterdam (like his father,
he initially trained in the construction of wheels) and in Venice he
seems to have introduced a type of bucket dredger that clawed across
the lagoon bed (the simpler version was man-powered, the more
sophisticated horse-powered). Some years earlier, in 1670, Gerhard
Reighemberg had obtained an identical patent, but for a floating
pontoon which the Senate judged to be less efficient than that
proposed by Meijer, whose dredger could fill up to thirty barges with

mud. This horse-powered dredger marked the state of the art in Venetian hydraulic technology; many archive sources confirm that it remained in use for a long time to come.[30]

Other Dutch imports of the day included the so-called *krabbelaars*. Large boats with steel 'combs' fitted to their hulls, these had been first built in Holland in 1435 and were used in dredging the port of Amsterdam. They were known to the Venetians not only thanks to a drawing presented by Meijer himself but also through the different versions whose employment was repeatedly discussed by the city's various *magistrature*. However, it is still an open question as to whether they were ever used in the lagoon as extensively as in Amsterdam.[31]

Dikes: Dutch Scientists and Dutch Technology

Development and application of Dutch technology in this area rested in part on the institutional role of expert technical personnel. Most representative of these institutional figures was the *dijkmeester* (dike engineer). If initially at the service of the monarchy and of the state – for example, Andries Vierlingh was *dijkmeester* to William the Silent – from the second half of the sixteenth century onwards, these engineers formed a professional body of technicians in the employ of the various companies set up to carry out land-reclamation projects. A no less important role was played by the *landmeters* (land-surveyors), who were to be found in each individual city, region or *hoogheemraadschap*.[32] These were not only responsible for measuring and drawing up plans of the area to be reclaimed, they also acted as overseers during the digging of canals, and the building of dikes and other constructions.[33]

A fundamental component of Dutch hydraulic technology, dikes were initially constructed as a defence for local inhabitants (numerous such defensive dikes were raised during the sixteenth century), and then employed in the delimitation and reclamation of agricultural land.[34] The safety of a polder was always linked to the presence of a stoutly-built dike, especially if the polder occupied reclaimed land on the coast (as was very often the case right up to the early years of the seventeenth century). And if the area of the polder was to be extended, this first dike might then be followed by a second, built closer to the sea. It is therefore easy to understand that a corrupt or inadequate *dijkmeester* – and the writings of Andries Vierlingh reveal that in the sixteenth century there were numerous examples of both – could have a disastrous effect on the well-being of the inhabitants and the prosperity of the polder.[35]

Like Venetian dikes, those raised in Holland were essentially composed of compressed earth.[36] However, it would seem that during the course of the sixteenth century the attention and care lavished on the Serenissima's sea defences were greater than those to be seen in the Low Countries. It should not be forgotten that this was the period in which Venice itself was being transformed from a city of wood to a city of brick and stone, and as a result the same transformation was taking place in its sea defences. The Venetian dikes were still protected with *palade* (walls of wooden piles), but these were now supplemented by a slightly inclined shelf facing the sea, which was intended to break the force of the waves. In Holland, on the other hand, the sea front of the dike still remained a sheer vertical wall, which – as engineers would later realise – provided excessively-rigid resistance to stormy seas.

An original feature of Dutch dikes was the use of seaweed as a construction material, the first example of this apparently dating from 1319. As Tommaso Contarini, the Venetian ambassador to the Low Countries, observed in 1610, this was a particularly successful way of preventing water from infiltrating the dike. And it is no coincidence that when, in 1692, the technician Matteo Alberti proposed the use of seaweed in the construction of the defences of the Venetian littorals, he used the expression 'defences in the Dutch style'. Reeds too might be used as a building material for these defences: for example, in 1402, Albrecht van Beyeren decided to use them in the Vier Noorder Koggen, precisely because there was a shortage of seaweed.[37]

Stone constructions would make their first – temporary – appearance along the coasts of Zeeland in the sixteenth century, though it was not until the eighteenth century that stone became the standard building material for sea defences in the Low Countries – and, for that matter, Venice.[38] It would seem that it was the need to withstand growing numbers of severe storms that led to legislators to focus on this question (the Feast of All Saints in 1570 saw the breach of numerous dikes, with disastrous consequences that became part of national folklore). Proof of this shift to stone can be seen in the introduction within sixteenth-century Friesland of a special tax – varying according to social class – designed to pay for such constructions.[39]

And just as the modernisation of ship-building had led to an individual vessel being constructed from various separate parts,[40] so the change in dike technology led to the structure being divided between a number of different contractors, each responsible for around 70 to 80 metres of dike.[41] The result was that it became possible to finish an entire dike in three-and-a-half months, which is a clear sign of economies of scale and a highly-specialised division of labour: in various regions – above all, the Delta and Zeeland, which were the most significant areas in the development of land reclamation – it has been possible to identify veritable family dynasties of 'bedijkingsde skundigen (dike engineers)'.[42]

With its sizeable polders and its early examples of fully-fledged capitalist enterprises supplying international markets with various crops (primarily turnips and madder),[43] Zeeland was also the Dutch region that set the pace as far as legislation was concerned: as early as 1250 the *comites in aggerum aquarum* had been set up, to evolve in the early fifteenth century into the *Suprema Collegia* which was the first step towards the institution of the *hoogheemraadschappen*, regional authorities that would play an essential role in dealing with affairs relating to water.[44] The importance of Zeeland in these matters did not escape that quite extraordinary observer Ludovico Guicciardini. After mentioning the high quantities of good-quality grain, coriander and madder which were exported from here throughout Europe, he underlines the key role played by dunes and dikes in the region's water defences. He also commented on the prohibition against the removal of peat – a substance which he calls *daring*, after the Old Dutch *darink* [45] – from the areas near the dunes, given that this provided the weight-bearing sub-stratum for these defences against advancing waters. And whilst the dunes provided natural defences against the sea, further inland were the dikes, built of clay (the same as used in producing pottery) reinforced with stone and timber and protected by a very effective layer of straw. To maintain and preserve these defences, Guicciardini concludes, the Dutch spared no effort or expense.[46]

Hydraulic science in Holland also had its distinctive, original characteristics, being more empirical and focused on practical results rather than on all-embracing theoretical questions. In fact, in summarising the technological and scientific exchange between the Low Countries and Italy (Venice, in particular), one might well conclude that the Dutch excelled in applied hydraulics, whilst the Italians were superior in the science of hydraulics.[47] This, however, does not mean that the sixteenth-century Low Countries – or, to be more precise, the southern provinces of the Low Countries – did not have their own theoretical scientists – for example, the Flemish Simon Stevin. At times compared to Leonardo da Vinci, Stevin has been considered a worthy successor in this field to the Italian's original research into many problems concerning hydraulic engineering and river locks. The area in which Stevin's scientific work is undoubtedly original in its own right is the study of winds and ways of harnessing wind power.[48] Obviously, this was an area of research that reflected the specific geographical features of the Low Countries and would continue to bear important fruit throughout the seventeenth and eighteenth century.[49]

Legislation: A Democratic Foundation?

Alongside this progressive development of adequate technology, the Low Countries were, at least as early as the Venetian Republic, also characterised by the presence of precise legislation governing hydraulic matters. In fact, the eleventh century has been given as the date for the beginning of that model of territorial organisation which involved the entire population in the struggle against an encroaching sea, with Van der Linden, for example, arguing that the processes of settlement enacted during the Middle Ages had a profound and lasting effect. It was in this century that the Counts of Holland took the decisive step of conceding extensive freedoms to the peoples from the Lower Rhine area who came to settle and cultivate these harsh, empty lands. On the basis of the 'contract' – *De cope* – signed between the Count of Holland and these settlers, Van der Linden speaks in terms of *landsheerlijke vrijheid*, i.e. of 'country-lordly freedom'.[50] These first settlers would form communities of free farmers, establishing *buurschappen* (farming districts) made up of settlers who each had their own farm (known as *ambacht* in the Southern Netherlands and *banne* in the North). It is important to stress that from the very beginning it was these local communities which concerned themselves with such necessary public-works schemes as the digging and maintenance of drainage channels and the construction of protective dikes.[51]

But is this a completely sustainable interpretation ? Was the situation here one of 'popular democracy' and therefore very different to that which is to be seen in the rest of Europe and in Venice itself ? Verhulst casts some doubt on this version of events, and denies 'the idea that rural communities generated the original inspiration for hydraulic projects', choosing instead to emphasise the role of private individuals and *l'individualisme agraire* in the establishment of farms and the construction of dikes in the late-medieval Low Countries.[52]

What is undeniable is that, at a regional level, popularly-based legal institutions and corporations – *heemraadschappen* – were established to defend the rights of the population.[53] It is also true that feudal powers quickly tried to impose their own authority on these bodies, and that when the *heemraadschappen* extended to embrace larger territories – forming the so-called *hoogheemraadschappen* – nobles and large landowners exercised ultimate control over them. Nevertheless, it does seem that this fact was not enough to erase the strong feeling of community within the *hoogheemraadschappen*, that popular basis of 'democracy' (if we are to accept the applicability of such a term) within administrative units which spearheaded the resistance against the threat posed by water.[54]

Nevertheless, even here – in discussing popular participation in the creation and maintenance of defences against water – one should not take the Dutch situation as being entirely unique. Although there was less institutional recognition of their role, the local population of the Venice littorals worked *en masse* as soon as the church bells warned of an unexpectedly high flood tide; and the people of the Loire valley had since the twelfth century taken spontaneous measures against the periodic flooding of the river, with the construction of embankments that they also used as roadways. True, after the disastrous 1527 flood, the monarchy responded to pressure from the *échevins* [municipal magistrates] by officially requiring the inhabitants of Moreau-aux-Près to rebuild their embankments, modelling them on those of the Val d'Orléans (with the costs to be borne by those landowners whose property was at risk of flooding 'unless these undertake in exchange to offer their labour as journeymen').[55] Dion, however, warns against excessive generalisation here, given that the monarchy often exempted villages from taxation as long as they undertook to exercise vigilance over the dikes built along the course of the Loire. In the following century, however, there is no doubt that the state took on a more *dirigiste* role, given that Colbert was convinced 'that public works always fall into decay when they are supposed to be kept up by local communities'.[56]

Yet while exemplary in a number of ways, the Dutch administration was lacking a central body, an equivalent of that *Waterstaat* (Ministry of Waterways and Roads) which was only set up at the end of the eighteenth century. An administrative and legislative body of this kind would have made it possible to overcome the predominance of local interests which was a characteristic of these centuries, given that as a federal organ present in all the different regions it could have mobilised the efforts of the population as a whole.

Dutch historians have charted the key phases in the emergence of such a body. Whilst the establishment of Rijnland by Willem I, Count of Holland (1168–1222), in the area around Leyden, laid the foundations for the earliest of the Dutch *hoogheemraadschappen*, it was Floris V (1256–96) who tried to set up a central authority for hydraulic matters throughout the country (in a period when the prime concern was the maintenance of dikes). These efforts towards centralisation would continue later under Charles V in 1544, without great success.[57] The central ministry, the *Waterstaat*, would only truly come into being in 1795, an expression of that élan and spirit of renewal resulting from the period of Napoleonic dominion.[58]

As for the polders, a certain common pattern can be identified in their structure; however, whilst there is no doubt such entities were precociously modern, it would be rather rash to define then as 'democratic' *tout court*. First set up in the twelfth century (the earliest Zeeland polders being established by local lords), they envisaged wide representation of landowners in open assemblies. There was in fact a more egalitarian, and extensive, degree of representation than that to be found in the later *heemraadschappen*, given that – from a legal point of view – the local nobility's right to vote in such assemblies rested solely on their status as land-owners, which they shared with all the other farmers of the polder.[59]

Dutch *regenten* and Venetian *rentiers*:
A Comparison of Two Patrician Classes

A comparison of Dutch *regenten* and Venetian *rentiers* immediately brings out the differences between the situations in the two states. In Venice – as in the Netherlands and other countries of northern Europe – the process of land reclamation which took place in the Middle Ages had been largely under the aegis of the great Benedictine monasteries (even if cities and rural communities did sometimes take an important role).[60] However, from the fifteenth and sixteenth centuries onwards, it would be the Venetian patrician class that became the driving-force behind land reclamation.

Here one must look at the ways drainage operations were carried out and at the limitations of the procedures followed. In the Low Countries, these projects were essentially carried out by a free coalition of land-owners determined to reclaim new land for agriculture, while in the Venetian Republic they were carried out by patricians, who could be said to have imposed relations of production that were much more feudalistic than capitalistic. The characteristic feature of such projects in Venice was that, thanks to legislation and the bodies in charge of organising such work and the laws applied by them, those who were enabled to make sizeable additions to their mainland estates were the city patricians, not the local nobility or other classes of landowners.[61]

However, social relations within the Republic of the United Provinces should not be made to fit a 'democratic' model that ill-reflects historical reality. For example, the open assemblies that were held within the polders did not prevent certain landowners from carrying more weight than others when it came to deciding upon key matters. What is more, the administration of the polders was almost entirely in the hands of such large property owners: the small landowners may have voted for the *college van hoofdingelanden*, but it was the *dijkgraaf* (lord of the dikes) and the *heemraden* who guided the decisions made by that collegial body.[62] Tensions could easily rise to the surface when it came to sharing out the cost of work amongst all the various land-owners, while no less serious conflicts at a territorial level could emerge between polders and villages when it came to the actual disposal of the water of the canals which enclosed village or polder.[63]

In effect, this may have been a precociously capitalistic model of agriculture, but when one comes to look at the economic exploitation of water there is evidence of conflict between large estate-owners and the local population: marshy areas here and elsewhere in Europe were connected with certain typical activities – fishing, hunting, the extraction of peat and salt, the harvesting of marsh grasses as fodder and the collection of raw materials for other craft products – and the presence of these resources could well serve to heighten conflict over land reclamation.[64]

Another parallel between Venice and Holland emerges from the historical literature which describes how landowners who lived in Amsterdam or other Dutch cities had large bourgeois and aristocratic homes built for themselves within the polders – residences that were not that different from the more famous villas of the Veneto. It is also true that in periods of crisis or economic stagnation these renowned entrepreneurs preferred to follow exactly the same policy as their more heavily-criticised Venetian counterparts: they simply rented out their land rather than working it themselves.[65]

Nevertheless, there is no question that in the seventeenth century the spirit of capitalistic enterprise was much stronger in Holland than in the Veneto – and that spirit was essentially bound up with the land; as one historian has observed 'capitalism in Holland grew out of the soil'.[66] For confirmation of this, one need only look at the *kavels* – those rectangular or square strips of land into which the polders were divided. They may not have been very big (when compared, for example, to the fields of the Ile-de-France), but they were always laid out with extreme regularity, which guaranteed a high level of productivity and – above all – reflected close links with organised markets. In Wieringerwaard, for example, 75 per cent of the agricultural land in 1611 was divided into plots that varied in size between 20 and 60 hectares; in Purmer in 1622, 87 per cent of the landholdings were no bigger than 60 hectares, with a good 46 per cent being between 32 and 40 hectares in size; and in Schermer (1635) three landowners controlled 14 per cent of the entire polder (4,872 hectares), while the rest was divided up between 272 owners. Figures in Beemster for 1612 were slightly higher, with 41 per cent of owners having landholdings varying from 80 to 120 hectares.[67]

One other essential feature is the extent of urban capital investment in recently-reclaimed land – a phenomenon which was not restricted to the Venetian mainland. Although the primary role of Venice (rather than the other mainland cities) in the reclamation of the terra firma has already been highlighted, the complex network of relations that would develop between the various Dutch cities has yet to be studied in full. For instance, in the village of Zijpe, in 1597, 47 per cent of the land was owned by just forty-six Amsterdamers, whose predominance would be slightly undermined in the centuries to come by landowners from other cities (Alkmaar, Den Haag, Haarlem and Utrecht), with these newcomers playing a more dynamic role.[68]

Although speculation and the stubborn defence of individual economic interests were more clearly a feature of land-owning on the Venetian mainland (it is no coincidence that the term *rentiers* is much more commonly used of the Venetian rather than the Dutch aristocracy), one would be wrong in seeing the situation in Holland as being entirely one of 'bourgeois capitalism'. Throughout the sixteenth and seventeenth centuries, the Counts of Holland – together with the various aristocratic authorities in the other provinces – continued to insist upon the payment of feudal-style dues upon newly-reclaimed agricultural land. It is true that these fiscal burdens gradually became much lighter as the nobility – much to their credit – realised the economic advantages, in terms of population growth and overall fiscal yield, of offering an – at least indirect – stimulus to the process already underway.[69] Similarly, as Faber's study of Friesland illustrates, the burden of church ownership of land did not disappear altogether. Another conservative factor was the role played by *regenten*, whose fortune originated in the exercise of political power rather than in Calvinist-inspired economic and entrepreneurial activities.[70] Further evidence of a feudal model can be seen in Drentha, where there were few farms owned by monasteries and nobility yet throughout the seventeenth century tithes remained relatively high (as did the various other payments many landowners were obliged to make to the nobility).[71]

This does not mean that during the course of the sixteenth and seventeenth centuries favourable economic conditions did not lead both the nobility and the *regenten* to join bourgeois speculators in investing in land-reclamation and dike-building projects. In effect, the small local landowners were left with only a minor role to play in the promotion of capitalistic agriculture.[72] As just one illustration of this point one might mention that when work began on the drainage of the Beemster and Purmer meres in the seventeenth century, four of the sixteen large landowners and investors involved were part of the ruling elite in Amsterdam: Pieter Boom, Barthold Cromhout, Janten Grootenhuis and Jacob Poppen.[73]

Venetian Land Reclamation and Dutch Polders: Two Different Trends

Land reclamation almost always goes together with an inclination to economic speculation, as can be seen in numerous projects in both the Veneto and the Low Countries, where population growth (particularly high in the sixteenth and seventeenth centuries) created a need for more agricultural land, and investors were looking for a greater return on their capital. Undoubtedly, a comparison of the two regions reveals that land had always been a more precious commodity in the Netherlands, which explains the early building of dikes along river banks and coastlines. In effect, geographical studies have revealed that up to the fourteenth century the main problems there were those posed by the sea, hence the focus had been on coastal defences rather than drainage dikes (though some such projects had been undertaken from the Middle Ages onwards).[74] Such studies have also highlighted the need to give due weight to climatic and geo-hydrological features rather than simply focusing on economic factors.[75] However, while it is easy to point out such requirements, it is much more difficult to actually chart the reciprocal influences at play between geography and economics.

What is beyond doubt is that by the end of the Middle Ages both Venice and Holland were undergoing commercial and economic growth, with territorial expansion being essential if necessary food supplies were to be guaranteed. In effect, medieval Venice had always been able to rely on its colonies for supplies of wheat, but from the sixteenth century onwards it could no longer take these for granted; hence it looked to its mainland in order to overcome reliance on overseas sources over which it no longer exercised unquestioned control. Although there are some differences in the timetable of events, it is essentially true that from the end of the fifteenth/beginning of the sixteenth century in both states one can see a sizeable increase in the areas of reclaimed land: in Holland, mainly along the coast, though with some inland areas; in Venice, in

Map 2. Land Drainage Project for the Schermeer (1635) by the Town of Alkmaar, Drawn Up by Claes J. Visscher. The regularity of the plots reveals the advanced agricultural strategy behind the scheme. Source: A.J. Haartsen et al., *Een verkenning van de cultuur-historische betekenis van het Nederlandse landschap*, 's-Gravenhage, 1989, p. 83.

the marshy plain areas. This means that the two regions are much more comparable than is often claimed.

It is true that Venetian drainage projects always relied on the force of gravity – rather than the mechanical power that was frequently used in the Low Countries – but this did not mean that the areas of land reclaimed by the two states during the course of the sixteenth century were not equally vast. It has, in fact, been estimated that the agricultural land reclaimed in Holland between 1540 and 1615 amounted to around 80,000 hectares: 70,000 through the construction of sea-barrier dikes (*bedijkingen*) and 10,000 through the drainage of inland terrain and meres (*droogmakerijen*);[76] Smith's figure for the total land reclaimed in this period is slightly lower 73,400 hectares.[77] In Venice over the same period it is estimated that around 77,000 hectares of low-lying or marshland were recovered for agriculture (above all in the areas of Padua and Rovigo, where the interests of the Venetian nobility were greatest).[78] It was only in the seventeenth and eighteenth centuries that the Venetian Republic would fall behind the United Provinces, with total estimates for the land reclaimed by the two states over the period 1500 to 1800 being 180,000 and 280,000 hectares respectively.[79]

Obviously, during the course of the seventeenth century the relative positions of Venice and Holland were inverted. The world economy had by then shifted to the North Sea, and Holland was not only playing the role that Venice had played in the fifteenth and sixteenth centuries, it also had a network of colonial links with Asia, Africa and the Americas (as has been observed, without that expansion westwards, expansion east and northwards would have been unthinkable).[80] Undoubtedly, the economic careers of the two states were now running in opposite directions: in both population flux and grain prices, the trend was upwards in Holland, downwards in Venice. What is more, Holland was now playing a fundamental role as a broker in the grain trade, handling the Baltic wheat supplies which began to arrive in the Mediterranean in the first decades of the sixteenth century.[81] As Jonathan Israel's research has shown, traditional historical accounts have tended to underestimate the size of the Dutch presence in the Mediterranean. All of these factors could not but have a negative effect on Venice's balance of trade – and on the attitudes of Venetian land-owners. It was almost inevitable at this point that these latter should become entrenched within economic conservatism.[82]

The 'Golden Age' of Dutch Land Reclamation: The Drainage of the Inland Meres

This conjunction of favourable circumstances would play a part in the 'Golden Age' of Dutch land reclamation, with the drainage of the large inland marshes during the first half of the seventeenth century producing terrain that would turn out to be amongst the most fertile in the entire country, particularly for the raising of livestock[83] (even if, immediately after draining, farmers initially preferred to fertilise the over-soft and over-humid land and use it for cereal crops).[84] In effect, this new land made a sizeable contribution to the 'agricultural revolution' within the Netherlands, and greatly boosted the country's output: in the seventeenth century, its productivity was double that of Eastern Europe and Scandinavia.[85]

The drainage of these marsh-lands also produced a remedy for the damage caused by the digging of peat, which was comparable to wind-power as a source of energy in the Netherlands (not only in the seventeenth and eighteenth centuries, but also in the nineteenth and twentieth). The massive quantities cut since the Middle Ages had led to subsidence and the flooding of agricultural land;[86] while the dangers peat-cutting posed had continued unabated (especially as the material was also used for building houses in the newly-drained polders).[87] The business was such that cutting and extraction had actually led to the formation of specialised companies managed according to capitalist criteria, which might also finance drainage operations but only rarely played a role in the later agricultural exploitation of the land. Typical examples of commercial capitalism, these companies moved from area to area, region to region, motivated solely by considerations of profit and making little investment in the means of production. It was only in the nineteenth century that their activities would come under some sort of state control, with central government imposing overall plans for territorial development (which up to that point had been largely in the hands of individual regions).[88] The economic importance of – and therefore increase in – peat-cutting, often carried out by settlements of peat-diggers and or, farmers, is well-illustrated by the fact that the 250,000 hectares of peat marshes in the Middle Ages had become 180,000 hectares by 1800; exploitation after that date would then increase even further, given that in the later decades of the twentieth century there were only 4,000 hectares of peat marsh.[89]

By the time the reclamation of the inland meres was undertaken, technological advances had made draining procedures much more efficient. At the beginning of the fifteenth century, a water-wheel (connected to a windmill) had made it possible to raise the water in the drainage channels from about 1.5 to 2 metres, but with the increasing use of Archimedes' screws in the following decades, that figure rose to 2 or 3 and even 4 metres; such technology was already used in draining the six small meres of Noorderkwartier in northern Holland in 1550. Around the same time, the Count of Egmont (the traditional nobility played an important role in such projects at this date) began the drainage of Egmondmeer, whilst the Baron of Brederode had the Bergermmer near Alkmaar-Limmen drained. However, it was the entrance of the mercantile bourgeoisie into such projects that led to significant progress in the amount of land reclaimed and the technology used in the process (for example, the use of the Archimedes' screw instead of the traditional water wheel).[90] And scholars have shown how the creation of the polders had an effect on the development of cartography, given that maps played an important – and very concrete – role in the sharing-out of the land within each polder and in the resolution of complex hydrological problems.[91]

The results in quantitative terms can be summarised using the following figures: in the period 1590–1615, the annual average of land reclaimed from the sea and inland meres was 1,448 hectares, which rose to 1,783 hectares in 1615–40 (the average from 1565–90 had been only 321 hectares, even if that from 1540–65 had been 1,474 hectares). The progress is even clearer when one looks at the draining of inland meres, which rises from an annual average of 9,149 hectares in 1590–1615 to 19,060 hectares in 1615–40, whilst the area of the polders reclaimed from the sea actually fell from 27,064 hectares in 1590–1615 to 25,513 hectares in the years 1615-40.[92] As the following table illustrates, the drainage depth of the *droogmakerijen* also increased over time.

The project that is perhaps most representative of this period of intense activity is that involving the Beemster mere, on which worked one of the most famous technicians and windmill-builders of the age, Leeghwater. In popular tradition, his name – which actually means 'to drain off water', *leeg water* – is associated with the early sixteenth-century trend towards agricultural development of the inland areas, just as around the end of the sixteenth century the name of Vierlingh and his treatise on dikes represented the opposite trend, towards the reclamation of coastal areas.

But if technology used all the means at its disposal for undertakings of this scale (a total of twenty-one windmills, for example, were set up around the shores of Beemster mere), there were a whole series of obstacles and problems to be overcome before the projects could be brought to completion. It was not uncommon, for example, for the schemes to have to be reviewed or re-financed: during the course of the seventeenth century, the necessary average investment in such work was considered to be around 1,500 guilders per hectare, but often the value of the land reclaimed fell short of this because it turned out to be 'too muddy or too peaty or too sandy'.[94] And then there was the problem of the dikes themselves, through which water began to seep, if it did not indeed overflow them or break through them entirely. Windmills could not of course work all the time as they depended on the presence of wind, so regular pumping could not be guaranteed; this meant that – perhaps at the end of the winter or the beginning of spring – water that may have been accumulating for weeks had to be drawn off. And once the polder had been reclaimed, it might be difficult to maintain satisfactory relations among the agents involved: if the land turned out to be not very profitable, tenants – as well as investors – faced difficulties, with insufficient earnings meaning they were unable to pay their land rents.[95]

Then there were the problems posed by the forces of nature, which apparently took every opportunity to reclaim the reclaimed. It

Mere	Drained	Drainage depth (metres)
Wogmeer	1607–1608	2–2.5
Beemster	1607–1612	3.5
Purmer	1617–1622	4
Wormer	1624–1626	4
Heerhugowaard	1625–1631	2.5
Schermer	1631–1635	3.5[93]

is true that, compared to the previous century, the first half of the seventeenth century saw a drop in the number of high tides. Yet the dikes of Beemster were seriously damaged by a north-eastern storm (1610) with the land being flooded (in 1625 the polders of Wormer and Wieringerwaard would suffer just as badly).[96] As a result, the number of windmills on the banks of the Beemster was doubled to forty-two to make up for lost time, so that by 1612 it was possible to fully exploit the recently-reclaimed land (all 7,100 hectares), with the peat dug from the bottom of the mere being used to build new farmhouses.[97] Thereafter would come the draining of the Purmer mere (2,756 hectares in 1622), of Heerhugowaard (3,500 hectares in 1630) and Schermer (4,770 hectares in 1635), thus completing an important period in such reclamation schemes. There would not be another comparable period of expansion until the early decades of the nineteenth century, with the drainage of the Zuidplaspolder in 1840 (4,143 hectares) and the Haarlemmermeer (18,100 hectares) making use of modern steam-driven water pumps.[98]

Eighteenth-Century Stagnation: An Unexpected Parallel

Around the middle of the seventeenth century the trend in land-reclamation in the Low Countries starts to become much more problematic. For example, Leeghwater's proposed scheme for the drainage of Haarlemmermeer came to nothing.[99] Is this clear proof that circumstances were no longer as favourable as they had been? This is just one area of activity covered by the on-going debates about the declining economic fortunes of Holland and the Venetian Republic. In effect, it is argued that whilst the term of 'decline' seems applicable to Venice as early as the start of the sixteenth century (with the *rentier* taking the place of the *entrepreneur*),[100] the same phenomenon does not appear to be observable in Holland until the second half of the seventeenth century. However, such interpretations always make one of two mistakes: either they offer too crude a picture of historical events, or they overlook the fact that the political and economic structures of the two states had become so consolidated over time that their accumulated resources (primarily financial resources) could hardly run out overnight. What is more, though the high salaries – and particularly the high cost of labour – in the two capital cities might well undermine competitiveness in a rapidly-changing international market, these very salaries reveal a high standard of living; thus the term 'crisis' is open to very different interpretations.[101] When one looks at Holland alone, what one sees is increasingly tough international competition, decline in demand for agricultural and industrial goods, and a standstill in population growth (Klein suggests that annual demographic growth in the period 1675–1860 was as low as 0.75 per cent). In such a situation, the shift of capital to other sectors is not necessarily the expression of merely passive economic strategies.[102]

This means that in the period of depression – normally given as the years 1650–1750 – Dutch agriculture continued to develop.[103] As for trade, more recent studies, for example, have argued that the 'zenith' point in Dutch economic development came a few decades later.[104] Nevertheless, during the eighteenth century both Venice and Holland were on the sidelines of the rapid economic development being enjoyed by some other countries, and this clearly had an effect upon the use and maintenance of agricultural land. It is no coincidence that the limited earnings of both the Dutch polders and the Venetian land-reclamation consortia reveal a chronic crisis. The Dutch economy in particular was brought to its knees by the drop in the price of grain, the loss of traditional markets (particularly in southern Europe) and the downturn in the prices of cheese and meat.[105] According to Ad van der Woude, the worst period of crisis in Noorderkwartier was from 1730–1755, paradoxically when agricultural prices in many European countries appeared to be taking an up-turn; this same region saw a 40–45 per cent drop in population over the period 1650–1750. Within the agricultural sector as a whole, the conversion of dairy to meat herds was probably intended to save on the costs of manpower; and anyway, many of the areas drained in the seventeenth century proved to be much more suitable for the raising of livestock than for intensive cultivation.

Whatever the truth, it is beyond doubt that the increasing difficulties in financing maintenance work on the dikes and other works of hydraulic engineering – together with a worsening in weather conditions, probably due to a new 'transgression phase' of climatic change – led to the introduction of heavy taxation (in the period of greatest expansion exactly the opposite policy had been followed). This greater fiscal burden inevitably made the land less profitable, with urban capital consequently seeking out other

economic sectors (primarily finance).[106] Two other – far from
negligible – factors made the situation even worse: salaries (which
remained high) and the fact that the cost of timber and other raw
materials necessary for the maintenance of hydraulic infrastructures
did not follow the same downward curve as grain prices.[107] C.
Baars's study of the Beijerlanden region reveals the following
development in the profit/cost ratios of dike-building:

Year	Costs (guilders per hectare)	Profit
1582	108	72
1615	204	104
1632	235	208
1653	383	85[108]

As one can see, the trend of increasing profitability had slumped
by the middle of the seventeenth century. It may well have been to
make up for the drop in private interest in such schemes that the
state intervened more and more often to take a guiding role in new
drainage projects (as Thurkow argues was the case in the polders of
Bleiswijk and Hillegersberg).[109]

More recent studies have tried to take a more optimistic tone
when talking about the Dutch economy – and particularly Dutch
agriculture – in this period. For example, in his comparative analysis
of the different interpretations of the Dutch crisis put forward by van
der Woude, Jan de Vries, Riley, Spooner and Johan de Vries, Van
Zanden has recently argued that the conclusions reached by Johan de
Vries should be re-assessed.[110] What is more, there was an up-turn in
the creation of polders (in both the south and north Netherlands)
during the second half of the eighteenth century.[111] Nevertheless, in
spite of the documentary evidence supporting a certain degree of
'revisionism', the overall impression is of financial and hydro-
geological decline in many polders (especially when compared with
the previous century). However, on the basis of some French eye-
witness accounts written during the Napoleonic period, the Dutch
remained true to their reputation for dedicating great care and
attention to the maintenance of dikes.[112] As a final note, one should
point out that the chronic situation of debt within the polders would

only be slightly alleviated by the increase in grain prices in the later decades of the eighteenth century.[113]

As has already been pointed out, the drainage canals and land-reclamation projects designed to protect the Venice lagoon were not always as advantageous as intended; but in Amsterdam, too, one sees a port that required canals and dredging which posed equally serious problems.[114] Nevertheless, although the Dutch administration was perhaps not as efficient as it had once been, there is no doubt that the situation was much more dynamic than it was in Venice. Think, for example, of the efforts made by the great hydraulic engineer Cruquius to establish a standard point of reference for all coastal and inland water-levels (a standard that would ultimately be fixed as the water-level of Amsterdam). The project involved measuring the height above water-level of all the shorelines, dunes, *boezems* and polders of Holland; and even though it would not be carried out for the whole of the country, it did begin for the region of Rijnland in 1743.[115] What is more, when Cruquius in Delft started to compile the oldest records of rainfall in the Low Countries – apparently for the period 1715–25 – he was acting a whole decade before Poleni began to keep similar records in Padua (1725); more systematic registers of rainfall would begin to be kept in Holland from 1735 onwards.

A few years later (1743) at 'Huize Zwandenburg' there would be statistical studies of another metro-hydro-geological phenomenon: evaporation, which had a direct effect on the problems involved in drainage projects and the time necessary for their implementation. There would also be serious statistical study of the winds as well; although these would only become truly systematic from 1840 onwards.[116]

Another similarity can be noted between the two states during this period of crisis, even if historians of both have seen this particular factor as being unique to one or the other. I am referring to the proliferation of a marine worm which, in Holland and Venice, became ever more voracious in its consumption of the timber used in dikes and thus highlighted the need to replace the traditional wooden defences with stonework. Looking at the series of projects whose results are still before us, one can perhaps say that the changeover in Venice occurred more slowly than in Holland. What is certain is that whilst Bernardino Zendrini was completing the Venetian *murazzi* [large rough-block sea defences at the Lido], Pieter

Straat and Pieter van der Deure were designing stone dikes for the
western coast of Friesland (naturally according to rather different
technical specifications). Other sea walls were also constructed along
the coast of Noorderkwartier, costing up to 5 to 6 million florins and
obtaining results that were in no way inferior to those Venetian
historians have claimed for Zendrini's *murazzi*; the advantages of
Venice's new construction mortar (*pozzolana*) were more than
counterbalanced by Dutch technological superiority in other
areas.[117]

In conclusion, therefore, one should point out that while the
tendency in the writings of contemporaries and subsequent
historians has been to consider each state as unique, focusing
attention upon the differences between them, such diversity should
not prevent us from seeing a close interconnection between the two,
both in their technological innovations and their technological
inadequacies.

Notes

1. Wittfogel, *Oriental Despotism. A Comparative Study of Total Power*; see also J.H.
   Steward, 'Initiation of a Research Trend: Wittfogel's Irrigation Hypothesis', in
   Society and History. Essays in Honour of Karl August Wittfogel, Ulmen ed., pp.
   3–10.
2. Glick, *Irrigation and Society in Medieval Valencia*, pp. 4–5.
3. In the Tokugawa period, the feudal powers of Japan were involved in such
   large projects of land reclamation and irrigation in the coastal areas; but
   there might also be the participation of rich merchants and wealthy
   landowners. A number of these projects were concerned with high-profit
   rice cultivation (F. Toshio, 'The Village and Agriculture During the Edo
   Period', in *The Cambridge History of Japan. Early Modern Japan*, J.W. Hall ed.,
   IV, Cambridge, 1997[2], pp. 498–502).
4. Guicciardini, *Descrittione di tutti i Paesi Bassi*, p. 184. On Guicciardini see
   the Proceedings of the Colloquium edited by P. Jodogne (*Lodovico
   Guicciardini, Florence 1521–Anvers 1589*, Leuven, 1991). The influence of the
   republican tradition in Venice upon political thought in seventeenth-century
   Holland is thoroughly examined in Haitsma Mulier, *The Myth of Venice and
   Dutch Republican Thought in the Seventeenth Century*.
5. Braudel, *Civilisation matérielle, économie et capitalisme*, III, p. 12ff.; Wallerstein,
   *The Modern World-system. Mercantilism and the Consolidation of the European
   World-economy*, II, p. 37ff. Some doubts have been expressed as to the effective
   standing of Venice as a 'world-economy' when compared to some other cities
   (primarily Antwerp in the second half of the of the sixteenth century). See the

fundamentally-opposed view in Israel, *Dutch primacy in world trade, 1585–1740*. It is true that in performing this role as a *world-economy* Venice is to be seen in conjunction with the whole of the Po valley and Florence.

6. Ciriacono, 'The Venetian Economy and its Place in the World Economy of the 17th and 18th Centuries', pp. 120–35. See Dodgsohn's claims regarding the changing characteristics of world-economies during the course of history (R.A. Dodgsohn, 'The Early Modern World-system: a Critique of its Inner Dynamics', in *The Early Modern World-system in Geographical Perspective*, Nitz ed., pp. 26–41).

7. J.A. Faber, 'De achttiende eeuw', in *De economische geschiedenis van Nederland*, J.H. van Stuijvenberg ed., Groningen, 1977, pp. 122–28; C. Vandenbroeke, 'Landbouw in de Zuidelijke Nederlanden 1650–1815', in *Algemene Geschiedenis der Nederlanden*, Blok and Prevenier eds., VIII, 1979, p. 73.

8. Berengo, *La società veneta alla fine del Settecento*, pp. 103–10.

9. Braudel, *Civilisation matérielle, économie et capitalisme*, III, p. 150.

10. Vierlingh, *Tractaat van Dijckagie*. Vierlingh's *Treatise* is fundamental to understanding the technology and techniques used in this period in building dikes; it also provides an original overall picture of the social context of such work and how it was organised: Baars, 'Andries Vierlingh', pp. 15–19.

11. Leeghwater, *Een kleyne Chronycke*, pp. 45–47. Leeghwater, a native of Rijp, describes himself as an engineer and a builder of windmills. Claes Arentsz. Coleveldt, a contemporary of Leeghwater's, does show a certain knowledge of what was happening in Italy, giving an informed description of the situation of the Arno: J.A. Leeghwater, *Haarlemmermeer boek*. I quote from the seventh edition (Amsterdam 1710), p. 3.

12. F. Cazzola, 'Le bonifiche', in *Cultura popolare nell'Emilia-Romagna. Strutture rurali e vita contadina*, L. Gambi ed., II, Milan, 1977, pp. 57–65; Wagret, *Les polders*, pp. 111–13.

13. Korthals Altes, *Polderland in Italië*, pp. 139–52, spec. p. 142. See also Baars, 'Landaanwinning door Nederlanders in Frankrijk en Italië', pp. 19–20.

14. Hoogewerff, *Bescheiden in Italië*, III, pp. 421–27.

15. O. De Smet, 'Willem de Raet', Biography in the *Nationaal Biografisch Woordenboek*, II, Brussels, 1966, kol.719–23.

16. G.J. Hoogewerff, *De twee reizen van Cosimo de' Medici*, (Amsterdam 1919), quoted by J. Belonie, *De Schermermeer, 1633–1933*, Wormerveer, 1933, p. 32. Thanks to Dutch technicians, the plain of Pisa and (temporarily) the Albenga region were reclaimed during the reigns of Granddukes Ferdinando I and Cosimo III in the seventeenth century: Wagret, *Les polders*, p. 113.

17. Korthals Altes, *Polderland in Italië*, p. 26.

18. Lambert, *The Making of the Dutch Landscape*, p. 213; A. Stella, 'Dalle bonifiche benedettine alla grande azienda agricola', in *La corte benedettina di Correzzola*, Padua, 1982, p. 10; L. Gambi, 'Acque ed ecologia', in *Agricoltura e trasformazione dell'ambiente*, Guarducci ed., p. 662.

186 *Building on Water*

19. A. Kaijser, 'System Building from Below: Institutional Change in Dutch Water Systems', in *Water Technology in the Netherlands*, Reuss ed. p. 531; Lingsma, *Les Pays-Bas: économie des eaux*, Rotterdam, 1970, p. 10.
20. Schultz, *Waterbeheersing van de Nederlandse droogmakerijen*, p. 228.
21. Doorman, *Patents for Inventions*, pp. 41–43 and 90–210; R.J. Forbes, 'The Drainage Mills. Introduction', in *The Principal Works of Simon Stevin. The Works on Engineering*, Forbes ed., Amsterdam, 1966, vol. V, pp. 311–13.
22. Keunen, 'Waterbeheersing en de ontwikkeling van de bemalingstechniek', pp. 571–606, esp. p. 76.
23. The historical and contemporary literature on windmills and their regional variations is vast. A classic work is L. van Natrus, J. Polly and C. van Vuuren, *Groot volkomen moolenboek*, Amsterdam, 1734, but see also T. van der Horst, *Théâtre universel des machines*, Amsterdam, 1737 and J. van Zyl, J. Schenk, *Theatrum machinarum universale*, Amsterdam, 1734; on the Middle Ages, A. Bicker Caarten, *Middeleeuwse watermolens in Hollands polderland 1407/'08–rondom 1500*, Wormerveer, 1990.
24. Schultz, *Waterbeheersing van de Nederlandse droogmakerijen*, p. 30. A good 52 windmills were used in draining the Schermer: Van der Linden, 'L'influence de l'eau sur les institutions rurales hollandaises', p. 678.
25. The first use of *boezem* was in the 1486 drainage project at Haastrecht, which used the small river Vliest (Keunen, 'Waterbeheersing en de ontwikkeling van de bemalingstechniek', p. 579).
26. Beekman, *Nederland als polderland*, pp. 8–9. A fundamental work is also Beekman *Het dijk- en waterschapsrecht in Nederland voor 1795*. On *boezems* see Monkhouse, *A Regional Geography*, p. 41 .
27. Doorman, *Patents for Inventions*, p. 81; R.J. Forbes, 'Hydraulic Engineering. Introduction', in *The Principal Works of Simon Stevin*, Forbes ed., V, p. 80.
28. Doorman, *Patents for Inventions*, p. 83.
29. A.S.V., S.T., *filza* 133, 18 September 1594. See also *Laguna, lidi, fiumi*, Tiepolo ed., pp. 67–69.
30. Berveglieri, 'Tecnologia idraulica olandese in Italia nel secolo XVII', pp. 81–97. It would, however, seem that a first version of Meijer's dredger had been used in Holland before the seventeenth century (Van Veen, *Dredge, Drain, Reclaim*, p. 79). An illustration of a sophisticated dredger (but not a horse-powered dredger) is in the Codex Grevembroich in the Library of the Museo Correr in Venice and quoted by B. Roeck, 'Wasser, Politik und Bürokratie. Venedig in der frühen Neuzeit', in *Die alte Stadt*, 20 (1993), p. 218.
31. Berveglieri, 'Tecnologia idraulica olandese in Italia nel secolo XVII', pp. 89–90; Van Veen, *Dredge, Drain, Reclaim*, pp. 76–80.
32. Klaas van Berkel, *In het voetspoor van Stevin. Geschiedenis van de natuurwetenschap in Nederland, 1580–1940*, Boom Meppel, 1985, p. 25; see also *Admissies als landmeter in Nederland voor 1811. Bronnen voor de geschiedenis van de landmeetkunde*, E. Muller and K. Zandvliet eds., Alphen aan den Rijn, 1987.

33. C. Baars, 'Leeghwater: een herwaardering', in *Spiegel Historiael*, 21 (1986), p. 3.

34. G.J. Borger, 'Ontgonnen, bedijkt, bebouwd. De agrarische voorgeschiedenis van het stedelijk gebied, 15e-17e eeuw', in *Amsterdam in kaarten. Verandering van de stad in vier eeuwen cartografie*, W.F. Heinemeijer et al. eds., Ede, 1987, pp. 16-19.

35. Vierlingh, *Tractaat van Dijckagie*, p. 219, quoted in H. van der Linden, 'De Nederlandse waterhuishouding en waterstaatsorganisatie tot aan de moderne tijd', in *Bijdragen en Mededelingen betreffende de Geschiedenis der Nederlanden*, 103 (1988), p. 550; see also Baars, 'Andries Vierlingh', p. 17.

36. A fundamental overview of dikes is given in Barentsen, 'De zeedijk van zijn ontstaan tot het jaar 1730'; see also J. van der Kley, *Polders en dijken*, Amsterdam, 1969, p. 206. On the sluices, Petra J.E.M. van Dam, 'Ecological challenges, technological innovations: the modernization of sluice building in Holland, 1300-1600', in *Water Technology in the Netherlands*, Reuss ed., pp. 500-20.

37. Tiepolo, 'Difese a mare', in *Mostra storica della laguna veneta*, pp. 133-35; Barentsen, 'De zeedijk van zijn ontstaan tot het jaar 1730', pp. 200-1.

38. Baars, 'Andries Vierlingh', p. 17.

39. H.T. Obreen, *Dijkplicht en waterschappen aan Frieslands westkust*, Bolsward, 1956, pp. 252-57; C. Baars, 'Willem Symonsz en Cornelis Jansz Scravelinck', in *Waterbouw*, 37 (1982), n.3, p. 17.

40. M. Aymard, 'L'arsenale e le conoscenze tecnico- marinaresche. Le arti', in *Storia della cultura veneta. Dal primo Quattrocento al Concilio di Trento*, Arnaldi and Pastore Stocchi eds., 3/II, 292-93.

41. De Hullu-Verhouven, 'Inleiding' to Vierlingh, *Tractaat van Dijckagie*, p. xxiii.

42. C. Baars, 'Geschiedenis van de bedijking van het Deltagebied', in *Landbouwkundig Tijdschrift*, 91 (1979), pp. 29-36.; idem, 'Geschiedenis van de dijkbouw in het Deltagebied', ibid., 92 (1980), pp. 15-23; idem, 'Nederlandse bedijkingsdeskundigen in de 16e-18e eeuw. Cornelis Claesz van Zuidkerke, Dirck Hendricxs en Jan Symonsz', in *Civiele Techniek*, 37 (1982), pp. 15-19.

43. H. van der Wee, 'Die Niederlande, 1350-1650', in *Handbuch der europäischen Wirtschafts- und Sozialgeschichte, 1350-1650*, W. Fischer ed., III, Stuttgart, 1986, p. 577; M.K.E. Gottschalk, 'Some Aspects of the Development of Historical Geography in the Netherlands', in *Tijdschrift van het Koninklijk Nederlandsch Aardrijkskundig Genootschap*, 77 (1960), n. 3, p. 320.

44. J. De Wal, *Specimen juridicum inaugurale de potestate legislatoria collegiorum curatorum*, Den Haag, 1850, p. 13.

45. From the old Dutch 'darink' and the modern Dutch 'derrie'.

46. Guicciardini, *Descrittione di tutti i Paesi Bassi*, p. 204. On Guicciardini, still considered a valuable and reliable source with regard to the Low Countries, see D. Aristodemo, 'La figura e l'opera di Lodovico Guicciardini:

prospettive di ricerca', in *Lodovico Guicciardini, Florence 1521–Anvers 1589*, Jodogne ed., p. 20 and n.

47. C. Maccagni, 'Mechanics and Hydrostatic in the Late Renaissance: Relations between Italy and the Low Countries', in *Italian Scientists in the Low Countries*, Maffioli and Palm eds., pp. 79 and 94–96. For example, Simon Stevin had direct knowledge of the theories of G.B. Benedetti. This does not change the fact that during the course of the seventeenth and eighteenth century links between the post-Galileo school in Italy and scientists in the North of Europe became more tenuous.

48. R.J. Forbes, 'Hydraulic Engineering. Introduction', in *The Principal Works of Simon Stevin. The Works on Engineering*, Forbes ed., V, pp. 67–72.

49. J.A. Brongers, 'Technische ontwikkelingen', in *Algemene Geschiedenis der Nederlanden*, Blok and Prevenier eds., VII, 1980, pp. 359–60; R.J. Forbes, 'The Drainage Mills. Introduction', in *The Principal Works of Simon Stevin. The Works on Engineering*, Forbes ed., V, pp. 319–20.

50. A 'country-lordly freedom ... which was new and unique in this period when compared with the surrounding countries of the continent': idem, 'History of the reclamation of the western Fenlands and of the organisation to keep them drained', in *Proceedings of the Symposium on Peat Lands below Sea Level*, H. de Bakker and M.W. van den Berg eds., Wageningen, 1982, p. 61.

51. Idem, 'L'influence de l'eau sur les institutions rurales hollandaises', pp. 668–69.

52. A. Verhulst, 'Compte-rendu' to *De Cope* in *Revue Belge de Philologie et d'Histoire*, 35 (1957), p. 161–66; idem and B. Augustyn, 'Deich- und Dammbau', Item in *Lexikon des Mittelalters*, III, München-Zürich, 1986, pp. 643–44.

53. Fockema Andreae, too, finds a significant example of this community spirit in medieval Spain, especially Valencia. There, as mentioned, the public authorities oversaw a rational and varied use of the canals (S.J. Fockema Andreae, 'Het Watergerecht van Valencia', in *Mededelingen der Koninklijke Nederlandse Akademie van Wetenschappen, afd. Letterkunde*, deel 23, 14 (1960), pp. 385–401).

54. Community organisations to oversee the control and management of water would also quickly developed in twelfth-century Flanders (even if they did not imply communal exploitation of the land). These *Wateringen* had their own representatives and their own accounts; but the initial impetus to set them up came from the nobility, on whom their administration depended. Verhulst and Augustyn, 'Deich- und Dammbau', cit., p. 642; S.J. Fockema Andreae, 'L'eau et les hommes de la Flandre maritime', in *Tijdschrift voor Rechtsgeschiedenis*, 28 (1960), pp. 181–96).

55. Dion, *Le Val de Loire.*, pp. 324–72, esp. p. 364.

56. Ibid., pp. 378–79.

57. C. Dekker, 'De vertegenwoordiging van de geërfden in de wateringen van Zeeland bewesten Schelde in de middeleeuwen', in *Bijdragen en Mededelingen betreffende de Geschiedenis der Nederlanden*, 89 (1974), pp.

351–52; P. van der Burgh, 'Ontwikkelingen op het gebied van het kwantiteitsbeheer', in *Waterschapschouw*, F.J. Kranenburg et al. eds., Deventer, 1977, p. 141; Fockema Andreae, 'Waterschaps-organisatie in Nederland en in den vreemde', in *Mededelingen der Koninklijke Nederlandse Akademie van Wetenschappen, afd. Letterkunde*, deel 14, 9 (1951), p. 318; idem, 'Embanking and Drainage Authorities in the Netherlands during the Middle Ages', in *Speculum*, 27 (1952), pp. 159–62.

58. In 1805 the Dutch government would set up a special body of State engineers, to be employed by the *Waterstaat* and work on the construction of public buildings, roads, bridges and canals. R.P.J. Tutein Nolthenius, *Netherlands Engineers and Contractors* (A general view of the Netherlands, II.14), The Hague, 1915, p. 3.

59. Van der Linden, 'History of the Reclamation of the Western Fenlands', cit., pp. 62–74; idem, 'L'influence de l'eau sur les institutions rurales hollandaises', pp. 675–77.

60. For England, Darby, *The Draining of the Fens*, p. 5. The Cistercians played a fundamental role in the organisation of numerous polders on the Belgian coast: J.A. van Houtte, *Economische en sociale geschiedenis van de Lage Landen*, Zeist, 1964, pp. 43–45; A. Verhulst, 'Die Niederlande im Hoch- und Spätmittelalter', in *Handbuch der europäischen Wirtschafts- und Sozialgeschichte*, H. Kellenbenz ed., II, Stuttgart, 1980, pp. 274–77; R. Tavernier and J. Ameryckx, *Kust, duinen, polders, Atlas van België*, Blad 17, 1970, pp. 15–18. About the Groningen, J.K. de Cock, 'De Middeleeuwen', in *Historie van Groningen. Stad en land*, W.J. Formsma et al. eds., Groningen, 1981, p. 603. On this point, also see De Vries, *The Dutch Rural Economy*, pp. 41–42.

61. Ventura, 'Considerazioni sull'agricoltura veneta', p. 519ff.; Romano, 'L'Italia nella crisi del secolo XVII', pp. 472–76.

62. Baars, 'Leeghwater: een herwaardering', p. 3.

63. Van der Linden, 'History of the Reclamation of the Western Fenlands', cit., pp. 65–67.

64. Ravensdale, *Liable to Floods. Village Landscape on the Edge of the Fens*, pp. 48–53; Spufford, *Contrasting Communities*, pp. 121–64; Hill, *Reformation to Industrial Revolution*, p. 120; Darby, *The Changing Fenland*, pp. 55 ss.; Lindlay, *Fenland Riots and the English Revolution*.

65. Lambert, *The Making of the Dutch Landscape*, pp. 220–24; Burke, *Venice and Amsterdam*, pp. 106–7.

66. De Vries, *The Role of the Rural Sector in the Development of the Dutch Economy, 1500–1700*, quoted by Braudel, *Civilisation matérielle, économie et capitalisme*, III, p. 148.

67. C. Baars, 'Oorspronkelijke verkaveling en grootte van de bezittingen in enige polders in Noord-Holland', in *Landbouwkundig Tijdschrift*, 93 (1981), n. 7, pp. 193–201.

68. A. Zijp, 'Hoofdstukken uit de economische en sociale geschiedenis van de polder Zijpe in de 17e en 18e eeuw', in *Tijdschrift voor Geschiedenis*, 70 (1957), pp. 33–35. For all their sometimes excessive celebration of national

achievements, numerous regional studies of polders (the real 'deep structure' of the nation) provide illuminating detailed accounts: J. Bouman, *Bedijking en bloei van de Beemster*, Amsterdam, 1857; B.W. van der Kloot-Meybrug, *De economische ontwikkeling van een Zuid-Hollands dorp (Oudshoorn)*, 's-Gravenhage, 1920; G. 't Hart, *Historische beschrijving der vrije en Hoge Heerlijkheid van Heenvliet*, Den Helder, 1949; H. Sannes, *Geschiedenis van het Bildt*, 3 dln., Franeker, 1951-1956; A. Vuyk, *Boskoop. Vijf eeuwen boomkwekerij*, Boskoop, 1966.

69. A.J. Thurkow, 'De overheid en het landschap in de droogmakerijen van de 16e tot en met de 19e eeuw', in *Historisch-Geografisch Tijdschrift*, 9 (1991), pp. 49-50.

70. J.A. Faber, 'De oligarchisering van Friesland in de tweede helft van de zeventiende eeuw', in *AAG Bijdragen*, 15 (1970), pp. 39-64: The same process can be seen in the Drentha, even if there were relatively few concerns belonging to the nobility or to monasteries.

71. J. Bieleman, *Boeren op de Drentse Zand 1600-1910* (A.A.G. Bijdragen, 29), Wageningen, 1987, p. 682.

72. C. Baars, 'Geschiedenis van de bedijking van het Deltagebied', in *Landbouwkundig Tijdschrift*, 91 (1979), pp. 33 and 36; idem, *De geschiedenis van de landbouw in de Beijerlanden*, p. 213.

73. Burke, *Venice and Amsterdam*, p. 59.

74. Monkhouse, *A Regional Geography of Western Europe*, p. 31.

75. Gottschalk, 'Some Aspects of the Development of Historical Geography', cit., p. 321

76. Cools, *Strijd om den grond in het lage Nederland*, p. 131; J. van Veen, 'Grafieken van indijkingen in Nederland', in *Tijdschrift van het Koninklijk Nederlandsch Aardrijkskundig Genootschap*, 65 (1948), pp. 19-25; Pounds, *An Historical Geography of Europe*, pp. 195-96. Sizeable dike-building was undertaken in Zeeland in the Late Middle Ages, even if there were losses between 1450 and 1570. On these issues, see Dekker, *Zuid-Beveland. De historische geografie en de instellingen van een Zeeuws eiland in de Middeleeuwen*, espec. pp. 98-212 and 312-13. Further data regarding the division of land can be found in Schultz, *Waterbeheersing van de Nederlandse droogmakerijen*, pp. 48-49, 115, 213, 214-15, 229.

77. Smith, *An Historical Geography*, p. 507.

78. Ventura, 'Considerazioni sull'agricoltura veneta', pp. 534-37.

79. Cools, *Strijd om den grond*, p. 131; Smith, *An Historical Geography*, p. 507.

80. J.R. Bruijn, 'Scheepvaart in de Noordelijke Nederlanden', in *Algemene Geschiedenis der Nederlanden*, Blok and Prevenier eds., VII, 1980, p. 151.

81. Aymard, *Venise, Raguse et le commerce du blé*, p. 7ff.

82. J. Israel, 'The Phases of the Dutch 'straatvaart' (1590-1713). A chapter in the economic history of the Mediterranean', in *Tijdschrift voor Geschiedenis*, 99 (1986), pp. 3-4. Van der Wee, 'Die Niederlande, 1350-1650', cit., pp. 570 and 587-89. See also P.W. Klein, 'De zeventiende eeuw', in *De economische geschiedenis van Nederland*, van Stuijvenberg ed., cit., pp. 86-90; Braudel, *La Méditerranée et le monde méditerranéen à l'époque de Philippe II*, I, pp. 568-69.

83. J.B.L. Hol and H. van Velthoven, 'La Néerlande. Etudes générales sur la géographie des Pays-Bas ', in *Tijdschrift van het Koninklijk Nederlandsch Aardrijkskundig Genootschap*, 55 (1938), n. 4, p. 601.

84. Thurkow, 'The Draining of the Lakes in the Netherlands (18th-19th centuries)', in *Eau et développement*, Ciriacono ed., pp. 103-16.

85. Klein, 'De zeventiende eeuw', *De economische geschiedenis van Nederland*, van Stuijvenberg ed., cit., pp. 90-91. Richard Weston claimed that around the middle of the seventeenth century the Waasland was the most fertile area in Europe (Weston, *Verhandeling over de landbouw in Vlaanderen en Brabant 1644-1645*; see also Vandenbroeke, 'Landbouw in de Zuidelijke Nederlanden', cit., p. 78.)

86. De Zeeuw, 'Peat and the Dutch Golden Age', pp. 3-27.

87. Hol and van Velthoven, 'La Néerlande. Etudes générales sur la géographie des Pays-Bas', cit., p.607; G.J. Borger, *De Veenhoop*, Amsterdam, 1975, pp. 234-38.

88. T. Stol, 'Overheden en het ontstaan van veenkoloniën', in *Historisch-Geografisch Tijdschrift*, 9 (1991), pp. 57-64; idem, 'Fuel, Peat and Peat Companies in the Low Countries (16th-18th centuries)', in *Eau et développement*, Ciriacono ed., pp. 155-68; Woude and de Vries, *The First Modern Economy*, pp. 37-40.

89. S. van der Hoek, *Het bruine goud. Kroniek van de turfgravers in Nederland*, Amsterdam, 1984, p. 7.

90. Lambert, *The Dutch Landscape*, pp. 213-14.

91. M. Casciato, 'La cartografia olandese tra Cinque e Seicento (Nota introduttiva di Hendrick van der Heyden)', in *Storia della città*, 12/13 (1979), p. 7.

92. Cools, *Strijd om den grond*, p. 131.

93. Lambert, *The Dutch Landscape*, p. 215.

94. Thurkow, 'The Draining of the Lakes in the Netherlands (18th-19th centuries)', in *Eau et développement*, Ciriacono ed., p. 113.

95. Ibid., p. 108. This happened at the end of the sixteenth century, when Johan van Oldenbarnevelt, Secretary to the State of Holland and to the Republic of the Seven Provinces, had to send in the bailiffs because 12 tenant farmers had not paid their rents 'as a result of crop failures and waterlogged conditions'.

96. Gottschalk, *Stormvloeden en rivieroverstromingen in Nederland. De periode 1600-1700*, III, 1977, pp. 156-57.

97. Lambert, *The Dutch Landscape*, pp. 215-16.

98. Schultz, *Waterbeheersing van de Nederlandse droogmakerijen*, p. 49.

99. Leeghwater's project was opposed by C.A. Coleveldt, who set out his arguments in *Bedenckingen over het droogmaken van de Haarlemmer en de Leydtsche meer*, a pamphlet which certainly enjoyed less success than Leeghwater's *Haarlemmermeer boek* given it was not published until 1727 (in Leyden), by which date there had been countless editions of Leeghwater's work. The latter's excessive confidence in his scheme is revealed by the fact that the Haarlemmer lake would not be drained until the nineteenth century, using steam-driven pumps (a total of 18,100 hectares of agricultural land were reclaimed by 1852). The first modern steam pump was tried experimentally near Mijdrecht in 1794 (Schultz, *Waterbeheersing van de Nederlandse droogmakerijen*, p. 30).

100. U. Tucci, 'The Psychology of the Venetian Merchant in the Sixteenth Century', in *Renaissance Venice*, J.R. Hale ed., London,1973, pp. 346-78.
101. On the decline in seventeenth-century Venice as relative rather than absolute, see Rapp, *Industry and Economic Decline in Seventeenth-century Venice*, p. 4. Jan de Vries also holds this view('An inquiry into the behaviour of wages in the Dutch Republic and the southern Netherlands from 1580 to 1800', in *Dutch Capitalism and World Capitalism*, Aymard ed., pp. 37-61), supporting his argument on the fact that salaries remained high because of high levels of productivity. See also my own 'Mass consumption goods and luxury goods: the deindustrialization of the Republic of Venice from the sixteenth to the eighteenth century', in *The Rise and Decline of Urban Industries in Italy and in the Low Countries*, Van der Wee ed., pp. 41-61.
102. P.W. Klein, 'Stagnation économique et emploi du capital dans la Hollande des XVIIIe et XIXe siècles', in *Revue du Nord*, 52 (1970), n. 204, pp. 34-41.
103. W.M. Zappey, 'De economische crisis van de zeventiende eeuw', in *Kernproblemen der economische geschiedenis*, H. Baudet and H. van der Meulen eds., Groningen, 1978, pp. 104-6; E.H. Kossmann, 'Some Meditations on Dutch Eighteenth-century Decline', in *Failed Transitions to Modern Industrial Society. Renaissance Italy and Seventeenth Century Holland*, F. Krantz and P.M. Hohenberg eds., Montreal, 1975, pp. 49-50; Johan de Vries, *De economische achteruitgang der Republiek in de achttiende eeuw*, pp. 150-66; H.K. Roessingh, 'Landbouw in de Noordelijke Nederlanden 1650-1815', in *Algemene geschiedenis der Nederlanden*, Blok and Prevenier eds., VIII, 1979, p. 70.
104. Israel, *Dutch Primacy in World Trade*, p. 377ff.
105. J.G. van Dillen, 'Economic Fluctuations and Trade in the Netherlands, 1650-1750', in *Essays in European Economic History, 1500-1800*, P. Earle ed., Oxford, 1974, pp. 202-3.
106. Van der Woude, *Het Noorderkwartier*, II, pp. 593-601 and 612-13; idem, 'De contractiefase van de seculaire trend in het Noorderkwartier nader beschouwd', in *Bijdragen en Mededelingen betreffende de Geschiedenis der Nederlanden*, 103 (1986), pp. 395-96.
107. Idem, 'The Long-term Movement of Rent for Pasture Land in North Holland and the Problem of Profitability in Agriculture (1570-1800)', in *Productivity of Land and Agricultural Innovation in the Low Countries (1250-1800)*, H. Van der Wee and E. Van Cauwenberghe eds., Leuven, 1978, pp. 172-73.
108. Baars, *De geschiedenis van de landbouw in de Beijerlanden*, p. 213.
109. Thurkow, 'De droogmakerij van Bleiswijk en Hillegersberg', pp. 35-44. Set up by the States of Holland and West Friesland between 1772 and 1779, these new polders would encounter a great number of problems. The scheme involved the use of a new oblique-angled waterwheel designed by the highly-considered technician, Anthonie George Eckhardt, who also designed a new type of windmill (ibid. p. 38 and note).
110. J.L. van Zanden, 'De economie van Holland in de periode 1650-1805: groei of achteruitgang ? Een overzicht van bronnen, problemen en resultaten', in *Bijdragen en Mededelingen betreffende de Geschiedenis der Nederlanden*, 102

(1987), pp. 562–609; idem, *The Rise and Decline of Holland's Economy*, pp. 35–41. Arguing that the decline only becomes evident after 1780, Johan de Vries suggests a period of relative economic stability in the period 1700–1780. Jan de Vries does not even rule out 'modest growth or, at worst, stagnation from 1740 to 1806' (see *Barges and Capitalism: Passenger Transportation in the Dutch Economy, 1632–1839* (A.A.G. Bijdragen, 21), Wageningen, 1978, p. 359. J.C. Riley, too, sees the Dutch economy as suffering no radical decline after 1650 (J.C. Riley, 'The Dutch Economy After 1650: Decline or Growth?', in *The Journal of European Economic History*, 13 (1984), pp. 521–69). Jonathan Israel concludes 'despite a growing mass of statistical data on the Dutch economy of the eighteenth century, scholars continue to arrive at strikingly different conclusions' (Israel, *Dutch Primacy in World Trade*, p. 377). This comment itself comes in a work that offers another timetable for the growth and decline of Dutch commerce.

111. Verhulst, *Précis d'histoire rurale de la Belgique*, pp. 163–65; M. Goossens, 'Modificazioni del paesaggio agrario nei Paesi Bassi, 1750–1900', in *Annali dell'Istituto Alcide Cervi*, 10 (1988) (Proceedings of the Colloquium on 'Studi sul paesaggio agrario in Europa', R. Villari ed.), Bologna, 1989, pp. 121–22.
112. ANP, F14, liasses 1114, 1115,1119,1131; M. Courtin, *Travaux des Ponts-et-Chaussées depuis 1800, ou tableau des constructions neuves*, Paris, 1812, pp. 241–53; A. Guillerme, *La cervelle de la terre. La mécanique des sols et des fondations en France, 1770–1840*, Paris (E.N.P.C., Laboratoire 'Théorie des mutations urbaines et pays développés'), 1986, pp. 87–91.
113. Roessingh, 'Landbouw in de Noordelijke Nederlanden 1650–1815', in *Algemene geschiedenis der Nederlanden*, Blok and Prevenier eds., VIII, 1979, cit., p. 59.
114. J.A. Faber, H.A. Diederiks and S. Hart, 'Urbanisering, industrialisering en milieu aantasting in Nederland in de periode van 1500 tot 1800', in *AAG Bijdragen*, 18 (1973), p. 269.
115. Van der Linden, 'De Nederlandse waterhuishouding en waterstaatsorganisatie', cit., p.551; see ibid. p. 552 on the embankment work on the Rhine and other Dutch rivers in the eighteenth century.
116. Schultz, *Waterbeheersing van de Nederlandse droogmakerijen*, p. 27.
117. M. Dendermonde and H.A.M.C. Dibbits, *De dijken*, Amsterdam, 1957, pp. 73–75.

Technological Transfer within Europe: From Holland to Germany, France and England

Towards a History of Land Reclamation in Europe

Venice and, even more so, Holland are exceptional cases of water management. However, though Europe as a whole presents a wide variety of environmental, geographical, social and political situations in land reclamation – under either authoritarian or 'bourgeois' governance – each project of this kind does seem to share a number of concomitant features[1]: (1) population increase, (2) a demand for cereal crops or other produce likely to increase agricultural earnings; (3) changes in climate that affect the land reclamation work itself; (4) a 'non-conflictual' political situation, necessary to guarantee the smooth running of operations requiring sizeable technical, financial and organisational investment; (5) the presence of certain basic technical knowledge[2]; (6) the availability of the funds necessary to finance such schemes. One should also consider the role which the country implementing the project played in the world economy of the day, because that had a clear effect on the choice of crops to be grown on the reclaimed land.

During the Middle Ages it was the large monasteries and abbeys – especially those of the Benedictine, Cistercian and Premonstratensian orders – that were the main financiers of land reclamation. And though such schemes were carried out using rudimentary methods and limited capital, they are to be seen throughout Europe – in an area ranging from Groningen in the north of the Netherlands to the Po Valley, from Cambridgeshire to the Papal States. At the beginning of the sixteenth century, the financing and execution of these projects started to pass into the hands of more dynamic groups, syndicates of entrepreneurial land-reclaimers who worked parallel (or in tandem) with the government.[3] After the sizeable land-reclamation projects of the twelfth and thirteenth centuries, it was the population increase of the sixteenth that led to the search for new areas of pasture and arable land that would, thanks to presence of reed compost, salts and other minerals, prove to be more fertile than other marginal areas of cultivation. Alongside these agricultural and economic considerations, there is also the fact that the nascent modern states of this period were actively following policies of territorial expansion. So the concomitant features listed above worked in conjunction with the very aspirations that led to the emergence of the modern state.[4]

Government policies therefore played a fundamental role within the land-reclamation projects implemented in numerous areas of Europe. In Spain, for example, there was not only the question of land irrigation – where, as we have already seen, the country in many ways led the rest of Europe – but also the problems linked with the deltas of various large rivers: for example, the Bas Llobregat of the lower Ebro (Barcelona), the Marismas of Seville and the Albufera at Valencia. There were also inland areas of reclamation, for example at the Llanos d'Albacete upriver from Murcia. There one can note the influence not only of the ecclesiastical authorities, which remained important throughout the eighteenth and nineteenth centuries, but also of climatic changes, which were the original motive for the reclamation at the end of the eighteenth century.[5]

Another interesting region is that around the Vistula, where of the 212,000 hectares of marshy land that made up the area, some 172,000 were reclaimed for agricultural use.[6] A first wave of reclamation and settlement had come in the thirteenth and fourteenth centuries, but then in the sixteenth came a second in which the Dutch Mennonite communities played a key role. Occupying the river islands of the Werder, these closely-knit settlements encountered geographical and economic conditions that were similar to those they had left behind them, even if they often found themselves in conflict with juridical structures that were still heavily feudal in character.[7]

As the extensive literature on the subject of this far from uniform 'European model' has shown, the presence of Dutch-Flemish communities and the drainage technologies they brought with them seems to have been a significantly constant feature. In a series of migratory waves that coincided largely with the periods of economic and demographic growth in the eleventh/twelfth and sixteenth centuries, emigrants from the Low Countries (and particularly the more dynamic Holland) managed to exert considerable influence on numerous areas of Europe: they brought with them not only

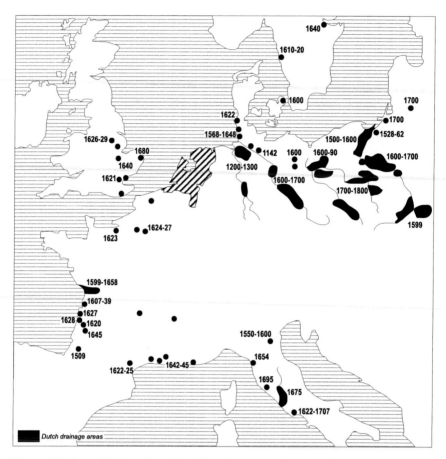

Map 3. Drainage Projects Developed by the Dutch in Early Modern
Europe. Note the extensive activity of the Dutch in Eastern Europe and even
Russia. A.J. Haartsen et al., *Een verkenning van de cultuur-historische betekenis
van het Nederlandse landschap*, 's-Gravenhage, 1989, p. 105.

technological know-how, labour skills and the financial instruments
necessary for the various stages of such projects, but also their own
models of legislation and of social organisation. Historians from
Holland and elsewhere have traced the effects of this *Nederlandse
expansie* in four countries in particular: Italy, Northern Germany,
France and England (though from the seventeenth century onwards,
that influence can also be seen in the flatlands of Russia). [8]
Obviously it would be impossible to discuss such an enormous area
in any detail, so I will look here at the problems of land drainage as

tackled in three large countries of Europe: Germany, France and England. These are significant not only because of the sizeable Dutch presence there over at least two centuries (the sixteenth and seventeenth), but also because land reclamation and drainage affected sizeable numbers of the population, with large capital investment and extensive involvement of political institutions.

Dutch-Flemish Settlers and the Polder-Fürsten: The Marschen of Northern Germany (Sixteenth and Seventeenth Centuries)

After a first wave of immigration in the eleventh and twelfth centuries[9], the new period of settlement of northern Europe during the sixteenth century is particularly significant because of the presence of a new influx of settlers from the Low Countries. In this expansion northwards and eastwards, one of the first areas to be settled was the marshy regions that ran from eastern Friesland to Schelswig-Holstein. Given that the manpower and know-how resources of the settlers were insufficient by themselves, there was an influx of capital investment (largely of Flemish origin) during the course of the sixteenth century, and the implementation of an active policy of colonisation by such states as Denmark and Prussia. In the following century would come a series of projects which, in Prussia, aimed to reclaim the marshy lands along the banks of the rivers Netze (1606) and Havel (1650), and, in Central Poland, those along the rivers Weichsel and Bug.[10] Such settlements would not be restricted solely to central-eastern Europe: beginning with the Weder colony of the Mennonite community, they would during the eighteenth century spread as far as southern Russia. There, the 'farmers of the marshes' would become 'farmers of the steppes', introducing sheep-farming (their first area of activity) and then the cultivation of grain crops (for example, in the Black Sea area).

The forms of contract introduced in these areas were typical of the Low Countries. If, for example, resort had to be made to urban and commercial capital in order to finance such projects, then the investors rented out the reclaimed lands in long-term contracts to Flemish and Dutch peasant farmers, who unlike the peasants of Central Europe retained all their personal liberties. So, along with different economic relations, different types of legal relations were also introduced.[11]

The area in which Dutch immigration played a role of fundamental importance was – for obvious reasons – that of the *Marschen* in Northern Germany. Here, the settlers brought with them not only technology and capital, but also religion and outlook. The influx of Mennonite and Anabaptists – as a result of religious persecution and the fall of the legendary peasant republics in the Low Countries – was not always a peaceful affair, arousing wariness or open hostility amongst the native German communities and the official Calvinist church. However the benefits these groups brought with them were considerable; it has been calculated that the dikes along the coastal strip from the mouths of the Rhine and the Moselle to the coasts of Jutland doubled in length and tripled in volume during the sixteenth and the first half of the seventeenth century, protecting some 10,000 km^2 of terrain (in Schleswig-Holstein alone, it has been said that some 4,000–5,000 hectares of marshy land were reclaimed for agricultural use).[12]

The studies by Nitz have also shown how in the entire coastal strip from Groningen to the *Köge* (polders) of Schleswig-Holstein, an international market economy was emerging, based on the sale of livestock and cereal crops. Regional case-studies have confirmed the interpretation put forward by Abel and Slicher van Bath, that there was a close relation between the market price of cereal crops and the impetus towards land reclamation. And the canals dredged as part of such projects served not only for drainage but also for the transport of the crops themselves, which from the ports set up at the mouths of the canals were exported to Holland or to wherever international demand was greatest.[13]

It is true, however, that distinctions have been made between various sub-regions, some of which focused mainly on the raising of livestock, others on the growing of crops. In Butjadingen, for example – which lies between the river Weser and the Jade – the production of dairy produce and meat had by 1550 emerged as much more profitable than the growing of wheat. Through their trusty stewards (*Meyers*), the Counts of Oldenburg, for example, used their own lands to fatten bulls imported from Denmark; and the rural population was obliged either to pay a feudal tax (the *Futtergeld*) or feed the lord's cattle in their own barns and stables over the winter months.[14]

The variations within the region of Eastern Friesland are no less interesting. The Jeverland, on the northern coast, had during the sixteenth century firmly established its place as a grower of commercial cereal crops, whilst the inland areas (Friesische Wehde and Ammerland) specialised in cash crops (hemp, hops, chicory), which supplied raw materials for proto-industrial cottage industries (see the arguments put forward by Wallerstein and von Thünen). Research has also revealed the existence of a more marginal – even if geographically more extensive – area in which the production of modest-quality wool went together with almost subsistence agriculture and peat-digging (the latter a key source of fuel for many areas of Germany in this period). This latter was the area of what one might call 'fen-colonies', settlements which expanded sizeably from the middle of the sixteenth century onwards to occupy not only parts of eastern and western Friesland but also such inland areas as those which were part of the Bishopric of Münster. The capital necessary to finance these small settlements (which are said to have ranged from 1 or 2 hectares to a maximum of 5 hectares per smallholding) could only have come from speculators in the nearby cities, who were interested in the income from the sale of peat. However, when there was a sharp drop in the demand for peat (or the ground reserves had been exhausted), the peasant-settlers (the *Fehntjer*) no longer drew enough from the land to meet their own food needs. [15] Here, as in the peat-fields exposed by the draining of the Dutch *meres* or in those of the Kempen area[16], peat-farming was yet again a sad chapter in the social history of Europe, with the workforce obliged to live in the most wretched of conditions.

In the coastal areas, large aristocratic estates (*Gutswirtschaft*) took over direct or indirect control of agricultural production. It is no coincidence that in the Rheiderland, a region between the river Ems and the bay of the Dollart, the settlements of the Early Modern period were very different from those of the Middle Ages, a characteristic feature of which had been long narrow parcels of land that ran at right angles to the dikes; these were now replaced by larger holdings (even if the labour force for the drainage was still supplied by feudal *corvée*). The *Polder-Fürsten* who oversaw the work of drainage preferred to then sell or rent the new land to bourgeois entrepreneurs, who in their turn received a very quick and sizeable return on their investment due to the great international demand for cereal crops.

The increase in size – and number – of aristocratic estates also went hand in hand with an increase in the production of wheat and butter, whilst the fattening of livestock (bulls from the Low Countries) led to

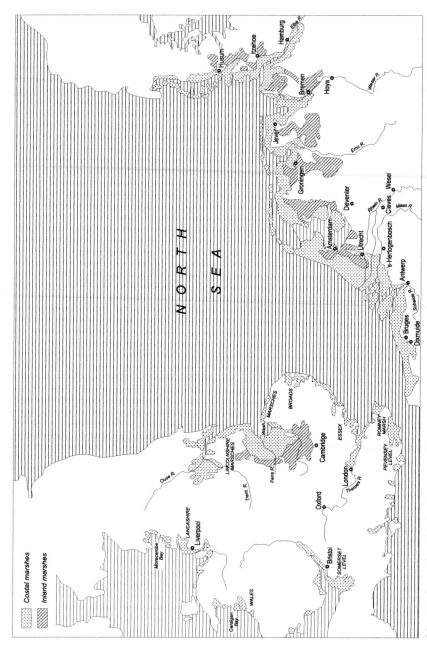

Map 4. Coastal and Inland Marshes in Northern Germany, the Low Countries, Belgium, England and Wales.
Source: J. Klasen, *Vergleichende Landschaftskunde der englischen Marschen*, Köln, 1967.

an extension of pasture land. What is more, the increase in milk production during the seventeenth and eighteenth centuries led to economic rationalisation of resources, so that the size of the herds was now reflected in the size of the workforce and the number of farms.[17]

Throughout the sixteenth century, therefore, the feudal nobility and the local aristocracy played a key role in the organisation of drainage and sea-protection projects. With their motto of *'So viel Land, so viel Deich'* ('So many dikes built, so many acres reclaimed') the *Polder-Fürsten* took over the role of the parish and community organisations which had previously been responsible for the erection and maintenance of dikes (be they for military protection or agricultural purposes). By the middle of the sixteenth century, the *Spadelandsrecht* – that body of regulations which governed the construction of the dikes – had taken on a fixed, definitive form, and it was this which provided the nobility of the region with the main legislative instrument for their intervention in this field.

These sixteenth-century efforts at land reclamation also benefited from the fact that the sea seems to have been receding during this period; thus at least some of the terrain that had been lost during the fourteenth and fifteenth centuries could be recouped. However, Abel has calculated that some 100,000 hectares of the coasts of Lower Saxony, Dithmarchsen, the Eiderstedt peninsula and North Friesland had gone underwater during those two centuries, whilst only 40,000 hectares were to be recovered in Jeverland, the Harlebucht and Leybucht and other coastal areas during the course of the sixteenth and seventeenth. Hence, the overall picture for this period is contradictory and fragmented, with loss of terrain in one area alternating with significant recoveries in another.

There were also similar contradictions at an institutional level. The Duchies of Schleswig-Holstein mixed together state capitalism and feudal rights, and even at the beginning of the seventeenth century were asserting their right of taxation on all lands that had been reclaimed by the erection of dikes (*Anwachsrecht*). Similarly, in the neighbouring Oldenburg, where only the local aristocracy had the right to construct dikes or other waterworks, each new area of land reclaimed from the sea or marshes was seen as coming under the feudal jurisdiction of the Counts of Oldenburg.

Dutch Capital and Technology in Germany: The Seventeenth Century

Greater dynamism in land reclamation at the beginning of the seventeenth century was the result of a further influx of Dutchmen, bringing with them 'revolutionary' technology and, above all, capital. In the case of the *Köge* of Schleswig-Holstein most historical studies have focused on the figure of Claeß Rollwagen, with slightly less attention being paid to Jan Barentsz. Westerdijck (whom we will meet again in the English Fens) and Johannes Sems.

In 1603–05 Rollwagen was at work in the Leybucht and the Dollart areas of Ostfriesland (the polders of Schoonorth and Bonder, the Freepsumer mere and the Newlandpolder). In 1610 his work would take him to the Eiderstedt peninsula, where he would construct a dike that led to the recovery of some 2,000 hectares of land. He is credited with having introduced into this area a new type of dike amply studied by German historians – much more gradually sloped towards the sea than traditional dikes, this was more efficient at breaking the force of incoming waves – and with having rationalised systems of construction and the transportation of materials. However, some have argued that the impact of these technological innovations was not as great as has been claimed, whilst others have underlined how the driving-force behind them was more the desire to turn a quick profit rather than an interest in constructing solid structures. It may well be no coincidence, therefore, that a number of Rollwagen's schemes met with violent opposition from the local population of Eiderstedt.

It is, however, clear that Rollwagen was just one of the first of those many Dutchmen who would invest their venture capital in numerous polders in the region, from Eiderstedt to the island of Nordstrand, and from Dithmarschen to Stapelholm – areas which also attracted investment capital from Flanders and the Brabant. The latter, for example, is known to have been a source of technology and capital for the northern Low Countries; the Brabant family of De Cortes played a decisive role in the reclamation of the Maria Elisabeth Koog on the island of Nordstrand (which was, in fact, referred to as 'Brabantine territory').

There were also some French investors in the region. The names of Pontchasteau, Louis Gorin, Angran, Lalane and Nicole figure amongst those involved in the drainage of the Maria Elisabeth Koog, the Friedrich Koog and the Trindermarsch Koog over the period 1654–63; unfortunately, we know little more about these men than the sums they invested (78,000 florins, 12,000 florins and 40,389 florins in the three projects respectively).

Investment in these agricultural concerns thus varied noticeably, with such venture capitalists as participated enjoying long-term returns; they were granted 'perpetual and hereditary rights'.[18] However, the risks involved should not be underestimated, given that the unsuccessful far outweighed the successful schemes – success depending upon various factors outside the control of the investors themselves (fluctuations in market prices; the inertia or diffidence of local peasant communities). Nor should one underestimate the disastrous effects of the worsening in the climate due to the 'Small Ice Age' at the end of the sixteenth century, when even the stoutest dikes might be broken by sudden and violent storms.[19] One victim of these conditions was the 1626 attempt by the Dutchman Christian Becker to drain the meres of Megger, Börmer and Bergenhuser in the Stapelholm, which ended in total failure. Organised at the behest of Duke Friedrich III of Holstein-Gottorp, whose interest is commemorated by the construction of a Friedrichstadt in perfect Dutch style, that project had drawn not only on Dutch capital but also on the newest technologies to be developed in Holland: large-scale drainage canals, which only the Dutch engineers seemed capable of creating, and windmills equipped with the new Archimedes' screw instead of the traditional waterwheel. Later, the scheme would also attract further investors and participants (including the famous Leeghwater), but the effects of the Thirty Years' War and of a terrible storm in 1634 would, in 1654, lead to the undertaking being abandoned once again. And so, overall, while some 8,000 hectares were reclaimed from the sea in this area during the sixteenth and the first half of the seventeenth century, those gains remained smaller than the terrain lost to the sea at the end of the Middle Ages.[20] It is hardly surprising, therefore, that during the eighteenth century it was the state which had to step in, commissioning the drainage of the Kronprinzenkoog and the less extensive Sophienkoog.[21] In effect, although the duchies in the region had shown a certain openness to foreign investment capital, the political authorities had always taken a co-ordinating role in these schemes, maintaining their right to intervene whenever they thought necessary (especially when the projects were encountering difficulties).

German Land Reclamation during the Eighteenth Century: The Return of the State

In spite of the problems faced by German land-drainage schemes during the second half of the seventeenth century, notable progress was made during the course of the following century – not only in the land reclamation itself, but also in the agricultural and economic exploitation of the land reclaimed. This was a period when most of the German states benefited from the increase in the amount of land under cultivation, which was a direct consequence not only of their population policies but also of the greater attention paid to hydrographical problems. Eastern Friesland (after 1744, a part of Prussia) continued the efforts which had long been made to drain the numerous lakes and meres within its territory. Like those in the Gronigen area, these drainage projects had for some time now been attracting Dutch capital and know-how. For example, as early as 1611 Rollwagen had, unsuccessfully, endeavoured to drain the Freepsummer Meer; and though the Dutch companies of investors who worked on the project after him did not enjoyed much greater success, 1631 did see the beginning within East Friesland of the drainage – and subsequent exploitation – of the peat bogs of Papenburg, which would continue to supply peat throughout the eighteenth century. What is more, the drainage work on the extensive marshes of the Emden region, which began in 1765, would by the end of the century have produced around 2,500 hectares of new agricultural land.

The policy followed in this region by Frederick II proved to be decisive. In 1764 he passed the *Urbarmachungsedikt*, which was expressly intended to stimulate land reclamation in Eastern Friesland; chance of a sure profit led a number of Prussian investors to now take an interest in such schemes. The sort of return on investment to be expected can be seen from that fact that in 1752 the Kurmark Agricultural Savings Bank loaned some 100,000 *thalers* for the building of dikes on one specific polder, where the reclaimed agricultural land rendered three times that sum (as early as the end of the seventeenth century there were, as Abel has pointed out, some schemes – for example, in certain polders of Schleswig-Holstein – that paid a fourfold return on investment).[22] As a result of this renewed interest, the Freepsumer Meer was eventually drained by a consortium set up in 1768 under Logemann and Creutzenberg, who were granted a perpetual lease on the land reclaimed.

In this area to the west of the Elbe, where the prevalent system of *Grundherrschaft* meant that the peasant communities enjoyed greater independence than their counterparts to the east of the river, what one sees is the joint action of private investors (of whom there was apparently no shortage) and the state (which remained the main financier in such schemes). Encouraged or directly promoted by the state, the resultant settlements would, during the eighteenth and nineteenth centuries, lead to a 100–400 per cent increase in the number of farms in some of the plain areas of north-western Germany.

The same state involvement can be seen in the *Donaumooskultursozietät*, founded in 1790 by the Duke of Bavaria to drain and cultivate a large marshy area to the north of Munich (the Donaumoos); the monarchy itself owned a substantial number of shares in the company. Here again, as in the fen-colonies between the Ems and Münsterland, the tendency was towards the setting-up of small – or very small – peasant holdings. The first settlements of the Karlkron colony were no bigger than 3 hectares each, whilst the later Karlshuld settlements envisaged an increase only to four hectares (with 9 hectares being fixed as a maximum). For the period up to 1816 it is estimated that this scheme drained and reclaimed some 19,000 hectares of agricultural land, thus meeting its initial purpose of giving limited means of support to the numerous peasantry of Bavaria as well as increasing the fiscal returns of the monarchy.[23]

Again in the south of Germany, the reform period in Baden had seen the introduction of a policy that was equally concerned with the reclamation for agricultural use of marginal land – approximately 3,000 hectares – and with the raising of defences against the periodic flooding of the river Dreisam. And even where population densities were lower and more uncultivated land was available – for example, in the north German area stretching from the Kurhannover to the Prussian-Polish lowlands – the policy was the same. For example, in the 1770s in the Kurhannover, the *Moorkommisar* J. Ch. Findorff focused on a programme of *Moorkolonisation*, aiming to reclaim the extensive tracts of marshy swamp and lowland in the region; in the area of Bremen and Verden alone such terrain accounted for some 180,000 hectares, so there was an obvious need for projects of this kind. To achieve the purpose Findorff set himself, agricultural enterprises based on a Dutch model were set up, for example at Stade. These proved more productive than their counterparts in eastern Friesland because the settlers were given smallholdings of at least 15 hectares; however, the main source of income from the land remained peat, which was sold through the port of Bremen.

Even further north, in Mecklenburg, there was a general improvement in hydro-geological conditions from the end of the Thirty Years' War onwards. What is more, like Brandenburg, this was a German province that offered scope for colonisation and settlement, given that in 1700 more than half of it was woodland and uncultivated terrain.[24]

The Case of Prussia

In general terms, if one includes within one's calculations those areas of land that had previously been left untended or as woodland, it emerges that the scale of reclamation in Germany as a whole bears comparison with what one sees throughout Europe – even if, on the basis of the information at present available to us, it would be impossible to draw up a table of the actual value of the land drained and reclaimed in each country; how could one when there are such variations in geographical location and soil quality? What is beyond question is that Prussia was the greatest success story in German land reclamation, though this is not the place for even the broadest outline of the agricultural policies behind it nor of the historical debate to which it has given rise.[25]

One of the tactics employed by the monarchy as part of its general strategy of territorial expansion, there was inevitably a centralist approach to land reclamation in Prussia, with the bases of policy being laid down in the early decades of the eighteenth century by Frederick William I, and then continued and developed by his successors: Frederick the Great, Frederick Wilhelm II and Frederick Wilhelm III. The first of these rulers had already managed to reclaim some 15,000 hectares by draining the Havelländer Luchs marshes to the north-west of his capital, while Frederick II would pursue this policy with even greater success (though the historical accounts of this are often tainted by excessive panegyrics to the achievements of the Hohenzollerns).[26] What is beyond doubt is that the projects of settlement were backed up by substantial canal-building schemes. These included the 1743–46 creation of the Plauerkanal and the Finowkanal (which resulted in a multi-functional system of canals embracing Berlin); the straightening of the course of the Oder; and the works on the rivers Madue and Plöne in Pomerania (1771). Similarly, it is true that thousands and thousands of hectares of good — indeed, excellent – farming-land were reclaimed for the raising of livestock. However, some estimates do seem a little inflated, even if in correcting them one must be careful not to go to the opposite extreme and underestimate the areas of land reclaimed.[27] It has been argued that during the course of the eighteenth century some 400,000 hectares of farmland were recovered in Oderbruch (Frankfurt-an-der-Oder), Netzebruch, Wrathebruch and Lower Pomerania; whilst in the five provinces of Prussia and Brandenburg the gains totalled something like 600–750,000 hectares. However, more modest estimates put the land reclaimed by drainage projects alone at no more than 100,000 hectares.[28] Similar differences can be seen with regard to the supposed results of another Hohenzollern policy, that relating to population, which aimed to attract thousands of new settlers from all the most remote areas of Germany and thus create hundreds of new villages. Exaggerated figures put these new arrivals at around one million, whereas a more soundly-based estimate is that they totalled something like 285,000.[29]

There is a problem, however, as to exactly how productive these new farms and settlements were. Frederick II certainly strove for innovation (for example, aiming to boost milk production – from Dutch-inspired model-farms – in order to supply urban demand), yet the policies followed had certain limits and contradictions. After the drainage work, paid for by the state, the size of the holdings given to the new farmer-settlers were far too small to stand as solid capitalistic enterprises, the bases for that new type of agriculture which was becoming established elsewhere in Europe. As had happened in various places throughout the continent – for example, Venice several decades earlier – the real beneficiaries of the drainage schemes were the traditional estates of the nobility and monarchy, even if it cannot be denied that these might be run dynamically as market-oriented concerns.[30]

The large aristocratic estates expanded and occupied those marshlands that had once been the traditional resources of fisherman and hunters, who certainly put up unexpectedly strong resistance against this destruction of their livelihood – opposition that is not usually mentioned in official documentation.[31] As we shall see later, such opposition was a common reaction to these schemes throughout Europe, and could sometimes take very violent forms (as in the English Fens).

All in all, therefore, land reclamation was a good deal not only for the Prussian monarchy, which gained from the increase in its fiscal revenues due to the population and mercantile policies followed by Frederick II, but also for other investors as well. For example, the return on investment in the 1768 drainage scheme involving the Madüsee, between Pyritz and Altdamm – which yielded some 19,000 *morgen* (about 4,500 hectares) – was said to have been over 7 per cent, whilst the return on the Great Camminer Bruch scheme (yielding some 25,000 *morgen*, around 6,000 hectares) was estimated by the Chamber of Stettin as being around 14 per cent, which must however be taken as a truly exceptional figure.[32]

Humphrey Bradley's Company in France

The situation with regard to land reclamation in France was broadly similar to that in Germany, even if one can identify certain specific features and a level of local conflict that probably had much more damaging consequences than it did over the border; in effect, Germany was probably a place of greater state control, with the authorities responsible for carrying out territorial policies being a more effective local presence. Nevertheless, in France, too, financial and entrepreneurial commitment on a large scale were required for such projects – so much so that a French geographer commented 'marshlands will be drained *en bloc* or not at all'.[33]

At the end of the sixteenth century, France relaunched the projects of land reclamation which would then continue, with variations in intensity, for many years to come. It was Henri IV who set up the *Association pour le Dessèchement des marais et lacs de France*, which drew on Dutch finance and technology to implement an entirely new agricultural policy on a national scale. Clearly, this reclamation of new terrain was only one part of a mercantile policy predicated on increase of output, extension of the transport network necessary to bring produce to market, and increased fiscal revenue for the state. But what was new here was the national scale of the association. Backed by what we today might call a holding company, this may – as Braudel pointed out[34] – have been an imperfect form of capitalism, but it still represented a novelty within the Europe of the day. As the ample literature on the subject has shown, the key figure here was Humphrey Bradley, from the Brabant. A well-known military engineer, he was called to France by Henri IV and soon showed himself to be a more astute organiser-entrepreneur than he was a skilled engineer of land-drainage and reclamation projects: this is clear from the fact that the completion of any number of projects was due to the various land-surveyors and engineers that Bradley had to import from his homeland.

The royal edict of 1599 granted Bradley and these associates the rights to drain 'all marshes and swamps, be they part of royal demesnes, or the property of the Church, the nobility or commoners', and this nationwide concession involved a structure comprising a parent company and a number of associate companies. A land-owner who wished to drain his *marais* would apply to the Dutch group linked with the parent company, which would then divide the reclaimed territory between all the various participants according to the size of their individual investment and the contract drawn up with the landowner himself, the terms of which could vary from situation to situation. Given that at the time most of the reclaimed land was within feudal estates, the speculators still had to pay seigniorial dues, as well as undertake to maintain the various hydraulic structures. However, the 1599 edict did abolish the *droit d'aubain* (taxation on alien residents) for settlers on the reclaimed land, promising them the right to naturalisation within two years, without the payment of any special tax. The great influx into France of people fleeing the religious persecution then taking place in Flanders and Holland would meet a crucial requirement of such land-reclamation projects: 'the settlement of an abundant labour force to guarantee the cultivation of the land ... and the maintenance of drainage works'.[35]

Dutch capital, too, made an essential contribution, making up for the shortage of French capital available for such schemes (even though it would be wrong to say there was no French investment here). As in the case of Germany, the influx of the Dutch also had an influence on the legislative and organisational aspects of the 'polder', so that the newcomers tried to import with them such figures as a *maître des digues*, paid by and answerable to a *directeur* or *polder maître*, who was elected to this unsalaried position by a meeting of landowners; it is no accident that in the French literature on this subject one often encounters the use of the Dutch term *waterschappen* (Water Administration).[36]

What is beyond doubt is that the new, more modern, juridical forms which began to emerge broke with the models inherited from serfdom and guaranteed the 'undertaker's' right to expropriation: he could, for example, demolish anything that interfered with the effectiveness of the drainage project (locks, mills, or other buildings).

The drainage canals themselves were especially profitable because they had a double function, both agricultural and commercial (they lowered the costs of transporting the produce of the polders themselves). However, although the hope was expressed that this reclaimed land would be used for more speculative and adventurous agriculture, producing 'Milan-style cheese, peat and earth-dug coals for burning, as well as sugar cane, rice and fishing', there is some doubt as to whether this actually happened. For example, Delafosse's study of the rental contracts drawn up for the exploitation of the *marais* of Aunis in the years 1639–43 shows how the tenant farmers were largely required to concentrate solely on cereal crops. Nor should one forget that in these decades 'wheat is expensive, and yields well as a crop' – particularly in those *marais* areas that lay along the coastline, from where grain and wheat could be most easily shipped. Jean Meuvret in fact observes that 'the marshlands of Blaye and Médoc would thus during the seventeenth century become the granaries of Bordeaux'.[37]

The heritage left by the Dutch at the beginning of this century was important, but not always long-lasting. It involved the reclamation of numerous marshy areas – both inland and coastal – spread over most of the regions of France: from Picardy to Normandy in the north, through Poitou and the Auvergne in the Centre to Languedoc and Provence in the south. The division of this land was generally very uniform, with the creation of rectangular lots that varied in area from 3 to 10 hectares. As records show, in some cases – for example, the Moëres, between French Flanders and the southern Low Countries – Dutch-style windmills were in use (to pump the drained water out towards Dunkirk). This particular scheme envisaged the draining of both the Grande Moëre (3,150 hectares) and the Petite Moëre (176 hectares); carried out in the years 1622–1626 by the Flemish engineer W. Cobergher, it drew on a very unusual source of finance – the *mont-de-piété* of Antwerp – a clear indication of the multiple social and financial resources that came into play during land reclamation. The drained land in this area would ultimately produce abundant crops of hay and rape, with one hundred and forty new farms arising on the rectangular plots divided by dikes and roads. However, the problems on the borders between French Flanders and the southern Low Countries – together with the military events of those decades – would lead Cobergher to cede his rights over the western Moëres to the local nobles, reserving for himself solely the pastureland. Harvests here would continue to be good right up to 1646, but following the rupture of the dikes during the French siege of Dunkirk, the Moëres would disappear under water again for more than a century – until, that is, various entrepreneurs (Antoine de Ricouart, M. d'Herouville and an advocate of The Hague known to us solely as 'Vendermey') would in the second half of the eighteenth century take an interest in the reclamation of the area. It would appear that during the late 1600s neither Colbert nor Louvois showed any serious interest in draining this land.[38]

The Results of Land Drainage in France during the Sixteenth and Seventeenth Centuries

Not all the projects drawn up for the various regions of Frances were equally successfully, either in performance or in financial returns. If, for example, at Blanquefort and Bordeaux, around 2,000 hectares were reclaimed thanks to the investments of Conraad Goosen, by the time he died in 1625 the project was doomed to end with serious financial losses. In the areas known as La Petite Flandre, near Rochefort, the Oudenaerde-born Coymans brothers (Jerôme, Marc and Gaspar) invested a total of 90,000 *livres tournois* in the reclamation of a polder of around 7,000 hectares, but soon found

Map 5. Lakes and Marshes Drained in France before 1789. Source: Tutein
Nolthenius, 'Mededelingen over meren en moerassen in vorige eeuwen in
Frankrijk door Nederlanders drooggelegd', in *Algemeen Verslag der
werkzaamheden van het Koninklijk Instituut van Ingenieurs*, 1891–92, Plate VI.

themselves coming up against strong opposition from the local inhabitants of these *terres marécageuses* and had to abandon the project. On the other hand, the area to the north of Bordeaux was to be much more remunerative for the Dutchmen Cat and Van Bommel, who drained the 3,200–hectare polders of Lesparre and Civrac (the latter actually called the 'Polder de Hollande') . This project is known to us through the *Cronycke* written by Leeghwater, who in 1627 sent an encouraging report upon it to the actual owner of the land, the Duc d'Eperon.

Another successful scheme was the digging of the *Ceinture des Hollandais* in 1642, which at Luçon on the Atlantic coast served to draw off the water that tended to settle in the depressions of the Petit Poitou area. The entire polder, covering a total of 6,670 hectares divided into holdings of some 50 hectares each, was drained of water by two canals that ran at right angles to each other and totalled 13 kilometres in length. A few years later, in 1651, the nearby polders of Champagné and Bois-dieux en Vix were created, whilst 2,700 acres were drained in the seigneury of Marans near La Rochelle by Remy Macquart, a pupil of Dutch hydraulic engineers: a total of sixteen farms thus became operative, bringing in some 20,000 *livres tournois* a year for an initial investment of about five times as much.

Other projects on the same coast had a more troubled history – for example, those involving the marshlands of Dol, Blaye and the Etang d'Orx, as well as the Marais Vernier in the lower Seine basin: here, in spite of the construction of the *Digue des Hollandais*, the marshlands won out.[39] And by the beginning of the eighteenth century it was clear that whilst livestock, crops of hay and 'quite good pasture' were an important source of income for the regions of Aunis, Saintonge and the areas along the Charente, there was still a lot left to do. For example, the *marais* to the south and north-west of the Tonnay Boutonne were considered as lost; whilst it was hoped that drainage could reclaim the *marais* to the north of Montreau (near Rochefort and the river Surgère) and the enormous marshy expanses along the banks of the Landes (which would not actually be drained until the nineteenth century).[40]

In Bas-Poitou itself, there may have been substantial investment in the creation of canals (measuring a total of 24 kms, not counting the short canals which divided the polders), locks (at least fifteen or sixteen of them were stone-faced), bridges, aqueducts and dikes (again made in stone, a very expensive material in this region), yet it remained true that more than half of the polders were underwater for a large part of the year. One of the reasons for this was that the narrow torrents and streams of the estuaries meant there was insufficient flow of the drainage waters towards the sea (possibly a technical oversight on the part of the Dutch).Yet of all the canals and *ceintures* that were dug, only the Chenal de Luçon was perfectly navigable. According to Bourde, who does not however fully analyse the data he provides, one half of the *dessèchements* undertaken in Poitou, Limousin, Angoumois and Aunis can be considered as successful; the other half – that is, an area of more than 100,000 acres – would have to wait for the completion of work in 1780.[41] Of course, such figures can only be taken as indicative, given that areas might be temporarily reclaimed and then abandoned. And all of this in spite of the fact that more attention was lavished on the Atlantic seaboard than other areas of France because of its strategical importance (see, for example, the amount of material regarding this area in the *Archives de la Marine et du Génie* [Naval and Military Engineers Archives] that dates from the period of Colbert onwards).

Financial Backing: Dutch Protestants and International Capitalism

From the financial point of view, Bradley's company certainly broke interesting new ground, even if its innovations were not to have a decisive influence on the development of the kingdom's agriculture. The financier-entrepreneurs behind the company would ultimately become the founders of veritable dynasties, anxious to establish themselves as an integral part of the kingdom's financial and economic structure. At the same time, a complex network of international finances was at work, involving families from different countries of origin and not just the Low Countries. The capital then fleeing the troubled Flanders did not only end up in the Low Countries of the north (as traditionally claimed)[42] but also found its way to France. And the influx of this capital was all the more essential because drainage projects were financially-demanding, having to overcome not only geographical and natural difficulties but also social and institutional opposition of various kinds (which could well add to investment and management costs).

One of these families of investors were the Coymans, who moved to France from Antwerp in the early 1600s and were originally interested in setting up manufacturing concerns (in particular, tapestries that could rival those of the Van Uffe and the De La Planche); they would only subsequently become directly involved in land drainage and reclamation (for example, in La Petite Flandre).

For their part, the Hoeufft family were to play no less an important role. The head of the dynasty, Jan Houefft, was the son of a family of Protestant *regenten* in Roermond, who had been born in 1578 in Liège, where the family had taken refuge from the war against the Spaniards. Having moved to Rouen, he took French nationality and would buy the office of the Secretary to Henri IV; later, he would be a representative in Paris of the Dutch state, also opening a bank that played an important role in large-scale Franco-Dutch financial operations. Hence it is no surprise that, given the favourable economic climate, he was in 1627 happy to form a company with other Dutch investors for the drainage of Sacy-le-Grand to the north of Paris, and from 1642 onwards would be involved in land reclamation in the Petit Poitou and around Arles in the Midi.

And finally, there is the Herwart family, which was of Augsburg origin but moved to Lyons towards the end of the sixteenth century and would subsequently be involved in drainage projects in Provence. In fact, Jean Henri Herwart was an important partner of Jan Houefft and, above all, of Jan van Ens, who was an Amsterdam-born royal counsellor to Louis XIII and seems to have been the original driving-force within the land-reclamation projects around Arles. Together with his brother Barthélemy, Jean Henri also occupied an important place in the financial world of seventeenth-century France; Barthélemy Herwart, for example, became *Contrôleur Général des Finances* in 1657, and was involved in the reclamation of certain *marais salants* [saline marshes].[43] The network of international involvement in these projects is further illustrated by the fact that at the death of Van Ens in 1652, it had been an important figure from the world of German finance who became Director of these very land-reclamation schemes: Octavius de Strada, whose father (of the same name) had come from a famous family of antiquarians, imperial counsellors and army commissars.[44] Nevertheless, despite this interweave of connections, from its very foundation Bradley's *Société* had brought together investors of clearly distinct interests[45]; and as the various associates began to draw up individual contracts with landowners and communities in different parts of the country, they ended up taking less and less interest in the affairs of each other, as it was only in the meetings concerning the areas of their own polders in which they took an active part. What is more, the fact that many of the *dessicateurs* lived abroad, or were perhaps suspected of having relations with an enemy power – a definition which fitted Holland itself after the Revocation of the Edict of Nantes – further added to the difficulties they had to face. The case of the confiscation of the late Jan Hoeufft's estate in 1685 (with only partial restitution to his innumerable heirs in 1713) is simply the most striking case of what could result from such diffidence; there are numerous examples of Dutch entrepreneurs and/or their heirs being forced into bankruptcy or the sale of their property.[46]

The French Midi

The development of such projects in the south of France was a special case; as is well known, different variables affected the drainage and land reclamation schemes here, with Italian hydraulic engineers exerting a decisive influence upon the local school of land reclamation in the fifteenth/sixteenth century. The most representative local figure is Adam de Craponne, the design of whose canals was clearly influenced by what had been created along the rivers of Lombardy and the Veneto (the Adda, the Ticino and the Brenta); the locks designed by Leonardo da Vinci, for example, certainly provided a technological model of undoubted significance.

Although the famous Canal du Midi was not dug until the second half of the seventeenth century, the canal off the river Durance came much earlier, in 1557. Intended to irrigate the Crau plain, this waterway was undoubtedly Craponne's most important project, even if not everything went as it was supposed to: for example, the canal did not manage to bring water to Marseilles and Aix-en-Provence, nor did it make it possible to use the *colmatage* technique to reclaim some 52,000 hectares of farming land within the plain itself (given that the Durance canal carried an annual quantity of mire which, it was calculated, could be used to cover 163 hectares to a depth of 0.25 metres). Similarly, Craponne failed to drain the Fréjus *marais* or the complex marsh environment of the Camargue.

Nevertheless, he did take a first step in this work, as well as initiating drainage in the area on the left bank of the Rhône (near Arles and Tarascon), where there were extensive areas of marshland. In fact, it was there that as early as 1486 a dike had been built which divided the alluvial waters into two parts (one running towards Arles, the other towards Tarascon), with the intention of thus draining them off towards the river Rhône. However, the project had not been a success, and in 1642 the Dutchman Jan van Ens was commissioned to drain the marshland, in which the temporarily or permanently immersed land totalled some 19,000 hectares. In 1619 Arles and Tarascon had signed an agreement that was now put into effect when, at his own expense, Van Ens dug two new drainage canals: the Viguirat canal that was to drain the marshland of Tarascon, and the Vuidange (further to the south) that was to perform the same service for Arles. It is true that Van Ens received two-thirds of the drained land (the reclaimed terrain is given as measuring 2,415 hectares), but it is also true that the project cost a total of 1,400,000 *livres tournois*. The fact that these costs were borne entirely by the entrepreneur probably led him to opt for the cheapest form of work, which naturally had an effect upon quality; and the traditional rivalry between Arles and Tarascon did the rest. Suspicious of the *Arlésiens* and of the way in which they had dug the drainage canals, the inhabitants of the latter actually began to rupture the more northerly dikes, which inevitably led to an abandonment of the project and brought to a head the financial crisis facing Van Ens. What is more, after the death of the Dutchman it became clear there were some planning flaws in the canals that ran into the Rhône and to the sea, with inevitable consequences for the hydro-geological balance in an area where water-logged terrain was a chronic problem.[47] Such errors were repeated just about everywhere in this period, with Dutch – and non-Dutch – engineers being defeated by the difficulties of the challenging situations they had to tackle.[48]

Land Drainage Policy in France

The number of unresolved – political and economic – problems in seventeenth-century France naturally affected land reclamation. Languedoc, for example, had been ravaged by plague and civil war (1631–1638), with consequent neglect of the drainage canals and protective dikes.[49] What is more, the agricultural and industrial policies implemented by Lafférnas and Sully failed to have decisive results (the case of the silk industry is typical) and left a situation of uncertainty that was to last for a long time. However, it would be an exaggeration to see the seventeenth century as a period of unmitigated crisis for France; with regard to the *Basse Provence rurale*, for example, René Baehrel offers precise quantitative data to support his argument that this was a period of growth.[50] As for drainage schemes, one should not forget that, even if their impact upon French agriculture and the nation's economy were not necessarily very sizeable, the edicts in support of such schemes continued throughout this and the following century. In 1641 Louis XIII would confirm further fiscal privileges for those engaged in land drainage in Poitou, Saintonge and Aunis, whilst in 1699 Louis XIV would present Colbert and Louvois with concessions of land in the Flemish Moëres and the Duke de Noailles with the *marais* of the Bas Languedoc 'as this area lacks livestock for the cultivation of land and the nourishment of the inhabitants, due to the scarcity of forage and all that which these lands would provide more abundantly, if it were not for the fact that – being occupied by marshland and swamp – they only produce reeds, which are ill-suited as grazing'. The same intention to stimulate development – and fiscal revenue – can be seen in Louis XV's concession to the Marquise de Maisons and the Marquis de Caillac of the *marais* that Colbert and Louvois had not managed to exploit successfully. In 1746 that same king would present the États de Languedoc with all the *marais* of Beaucaire and Aigues Mortes.[51]

There were still, however, a number of obstacles hindering drainage schemes from being fully implemented or fully effective. Such land reclamation clashed with the economic needs and activities of others whose livelihood depended on these marshy areas. For example, salt production was important all along the coasts of France, particularly on the west coast from southern Brittany to the Landes, but also in the Mediterranean Languedoc. Hence the owners of the salt-works, which would disappear as a result of the drainage of the *marais*, put up determined resistance. Sometimes, as in the island of Ré off the coasts of the Bas Poitou, a perfect balance could nevertheless struck between the exploitation of saline *marais* and of terrain reclaimed for vineyards and wheat fields, all uses of land that were highly profitable.

Then there was the effect on shipping: for example, the drainage of the coast between the Artois and Calais might have comprised navigation through those coastal waters, whilst the reclamation of the *terres marécageuses* in the Sambre affected the traditional source of forage for the king's cavalry and thus conflicted directly with the interests of the monarch.[52] And even without such protests from those who opposed drainage schemes, there was also a real risk of finding that the end-result was excess production of cereal crops and a continual drop in prices.

The *marais*'s wild fowl and *pacage estival* (those grasses and reeds harvested in the summer to be used in basket-weaving, stable litters and thatching) were undoubtedly important economic resources for those who lived in these marshy regions. For example, the authorities themselves recognised that the draining of the *marais* on the Haute Somme in Picardy resulted in the impoverishment of eight hundred households, as hunting and fishing enabled a *maître pêcheur* to earn more than a farm labourer (not that any fisherman would even have considered working the land). What is more, the authorities had to take into account that – as a result of the concessions granted to speculators and the time necessary for full exploitation of the new farm land – reclamation meant the *marais* ceased to be a source of fiscal revenue for at least forty years.

The situation was little different in the south of France, where peasant communities were just as afraid of losing the rights they had once had over the marshlands: the inhabitants of the area between Beaucaire and the Aigues Mortes, for example, protested vociferously against any kind of drainage project (the marshlands in this region produced enough fine quality fodder for more than 100,000 head of livestock).[53] Hence the initial forms of agrarian capitalism came up against a mix of collective interests, consolidated rights, local rivalries and feudal legacies. Mention has already been made of one example of such local rivalry, between Arles and Tarascon, and these clashes could involve entire regions (for example, Contado and Provence) or an individual village and a group of investors, with the result frequently being the sabotage of essential hydraulic structures. What is more, in Provence irrigation may have been a real necessity but proved to be largely impossible due to the fragmentation of the political authorities that exercised rights over public land.[54] The *dessicateurs* therefore had to deal with not only civil but also ecclesiastical authorities – for example, in the cases of the Marais Vernier at Boureaux in the Petit Poitou – and these bodies continued to insist that their ancient rights gave them a say in the drainage operations. The same assertion of traditional privileges came from the never totally undermined feudal forces in the country. In the Vallée des Baux, for example, the Prince of Monaco – to whom Louis XIII had ceded this seigneury after Van Ens began work on his drainage scheme – called into question the terms of the contract, refusing to share his feudal rights over these *marais* with anyone. This meant that the marshlands remained as bleak and desolate as ever, given that the first result of this challenge of Van Ens's contract was that work on all the hydraulic structures was abandoned. Sometimes it was actually the financiers and entrepreneurs who were tempted to set themselves up as feudal lords of the drained territories: for example, Otto Fabrice De Gressenich became Lord of Fontaine-le-Comte in Picardy, and Thierry Hoeufft of the nearby Fontaine Peureuse.[55]

As has been amply shown for the polders of the Bas Médoc, those responsible for administering the reclaimed land often argued amongst themselves. With regard to these polders, it has been observed that as long as the Dutch alone were involved in their management, the maintenance of the hydraulic structures was guaranteed; but once their place began to be taken by other proprietors there was a gradual decline.[56]

The Recovery of the Eighteenth Century

Although careful studies dedicated to the seventeenth century have shown that, in some ways, this was not a period of total stagnation, there can be no doubt that land reclamation – and the profitable exploitation of reclaimed land – was pursued much more vigorously in the following century. Here two main factors come into play: population increase and the ideas of the Physiocrats. Inevitably the former – with the passage from 22 million to 28.1 million during the course of the century[57] – led to the quest for higher returns on investments and higher levels of agricultural production. And though the apparent synchrony between the trends in demography and agriculture is still no more than a hypothesis, there does seem to have been a substantial link between population growth and the increase in the number of publications dedicated to such themes as water resources, fertilisers, crop rotation, livestock, farm management, and other factors that could make a contribution to efficiency.

Though obviously a resource to be exploited in agricultural development – for example, in irrigation – water could also be a hindrance. The Marquis de Turbilly, for one, listed it – together with rock and deeply-embedded plant roots – as one of the physical obstacles to the proper exploitation of land, recommending the use of 'fossés, des signeés, dcs rigoles el des puisards profonds' [ditches, trenches and deep drainage wells] to eliminate the excess. What is more, it became apparent that it was not enough to simply drain marshes and bogs to obtain new farmland for the cultivation of crops: the resultant terrain was fine as pasture-land, but animal manure and fertilisers were required before one could start growing such crops as rye. Hence, a whole series of studies was published on the different types of terrain (marl, chalky, tufa, rocky and limestone – the latter reclaimed through a complex and, above all, costly process) and the fertilisers that were most suitable for them.[58] As Herbert wrote, it was his incapacity in applying such modern techniques of fertilisation that led the peasant to concentrate his attention only on the best-quality land and to neglect all the rest. This, he claimed, was why productivity in France remained stagnant, whilst in England 'which is about half the size of France and, proportionally, much more densely populated, the inhabitants enjoy a higher standard of living'.[59]

Obviously, drainage was one of the techniques to be used in those *défrichements* around which a whole literature developed in France from the 1750s onwards; from Duhamel du Monceau to De La Salle, from Herbert to Dangeul, from Mirabeau to Quesnay, there was no French agronomer who did not discuss the fundamental theme of ridding terrain of water in order to produce fertile agricultural land.

Such schemes might also have an effect on manufacturing industries: for example, Dangeul – a most enigmatic economist – pointed out that the English marshlands (in the areas around Rumney, Leicester and Lincoln) were the source not only of valuable agricultural produce but also of the much-sought-after long-haired wool that was employed by the weaving industries of Norwich, as well as those of northern France (Amiens, Abbeville and Lille),

Flanders and Holland. In fact, the marshland of Rumney was said to have a good 133,000 head of such livestock on an area of 44,000 acres – that is, to achieve a grazing intensity of 3 head per acre.[60]

Comparisons with England were an obsession in the French agronomic writing of the day, especially when it came to pointing out how, employing the same area of terrain, England managed to enjoy substantially larger crop yields. As Pattullo noted so polemically, England was overall one-third smaller than France, but its annual production of cereal crops and fodder was at least double. Comparison with Holland was no less disheartening, given that – including Zeeland – the Low Countries had a surface area one twenty-fourth that of France, but its agricultural production was equal to one third the entire French output.[61] And though France should have been able to feed a population of 28 million, it proved incapable of meeting the food needs of a population which, at the middle of the century, is estimated at somewhere between 16 and 21 million. Of course, it may be the case that such open pessimism was in fact a propaganda tactic used by the Physiocrats to strike their message home; for example, Mirabeau goes so far as to say that in his day French agriculture did not produce 'more than an eighth of what it produced in the days of Sully – a drop that is as incredible as it is real'. In this dramatic situation, even before one tackled the question of agricultural output in general, everything possible had to be done to stimulate the production of cereal crops (in such desperate shortage because of the population increase). As outlined in the works of Turbilly and Duhamel du Monceau, the *défrichements* and the cultivation of the newly-reclaimed land were the keys to the solution of this problem; the means employed in these projects were in part the same as in the previous century, in part derived from the new resources that were the result of developing 'native' social and economic forces, which in Henri IV's day had shown themselves incapable of taking up the challenge posed by ambitious drainage projects. In the eighteenth century, however, *dessèchement* could vary in character. For example, where the ownership of the *marais* was uncertain or unknown, then – to use Bourde's expression – it was concerned with the exploitation of 'terres vaines et vagues' (wasteland); but where the *marais* was clearly the property of a particular village, it was concerned with the exploitation and division of these commonlands. Similarly in the case of meadow land that was subject to flooding, *dessèchement* was little more than land improvement, but in the case of privately-owned *marais* it was often employed as a means of increasing the output of agricultural land already in use. Obviously, in each of these cases one might see the various key issues associated with eighteenth-century agriculture: the problem of the closures; the creation of capitalistic private ownership; the importation of the English-Dutch 'agricultural revolution'; the application of a state policy to encourage reform; the need for one or two social classes capable of implementing new approaches to agronomy.

It was the traditional fiscal approach of tax exemptions that put new energy into projects of *dessèchements* and *défrichements*. From 1761 onwards there were royal decrees concerning uncultivated land that had not yielded any crops for forty years. With their substantial fiscal encouragements – exemptions (generally for a twenty-year period) from the payment of the *dîme*, the *franc-fief* (paid for the right to alter land-use) and the tax on first land purchases by poor peasants; the abolition of existing mortgages and a supply of credit for individual communities – these led to the exploitation of the vast areas of common and privately-owned land in France that had previously lain unused.[62]

In his fundamental entry concerning 'Grains' written for the *Encyclopédie*, François Quesnay calculated that in 1757 some 36 million *arpentes* (around 18 millions hectares) of land were being used for grain crops in France, whilst the *Tableau économique* put the figure as high as 60 million *arpentes*. More pessimistically, the Marquis de Turbilly argued that though the country had the best climate of God's universe, only half of the available farming land was being cultivated. Probably, there was more than a little exaggeration here; as Ferdinando Galiani comments: 'There is a lot less land lying uncultivated than the writers claim'.[63] However, one could not deny that as one moved away from the vast plain around the capital (towards the regions of Anjou, Maine, Touraine, Poitou, Limousin, Marche, Nivernais, Bourbonnais and Auvergne) one encountered 'immense plains that could all come under the plough'. And that is without including Brittany, where two-thirds of the land was still uncultivated.[64]

With these large areas and a continual upward tread in agricultural prices, there were all the necessary theoretical and economic premises for a successful land reclamation campaign, involving not only coastal and inland marshlands but also the vast tracts of uncultivated terrain within feudal estates and common lands. However, such a process was to be neither painless nor easy. As far as the common lands were concerned, the resistance encountered in the seventeenth century persisted, with the assertion of the usual customary rights. But there was also resistance within feudal properties, though of a different nature (here concerned with the defence of the local nobility's privileges and incomes). Deeply imbued with the notion of 'nulle terre sans seigneur', these feudal land-holders did everything they could to obstruct the land reclaimers who posed a challenge to their rights of ownership over what was clearly abandoned land. It is true that La Maillardière, the most convinced champion of the need for canals and drainage systems to boost agricultural progress, argued that the privatisation of the drained *marais* was a necessary juridical step if the land-reclamation projects were to have lasting results.[65] But it is also true that the new land reclaimed in Brittany – where the *défrichements* were amongst the most extensive in the country – was cultivated under the system of feudal concession – *afféagement* – as it was currently defined by law. The Breton nobles received 5 *soldes* for each *journal afféagé* (a *journal* being about half a hectare), and hence had a real incentive to support the land-reclamation projects, which enjoyed equal support from the monarch (who opened the entire *domaine royale* to such *afféagement*), the Breton *états* and – by the middle of the century – most of those writing on such matters in Brittany. In effect, the *défrichements* here were relatively painless (though not entirely so, as we will see shortly): whilst in other areas of France, agricultural progress involved the suppression of *vaine pâture* [customary grazing rights] and the traditional rights of way across land, in Brittany such legal measures were made unnecessary by the very size of the areas to be reclaimed and the fact that since time immemorial owners had enjoyed the right to enclose their land[66] (with regard to the first point, it is estimated that a total of 130,000 *arpentes de Paris* – that is, around 45,000 hectares – were reclaimed in Brittany between 1758 and 1780).

However, even in this region land reclamation and, in particular, drainage projects (probably involved in most of the recovery of the 45,000 hectares cited above) resulted in some degree of conflict and social distress. Here again, those who tried to drain land (feudal land owners, the Breton *états*, the bourgeoisie and sometimes even wealthier members of the peasantry) clashed with those who feared its effects; foremost amongst these were the peasant communities, who reacted negatively to every measure they took as threatening their established rights (be it the deepening of a drainage canal or the demolition of an old corn mill). However, short of experience, education and capital, in the short term they were at a disadvantage compared to the local nobility and town bourgeoisie who were interested in seeing such projects through. Between 1770 and 1789 four companies were set up by four upwardly-mobile social figures: merchants from Versailles, Rouen and Nantes, a manager working for the state mining corporation and the head engineer of the government *Ponts et Chaussées* [Ministry of Bridges and Roads]. Setting themselves the aim of draining all the *marais* around the gulf of Morbihan, those in Saint-Gildas and in the Vicomté de Donges, they made a sizeable capital investment (400,000 *livres*) and developed a strategy that covered the region as a whole. However, not everything went according to plan. Local communities determined to defend the existing status quo took measures that seriously impeded the progress of work; and faced with peasants who 'filled in the canals, destroyed the ditches, cut and took away the crops, carried off the gathered hay', the companies found themselves having to employ guards to protect their investment. And in such a situation attempts to attract new funds were hardly likely to succeed. In fact, of all the *marais* which the companies tried to drain – stretching from the region of Dol to that of Saint-Malo – only those projects involving the Donges enjoyed even partial success. Financial backing and technical expertise alone proved to be insufficient: once again, it was clear that 'le soutien paysan' [the support of the peasants] was indispensable for the ultimate success of such projects.[67]

The Results of *Dessèchements* (Land Drainage) and *Défrichements* (Wasteland Cultivation) in Eighteenth-Century France

The partial failure described above – together with the limitations inherent in all of these projects – should not however blind one to the fact that the decrees of 1761–1764 and the 1766 declaration regarding *défrichements* (all of which envisaged a whole series of regionally-adapted measures) did make a significant contribution to agricultural improvements and land drainage in many regions of France by stimulating the entrepreneurial and financial resources already existing within the country. It should also be pointed out that these resources were not the preserve of one class only, being found sometimes in state functionaries, sometimes in the 'enlightened' nobility and bourgeoisie, sometimes in local communities and merchants.

As has already been mentioned, land-reclamation projects never really came to a full stop at all; and there was a clear upturn in such activity in the early decades of the eighteenth century. For example, in 1739 a convent in La Rochelle applied for 'exemption from various duties for the drainage work that they plan to carry out on various pastures flooded by the Charente', whilst in 1751 a certain 'Sieur Mansard et Compagnie' applied for the tax relief offered in the (repeatedly confirmed) decree of 8 April 1599 as they were to about to engage in the drainage of the lake and *marais* of Grandlieu near Nantes (once the area was drained, it was intended to dig a canal linking Nantes with the sea – a project that significantly did not draw on Dutch capital but on investment by local land-owners and merchants). As further proof of such work, look at the calculations and surveys prepared for a canal which was to have been dug in the Laon region (northern France) and carry the drainage waters from the *marais* in that area into the Ailette canal. This project was undertaken by Nicolas Charbise, head military engineer in Hainaut, and Claude Fontbouillant, a rich land-owner who possessed the rights over the marshland concerned. The two envisaged not only profitable production of vegetables and other crops (rendering at least 75,000 *livres tournois* annually) but also the possibility of using the canal to transport timber, iron, marble and slate over an interregional area that included Flanders, Hainaut, Picardy, Artois and Cambresis. Estimating that the income from this waterway could amount to 146,895 *livres tournois*, they calculated total annual yield at around 221,895. Given that initial project costs were put at 504,360 *livres*, this meant the scheme would have paid for itself in just two to three years.[68]

In effect, as was argued by Goyon de la Plombanie – one of the staunchest champions of drainage projects – if one really wanted to resolve the problems posed by the numerous marshy areas of France (the Bas Médoc, the Upper Périgord, the Quercy, the Rouergue, the Comté de Foix – and, of course, the landes of Bordeaux and Bayonne), then irrigation and drainage canals had to be exploited as routes of commercial navigation as well. The main concern of land-reclamation treatises in this period was the canal, which served not only to develop agriculture, but also provided transport for agricultural produce, stimulated port development (especially along the Atlantic seaboard) and encouraged the growth of manufacturing industries.[69]

Another feature of these decades was the formation of companies made up exclusively of French investors. Whilst there was still talk of Dutch expertise – for example, in the proposal that they might be used as settlers in the South of France, where they could carry out the necessary drainage work and find themselves in their 'natural milieu' (*sic*) – there was a noteworthy decline in the number of investors from the Low Countries; though, as we have already seen, the drainage of the Moëres in the second half of the eighteenth century did involve investment by Vandermey, an advocate from The Hague, whilst engineers from Holland, Flanders and other foreign countries continued to serve as consultants or directors of works on numerous land-reclamation projects[70] (in the south of France, schemes still envisaged the use of Dutch-style windmills).[71] Nevertheless, it is true that the financing and execution of drainage was passing increasingly into the hands of the French themselves. This gradual disappearance of Dutch entrepreneurs, which undoubtedly accelerated after the Revocation of the Edict of Nantes (1685), was accompanied by slower-paced modernisation within France as a whole, so it can hardly be considered as an unambiguous step forward.

French-based investment companies sprang up all over the country, with the key focus for these projects being the areas along the Atlantic seaboard. For example, in 1762 Vallet de Sallignac and Chaube de Chazelles set up a company for the drainage of an entire series of *marais* around Bordeaux; whilst in 1787 around 2 million *livres tournois* were invested in the drainage of some 64,000 *arpentes* around Rochefort (partly, it was stressed, to make the region more salubrious, but also to provide land for the cultivation of hemp and flax – for which there would be a nearby market in the ports of the Atlantic seaboard – and the raising of horses and livestock). The result of this latter scheme, it was calculated, was that the price of an *arpente* would jump from 10 to 300 *livres tournois*.[72]

Renewed interest in land reclamation can also be seen in the Midi, which had long been trying to resolve the problems caused by its shortage of irrigation and farmland. According to the figures provided by L. Dutil, within the Languedoc between 1779 and 1788 some 55,371 *arpentes de Paris* (that is, 18,925 hectares) were reclaimed for crop cultivation as a direct result of the measures taken to encourage *défrichements* and *dessèchements* (it should be noted, however, that numerous fiscal exemptions had been granted to the region in previous periods as well). As has been underlined, it would seem that the more areas of land there were involved in such reclamation projects, the more numerous became those where conversion to agricultural use became perceived as a necessity.[73]

In the Généralité de Montauban, the land reclaimed for cultivation in the years 1766–1768 amounted to 19,373 *arpentes* (6,624 hectares), whilst the figure for the Pays de Foix over the period 1770–1782 is 11,584 (3,960 hectares); but in both cases large-scale *défrichements* required investment on a scale that was quite beyond the reach of small landowners.[74] Similarly large sums were required for drainage and irrigation projects which could be put off no longer. For example, in 1746 the king had granted the province of Languedoc all the ponds and marshes that ran from Beaucaire to Aigues Mortes, but far too many of them were still marshland that had yet to be properly reclaimed. In 1761, François Antoine Roudit de Berriac made an offer to drain the Etang de Marseillete near Carcassonne, making explicit reference to the privileges that Henri IV had granted to whoever would undertake the project.[75] However, his scheme does not seem to have produced significant results.

It was a Parisian architect, Sieur de Beaumond, who made a similar offer to drain the troublesome *marais* around Arles and Tarascon; however, once again, the local communities of Arles and Baux feared the results of that project more than the existing status quo, which provided them with marsh grasses (for example, the characteristic local *sagne*) that they used as fodder for their flocks and as fertiliser.

The schemes undertaken by such large-scale entrepreneurs as Fabre, Floquet and Deyssautier proved even more costly, and it is no accident that they came to nothing. Their aim was to irrigate dry land and at the same time resurrect the old project of linking up Aix-en-Provence and Marseilles with the Durance. To finance the scheme, Floquet issued some 3,200 shares in 1749, raising a total of 1,920,000 *livres tournois*. When that first project soon came to grief, a second company – headed by Deyssautier – was set up in 1769. Once again, the costs went far beyond the initial estimates: a major in the Dutch Army Engineering Corps, Van Sugtelen, calculated the ultimate costs that would have to be borne at around 9,000,000 *livres*, a figure that went way beyond previous forecasts. Given this, it was inevitable that the company fell back on less demanding projects – for example, the digging of the Boisgelin canal to link up with the old Craponne canal.[76]

The difficulties encountered in the Midi were no exception, and so serve as a measure by which to evaluate the land-reclamation and drainage policy which had been enthusiastically pursued throughout the nation in the previous decades. Further proof of the disappointing results ultimately achieved can be seen in the hundreds of thousands of hectares of uncultivated and marshy land that the Abbé Rozier records in his 1809 *Cours complet*;[77] French historians have, almost unanimously, spoken of the 'overwhelming failure of land reclamation based on the granting of privileges'. With figures to hand, Labrousse calculated that (including drained terrain) a maximum of one and a half million *arpentes* of land had been reclaimed for cultivation. The data in nineteenth-century and Napoleonic land registers reveal that the total of *terres labourables* in the last years of the French monarchy was around 60–65 million *arpentes de Paris*, and thus the historian shows that 'the wasteland reclaimed for cultivation between 1766 and 1789 accounted for around 2.5 per cent of the total of agricultural land at the end of the Ancien Régime'. The ambitious policies introduced in 1761–66 ultimately produced a derisory increase in the land under cultivation.[78]

The Period of the Revolution

Naturally the question of land-reclamation policy was one that the Revolutionary period had to deal with. Indeed, there was renewed interest in the issue, largely because of the need to feed a population at war, whose requirements were greater than they had been in the previous time of peace. This situation resulted in a new flurry of statistical and on-site studies: according to Rougier de la Bergerie, for example, the reclamation of marshland alone would led to the recovery of around 100,000 hectares (308,220 *arpentes*) of agricultural land for the cultivation of crops, whilst the *Tableau général des marais à déssecher en France* (published in 1817) gives the area of the marshland yet to be drained at that date as totalling 730,216 hectares.[79] Meanwhile the memoranda written regarding the *dessèchements* continued to pile up, and the revolutionary assemblies – primarily the Convention – showed growing interest in drainage schemes that would meet ever more pressing food needs.[80]

Writing in 1791, Boncerf claimed that he had realised a full fifteen years earlier how essentially important land reclamation was, and that his ideas had been confirmed by the events of subsequent years. His painstaking analyses of the areas yet to be drained left the reader in no doubt as to how profitable such undertakings might be: there were some 20 million *arpentes* of uncultivated land, 1,200,000 of them being made up of *marais*. 'Turned into pasture, meadow or fields of flax, hemp, rape and timber' yielding 20 *livres tournois* per *arpente*, they would render the state a return of 24 million *livres*. The rest of the uncultivated land (at least another 15 million *arpentes*) could be used to meet Revolutionary France's trading deficit in imports of meat, flax, butter, cheese and salted meat, which Bocerf calculated as amounting to 138 million *livres tournois* – plus another 66 million for the imports of manufactured goods. Underlining once more how the raising of livestock and the production of fodder were an essential part of the nation's wealth, his perceptive analysis showed a link between the agricultural sector, the expansion of manufacturing industries and the requirements of the navy (the most significant link between the three being the crops of flax and hemp).[81]

However, land-reclamation projects would come up against the same sort of difficulties in Revolutionary France as they had under the Ancien Régime, with a modern and rational policy for the management of water resources encountering a whole series of institutional, socio-political and technical problems. One of the former concerned the legislation governing the division of communal property, which was at the very basis of the establishment of solidly-based private property and yet clashed with a principle that the Republic wished to safeguard: that the *marais* were to be considered as a public utility.[82]

The 'Agricultural Revolution' in France

Whilst the theorists of French agronomy had written extensively on a huge range of subjects, the institutional, socio-political and geographical obstacles to the implementation of their theories had proved to be almost insurmountable.[83] Recent and less recent studies have cast light on each of these obstacles, but it is only a general survey that can give us a fair idea of the complexity of the situation in France. One has to bear in mind not only the 'original characteristics' of French agriculture but also the various kinds of significant progress that had been made at a regional level. Le Roy Ladurie, for example, focuses on the diversification in agricultural produce, the progress made in the transport system and the forms of economic compensation that emerged in Provence, Bourgogone and the Auvergne. And, elsewhere in France, there were high levels of yields and the use of 'English-style' crop rotation in the large farming concerns of the Ile-de-France basin and the northern regions bordering on the Low Countries.

Various regions specialised in specific crops: wheat (Brie, Beauce), vines (Auxerrois), garden vegetables (Vaucluse), bovine livestock and dairy products (Normandy);[84] as Mulliez has pointed out, wheat was far from being a *mal nécessaire* that had to be cultivated regardless of local suitability, and thus various regions could focus on more profitable produce or – as in the case of Normandy – livestock. [85] Nevertheless, it is undoubtedly the case that 'large-scale agriculture' and the Flemish methods used extensively in England were very slow in obtaining a solid foothold in the agricultural heartlands of France. [86] However Le Roy Ladurie argues that the medium-small agricultural concerns themselves generated certain types of development: contrary to what had happened in the sixteenth century, the small-scale farms did manage to resist the *rassembleurs de terres* [land accumulators], hence preventing any mass migration into the cities and excessive rural impoverishment; meanwhile seigniorial rights remained static, indeed diminished in importance due to inflation during the eighteenth century, and were anyway generally accepted without much resistance by most of the peasant population.[87]

There are similarly nuanced areas when it comes to evaluating the individual crops introduced into the *marais* and into French farming in general. True, clover (championed by Duhamel du Monceau) was widely grown in the Paris basin. However, the *jachère* system was not abandoned overall, and there was no widespread introduction of other hoe crops and leguminous plants in crop-rotation cycles – for all that Abbé Rozier was convinced that the key to being competitive with England was quality rather than quantity: 'we grow too much. Let us grow less, and grow better'[88] It is also true that the introduction of more speculative crops, the most representative of which is perhaps madder, was stimulated by decrees that offered incentives for drainage.[89] However, the conclusions that Barral reaches with regard to the irrigation projects in the Midi show this *'aménagement de l'eau'* fell dispiritingly short of the goals proposed by the *'éclairés'*: irrigation was poorly carried out in general, and profitable canal-building in the south of France would have to wait until the nineteenth century. Even Turgot, though he urged the extension of cultivated meadowland and recognised the essential importance of fodder, failed to see that water resources were the key to a fundamental boost in yield levels.[90] As a further sign of the discordant and contradictory opinions that were emerging from the French scientific community, one might look at what was being argued by La Maillardière and Rozier: whilst the former envisaged drainage as going hand-in-hand with the construction of viable canals and the privatisation of the reclaimed land of the *marais*, the latter – in a rather contradictory fashion – was hoping to see the development of small-scale rather than large agricultural concerns. In support of this view, he argued that where the farmer owned a lot of land he tended to use it solely to graze livestock; and even if he did cultivate crops, he only obtained a quarter of the yield that would be gained by twenty smallholders 'because it is only smallholdings that are well farmed'. Though there was some truth in this last statement, accepting it as a given did nothing to resolve the fundamental problem of the low yields and excessive fragmentation of far too much French farmland.

One of the contemporary writers on such matters who was clearly aware of these problems was Despommiers, who gave this description of a peasant smallholding: 'a farm of 30 *arpentes* can in a season nourish two horses, three or four cows and around sixty to eighty sheep. I know enormous areas of countryside like this: almost all those that I examined produced scarcely two Paris-measure *setiers* of wheat, and half as much of oats. Let one judge the living conditions of such farmers'.[91]

It was realised that England had overtaken France because it had appreciated the importance of manure, fertilisers, livestock and irrigated areas planted as meadowland.

Obviously the reasons for these weaknesses of French agriculture can only be understood by looking at a number of variables: urban demand and consumption, together with the socio-economic behaviour of both the farming communities themselves and of the political institutions above them. Focus on some of these factors to the exclusion of others leads to the emergence of a misleading picture; the more recent interpretations that tend to stress the role of institutions and of the micro-conflicts that hindered the implementation of efficient drainage and irrigation projects are not entirely convincing, as they tend to neglect a number of variables whose role was fundamental. However, analyses that owe a substantial amount to the approach of 'new economic history' have cast a great deal of light on the economic mechanisms at play in furthering or hindering land reclamation. In effect, by establishing a close relation between interest rates, land prices and possible profits one outlines the core of the problem – that is, the reasons why work or was not undertaken on the implementation of a particular drainage scheme or the creation of irrigation channels (again, it should be remembered that most of the work on these channels in the Midi only really began in the nineteenth century). However, given that feudal-type dues and duties continued to be such a burden on the economic life of eighteenth-century France, it is doubtful whether one can really speak of the country as having a credit system and a capital market comparable to such economic mechanisms as they exist nowadays.[92]

All in all, it seems difficult to argue with the conclusion that the obstacles to agricultural growth in France cannot be seen as due solely to social or institutional factors. If that had been the case, then the abolition of feudal factors and the very Revolution itself should have opened the way to unrestrained agricultural progress, whilst we know that not to have been the case: the Revolution did little to change the existing situation either in terms of the size of landholdings, the distribution of property or of the farming techniques used. Even in the first half of the nineteenth century there was no significant increase in yield levels, with little movement towards the introduction of commercial fertilisers and fodder crops, as well as only slow increases in livestock-breeding.[93] One reason for all of this was the low level of urbanisation in France, which naturally had an effect on the demand for meat and dairy produce, even if that explanation can also be turned on its head so that – like Cantillon – one can argue that urban development can be seen as an effect not a cause (with agricultural output and *rentier* income being the fundamental factors in determining the size of cities). One might also claim that the great distance between the areas to be converted to farming (many of them along the French coast) and the large urban market of Paris meant the capital had little effect as a stimulus on land reclamation. This does not mean that one minimises the importance of the abolition of feudal institutions – for example, that seigniorial *tirage*, which gave the local lord a right to one third of all land cultivated[94] – or denies that the advent of the Revolution created a totally new situation by undermining a whole series of customary laws. But what remains true is that technology and relations of production – that is, the structural features of French agriculture, with which 'jurisprudence and *a fortiori* the law dealt only in a tardy and patchy fashion'[95] – continued to be a part of the problem rather than the solution. One fact alone may illustrate this: in 1852, 85 per cent of French peasants still had small-holdings of less than 10 hectares and did not produce market crops. It has also been calculated that if in eighteenth-century Europe as a whole the average number of labourers required to work 100 hectares of cereal-crop land was around fifty, in France the number needed was exactly double that. A large part of farming still depended on small- to medium-scale concerns with rented land or sharecropping, with the *fermier* being much less inclined than his English counterpart to welcome innovation.[96] Here, the greater or lesser duration of land-rent contracts played an important role: for example, with regard to the Paris Basin, it has been observed that 'in inner parts of the Paris Basin where leases ran from nine to eighteen years, farmers were willing to pay interest on draining outlay. But in western *départements* where leases ran for nine years or less, it was recorded that farmers disliked paying extra rents for draining'.[97]

In the final analysis, it was financial restrictions that prevented people meeting the costs of drainage or of introducing techniques and technologies that could have had a decisive effect. What is more, the quality of soil and terrain varies much more in France than in England, which enjoyed the advantage of a high percentage of top-quality soil, more abundant and regular rainfall and greater potential for livestock breeding and crop rotation. And the very availability of abundant labour meant that in France there was more extensive cultivation of marginal land that in England had long ago been abandoned as pasture. Hence, output per farm in France was much lower than on the other side of the Channel, with French agriculture being unable to 'accumulate a stock of productive assets to match the capital-labour and capital-land ratios achieved in Britain'.[98] No one has shown more effectively than Meuvret how the French peasants had a deep-seated interest in maintaining *vaine pâture*, where they could freely graze livestock (sheep more than cattle) on the thin layer of stubble left in the fields; it is no coincidence that the French family seemed reluctant to change its diet away from cereal crops to milk and dairy products, potatoes, maize and turnips.[99] And here Marc Bloch's perceptive analysis of the socio-political reasons for France's lagging behind England remain valid, especially with regard to the point that as early as the Middle Ages large estate-owners in England had – by asserting their economic independence from the monarchy – served as agents to stimulate rather than hinder agricultural renewal. The French monarchy, on the other hand, had protected the small peasant farmer (the very basis of its fiscal revenues) from possible encroachments by the large aristocratic estate owners, whilst the peasant small-holders themselves did everything in their power to maintain their rights of access and control over the lands within communal properties. What is more, the failure of a number of land-reclamation projects in the seventeenth century had led to a return of 'concession of land either to individual communities where the land was found or to the state, which in turn gave it back to the local inhabitants'.[100] Only when owners of middle-scale or large estates had rid themselves of these handicaps – which, if the truth be told, were more a question of customary practice than legislation[101] – and ceased to use them as an excuse for simply living off land rents, would they be able to set up those farming concerns that could initiate a process similar to that which had taken place in the English countryside. In this context, drainage would – together with enclosure and the consolidation of bourgeois notions of private property – become one of the key factors, opening the way to thorough-going capitalist-based renewal of the countryside. Undoubtedly, increases in the price of wheat and the theories of the Physiocrats all served to make agriculture more dynamic, focusing attention on the farmer-entrepreneur and encouraging a break with customary communal bonds and ties. However, there were various factors that cast doubt on whether this step forward could be consolidated: the poor market structure of French agriculture, the types of crops chosen, variations in soil quality and the relations of production within the countryside itself.

Italian and Dutch Expertise in England at the End of the Sixteenth and Beginning of the Seventeenth Centuries

With the exception of Holland, which represents the most advanced model of land reclamation through drainage, England is probably the country in which land reclamation is most clearly linked with the process of modernisation and the penetration of capitalism into the countryside. Drainage itself is apparently indissolubly linked with the question of 'enclosures' and the consolidation of bourgeois property, and finds a place in the unflagging debate regarding the 'agricultural revolution' in England and the social resistance to that process put up by the peasant classes. The recent arguments put forward by Robert C. Allen are here very significant: contrary to the claims of a long-established historical tradition, not only were the enclosures not much more productive than communal land, but the profits realised from drained land were higher than those achieved within the enclosures themselves. What is more, drainage projects were cheaper if carried out on open land, as – in terms of return on investment – the collective benefits of two or three landowners were greater than those which might be achieved by a project undertaken by a single individual.[102] In effect, it has been claimed that drainage was 'second only in significance to the supersession of permanent tillage and grass by up-and-down land ... between 1560 and 1720, particularly before 1660'.[103]

The first to undertake land-reclamation schemes were the large land-owning religious houses. However, when substantial gains were made in the reclamation of British marshlands – primarily from

1536–39 onwards – the impulse for such projects came from the increasing prices of agricultural produce and the increasing value of drained land (which soon outstripped the value of existing farming land).

Among the European technicians present in the English countryside, one of the main groups to influence the development of land reclamation work around this time was that of Italian military engineers, who made their mark some time before Dutch capital and know-how began to dominate the scene. Clive Holmes, for example, has illustrated the key role of the political-religious refugee Jacopo Aconcio, who arrived in England in 1559 and was therefore at work on land reclamation some twenty years or so before Humphrey Bradley. A native of Trento, Aconcio – who was a philosopher, jurist and mathematician as well as a military engineer – would in 1565 apply for patents on various types of hydraulic machinery, and also proposed a scheme for the reclamation of 800 hectares of land around Plumstead which was subject to occasional flooding by the Thames. Although that scheme did not produce any permanent results, the group of investors associated with Aconcio was highly significant (and varied): Giambattista Castiglione, Giacomo Guicciardini and a certain Ferdinando Poyntz (who is described as an 'English merchant', had business connections with the Low Countries and would subsequently play an essential role in bringing to England Humphrey Bradley, the son of an English merchant who lived in Bergen-op-Zoom in the Brabant). Other foreigners involved in such schemes at the time of Aconcio include such French technicians as Latreille and Mostart, the German engineer Wilhelm Engelbert, the Dutchman Peter Morrice, and the Frieslander Gherard Houricke – presences which clearly bear out Clive Holmes's insistence on the international nature of land reclamation in Elizabethan and Stuart England.[104] As far as Aconcio is concerned, another innovative contribution was his recognition of the need for legislative as well as technical development: he argued that one could only overcome the clear conflicts that such speculative private projects would continue to arouse throughout the first half of the seventeenth century if one found some way of dealing with the customary use-rights associated with common land.

In effect, in England more than anywhere else one has to see such land-reclamation projects within the context of a rapidly changing

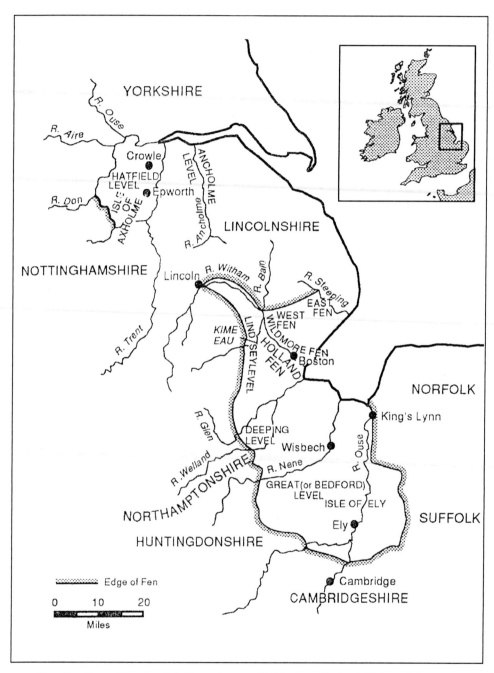

Map 6.   Map of the English Fens. Source: K. Lindley, *Fenland Riots and the English Revolution*, London, 1982.

socio-economic situation, which itself provided the stimulus and momentum for such schemes. The most widely studied case is that of the Fens, 'immense tracts of water-formed land', where in 1590 the Duke of Bedford would commission three Dutch technicians to assess the possibility of draining Thorney Fen, where various substantial areas of farm land would be reclaimed around Milton Fen, Ely, Conington and Upwall Fen, which were all significantly referred to as the 'Londoner's Fens'. However, only a few decades later place-names would begin to reflect the Dutch role in the area: Great Holland, Great Holland Common, Holland Haven and Little Holland. Rudimentary windmills and other machinery ('screwers, pullies, poizes...') had been introduced by the end of the sixteenth century, though it is difficult to assess just how crucial a role this transfer of Dutch technology played here, in a region where a certain Captain Thomas Well invested £12,000 (in 1599) in the largely unsuccessful project to drain the Deeping and Crowland Fens (a project into which the Duke of Exeter would subsequently pour a further £17,000). Nevertheless, there was some measure of success, given that the fens of 1619 have been described in these terms 'although only about a third of the fenland around Peterborough was dry, and only half that south of Holland and Marshland, very little remained drowned east or south of the Ouse, south-east of Ely or about Somersham'.[105]

The fact that there was rapid deterioration in the areas where such schemes had been completed ultimately made recourse to Dutch technicians and engineers inevitable. In 1588 the famous Humphrey Bradley presented a general project involving the whole of the fens, which included the suggestion of a long drainage canal as well as work on the rivers Ouse, Nene and Welland (though subsequent experience would show that Bradley's belief that such drainage could rely solely on gravity was incorrect).[106] This scheme would not be put into effect, but the 1626–27 project drawn up by Vermuyden for Hatfield Chase and the Isle of Axholm (in the northern part of the fens) was probably the first of its kind to attract a massive influx of investment from abroad (funding that was largely gathered by Vermuyden himself). The entire area covered around 70,000 acres, of which some 24,500 would be assigned to the (mainly Dutch) investors. However, here again the project was largely unsuccessful, due mainly to the difficulties that would emerge during the later – more ambitious – schemes involving the fens proper. Along with technical errors and miscalculations there was also the effect of stiff resistance from 'commoners', for whom the land which lay between one village and the next had traditionally been a source of pasture-land, marsh herbs, material for boat-building and plentiful wild fowl; as one contemporary source puts it, the inhabitants of the fens might earn 16 shillings 'by [the] cutting down of three or four loads of reed for thatch and fuel to bake and brew withal'.[107]

Already looked upon with suspicion as a foreigner, Vermuyden thus found himself having to deal with a very hostile local population. His problems only got worse when, to cope with the constant overflowing of the rivers, he had a spillway built; partially funded by the engineer himself, this nevertheless ate substantially into the profits of the scheme. Ultimately, Vermuyden – who had previously enjoyed royal backing; the Crown saw the scheme as a resulting in a new source of fiscal revenue – not only found himself facing financial difficulties but also became a scapegoat caught in the middle of the clashes between Parliamentarians and Royalists (the former, in 1642, organised a decisive campaign of dike destruction which would result in a loss for the 'Hatfield settlers' of around £20,000).[108]

Commoners and Drainers in England: Capitalism in the Countryside

Drainage, enclosures and land speculation were in this period both a cause and a reflection of social malaise resulting from changes in the system of land ownership. The proof of this is provided by the fact that in these decades the Hatfield Chase area was in fact much less troubled than other areas affected by drainage schemes: where commoners and individual villages managed to organise themselves and reach some sort of negotiated compromise with investors/land reclaimers – and make their voice felt in Parliament – they could save a large part of their customary rights and of the traditional structure of the community.[109]

The decisive clash between the interests involved came south of Hatfield Chase, above all in the Great Level, where it was the land-owning aristocracy that was most concerned to further exploitation of these vast areas of marshland – all in all, some 400,000 acres traversed by the rivers Welland, Glen and Witham, with another 360,000 acres lying further north in Lincolnshire. In 1621 the king himself had become committed to the project for the reclamation of the Great Level, taking upon the Crown the task of reconciling the 'commoners [to the work of] the commissioners, as experience had shown that the common sort of people are apt to be jealous of anything that is new'.[110]

The project was taken up again in 1630 by the Duke of Bedford, who headed a consortium of fourteen investors and commissioned Vermuyden as chief engineer (he was to get 90,000 acres, whilst the Crown would get 30,000 acres and the syndicate the rest). Due to violent opposition from the commoners, however, Vermuyden was soon replaced by the Duke of Bedford himself, with significant changes being made in the share-out of the allotted land. But the persistent difficulties encountered by the project would then, in 1638, lead to the king re-appointing Vermuyden as head engineer, with the Crown taking over from the Duke of Bedford as the general manager for the scheme (at which point the 30,000 acres assigned to the monarch in 1630 increased to some 152,000 acres). Events of this period reveal how the interests of the ruling classes (aristocracy and monarchy) could differ, converge and become interwoven in complex temporary alliances. There is also evidence of manoeuvring and attempts at parliamentary corruption in order to create cartels and pressure groups, which rather clumsily attempted to disguise their aims beneath a veneer of patriotism and appeals to the 'common good'.

Proof of the favourable economic climate at the time is provided by the fact that the monarchy and the aristocracy were joined in these schemes by small local entrepreneurs and courtiers who could raise sufficient capital to finance reasonably large landholdings. This is the case with the Killigrews, an 'archetypal courtier family' who in 1646 – together with such squires as Robert Long and George Kirke – invested more than £30,000 in the drainage of the Lindsey Level (some 70,000 acres in South Lincolnshire). The scheme was, with clear ulterior motives, supported by the Crown and other influential members of the government, the king receiving some 3,000 acres of reclaimed agricultural land, the queen 500 acres, and the Lord Keeper, the Chancellor of the Exchequer and the two Secretaries of State further sizeable parcels of land.

A few years later the same consortium was involved in the drainage of the around 21,500 acres of Holland Fen (between

Lindsey Level and the river Witham in Lincolnshire). The king here asserted his status as the legal owner of the Fen, thus confirming his right to expropriate the commoners; however there was an inevitable clash over the matter. In fact, the commoners both contested the king's right to be recognised as 'lord' of the area and also did everything they could to maintain their traditional communal rights. It is no accident that this region revealed the great rift between the monarchy and local communities that would find more violent expression a few years later in the Civil War, though it would be going too far to see this conflict between monarchy and 'undertakers' and local communities as one of the causes of the English Revolution (even if it does help to explain why, at the moment of its decisive confrontation with Parliament, the Crown found itself largely deprived of popular support in this area).[111]

Significantly, resistance within Holland Fen against encroachments on traditional rights would continue for decades into the following century. And even though the silent sabotage of dikes, canals and embankments was much more prevalent than open violence against land-owners, the rebellion obviously created a situation of great uncertainty in the area. As historians have pointed out, such peasant revolts against 'improvements' were surpassed in intensity only by those that had greeted the enclosures.

However, as in the previous case, land-drainage projects revealed capitalism refining the legal strategies and other means at its disposal in order to gain a firm foothold in the countryside and undermine the position of its opponents. The first step was to deprive 'the commoners of their authority to govern the fen, or to raise money to defend suits and oppose the king in the work of drainage'. Then would come the move 'to inquire into certain particulars', which might result in the 'legal prosecution of some principal opponents'. From the formal point of view, the steps taken were more cautious, but they nevertheless proved equally fatal to these local rural communities: parishes were taxed in order to finance drainage projects that were described as intended for 'the common good'; and when sufficient monies could not be raised this way, land was expropriated and the fen assigned to the drainage company itself.[112]

So, for all the differences of circumstances, the policies followed were not that different from those applied in other areas of land reclamation, including Venice, even if historical records seem to show that the English peasants and local communities put up stiffer resistance against this process of privatisation of land resources. In effect, the course of events in England reveals both strong opposition to modernisation at the bottom of the social scale and substantial success in actually carrying out such projects; and it is more than probable that the former was the due to the powerful stimulus for change resulting from the latter.

A Technological Impasse: The Halt in Drainage Projects in Eighteenth-Century England

As has been pointed out, the capitalist surge in English agriculture came in precisely the same decades as the major fen drainage projects, culminating in the 1672 Corn Law (which occurred long before Adam Smith became the champion of economic liberalism).[113] Thanks to these strategies, important results were achieved in more than one area of land reclamation in England: for example, in the Ancholme Level project (involving around 18,000 acres in the north of Lincolnshire), where Sir John Monson and a consortium of fourteen other aristocrats totally overcame the opposition of the local commoners and ultimately turned this fen into one of the most peaceful in the region. In effect, both Parliament and the agronomists who were concerned to increase agricultural yields – for example, Walter Blith, who published his *The English Improver Improved* in 1652 – unhesitatingly took the side of the improvers, for all that they were aware of the social equilibrium disturbed by their projects.[114] Of course, there were exceptions – for example, radical Parliamentarians such as John Wildman and John Lilburne – but their support for the commoners could do little to halt the course of events; and passive resistance from local communities – for example, refusing to supply the manpower necessary to work the new farms – proved counterproductive because new settlers were imported from Scotland and the Netherlands to replace them. However, as Joan Thirsk points out, the overall situation is far from clear-cut or standardised, as the absence of precise government rulings on the matter meant that the size of settlements varied from area to area, with some smallholdings being no more than 15 acres[115] – a clear sign that even in the more advanced context of English agriculture, individual land speculation existed alongside more solidly-based capitalistic investment. And this should come as no surprise because, as more recent studies have shown, the English aristocracy was not always the champion of 'improving' and innovation that it appears to be in more traditional accounts.[116]

Whatever the truth, the need for food and the desire to make the country self-sufficient in grain production obviously aroused interest in the 'drowned' areas of potentially fertile soil that might produce not only corn but also fodder, rape (with a wide variety of applications, from soap-making to the production of oil for the treatment of fabrics), flax, hemp and plant dyes (for example, madder and woad), which had obvious consequences for the weaving industry. The agronomists of the time seemed to have no doubts that the drained land would produce much more fodder than the common-lands left open to temporary flooding. At the same time, various writers put forward new organisational models for the farming of the fens in order to make them as productive as possible. One such was the agronomist Cressey Dymock, who was deeply influenced by the ideas generated in the 1650s within the group centred around Samuel Hartlib.[117] Like the later – and more famous model – put forward by von Thünen, Dymock proposed a concentric layout of land around a central farm, with the first circle being used from cereal crops, and the second, more distant circle, being used as pastureland.[118]

While new forms of agricultural organisation were undoubtedly tried out in such reclaimed areas as the Isle of Axholme, the rapid conversion of pasture to cereal crops ultimately lead to a market glut, which then had an effect on prices; this was particularly clear after 1700 and resulted in a decline in interest in the draining of other fenlands or marshy areas. The need to maintain prices became of such importance that the owners of chalky or hilly terrain began to look with suspicion on their fenland rivals, the 'improvers', who were a serious threat because they produced 'more corn, more wool and more meat from more fertile soil'.[119] The stagnation resulting from a drop in prices naturally led to a falling-off in speculative investments in such projects; indeed, this was a period in which 'the constant cry was for money'.[120]

Another problem was the safeguarding of the hydraulic works that had already been carried out. This obviously required an efficient system of taxation and of juridical and legislative control. Such efficiency was undermined by the conflictual relationship that inevitably existed between the various bodies which had a say in such matters – for example, the 'Conservators of the Great Level of the Fens,' the 'Court of Sewers for the Northern Fenlands of Lincolnshire', the 'Earl of Manchester for the Deeping Fen', and so on. And as numerous landowners began to make insufficient profits from their reclaimed land, they were unable to pay the taxes due, with the result that failure of maintenance led to a decline in the state of the drained terrain (exactly the same state of affairs as obtained at around the same time in Holland; though in England the situation was even more confused because of the absence of such control bodies as the polders and the *hoogheemraadschappen*).[121]

As in numerous other areas of Europe, there was also a situation of chronic conflict between various factors: the technological limits of windmills; the need to keep reclaimed land from once more going under water; and the dual use of canals for both drainage and transport. As is well known, only very gradually were canals restricted to one specific use – the process concluding with a veritable revolution in England's transport system, the basis for which was laid around this time. What is more, the years 1630–1650 saw the emergence in the fens of various specific technical problems (just how insurmountable these were is still a matter of debate amongst historians). In effect, the Dutch technicians had no experience of dealing with areas in which there were a large number of rivers – as was the case in Hatfield Chase or the fens (in the Low Countries drainage schemes had mainly involved large inland lakes) – so Vermuyden and his colleagues found themselves having to tackle a number of unforeseen problems. For example, the former had various drainage canals dug for his reclamation schemes (the Old Bedford River and then the New Bedford River) which led to the drying out, shrinking and thus lowering of the local peaty terrain; the result was that, when the banks of the canal shrank, the canals themselves began to overflow. Attacked on this question by another Dutch hydraulic engineer (Jan Barentsz. Westerdijck), Vermuyden would, in 1642, write his *Discourse Touching the Draining of the Great Fens* in his own defence – an act for which there are various interesting historical parallels: in the early decades of the sixteenth century, the Paduan Alvise Cornaro had written his own *Scritture sulla Laguna* with the same purpose, whilst around a century later it would be the

Dutchman Leeghwater who defended his own land-reclamation schemes with his *Haarlemmermeer Boek*.

But quite apart from these technical questions, the Dutch contribution to which has been widely studied by historians, the main point to be stressed is how long the conditions in the fens and the other marshlands of England remained precarious. In the Bedford Levels, for example, 'the problems of peat shrinkage and silting outfalls seemed to be insuperable, and flooding relentlessly increased in frequency and severity'; in the North Level there was a series of floods between 1753 and 1770, with the phenomenon – due to the above-mentioned shrinking and silting – re-occurring in 1795, 1799 and 1800; and in the Middle Level the situation was throughout the period 1760–1840 one of gradual decline, in spite of the erection of a number of drainage windmills (in 1760 Deeping Fen, to the north of the river Welland, was drained using 50 windmills, but just thirty years later these pumps were powerless to stop the constant flooding). When, in 1800, Arthur Young visited the area between Whittlesey and March he described a situation of chronic environmental instability, with fertile fields having to be abandoned at the first sign of flooding.[122]

The slow improvement in the state of the fens would only begin in the 1820s and 1830s, when an up-turn in agricultural prices[123], the incorporation of technological change encouraged landowners to install more efficient hydraulic machinery – for example, steam-driven water pumps. The first of these was introduced in the Bedford Level as early as 1817, whilst the South Level would have to wait for the early years of the following decade (however, the six-foot drop in the level of water in the main spillway there was also due in part to the creation of a new drainage canal – the Eau Brink Cut – in 1821).[124]

Conclusions

The seventeenth and eighteenth centuries saw a standstill in drainage and land reclamation that affected not only England but a number of countries on the continent. This would seem to support the notion that drainage and land reclamation should be considered as a European phenomenon, in which there are individual national variations but also a number of common characteristics. From the technological point of view, for example, both the English fens and the Dutch polders came up against the difficulties in overcoming the limitations of the traditional drainage windmill (*wipmolen*) that had first been developed in the Low Countries. True, this technology was not used everywhere – its absence in the Veneto was to put a severe limitation on land reclamation in that region – but there is no doubt that windmills, fitted with either waterwheels or Archimedes' screws, were introduced to, and then further developed in, the English fens; Darby would even go so far as to speak of England, too, as having its 'windmill age', which extended up until the first decades of the nineteenth century. The first such windmill, almost certainly based on a Dutch model, seems to have been set up at Satterday Bridge (Holbech) in 1588; but eventually – as in the German *Köge* and the Dutch polders – windmills would reveal their inability to provide a conclusive solution to the problem of draining – and above all, keeping drained – large areas of marshland (almost everywhere it was taken for granted that some of the recently-drained terrain would be lost). It was not until the advent of the steam pump – first developed in Holland at the end of the eighteenth century and then adopted throughout Europe in the first decades of the nineteenth – that this technological stalemate was broken. This decisive turning-point made it possible to finally establish complete control over the key areas of drainage and land reclamation in Europe. In 1852, for example, it was observed that 'in the whole of the Fens, the number of windmills formerly at work between Lincoln and Cambridge' had dropped from 700 to 220,[125] with steam-powered drainage managing to increase not only the area of land drained but also the cost efficiency of the entire operation (though, of course, sizeable initial investment was required; it is no coincidence that the use of steam pump meant the setting up of sizeable consortia that could draw on adequate financial backing).

However, the history of land drainage is not only the history of technological developments, involving as it does economic, financial and agricultural factors. Prices, climate, migration and agricultural circumstances all affected – and were affected by – drainage projects; and this interaction within individual regions should be studied in greater depth.

From the financial point of view there was an increasing internationalisation of funding that has yet to be studied extensively.

Moved by speculators and family dynasties of financiers, sizeable amounts of capital shifted between different economic sectors and different nations; clearly, drainage and land reclamation was attractive to investment capital. The case of France here seems the most stimulating area for study, given the large presence of Dutch bankers within the nation; probably it is no coincidence that there seems to be a direct link between Protestant bankers and such high-risk investments as land drainage. However, further attention should also be paid to other, rather surprising, channels of investments – for example, the French capital invested in the German *Köge*, or the funding for land reclamation provided by an Antwerp *mont-de-piété*. To what extent were other banks – and even monasteries – involved in this sector?

Emphasis has been put on the fact that land reclamation involved not only the 'conquest' of new terrain (in which case it would simply be an episode in an age-old history) but also the advent of capitalist agriculture. It is clear that capitalism – that is, the investment of large sums of capital – can take many forms, and so it should come as no surprise that many operations of land reclamation and drainage could co-exist with feudalist structures (indeed, sometimes even strengthen them – as would seem to have happened in parts of France and Prussia). Nor should one overlook the fact that within many areas of reclaimed land traditional relations of production continued to exist, with the focus still on the traditional crops (primarily cereals) intended to meet internal demand (this was the case, for example, within the Venetian Republic). In pre-industrial societies, food requirements accounted for a large amount of production, and thus they had an extensive effect on policies regarding the environment, and on those governing land drainage and irrigation. Within the areas of sharper economic acceleration, such as Holland and England, there was greater market awareness, with the introduction of crops that produced higher profits and would also open the way to significant social transformations. All in all, agriculture seems to have played a much larger role in stimulating drainage and land-reclamation projects than did various other considerations – for example, the determination to root out malaria and similar diseases associated with marshy terrain.

When one looks at the social aspects of these actions, one sees levels of polarisation and violent opposition that vary according to the degree of cohesion within rural communities and the extent of privatisation within individual reclamation schemes. Given that they were predicated on domination of, rather than symbiosis with, the natural world, capitalistic agriculture and 'modernisation' had high social costs and undoubtedly led to changes in the natural habitat that were not always desirable. In fact, some of the agricultural and economic decisions dictated by so-called 'economic rationality' at certain points in history have not always been justified by later events.[126] More and more frequently, the question is posed whether the agricultural use of the maritime polders and the drained inland marshes was really such an economically 'rational' decision, let alone whether it was environmentally desirable for the defence of these coastal areas. Along the North German coast nowadays 'environmentalists [object] against any reclamation projects. Their main argument has been the ecological richness of the tidal marshes and the negative effects of embankments on the Wadden Sea'.[127] All things considered environmental historians have little difficulty in arguing that the loss of this natural heritage of marshlands, woods and moors is to be regretted. However, whilst that is undoubtedly the case, one should also ask what role this same atmospheric and fertile landscape had played in perpetuating such endemic diseases as malaria.[128] What is more, one is justified in doubting that pre-industrial villagers and the gleaners of the 'commons' held the same views as our contemporaries on the historical necessity of preserving natural resources and environmental equilibria.

As for the state, it intervened only very rarely to mediate between privatisation of resources and the attempts by local people to maintain traditional rights over marsh and common land. Much more frequently, it took an active role in support of such land reclamation, granting investors fiscal privileges and co-ordinating the institutional and juridical re-definition of the status quo. In doing this, it was pursuing one of the principal aims that the modern state set itself at the time: an increase in agricultural production that would boost national wealth and provide the increase in population necessary to meet the manpower requirements of the military. What is more, a larger population meant a larger fiscal catchment area and thus guaranteed larger tax revenues – one of the linchpins of the mercantile and late-mercantile policies of Germany and France in these years. The state thus became directly involved in the 'conquest' of new territory for agriculture, not only through the creation of the necessary infrastructures (canals, dikes, locks, windmills, bridges and roads) but also by stimulating the growth of new settlements and the arrival of new settlers (through sizeable monetary and material incentives). However, there were differences – for example, speculator-entrepreneurs in Holland and England clearly enjoyed greater autonomy of action than their counterparts in France and Germany. As for the Venetian Republic, one can see that – though acting under the control exercised by the various *magistrature* – the patrician classes there had ample opportunity to obtain satisfying return on speculative investment; after all, they themselves made up those very *magistrature*. This latter point should perhaps encourage one to look more carefully at the importance of conflicting and vested interests in Holland and England. Undoubtedly, these two countries were more open to capitalistic developments in agriculture, but one is more than justified in questioning the degree of neutrality shown by the state and the elites of power in matters relating to drainage and land-reclamation projects.

Notes

1. One should never forget Bloch's insistence on the importance of comparative studies: M. Bloch, 'Pour une histoire comparée des sociétés européennes' (1928), in *Mélanges Historiques*, Préface de Ch.-E. Perrin, I, Paris, 1963, p. 17.

2. Ester Boserup's arguments highlight the importance of demographic growth in stimulating the development of agricultural techniques required to feed the population (E. Boserup, *The Conditions of Agricultural Growth: the Economics of Agrarian Change under Population Pressure*, London, 1965). However, her theoretical approach may appear too simplistic; Boserup herself recognises that the maintenance of demographic growth-rates involves not just agricultural technology but a number of social, economic and enviromental factors (Boserup, 'Environment, Population and Technology in Primitive Societies', in *The Ends of the Earth. Perspectives on Modern Environmental History*, D. Worster ed., Cambridge, 1988, p. 23). See also the observations of D. Grigg in *The Transformation of Agriculture in the West*, Oxford, 1992, pp. 22–31.

3. An illuminating case is that of England, where the suppression of the monasteries would lead to a change in the drainage policies up to then efficiently applied by the monastic orders themselves. However, in some areas – the Papal States, Brabant and the Iberian peninsula – church bodies would even in the Early Modern era continue to play a role in the protection and reclamation of agricultural land (F. Guarino, *Acque fluviali e bonifica*

nella pianura di Foligno durante il XVIII secolo, with an Introduction by A. Grohmann, Foligno, 1985; F. Bettoni, 'Bonifications et metairies dans les régions de l'Italie centrale à l'époque moderne', Unpublished Paper presented at the Colloquium on 'Techniques de drainage et politiques agricoles en Europe', organized by S. Ciriacono, Paris, 1992; Verhulst, *Précis d'histoire rurale de la Belgique*, pp. 163–65).

4. The fundamental work on the role of bureaucracy in the formation of the modern State is still M. Weber, *Wirtschaft und Gesellschaft. Grundriss der verstehenden Soziologie*, II, Tübingen, 1956[4], pp. 833–34.

5. G. Lemeunier, 'Drainage et croissance agricole dans l'Espagne méditerranéenne (1500–1800)', in *Eau et développement*, Ciriacono ed., pp. 19 68; M.T. Pérez Picazo, G. Lemeunier, *Agua y coyuntura economica. Las transformaciones de los regadíos murciano (1450–1926)*, Barcelona (Geo Critica, 58), julio 1985; G. Pérez Sarrión, 'Hydraulic Policy and Irrigation Works in the Second Half of XVIIIth century in Spain', in *The Journal of European Economic History*, 24 (1995), pp. 131–43. A. Maczak, *Gospodarstwo Chłopskie na Żuławach Malborskich w Początkach XVII Wieku (Peasant Farms and Farming in the Vistula Fens at the Beginning of the 17th century)*, Warszawa, 1962, pp. 307–9.

7. A. Rybak, 'The Significance of the Agricultural Achievements of the Mennonites in the Vistula-Nogat Delta', in *The Mennonite Quarterly Review*, 66 (1992), pp. 214–20. The Mennonites also introduced the Archimedes' screw amd various new types of settlement (E. Kizik, 'A Radical Attempt to Resolve the Mennonite Question in Danzig in the Mid-eighteenth Century', ibid., pp. 127–54, esp. p. 129). See also Z. Chodyla, 'Holländersiedlungen in Großpolen in den Jahren 1597–1672', in *Auf den Spuren der Niederländer zwischen Berlin und Warschau*, Berlin (Vorstand der Deutsch-Niederländischen Gesellschaft), 1997, pp. 84–91.

8. Van Veen, 'Inpoldering in vroegere eeuwen door Nederlanders in het buitenland', pp.215–19; S.J. Fockema Andreae, 'Waterschaps-organisatie in Nederlanden in den Vreemde', in *Mededelingen der Koninklijke Nederlandse Akademie van Wetenschappen*, 14 (1951), pp. 309–30.

9. C. Higounet, *Les allemands en Europe centrale et orientale au Moyen Age*, Paris, 1989, pp. 101–4.

10. W. Kuhn, 'Die niederländisch-nordwestdeutschen Siedlungs-bewegungen des 16. und 17. Jahrhunderts', in *Geschichtliche Landeskunde und Universalgeschichte. Festgabe für Hermann Aubin*, Hamburg, 1950, pp. 250–51; J. Peters, 'Historische Einführung: Neuholland von den Anfängen bis zur Mitte des 18. Jahrhunderts', in *Märkische Bauerntagebücher des 18. und 19. Jahrhunderts*, J. Peters, H. Harnisch, L. Enders eds., Weimar, 1989, pp. 18–19. Peasants from North Holland would settle the island of Amager, near Copenhagen, in 1519; and in 1527 the Duke of Prussia would rely on settlers from Zeeland, Holland and Friesland to instill new life into the waning villages of Western Prussia (Preussisch-Holland).

11. Kuhn, 'Die niederländisch-nordwestdeutschen Siedlungs-bewegungen des 16. und 17. Jahrhunderts', cit., p. 251.

12. O.S. Knottnerus, 'Moral Economy behind the Dikes: Class Relations along the Frisian and German North Sea Coast during the Early Modern Age', in *Tijdschrift voor Sociale Geschiedenis*, 18 (1992), pp. 333–52; idem, 'Deicharbeit und Unternehmertätigkeit in den Nordseemarschen um 1600', in *Deichbau und Sturmfluten in den Frieslanden: Beiträge vom 2. Historiker-Treffen des Nordfriisk Instituut*, T. Steensen ed., Bredstedt, 1992, pp. 60–72. Contrary to common belief, this area was as exposed to periodic outbreaks of malaria as the areas of Southern Europe.

13. Abel, *Agrarkrisen und Agrarkonjunktur*; Slicher van Bath, *The Agrarian History of Western Europe*; H.-J. Nitz, 'Old Elements Changing and New Structures Introduced in the Rural Landscape of Europe. General Introduction', in *The Medieval and Early-modern Rural Landscape of Europe*, Nitz ed., pp. 84–86; see also idem, 'Trasformazione delle antiche e formazione di nuove strutture nel paesaggio rurale dell'Europa centro-settentrionale fra il XVI e il XVIII secolo', in *Annali dell'Istituto Alcide Cervi*, 10 (1980) (Atti del Convegno di 'Studi sul paesaggio agrario in Europa', edited by R. Villari), Bologna, 1989, pp. 55–81.

14. J. Ey, 'Late Medieval and Early-modern Reclamation: the Role of the State and of Village Communities. A Case Study of the North-Western Weser Marshes under the Counts of Oldenburg', in *The Medieval and Early-modern Rural Landscape*, Nitz ed., p. 215. Similarly, in England the peasants were expected to graze and fatten livestock in the upland summer pastures; however, for this they received a payment known as the *agistment* (see Klasen, *Vergleichende Landschaftskunde der englischen Marschen*, pp. 188–89).

15. Nitz, 'Die mittelalterliche und frühneuzeitliche Besiedlung von Marsch und Moor zwischen Ems und Weser', in *Siedlungsforschung. Archäologie-Geschichte-Geographie*, 2 (1984), p. 68–73. Similar social problems would emerge in the nearby *Marschen* of Jeverland and Butjadingen, to the north of Oldenburg. During the course of the seventeenth and, above all, the eighteenth century, these areas saw a social divide open between the relatively wealthy peasant farmers who owned at least 25 hectares of land, and a class of poorer peasants who had access to less and less land and thus sank deeper and deeper into poverty (E. Hinrichs, R. Krämer, C. Reinders, *Die Wirtschaft des Landes Oldenburg in vorindustrieller Zeit*, Oldenburg, 1988).

16. B. Augustyn, 'Traces of a Proto-industrial Organization of the Medieval North Flemish Peat Region', in *The Medieval and Early-modern Rural Landscape*, Nitz ed., p. 61.

17. Abel, *Agrarkrisen und Agrarkonjunktur*, p. 102; E. Ennen, W. Janssen, *Deutsche Agrargeschichte. Vom Neolithikum bis zur Schwelle des Industriezeitalters*, Wiesbaden, 1979, p. 199.

18. E. Siebert, *Entwicklung des Deichwesens vom Mittelalter bis zur Gegenwart*, in *Ostfriesland im Schutze des Deiches*, J. Ohling ed., II, Sitz Pewsum, 1969, pp. 117–21; Abel, *Agrarkrisen und Agrarkonjunktur*, pp. 101–2; O. Fischer, *Das Wasserwesen an der Schleswig-Holsteinischen Nordseeküste. Sonderprobleme und Einzel-fragen des Küstenraumes*, I, Berlin, 1955, pp. 137–41; ibid., II, pp. 145–46; idem, *Das Wasserwesen an der Schleswig-Holsteinischen Nordseeküste*.

Nordstrand, Berlin, 1936, pp. 10–37; Ey, 'Late Medieval and Early-modern Reclamation', cit., Nitz ed., p. 214.

19. Le Roy Ladurie, *Histoire humaine et comparée du climat*; Gottschalk, *Stormvloeden en rivier-overstromingen in Nederland*, III.

20. Van Veen, *Dredge, Drain, Reclaim*; C. Degn, U. Muuß, *Topographischer Atlas Schleswig-Holstein (Die Landschaft Stapelholm, n.41)*, Neumünster, 1966, p. 104; Abel, *Agrarkrisen und Agrarkonjunktur*, p. 102.

21. Mayhew, *Rural Settlement and Farming in Germany*, pp. 160–61; Fischer, *Das Wasserwesen an der Schleswig-Holsteinischen Nordseeküste. Eiderstedt*, Berlin, 1956, pp. 133–36.

22. *Die Mündungs- und Unterschöpfwerke im I. Entwässerungsverband Emden – Sitz Pewsum*, J. Ohling ed., Pewsum, 1973, pp. 20–21; Berthold, 'Wachstumsprobleme der landwirtschaftlichen Nutzfläche im Spätfeudalismus', p. 21–24; H.-J. Nitz, 'Small-Holder Colonization in the Heathlands of Northwest Germany during the 18th and 19th century', in *Geografia Polonica*, 38 (1978), p. 209; Abel, *Geschichte der deutschen Landwirtschaft*, p. 294.

23. Franz, *Geschichte des deutschen Bauernstandes*, Stuttgart, 1970, pp. 89–95; Nitz, 'Small-holder Colonization', cit., p. 207; Mayhew, *Rural Settlement*, pp. 161–62.

24. C. Zimmermann, *Reformen in der bäuerlichen Gesellschaft. Studien zum aufgeklärten Absolutismus in der Markgrafschaft Baden 1750–1790*, Ostfildern, 1983, pp. 139–40; *Topographischer Atlas Niedersachsen und Bremen*, H.H. Seedorf ed., Neumünster, 1977, p. 86; R. Oberschelp, *Niedersachsen 1760–1820*, I, Hildesheim, 1982, pp. 62–63. On the settlements in Schleswig-Holstein, which in this period were still rather small, see W. Prange, *Die Anfänge der großen Agrarreformen in Schleswig-Holstein bis zum 1771*, Neumünster, 1971, pp. 465–66; F. Mager, *Geschichte des Bauerntums und der Bodenkultur im Lande Mecklenburg*, Berlin, 1955, p. 308.

25. A generous estimate puts the area of marshy and river-flooded land reclaimed at this time in Holland at around 1/3 of the entire country – that is, 15,000 Km^2. For Northern Germany the figure is given as 6,000 Km^2, for Belgium 970 Km^2, and for French Flanders and Denmark 650 Km^2. Adding the 7,090 Km^2 in England, one has a figure of around 30,000 Km^2,: Klasen, *Vergleichende Landschaftskunde der englischen Marschen*, pp. 13–22.

26. R. Stadelmann, *Friedrich Wilhelm I. in seiner Thätigkeit für die Landescultur Preussens*, Leipzig, 1878, pp. 62–72; idem, *Preussens Könige in Ihrer Thätigkeit für die Landescultur. Friedrich der Grosse*, II, Leipzig, 1882; *Friedrich Wilhelm II.*, Leipzig, 1885; *Friedrich Wilhelm III (1797–1807)*, Leipzig, 1887; Abel, *Geschichte der deutschen Landwirtschaft*, p. 296; H. Kisch, 'Apologia Borussica', in *From Domestic Manufacture to Industrial Revolution*, New York, pp. 89–90.

27. Corni, *Stato assoluto e società agraria in Prussia*, pp. 121–51; B. von Knobelsdorff Brenkenhoff, *Eine Provinz im Frieden erobert. Brenkenhoff als Leiter d. friderizian. Retablissements in Pommern 1762–1780*, Köln, 1984, p. 100ff.

28. Franz, *Geschichte des deutschen Bauernstandes*, p. 200; D. Blackbourn, 'Besiegte Natur. Wasser und die Entstehung der modernen deutschen Landschaft', in *Wasser*, Busch ed., pp. 440–53; M. Kaup, 'Melioration und Umweltveränderung vom 18. bis 20. Jahrhundert am Beispiel des Oderbruchs', in *Kulturlandschaftsforschung und Umweltplanung*, U. Harteisen, A. Schmidt and M. Wulf eds. (Kulturlandschaft. Zeitschrift für Angewandte Historische Geographie, 10 (2000), Heft 2), pp. 149–59; Berthold, 'Wachstumsprobleme der landwirtschaftlichen Nutzfläche im Spätfeudalismus', p. 22; Mayhew, *Rural Settlement*, p. 164.

29. Abel, *Geschichte der deutschen Landwirtschaft*, p. 303; R. Berthold, *Die Entwicklung des Ackerbaues* (1963), quoted by Corni, *Stato assoluto e società agraria in Prussia*, p. 133. See also W. Rösener, *Die Bauern in der europäischen Geschichte*, München, 1993, pp. 170–71.

30. Stadelmann, *Friedrich Wilhelm II*, cit., p. 58; Abel, *Geschichte der deutschen Landwirtschaft*, p. 296; Corni, *Stato assoluto e società agraria in Prussia*, p. 147ff.; T. Pierenkemper, 'Englische Agrarrevolution und Preussisch-Deutsche Agrarreformen in vergleichender Perspective', in *Landwirtschaft und industrielle Entwicklung*, Pierenkemper ed., pp. 19–21.

31. Kaup, 'Die Urbarmachung des Oderbruchs. Umwelthistorische Annäherung an ein bekanntes Thema', pp. 128–29. For a brief comment on this, see Stadelmann, *Friedrich Wilhelm II*, cit., p. 52.

32. Such investments were, however, veritable speculations. See those made by Brenkenhoff, who seems to have been Frederick II's main collaborator in a number of land-reclamation projects (Corni, *Stato assoluto e società agraria in Prussia*, p. 129; Abel, *Geschichte der deutschen Landwirtschaft*, p. 294).

33. R. Livet, *Habitat rural et structures agraires en Basse-Provence*, Aix-en-Provence, 1962, p. 85.

34. F. Braudel, *L'identité de la France, II, Les hommes et les choses*, Paris, 1986, pp. 59–67.

35. Baars, 'Landaanwinning door Nederlanders in Frankrijk', p. 16.; De Dienne, *Histoire du dessèchement des lacs et marais en France*, pp. 15–19 and 34; P. Massé, 'Le dessèchement des marais du Bas-Médoc', in *Revue Historique de Bordeaux*, 6 (1957), pp. 25–38; Meuvret, *Le problème des subsistances à l'époque Louis XIV, II. La production des céréales et la société rurale. Texte*, pp. 187–88.

36. To stimulate effective exploitation of the land, owners were encouraged to rent their half of the reclaimed terrain to the *dessicateurs* themselves (that is, in those cases where the drainage contract envisaged a 50–50 split of the *marais* between financial backer and land-owner): De Dienne, *Histoire du dessèchement*, pp. 428–29; ANP, F10 208, Mémoire historique sur les dessèchements des marais, date of publication unknown but almost certainly the second half of the eighteenth century. See also L.E. Harris, *The Two Netherlanders, Humphrey Bradley and Cornelis Drebbel*, Leiden, 1961, p. 88ff.).

37. 'Edict du roy pour le dessèchement des marais, donné à Paris au mois de janvier 1607', in Jeune Poterlet, *Code des dessèchements ou Recueil des réglements rendus sur cette matière depuis le règne d'Henri IV jusqu'à non jours*,

Paris, 1817, pp. 34-35; on the different legislation involved, see *Recueil des édits, déclarations, arrests et réglements concernant le dessèchement des marais [...] depuis 1619 jusqu'à présent*, Paris, 1735; Meuvret, *Le problème des subsistances*, II, *Notes*, pp. 238-40, esp. p. 238.

38. Though the first work of drainage began in such areas as Poitou and Normandy as early as the Middle Ages, appreciable reclamation really got under way with the arrival of Dutch capital and technology; even then there were setbacks (R. D'Hollander, 'Le marais poitevin', in *Etudes Rurales*, 3, (1961), pp. 81-90); ENPC, Ms. 2584, *Précis historique sur les moëres*, Dunkerque, 24 janvier 1791, par Duclos; H.D. Clout, 'Reclamation of Coastal Marshland', in *Themes in the Historical Geography of France*, Clout ed., pp. 199-201.

39. Baars, 'Landaanwinning door Nederlanders in Frankrijk', p. 18; E. De Dienne, *Un épisode de l'histoire de l'agriculture au XVIIe siècle. La société de dessèchement général des marais et lacs de France en Basse Auvergne*, Clermond-Ferrand, 1886, p. 11 n.; Clout, 'Reclamation of Coastal Marshland', pp. 194-201.

40. AGP, Art.4, Section 2, §4, Cart. 1, *Mémoire [...] de la province de Saintonge [...] le Pays d'Aunis [...], partie du Bas Poictou...*, 10 December 1721, par Masse; ibid., *Mémoire sur la carte [...] de la Charente*, 19 June 1704; ibid., *Mémoire sur la carte [...] du bas Poitou, Pais d'Aunis et Saintonge*, 5 February 1719.

41. Though dikes in Poitou were built in stone before those in Hoilland and Venice, they were much more rudimentary structures than the late-seventeenth-century Dutch dikes with their sharply-defined outlines (Bibliothèque du Génie (Vincennes), Ms.183 (4a 133), *Mémoire qui accompagne la carte de l'isle de Ré pour expliquer l'estendue des digues* (date of publication unknown); see also ibid., *Mémoire géographique de Masse sur partie du Bas Poitou, Pays d'Aunis et Saintonge*, 1715) and *Mémoire sur la carte des costes du bas Poictou, et partie du Pays d'Aunis & Bretagne*, 28 March 1704; Bourde, *Agronomie et agronomes*, I, p. 534.

42. H. Lüthy, *La Banque Protestante en France, 1685-1794*, Paris, 1959, but see also *La Repubblica internazionale del denaro tra XV e XVII secolo*, A. De Maddalena and H. Kellenbenz eds., Bologna, 1986; W. Brulez, 'De diaspora der Vlaamse kooplui op het einde der XVI eeuw', in *Bijdragen voor de Geschiedenis der Nederlanden*, 15 (1960), pp. 279-306; J.G. Briels, *De Zuidnederlandse immigratie 1572-1630*, Bussum, 1978, espec. pp. 33-34. Due to these political and financial difficulties, the Flemish presence in late-sixteenth/early-seventeenth-century Venice would also increase (*Marchands flamands à Venise, II, (1606-1621)*, G. Devos and W. Brulez eds., Rome, 1986).

43. De Dienne, *Histoire du dessèchement*, pp. 35-37; Baars, 'Landaanwinning door Nederlanders in Frankrijk', pp. 17-18; D. Dessert, *Argent, pouvoir et société au Grand Siècle*, Paris, 1984, p. 605.

44. In spite of van Ens' work, the value of the Arles *marais* never topped 600,000 *livres tournois*, even if the work itself had cost double that. Van Ens would, in fact, die insolvent (Meuvret, *Le problème des subsistances, Notes*, p. 237); De Dienne, *Un épisode de l'histoire de l'agriculture*, cit., p. 28.

45. As a result, Jan Hoeufft and his heirs were present in Poitou and Provence (but also in Picardy, working with the Van Ens, the De Strada and Fabrice de Gressenich), whilst the De Strada worked on drainage in the Languedoc, the Auvergne, Poitou and Provence. Van Ens is to be found in Picardy, the Comans in Normandy, Poitou, Saintonge and the Languedoc, and the Beringhem were invovled in numerous projects in the Bordolais (as well as collaborating with other speculators on projects in the Languedoc). As for the Van Gaugelt, they are to be seen in Poitou and Provence, whilst the Midorge were in Normandy and in Picardy (De Dienne, *Histoire du dessèchement*, pp. 35–57).

46. W.H. Hoeufft, *Genealogie van het geslacht Hoeufft* (Middelburg 1905) quoted by Baars, 'Landaanwinning door Nederlanders in Frankrijk', cit., p. 18; Braudel, *La Méditerranée*, I, p. 57; F. Martin, *Adam de Craponne et son oeuvre*, Paris, 1874, pp. 18–22 and 46–50.

47. ENPC, Ms. 2634, *Mémoire sur le projet de canal pour le faire servir au dessèchement des marais d'Arles*, Beaucaire 25 January 1826; R.P.J. Tutein Nolthenius, *Mededelingen over meren en moerassen in vorige eeuwen in Frankrijk door Nederlanders drooggelegd*; idem, *Hollandse dijken op Franse grondslag*, quoted by Baars, 'Landaanwinning door Nederlanders in Frankrijk', pp. 18–19; P. Masson, 'Le canal de Provence au XVIIe siècle', in *Revue Historique de Provence*, 1 (1901), p. 350; J. Rigaud, *Les grands problèmes d'hydraulique et la prospérité du département des Bouches-du-Rhône*, Aix-en-Provence, 1932, p. 1.

48. The Genoese engineers working on the draining of the Anguilaggio marsh at Aleria (Corsica) were accused of the same errors of planning. The main purpose of that project had been to boost cereal production, though health/sanitary considerations had also played their part (A.M. Salone, *Tentative de bonification de la plaine d'Aleria au XVIIe par l'assèchement de l'étang Del Sale*, Bastia (Cahiers Corsica, 122), 1988, p. 1ff.).

49. ANP, F^{10}, Carton 319, *Mémoire sur le dessèchement de l'Etang appelé de Marseillete*, date of publication unknown.

50. Baehrel, *Une croissance. La basse Provence rurale*, I, pp. 115–16; see also the Introduction by Maurice Aymard, with its timely reminder that mainstream historians have tended to deny such ideas due consideration.

51. La Maillardière, *Traité d'économie politique*, pp. 100–1; the city of Beauvais itself was described as 'sunk in its *marais*' (P. Goubert, *Beauvais et le Beauvaisis de 1600 à 1730*, I, Paris, 1960, p. 5; AGP, Art.5, Section 7, §4, Carton 2, *Mémoire de Mrs. les proprietaires des salins de Pecais*, 1742).

52. AGP, Art.4, Section 2, §4, Carton 1, *Mémoire sur la carte générale [...] du Bas Poitou*, 15 March 1702; ibid., Art.5, Section 7, §1, Carton 1, *Rapport sur le dessèchement du Bas Artois*, 13 agosto 1791; ibid., §3, Carton 1, *Mémoire pour le dessèchement à faire des prairies depuis Landrecy jusqu'à Castillon*, 1693. See also P. Lemonnier, *Les salins de l'ouest. Logique technique, logique sociale*, Lille, 1980, pp. 24–27.

53. Meuvret, *Le problème des subsistances. Texte*, p.188; AGP., Art.5, Section 7, §3, Carton 1, *Mémoire au sujet des marais de la rivière de Somme*, par M***, Lieutenant de Roi de la ville de ***, date of publication unknown; Clout, 'Reclamation of Coastal Marshland', p. 198.

54. Rosenthal, *The Development of Irrigation in Provence, 1700–1860*, pp. 614–15.

55. De Dienne, *Histoire du dessèchement*, pp. 50, 72 and 117; P. George, *La région du Bas-Rhône. Etude de géographie régionale*, Paris, 1935, pp. 315–17.

56. P. Massé, 'Le dessèchement des marais du Bas-Médoc', cit., p. 38.

57. Le Roy Ladurie, 'L'historiographie rurale en France', p. 238.

58. Louis François de Turbilly, *Pratiques des défrichements*, Paris, 1811[4], p. 5; ANP, AD IV 22/121, *Idées d'un agriculteur patriote*, without date but of the revolutionary period; Duhamel du Monceau, *Traité de la culture des terres, suivant les principes de M.Tull anglois*, VI, Paris, 1761, pp. 214–16 ; De la Salle de l'Etang, *Les prairies artificielles ou moyens de perfectionner l'agriculture dans toutes les provinces de France*, Paris, 1762, p. 12.

59. Claude Jacques Herbert, *Essai sur la police des grains*, London, 1754, pp. 20–21, 47 and 52.

60. Dangeul wrote his treatise under the English pseudonym Jack Nickolls, presenting it as a translation. The work is, in fact, so well-informed on the situation in England that it strikes one as written by an English agronomist: Plumard de Dangeul, *Remarques sur les avantages et les désavantages de la France et de la Grande Bretagne*, Leyden, 1754, pp. 109–11.

61. Bourde, *Agronomie et agronomes*, p. 522; Henri de Pattullo, *Essai sur l'amélioration des terres*, Paris, 1758, pp. 259–61.

62. Weulersse, *Le mouvement physiocratique en France*, I, p. 319; Bourde, *Agronomie et agronomes*, pp. 517–19 and 532.

63. Weulersse, *Le mouvement physiocratique en France*, I, p. 318; see also on this point K. Sutton, 'Reclamation of Wasteland during the Eighteenth and Nineteenth Centuries', in *Themes in the Historical Geography*, Clout ed., p. 256. This calculation uses the *arpent d'ordinance*, equal to 51 *ares* (the *arpent commune* was equal to 42, whilst that of Paris was equal to 34): J.C. Perrot, 'Introduction' to Lavoisier, *De la richesse territoriale du Royaume de France. Texte et documents*, Paris, 1988, pp. 77–78).

64. Weulersse, *Le mouvement physiocratique en France*, I, pp. 316–18.

65. Bourde, *Agronomie et agronomes*, pp. 514 and 535.

66. E. Labrousse, 'L'expansion agricole: la montée de la production', in *Histoire économique et sociale de la France*, II, Braudel and Labrousse eds.,, p. 428; Meyer, *La noblesse bretonne*, pp. 533–34; H. Sée. *Les classes rurales en Bretagne du XVIe siècle à la Révolution*, Paris, 1906, p. 443.

67. Meyer, *La noblesse bretonne*, pp. 550–75, espec. p. 573. However, as A. Young would point out at the end of the century, about a 1/3 of the province remained uncultivated, with abandoned fields edging right up to the outskirts of a rich city like Nantes (Sée, *Les classes rurales*, cit., p. 443; G. Debien, *En Haut-Poitou. Défricheurs au travail, XVe–XVIIIe siècles*, Paris, 1952, pp. 86 and 93).

68. ANP, F[10], Carton 318, 1739; ibid., juillet 1751; see also ibid. *Observation sur le dessèchement du Lac de Grandlieu*, without date but probably 1756, on the *riverains*' resistance to harrassment by *dessécheurs*; AGP, Carton 1/11, Art.5, Section 7, §5, 11 April 1741; see also ibid., Carton 1/9, for the company formed by the two entrepreneurs.

69. Goyon de la Plombanie, *La France agricole et marchande*, I, Avignon, 1762, p. 127ff.; II, pp. 198–205.

70. ANP, F¹⁰ 316, *Observations sur le projet d'établir les hollandais en Provence*, date of publication unknown but around 1783–1786. The Flemish Jacobs was responsible for various projects caried out in the coastal area of Bourgneuf Bay in the first decades of the second half of the century (Clout, 'Reclamation of coastal marshland', in *Themes in the Historical Geography of France*, Clout ed., p. 203). In 1772 it was decided to consult an English engineer on the possible construction of a dike to protect a *marais* in Poitou (cfr. ANP, F¹⁰, Carton 318, Agosto 1772).

71. ANP, Art 5, Section 7, §4, Carton 1, *Mémoire relatif aux ouvrages à faire pour dessécher les marais [...] d'Aigues-Mortes jusqu'au Rhône*, 1701, by Niquet.

72. F. Wolters, *Studien über Agrarzustände und Agrarprobleme in Frankreich von 1700 bis 1790*, Leipzig, 1905, p. 197; ANP, F¹⁰, Carton 318, *Mémoire sur les travaux des dessèchements d'Aunis et Saintonge (villes de Rochefort, Marennes et St. Jean Dangely)*, 1787.

73. L. Dutil, *L'état économique du Languedoc à la fin de l'ancien régime (1750–1789)*, Paris, 1911, pp. 106–21, espec. p. 114: for example, in 1786 4,920 *arpents* were reclaimed, leaving 148,626 *en friches*, whilst in 1787, 8,284 were reclaimed (still leaving 316,973 uncultivated).

74. G. Frêche, *Toulouse et la région Midi-Pyrénées au siècle des lumières vers 1670–1789*, Paris, 1974, p. 267. Further data on the Orléanais (45.150 *arpents* reclaimed for agriculture between 1760 and 1785) can be found in L. Guerin (*L'intendant de Cypierre et la vie économique de l'Orléanais, 1760–1785*, Mayenne, 1938, p. 94). For archive and bibliographical references regarding *défrichements*, see J.-Y. Grenier, *Séries économiques françaises (XVIᵉ–XVIIIᵉ siècles)*, Paris, 1985, pp. 143–44.

75. ANP, F¹⁰, Carton 319, Arrêt du Conseil d'Etat, 15 novembre 1746; F¹⁰, Carton 319, *Mémoire pour appuyer les demandes que fait au Conseil le S. de Berriac*, 6 June 1761.

76. V.-L. Bourrilly, 'Le XVIIIᵉ siècle. Histoire économique', in *Les Bouches du Rhône. Les temps modernes (1482–1789)*, III, P. Masson ed., Marseille, 1920, pp. 223–24; J.A. Barral, *Discours sur les irrigations du département de Vaucluse. Extrait du Journal de l'Agriculture*, Paris, 1877, p. 5.

77. Rozier, *Cours complet d'agriculture pratique*, III, 1809, pp. 11–21, esp. p. 15: the *friches* in Poitou amounted to 100,000 hectares.; the *marais* of Bourgoin to 10,000, that of Ponthieu to 14,000, those of Gournay and Beauvais to 2,000, the Brêles *marais* in the Beauvaisis to 2,000; those of the Saintonge to 15,000, those around Nantes to 3,000, and those in the Charentan to 20,000. There were at least 200,000 hectares in the *landes* of Bordeaux and dozens of kilometres of coastal *marais* in Brittany and Saint-Quentin.

78. Labrousse, 'L'expansion agricole: la montée de la production', in *Histoire économique et sociale de la France*, II, Braudel and Labrousse eds., p. 429. For some data on the area of the *jardins maraîchers*, see J.-C.Toutain, 'Le produit de l'agriculture française de 1700 à 1958', in *Cahiers de l'Institut de Science Economique appliquée*, 115 (1961), p. 105. There is, however, no overall data

on the areas drained in France during these decades and, as G. Weulersse showed, in some regions the *défrichements* were far from excessive (Weulersse, *Le mouvement physiocratique en France*, II, pp. 299–302).

79. J.B. Rougier de La Bergerie, 'Tableau approximatif du nombre et de l'étendue des étangs dans la République', in *Rapport général sur les étangs, fait au comité d'agriculture*, Paris, 1795, année IIIe de la République; Jeune Poterlet, *Code des dessèchements*, cit., p. 1ff.

80. ANP, F^{10}, Cartons 313 and 317: Prints Proclamations and Enquiries solicited by the Convention, Year II of the Republic. However, attention was drawn to the fact that the damage to fishing and mills might not be counterbalanced by the advantages of land reclamation (ANP, F^{10}, Carton 314, *Observation faite sur le dessèchement dans le département de la Meurthe*, 29 Pluviose de l'année II de la République).

81. Pierre-François Boncerf, *Sur le dessèchement de la Vallée de l'Auge, lu à la séance publique de la Société Royale d'Agriculture le 28 décembre 1791*, Paris, 1791, pp. 1–15; idem, *Aperçu des effets qui résulteront des dessèchements, défrichements, plantations*, date and place of publication unknown (but almost certainly Paris and 1790-91), pp. 1 and 3-5; idem and Parmentier, *Marais de Bourgoin. Extrait des registres de la Société royale d'agriculture du 10 mai 1790*, Paris, 1790. This latter *marais* was in the Dauphiné, thus strategically close to Lyons and its industries – to which Boncerf attributed a fundamental role in the development of the economy of the Revolution.

82. ANP, F^{10}, Carton 2303, 20 août de l'année II de la République; A. Couladon, *Chazerat, dernier intendant de la Généralité de Riom et province d'Auvergne (1774–1789)*, Paris, 1932, espec. p. 118.

83. *Défrichements*, La Maillardière commented, were a European not solely a French problem, with land reclamation being carried on from England to the Papal States. The *Journal Politique* of 1779 pointed out how in this latter state 3,500 workmen had been employed in schemes to reclaim insalubrious marshland, opening new roads towards Naples and (partially) eradicating malaria (La Maillardière, *Traité d'économie politique*, pp. 104-6).

84. Le Roy Ladurie, 'L'historiographie rurale en France', pp. 238-40.

85. J. Mulliez, 'Du blé 'mal nécessaire'. Réflexions sur les progrès de l'agriculture, 1750-1850', in *Revue d'Histoire Moderne et Contemporaine*, 26 (1979), pp. 3-47. Mulliez argues that in not taking the enormous differences between regions into account, the Physiocrats were little more than a 'mince élite intellectuelle' in their call for the end of the *jachère* system, voicing solely the agricultural interests that had developed to the north of the Loire. Another French agronomist, also aware of the problems of land drainage, did pay more attention to these regional differences: Le Vassor, *Méthode générale et particulière [...] pour le dessèchement des marais et des terres noyées*, Paris, 1788, pp. 13 and 58ff.

86. See Michel Morineau, *Les Faux-semblants d'un démarrage économique*, which in my opinion remains a fundamental work, in spite of some vitriolic criticism from French historians.

87. Le Roy Ladurie, 'L'historiographie rurale en France', pp. 241-42.

88. Bourde, *Agronomie et agronomes en France*, p. 522; J.-R. Pitte, *Histoire des paysages français. Le profane du 16ᵉ siècle à nos jours*, Paris, 1983, pp. 54–55.
89. In 1756 those who had undertaken to produce madder in the *marais* were granted a twenty-year exemption (La Maillardière, *Traité d'économie politique*, cit., p. 102). This *arrêt* (24 February 1756) encouraged such figures as the Parisian entrepreneur Etienne Martin to invest in the crop: ANP, F¹⁰, Carton 318, Dossier 1757.
90. J.A. Barral, *L'agriculture, les prairies et les irrigations de la Haute-Vienne*, Paris, 1884, pp. 123–25; see also R. Price, *The Economic Modernisation of France (1730–'80)*, London, 1975, pp. 81–84.
91. Despommiers, *L'art de s'enrichir promptement par l'agriculture*, Paris, 1762, p. 3; La Maillardière, *Traité d'économie politique*, p. 183ff.; Bourde, *Agronomie et agronomes en France*, pp. 521 and 535; Jean Baptiste Miroudot, *Prairies artificielles*, Lyon, 1762.
92. Rosenthal, *The Fruits of Revolution: Property Rights, Litigation and French Agriculture*. Rosenthal argues that the internal rate of return rises as the price of arable crops rises and falls as the price of labour increases. However, how legitimately can one take the cost of labour into account within a system comprising *corvées* ? This does not rule out that interest rates and the availability of money were monetary variables that played a part in deciding whether land-reclamation projects were undertaken. Writing to the Contrôleur générale in 1706, De Foucault, Intendant at Caen, underlined this: 'It is certain that it would be very useful to take measures to drain the above-mentioned *marais* [...] but in my opinion these are projects for peacetime, when there is more money around' (Boislisle, *Correspondance*, quoted by Meuvret, *Le problème des subsistances*, II. *Notes*, p. 237).
93. Foster, 'Obstacles to Agricultural Growth in Eighteenth-century France', pp. 1613–15; O' Brien and Keyder, *Economic Growth in Britain and France (1780–1914)*, pp. 135–39.
94. Grantham, 'The Diffusion of the New Husbandry in Northern France', pp. 311–37; B. Lepetit, *Les villes dans la France moderne: 1740–1840*, Paris, 1988, p. 97; on regional variations in this legislation, see Rosenthal, *The Fruits of Revolution*, p. 167.
95. M. Morineau, 'Jean Meuvret et la vie rurale en France au temps de Louis XIV', in *Revue Belge de Philologie et d'Histoire*, 67 (1989), p. 773.
96. Foster, 'Obstacles to agricultural growth', p. 1600. As Arthur Young would note, if the large landowners in France were not able to 'plant wheat after a forage, they regard the forage as no good' (ibid., p. 1603). However, one must not exaggerate the entrepreneurial standing of English agriculture either: the agronomists of Norfolk showed little interest in 'agricultural machinery', focusing their research mainly on crop rotations (Bourde, *Agronomie et agronomes en France*, I, pp. 300–1). The continuing importance of manpower as opposed to machine power throughout the first half of the nineteenth century is stressed in G. Clark, ('Productivity Growth without

Change in European Agriculture before 1850', in *Journal of Economic History*, 47 (1987), pp. 419–32).

97. Clout, 'Agricultural Change', in *Themes in the Historical Geography*, Clout ed., p. 433.

98. O'Brien and Keyder, *Economic Growth in Britain and France*, pp. 109–38.

99. Meuvret, *Le problème des subsistances*, II. *Texte*, p.11ff. Drawing on ideas expressed in Buffon's *Histoire naturelle*, La Maillardière insisted that the pastureland created by drainage should first be used for cattle, who would graze on both long and short grass. These would be followed by horses, who only eat the short grass. Given their tendency to uproot grass altogether, sheep were undesirable (La Maillardière, *Traité d'économie politique*, p. 35; Foster, 'Obstacles to Agricultural Growth', p. 1603).

100. M. Bloch, 'La lutte pour l'individualisme agraire', in *Annales d'Histoire Economique et Sociale*, 2 (1929), pp. 239–83 and 511–56. For un update discussion on these issues, and for a more nuanced interpretation of the conditions of the French agriculture, see now Béaur, *Histoire agraire de la France au XVIIIe siècle*, pp. 300–2; Clout, 'Reclamation of Coastal Marshland', in *Themes in the Historical Geography of France*, Clout ed., p. 203.

101. Meuvret, *Le problème des subsistances*, II. *Texte*, pp. 16–19.

102. R.C. Allen, 'Enclosure, Farming Methods, and the Growth of Productivity in the South Midlands', in *Research in Economic History* (Supplement 5), 1989, G. Grantham and C.S. Leonard eds., pp. 80–82. See also *Agrarian Fundamentalism and English Agricultural Development*, in *Structures and Dynamics of Agricultural Exploitations*, E. Aerts, M. Aymard, J Kahk, G. Postel-Vinay and R. Sutch eds.(Proceedings of the Tenth International Economic History Congress, Leuven, Session B-2), Leuven, 1990, pp. 57–66 and Rosenthal, *The Fruits of Revolution*, p. 194. On the issue of open fields, and the reasons of climate and economy which led to the discontinuation of community farming, see the debate that developed during the 70s in the review 'Explorations in Economic History': S. Fenoaltea, 'Risk, Transaction Costs, and the Organitation of Medieval Agriculture' and his Reply ('Fenoaltea on Open Fields: a Reply') to Donald N. McCloskey, 'Fenoaltea on Open Fields: a Comment': 13 (1976), pp. 129–51 and 14 (1977), pp. 402–10.

103. Kerridge, *The Agricultural Revolution*, pp. 222–27, esp. p. 222. It has been roughly estimated that a good 700,000 hectares were reclaimed in this period in the Severn valley and, primarily, in the Fens: Klasen, *Vergleichende Landschaftskunde der englischen Marschen*, pp. 13–22; Darby, *The Draining of the Fens*, pp. 5–7.

104. C. Holmes, 'Drainage Projects in Elizabethan England: the European Dimension', in *Eau et développement*, Ciriacono ed., pp. 87–102.

105. Kerridge, *The Agricultural Revolution*, pp. 230–31.

106. Van Veen, 'Inpolderingen in vroegere eeuwen door Nederlanders in het buitenland', pp. 217–18; S. Smiles, *Lives of the Engineers* (1862), New Introduction by L.T.C. Rolt, I, New York, 1968, pp. 6–7. In 1621 Cornelis Vermuyden was commissioned to build some defensive dikes on the

Thames and to undertake control of the water resources of Windsor Park. As well as working on the reclamation projects in Hatfield Chase and the Isle of Axholme (in the Fens), he would also be active in Malvern Chase (Worcestershire) and at Sedgemoor. Other technicians from the Low Countries involved in such schemes included: the Flemish Freeston (in the Norfolk marshes) and the Dutchmen Joas Croppenburg (Canvey Island, in the Thames) and Cornelis Vanderwelt (Wapping Marsh).

107. M.E. Kennedy, *So Glorious a Work as this Draining of the Fens: the Impact of Royal Government on Local Political Culture in Elizabethan and Jacobean England*, Ph.D. Thesis, Cornell University (University Microfilms International, Ann Arbor, Michigan), 1985, pp. 24–25, kindly suggested by Clive Holmes. Conflicts between communities and aristocrats or rich landowners occurred when the latter grazed livestock other than their own on commonland, thus infringing consuetudinary law.

108. Korthals Altes, *Polderland in Engeland*, pp. 46–50; idem, *Sir Cornelius Vermuyden*, London-Den Haag, 1925, pp. 24–30; J. Thirsk, 'The Isle of Axholme before Vermuyden', in *The Rural Economy of England. Collected Essays*, London, 1984, p. 149ff.; L.E. Harris, *Vermuyden and the Fens*, pp. 41–47.

109. Lindley, *Fenland Riots and the English Revolution*, pp. 258–59; C. Holmes, 'Drainers and Fenmen: the Problem of Popular Political Consciousness in the Seventeenth Century', in *Order & Disorder in Early Modern England*, A. Fletcher and J. Stevenson eds., Cambridge, 1987, pp. 174–89.

110. Darby, *The Changing Fenland*, p. 133; Lindley, *Fenland Riots*, p. 23ff., esp. p. 40.

111. Holmes, 'Drainers and Fenmen', cit., p. 185; Kennedy, *So Glorious a Work as this Draining of the Fens*, cit., pp. 41–53 and 302–7.

112. *An Atlas of Rural Protest in Britain, 1548–1900*, A. Charlesworth ed., London, 1983, pp. 39–43; Lindley, *Fenland Riots*, pp. 54–55.

113. D. Ormrod, *English Grain Exports and the Structure of Agrarian Capitalism, 1700–1760*, Hull, 1985, pp. 20–21. See also the works of Alan Macfarlane, *The Culture of Capitalism* and *The Origin of English Individualism: the Family, Property and Social Transition*, though his emphasis on continuity with the Middle Ages tends to underestimate the changes that were taking place in this period.

114. Lindley, *Fenland Riots*, pp. 44 and 259. On the cultural and agronomical debate in England during these crucial decades, there are useful comments in Ambrosoli, *The Wild and the Sown*, p. 305ff.

115. J. Thirsk, 'Agricultural Policy: Public Debate and Legislation', in *The Agrarian History of England and Wales, 1640–1750. Agrarian Change*, Thirsk ed., V/2, 1985, p. 313.

116. P. O'Brien, 'Quelle a été exactement la contribution de l'aristocratie britannique au progrès de l'agriculture entre 1688 et 1789', in *Annales. ESC*, 42 (1987), pp. 1391–1409.

117. Thirsk, 'Agricultural Policy', cit., pp. 312 and 372. Hartlib would seem to have been influenced by Sir Richard Weston's picture of flourishing Flemish agriculture, echoing his conclusions in *Legacie or an Enlargement of*

the Discourse of Husbandry Used in Brabant and Flanders (London 1657): F. Bray, 'Agriculture', in *Science and Civilisation in China*, J. Needham ed., 6/II, Cambridge, 1984, p. 89.

118. R. Grove, 'Cressey Dymock and the Draining of the Fens: an Early Agricultural Model', in *Geographical Journal*, 147 (1981), pp. 27-37.

119. Thirsk, 'Agricultural Policy', cit., p. 373.

120. Darby, *The Changing Fenland*, p. 73.

121. H. van der Linden, 'L'influence de l'eau sur les institutions hollandaises', in *Agricultura e trasformazione dell'ambiente*, Guarducci ed., p. 665 ff.

122. H.C. Prince, 'The Changing Rural Landscape, 1750-1850', in *The Agrarian History of England and Wales*, Thirsk ed., VI, 1989, pp. 58-63; A. Parker and D. Pye, *The Fenland*, London, 1976; C. Taylor, *The Cambridgeshire Landscape*, Cambridge, 1974.; Korthals-Altes, *Polderland in Engeland*; idem, *Sir Cornelius Vermuyden*; L.E. Harris, *Vermuyden and the Fens*; idem, *The Two Netherlanders*.

123. Overton, *Agricultural Revolution in England. The Transformation of the Agrarian Economy*, pp. 197-207. For Overton 'although there is evidence of improvements in farming methods from the late sixteenth century, it was not until after 1750', and even the first half of the nineteenth century, that we can talk of 'an agricultural triumph'.

124. The failed attempts to drain the Haarlemmermeer in the Low Countries during the first half of the seventeenth century are emblematic here.

125. Darby, *The Draining of the Fens*, p. 225. Around this period 'the number of steam engines may be estimated at 17 in the Lincolnshire part, varying from 10 to 80 horsepower each, and upwards of 43 in the remainder of the level'.

126. J. Radkau, 'Was ist Umweltgeschichte ?', quoted by Kaup, 'Die Urbarmachung des Oderbruchs', p. 112; Ostrom, *Governing the Commons: the Evolution of Institutions for Collective Action*, quoted by Kaijser, 'System Building from below: Institutional Change in Dutch Water Control Systems', in *Water Technology in the Netherlands*, Reuss ed., p. 545; D. Worster, *Nature's Economy. Studies in Environment and History*, Cambridge, 1977, pp. X-XI; A. Caracciolo, *L'ambiente come storia*, Bologna, pp. 33-36; W. Blockmans, 'La lotta dell'uomo contro l'acqua nell'Olanda del tardo Medioevo', in *Ars et Ratio*, J.-C. Maire-Vigueur and A. Paravicini Bagliani eds., Palermo, 1990, p. 55.

127. L. Goeldner, 'The German Wadden Sea Coast: Reclamation and Environmental Protection', in *Journal of Coastal Conservation*, 5 (1999), pp. 23-30; idem, 'Réouverture de polders et restauration des marais salés en Angleterre', in *Revue de Géographie de Lyon*, 74 (1999), pp. 75-84.

 **Glossary**

Afféagement: feudal land concession, generally regarding uncultivated terrain, with payment in kind or in cash. This type of concession was very common in Brittany.

Ambacht: farm belonging to the Dutch settlers in the southern Netherlands.

Anwachsrecht: the right to possess newly-reclaimed land on behalf of the political authority.

Arpent: unit of surface area used in France, comprising an *arpent d'ordonnance* (= 51 ares and 7 centiares) and an *arpent commun* (= 42 ares and 21 centiares).

Arpent de Paris: unit of surface area, equal to 34 ares and 19 centiares.

Banne: farm belonging to the Dutch settlers in the northern Netherlands.

Barene: deposits of silt within the lagoon that have been harden by the action of sea water and are covered with vegetation; they are underwater only at exceptional high tides and some of them were converted for use as pasture or arable land.

Bari: acquatic plants, alghae-like.

Bas Médoc: region on the Atlantic coast of France.

Bassa: low-lying area of a Venetian province.

Bedijking: part of the seabed which is no longer flooded by the sea and which is surrounded by a dike. A 'bedijking' was also a polder of land which was particularly fertile because of the fresh seaclay on the surface.

Bedijkingsdeskundigen: dike engineers.

Boaria: agricultural contract within the Venetian Republic. Payment was in kind and/or cash, but no limits were placed on the actions of the actual land-owner.

Boezem: water control system in every polder. In general terms water is pumped 'over the side' into the *boezem*. The *boezem* consists of all waterways and lakes outside the polders but within the confinement of the outer sea dikes. From the *boezem*, surplus water has to be flushed out into the sea.

Boezemgebied: polder drainage area.

Bonifica: process of land-reclamation and/or improvement of soil fertility.

Botte-sifone: culvert that enabled a canal to run under another watercourse; aqueducts bearing the canal over the watercourse were called *ponte-canale*.

Brolo: was a field laid out for the cultivation of vegetables and occasionally fruit. The term might also be used to refer to a garden or park.

Buurschappen: village community of peasant farmers and land-owners, responsible, with a certain degree of autonomy, for the maintenance of dikes, locks, drainage canals and the banks of watercourses.

Campatico: tax on agricultural land within the Venetian Republic.

Campo: Venetian unit of measurement of agricultural terrain. It could measure from 3,862 m^2 (*campo vicentino*) to 5,204 m^2 (*campo trevigiano*).

Caratade: tax on agricultural land in the Venetian Republic; it was calculated on the basis of the extent and population of the area concerned.

Colmata or *colmatage*: the use of alluvial material carried by a river to fill in a land depression and thus obtain reclaimed agricultural land.

Colmellone: This regulated the water flow from one canal to another; it comprised a stout pillar on either side of the channel and one in the middle, in order to divide the water flow into two sections. One such important structure in the Veneto was at Limena, near Padua, and controlled the flow between the Bretella canal and the river Brenta.

Conferme di possesso: recognition of ancient use rights. They did not usually require payment.

Decima: tax on cultivated agricultural land – approximately one tenth (*decima*) of the yield. Sometimes this monetary payment was replaced by a labour requirement.

Défrichement: the reclaimation for agriculture of uncultivated land, both marshy and otherwise.

Dessicateurs: French agricultural entrepreneurs involved in land drainage.

Diversivo: canal or river drawn off a main watercourse to reduce its volume and therefore destructive potential.

Domaine royale: king's domain.

Donaumooskultursozietät: Private-public company set up to reclaim land along the river Danube (Bayer).

Droit d'aubaine: tax paid by foreigners (*aubain* = 'foreigner'). In France the king had the right to take over a foreign resident's property at his death. The law was only abolished in 1819.

Droogmakerij: reclamation project; area reclaimed from inland lakes. Classic *droogmakerij* landscape is very regular in layout.

Fehntjer: settler in the peatland areas of North Germany.

Fermier: tenant farmer.

Franc-fief: right paid by a commoner to 'alter' land-use, on newly cultivated land.

Grundherrschaft: noble landed estates in Germany. From the Early Middle Ages onwards these would be the basis of small and medium-sized agricultural concerns, which resulted in the loosening of the ties binding serfs to the land and thus stimulated the growth of a rural protoindustry.

Gutswirtschaft: a noble landed estate which – unlike a *Grundherrschaft* – resulted in the extension of the local lord's lands.

Huertas: irrigated gardens in Spain.

Jachère: fallowland, permanent or temporary.

Kavel: a part of the drained land in a Dutch polder. Destined for agricultural use, it figured in an overall plan of investment.

Koog (Köge): drained area along the German coast of the North Sea.

Krabbelaars: Dutch dredge, usually animal-powered.

Livre: French money of account.

Livres tournois: The *livre tournois* (or Tournoise pound) was currency used in France, named after the town of Tours, in which it was minted.

Maître pêcheur: master fisherman.

Marais: French term for marshy and swampy terrain.

Marezane: *golena*; muddy and sandy deposits along the sides of watercourses, rising to form banks for torrents/rivers.

Marschen: the stretch of coast between eastern Friesland and Schleswig-Holstein.

Mede: wooden piles indicating the course of a channel.

Mesta: powerful association of sheep-owners in the Kingdom of Castile.

Metayers: French share-croppers.

Minali: measure of weight for wheat, especially in the Verona area, equal to 28.601 kg.

Moeren (Les Moëres): (geographical name) drained lakes in the Belgian province of West Flanders that lie 3–4 m below sea level. Land reclaimed according the plans of the engineer Wenceslas Coberger since 1620. The Moeren were modelled on the Dutch Beemster polder.

Mont-de-piété: powerbroker.

Moorkolonisation: the agricultural settlement of marshy terrain.

Moorkommissar: government official overseeing the reclamation and exploitation of new land.

Morgen: old measure of surface area (before the introduction of the decimal system by the French). Originally, it was the area of land that could be ploughed in a morning (before midday). One *morgen* measures roughly one hectare. Among the different regional standards, the Rhenish (Rijnlandse) *morgen* equalled 0.85 hectares.

Murazzi: large rough-block sea defences on the Venice Lido, created during the second half of the eighteenth century.

Oncie: inches.

Palada: a wall or dike comprising two lines of wooden piles with the space between them filled with rubble and reeds.

Paradore: a line of piles set at equal distance along the bed of the river. They could sometimes, far from protecting the banks, actually cause breaches.

Pennello: dike made of canes, stones and mortar; laid out along the course of a river, it was designed to protect the banks and control the flow of current.

Pertica: unit of measure within the Venetian Republic, could vary from about 204 to 230 cm.

Piede lineare: one foot: 0.34 metre.

Piò: unit of measurement of agricultural land, equal to 3,255 m². 3.071 piò made up one hectare.

Polder Fürsten: rich land owners in northern Germany. These princes (*Fürsten*) grew rich thanks to the sale of the cereal crops produced on drained land.

Polder: a private body, even if subject to the state authorities (*Rijkswaterstaat*, cf.); it was responsible for a certain area of agricultural land reclaimed from the sea which was exploited by the residents who lived there.

Porta: moveable barrier set at either end of a lock for river shipping.

Pozzolana: material of volcanic origin comprising alum and silica. Mixed with lime it can harden even in the absence of CO_2. The discovery of *pozzolana*, mentioned by Vitruvius, marked a revolution in the use of cement in Classical architecture because the material hardened very quickly. Thanks to the formation of calcium silicates, pozzolana is particularly resistant to the action of water.

Proto alle acque: water engineer.

Provveditori sopra i beni inculti del Trevisano e sopra l'adacquatione dei terreni: a special agency set up in 1560 to exploit the uncultivated lands of the Treviso area. Subsequently it would disappear from archive records.

Punto: $\frac{1}{12}$ of an inch.

Quadretto: a square foot made up of 144 square inches.

Quadretto vicentino: was a variation of the *quadretto veronese*. In monetary terms it cost about one-third as much.

Regadío: irrigated lands in Spain, which were used for the cultivation of fruit, rice, vines, sugarcane, cotton and citrus fruits.

Regenten: Those who held public office in the cities of Holland; an exclusive social class.

Rentier: those who lived off agricultural income without running the risk of investment.

Rosta: a fixed or moveable barrier of wooden piles set along a river bed to deviate part of the water to be used for irrigation or as a source of power.

Ruota [wheel]: unit of measure usually equivalent to one *quadretto*.

Scudo: silver and gold coinage in the Venetian Republic. In 1598, one *scudo* was the equivalent of 6 *lire* and 4 *soldi*.

Secanos: this Spanish term applied to both arid and semi-arid lands. The *secanos aridi* had an annual rainfall of 500 mm or less, the so-called *secanos umidi* one of over 500 mm.

Setiers (of wheat): French measure equal to 156 l.

Sovescio: the digging-in of the plants of root crops in order to increase soil fertility.

Sovrabbondante or *superfluo*: the amount of water that became available when a river or torrent was in spate.

Spadelandsrecht: dike law or regulations for the maintenance of dikes along the north German coast, especially in Schleswig-Holstein. It originated from customary law but was formulated in written legislation in 1585.

Sperone: a littoral breakwater comprising two parallel walls of wooden piles. Sometimes assimilated with the *palada* (cf.).

Terpen: raised lands where early Dutch settlers took refuge from flooding.

Terres labourables: fields under cultivation.

Terres marecageuses: French term for marshy terrain.

Thaler: silver coin minted in Austria and the German states from the sixteenth to the nineteenth century.

Triage: legal right of the local lord to one third of all land cultivated.

Urbarmachungsedikt: edict issued in German states to encourage the cultivation of newly-reclaimed lands.

Vaine pâture: pasture use of land alongside roads and forests. Here, each member of a village community could graze their animals free of charge.

Velme: these form the 'lips of the canals', marking the limits of channels and the *barene* themselves.

Waterbouwkunde: hydraulic engineering.

Waterbouwkundige: hydraulic engineer.

Wipmolen: windmill. A modified form of the structures that had been used in Holland to mill corn, these were equipped with a water-wheel to raise water.

❧ Primary Sources

List of Abbreviations

AGP	Archives du Génie (Paris, Chateau de Vincennes)
ANP	Archives Nationales (Paris)
ASV	State Archives (Venice)
C.	Codex
c.	*carta* (folio)
ENPC	Ecole Nationale des Ponts et Chaussées (Paris)
M.C.	Museo Correr Library (Venice)
Ms.	manuscript
P. all'A.	*Provveditori all'Adige*
P.a.B	*Piovveditori alle Biave*
P.D.	*Provenienze Diverse*
Psbi	*Provveditori ai Beni Inculti*
r.	recto
reg.	register
s.	series
SEA	*Savi ed Esecutori alle Acque*
S.T.	*Senato Terra*
v.	verso

ASV

S.T., reg. 21, cc.43v.–45r., Senate decree of 21 July 1519.

S.T., reg. 22, cc. 107v.–108r., Senate decree of 15 July 1522.

S.T., reg. 40, cc.128r.–128v., Senate decree of 29 August 1556.

S.T., reg. 40, cc. 156v.–157r., Senate decree of 6 February 1556.

S.T., *filza* 32, Senate decree of 12 October 1560 and 6 February 1560.

S.T., *filza* 59, Senate decree of 2 August 1572.

S.T., *filza* 60, Senate decree of 3 December 1572 and attached document by Nicolò Cicogna, 22 November 1572.

S.T., *filza* 64, Senate decree of 16 September 1574.

S.T., *filza* 133, Senate decree of 17 September 1594.

S.T., *filza* 133, Senate decree of 18 September 1594.

S.T., *filza* 182, Senate decree of 2 August 1597 and Report enclosed by the Psbi, 26 February 1597.

S.T., *filza* 182, Senate decree of 29 May 1607.

S.T., *filza* 192, Senate decree of 7 November 1609.

S.T., *filza* 241, Senate decree of 17 August 1620.

S.T., *filza* 252, Senate decree of 20 May 1622.

S.T., *filza* 270, Senate decree of 15 October 1624.

S.T., *filza* 273, Senate decree of 17 April 1625.

S.T., *filza* 342, Senate decree of 20 February 1630 and Document of the Psbi 18 August 1622.

S.T., *filza* 465, Senate decree of 2 January 1642.

S.T., *filza* 628, Senate decree of 9 August 1656.

S.T., *filza* 699, Senate decree of 18 March 1662.

S.T., *filza* 676, Senate decree of 19 May 1670.

S.T., *filza* 967, Senate decree of 26 March 1678.

S.T., *filza* 899, Senate decree of 3 November 1674.

S.T., *filza* 1031, Application by the City of Verona, 10 April 1681 and Report by the *Presidenti del Collegio dell'Adige*, 11 March 1682 enclosed with the Senate decree of of 11 April 1682.

S.T., *filza* 1024, Senate decree of 24 June 1682.

S.T., *filza* 1024, Senate decree of 25 July 1682.

S.T., *filza* 1049, Report by Marchio Moretti, 14 August 1683, deputy expert on rivers, attached to Senate decree of 19 August 1684.

S.T., *filza* 1053, Senate decree of 16 December 1684.

S.T., *filza* 1074, Senate decree of 26 September 1686 and Report by the *rettori* of Padua, 14 September 1686.

S.T., *filza* 1021, Senate decree of 11 April 1687.

S.T., *filza* 1091, Senate decree of 12 February 1687.

S.T., *filza* 1637, Document from the Podestà and Capitanio of Este, 2 April 1725.

S.T., *filza* 2098, Senate decree of 9 August 1749.

S.T. *filza* 2701, Senate decree of 26 August 1779 and Report by the *Provveditori all'Adige*, 17 August 1779.

SEA, reg. 115, *Scritture circa porti, laguna e fiumi*, 1683–86.

SEA, reg. 300, *Scritture circa l'affare di Reno*, 15 September 1731, signed by I. Riccati, G. Poleni and B. Zendrini.

SEA, reg. 301, Document of the Savi, 26 April 1735.

SEA, reg. 303, Documents of the Savi, 16 June 1742, 12 August and 6 February 1743.

SEA, reg. 303, Document of the Savi, 3 November 1743.

SEA, reg. 304, Documents of the Savi, 5 December 1747 and 20 April 1748.

SEA, reg. 305, Document of the Savi, 9 December 1752.

SEA, reg. 305, Document of the Savi, 1749.

SEA, reg. 306, Document of the Savi, 3 September 1754.

SEA, reg. 306, Documents of the Savi, 28 September and 15 February 1754.

SEA, reg. 307, Document of the Savi, 2 May 1757.

SEA, reg. 314, Document of the Savi, 19 April 1779

SEA, reg. 315, Document of the Savi, 9 January 1782.

SEA, reg. 317, Documents of the Savi, 18 January 1787 and 7 May 1787.

SEA, reg. 317, Document of the Savi, 10 April 1788.

SEA, reg. 319, Document of the Savi, 26 April 1793.

SEA, reg. 320, Documents of the Savi, 10 June 1795 and 15 March 1796.

SEA, reg. 320, Document of the Savi 19 August 1795.

SEA, *filza* 22, Documents of the Savi, 19 December and 2 January 1787.

SEA, *filza* 85, Document of the Savi, 11 January 1550.

SEA, *filza* 129, Documents of the Savi, 17 March and 13 July 1677.

SEA, *filza* 565, *Scritture di scandagli e ricordi,* Ortensio Zaghi, 22 March and 8 May 1725.

SEA, *filza* 565, 'Report and drawings by Gaetano Folega', 12 June 1725; 'Report and drawing by Antonio Benussi', 2 August 1725; 'Report and drawing by Giovanni Cattaneo', 11 June 1725.

SEA, *filza* 566, 'Report by Giovanni Poleni', 3 March 1727.

SEA, *filza* 567, 'Report by Bernardino Zendrini', 2 December 1741.

SEA, *busta* 89, Decree of the Senate (copy), of 19 June 1545.

SEA, *busta* 89, Application by F. and G.B. Garzadori, 9 August 1565.

SEA, *busta* 89, Documents of the experts, 14 and 23 January 1573.

SEA, *busta* 128, Decree of the Senate (copy), 23 November 1672.

SEA, *busta*155, Document of Savi, 31 March 1760.

SEA, *busta* 269, Document of Savi, 28 June 1622.

SEA, b. 523, Documents of Savi and 'Relazione del matematico', 4 January 1770.

Psbi, *Catastico of Verona, Cologna, Vicenza, Padova, Treviso and Friuli.*

Psbi, *Capitolare secondo,* cc. 138r.–139v., Application from the ambassadors of Treviso to the Collegio, 27 July 1572; ibid., cc. 133v.–140r., Written documents by Nicolò Cicogna 22 June, 21 and 29 July, 1 August 1572.

Psbi, *Capitolare secondo,* c.98r., Ruling 22 February 1611.

Psbi, reg. 264, cc. 139r.–140v., Water concession, 27 March 1572.

Psbi, reg. 300, cc. 7v.–8v., Water concession, 8 April 1557.

Psbi, reg. 300, c.19r., Ducal decree by Girolamo Priuli to Psbi (copy), 21 November 1559.

Psbi, reg. 307, cc.58v.–59r., Report by Psbi, 16 March 1569.

Psbi, reg. 309, cc. 111v.–112r., Water concession, 22 June 1571.

Psbi, reg. 310, cc. 68r.–v., Water concession, 27 March 1572.

Psbi, reg. 312, cc.19v.–20r., Water concession, 23 March 1574.

Psbi, reg. 316, cc. 28v.–29r., Water concession, 12 August 1589.

Psbi, reg. 532, c. 17r., Water concession, 15 March 1589.

Psbi, reg. 550, c.81r., Report by Psbi (Michele Priuli), 24 September 1535.

Psbi, reg. 603, Report by Psbi, 8 September 1655.

Psbi, *busta* 9, Application 19 November 1569.

Psbi, *busta* 11, Applications 23 May 1570 (the concession was granted on 20 March 1568); ibid., 29 November 1591, 9 March 1592 and 29 April 1592.

Psbi, *busta* 11, Report by Antonio Glisenti il Magro, 17 April 1592.

Psbi, *busta* 13, Lawsuit against the Bonetti family by Leone Aleardi, 8 July 1561.

Psbi, *busta* 43, Water concessions to Grimany family, 16 September 1660, 29 March 1661, 20 November 1663 and 26 February 1664.

Psbi, *busta* 43, Water concession, 15 July 1689.

Psbi, *busta* 44, Water concessions, 23 April and 25 May 1570.

Psbi, *busta* 78, Report by Psbi, 20 August 1655.

Psbi, *busta* 81, Dossier Sagramoso, Secret report to the Psbi, 26 June 1598.

Psbi, *busta* 81, Applications 13 January 1561, 16 May 1572 and 19 June 1599.
Psbi, *busta* 89, Water concessions, 3 July 1570 and 27 June 1579.
Psbi, *busta* 94, Report by the expert Tommaso Fiorini, 4 July 1695.
Psbi, *busta* 262, Water concession, 15 July 1574.
Psbi, *busta* 262, Report by the expert Panfilo Piazzola, 15 July 1574.
Psbi, *busta* 263, Report by Psbi, 8 March 1583.
Psbi, *busta* 263, Report by the expert Feliciano Perona, 13 November 1595.
Psbi, *busta* 264, Water concession 23 September 1586.
Psbi, *busta* 378, Water concession 22 September 1595.
Psbi, *busta* 389, Report by Psbi, 5 September 1682.
Psbi, *busta* 391, Report by Psbi, 10 May 1691.
Psbi, *busta* 402 (1748-1752), Water concessions.
Psbi, *busta* 403 (1753-1759), Water concessions.
Psbi, *busta* 404 (1760-1767); Water concessions.
Psbi, *busta* 405 (1768-1775); Water concessions.
Psbi, *busta* 406 (1776-1782); Water concessions.
Psbi, *busta* 407 (1783-1788); Water concessions.
Psbi, *busta* 408 (1789-1793); Water concessions.
Psbi, *busta* 475, Application by Girolamo and Antonio Morosini, 9 March 1557.
Psbi, *busta* 376-409, Water concessions.
Psbi, *busta* 735, Report by Psbi, 18 May 1735.
Psbi, *busta* 736, Report by Psbi, 20 March 1728 and 6 May 1789 (Consortium Brancaglia).
Psbi, *busta* 736, 741, 767, 779, 781-82, 785-86, 789, 791-92, 796, 799, 806, 809-14, 817, 819, 827 bis, 828-29, 831-32, 917, Water concessions.
Psbi, *busta* 741, Report by Psbi, 19 September 1764.
Psbi, *busta* 745, Report by Psbi, 31 December 1657.
Psbi, *busta* 745, Report by Psbi, 28 November 1713 (Consortium Frassinella).
Psbi, *busta* 750, Report by Psbi, 18 September 1787 and 11 April 1788.
Psbi, *busta* 781, Report by Psbi, 21 May 1699 (Consortium of Brancaglia).
Psbi, *busta* 790, Report by the *Podestà* and *Vicecapitano* of Montagnana, 2 November 1778.
Psbi, *busta* 790, Report by Psbi, 4 July 1778 and 8 August 1790.
Psbi, *busta* 794, Information on the reclaimed land of the Gorzon – undated, undoubtedly from the second half of the eighteenth century.
Psbi, *busta* 794, Copy of Senate decree, 7 October 1679.
Psbi, *busta* 795, 2 August 1677, Appeal by the community of Monselice.
Psbi, *busta* 798, Note by Giacinto Corradin, agent of the *President of the ritratto of Lozzo*, 1687.
Psbi, *busta* 801, Report by Psbi, 4 July 1633 (Consortium of Lozzo).
Psbi, *busta* 804, Report by Psbi, 8 June 1696.
Psbi, *busta* 804, Reports by Psbi, 3 January 1634 and 17 April 1763.
Psbi, *busta* 812, Auction of the Consorzio del Piavon, 27 March 1748.
Psbi, *busta* 812, Report by the *Inquisitore alla sanità* Giacomo Nani, 3 June 1772.
Psbi, *busta* 827, Copy of Senate Decree 16 November 1589.

ASV

Archivio Proprio B. Zendrini, reg. 24, cc.56–59, C. Sabbadino, 'Per adacquar il Trevisan da Nervesa in zoso', between 1550 and 1558.

Archivio Proprio B. Zendrini, reg. 21, *Scritture in materia di acque,* 1679–87.

Archivio Proprio B. Zendrini, reg. 22, cc. 193–210, 'Relazione di D. Guglielmini, matematico di Padova, sopra la laguna di Venezia', 17 February 1699; ibid., cc. 213–438, for numerous other writings on the problems tackled by Guglielmini in the years 1699–1709.

Archivio Proprio G. Poleni, filza 8, 'Scrittura di D. Guglielmtni per la diversione della Bretella', 14 April 1707.

Archivio Proprio di Bernardo e Francesco Trevisan, reports on the rivers, littorals and lagoon gathered by Bernardo Trevisan.

Provveditori all'Adige, Disegni n. 28, *Corso generale delle acque da sette miglia inferiormente a Verona fino al mare,* 30 July 1784.

Provveditori all'Adige, busta 258 (Report by P.a.A., 3 February 1738); 259 (Water concessions); 260 (Note by the Presidency of the consortium of Castagnaro, Rovigo, 18 April 1794), 261 (Water concessions); 262 (Water concessions); 263 (Report by P.a.A., 10 marzo 1691).

Provveditori alle Biave, busta 34, Reports by P.a.B., 29 April 1670, 27 December 1670 and 5 January 1672.

P.a.B, *busta* 35, Report by P.a.B, 22 December 1693 and 11 June 1695.

Museo Correr Venice

Mss. P.D., C. 975/52, Concordate between the Republic and the Duke of Mantova, 15 March 1548.

Mss. P.D., C. 827/37, Water Applications 16 September 1678, 24 March 1679, 9 September 1679.

Mss. P.D., Codex 519/6, Water Applications 28 March 1590, 29 April 1589, 30 March 1590 and 4 June 1590.

ANP

AD IV 22/121, *Idées d'un agriculteur patriote,* without date but of the revolutionary period.

F10 208, Mémoire historique sur les dessèchements des marais, date of publication unknown but almost certainly the second half of the eighteenth century.

F^{10}, Carton 319, *Mémoire sur le dessèchement de l'Etang appelé de Marseillete,* date of publication unknown.

F^{10}, Carton 318, 1739; ibid., July 1751; see also ibid. *Observation sur le dessèchement du Lac de Grandlieu,* without date but probably 1756, on the *riverains'* resistance to harassment by *dessecheurs;* AGP, Carton 1/11, Art.5, Section 7, §5, 11 April 1741; see also ibid., Carton 1/9, for the company formed by the two entreprencurs.

F^{10} 316, *Observations sur le projet d'établir les hollandais en Provence,* date of publication unknown but around 1783–1786.

F^{10}, Carton 318, Agosto 1772.

F^{10}, Carton 318, *Mémoire sur les travaux des dessèchements d'Aunis et Saintonge (villes de Rochefort, Marennes et St. Jean Dangely)*, 1787.

F^{10}, Carton 319, Arrêt du Conseil d'Etat, 15 novembre 1746; F^{10}, Carton 319, *Mémoire pour appuyer les demandes que fait au Conseil le S. de Berriac*, 6 June 1761.

F^{10}, Cartons 313 and 317: Prints Proclamations and Enquiries solicited by the Convention, Year II of the Republic.

F^{10}, Carton 314, *Observation faite sur le dessèchement dans le département de la Meurthe*, 29 Pluviose de l'année II de la République.

F^{10}, Carton 2303, 20 août de l'année II de la République.

F^{10}, Carton 318, Dossier 1757, *arrêt* 24 February 1756.

F14, liasses 1114, 1115,1119, 1131.

Carton 1, Art.5, Section 7, § 4, *Mémoire relatif aux ouvrages à faire pour dessécher les marais [...] d'Aigues-Mortes jusqu'au Rhône*, 1701, by Niquet.

AGP

Art.4, Section 2, §4, Cart. 1, *Mémoire [...] de la province de Saintonge [...] le Pays d'Aunis [...], partie du Bas Poictou...*, 10 December 1721, par Masse; ibid., *Mémoire sur la carte [...] de la Charente*, 19 June 1704; ibid., *Mémoire sur la carte [...] du bas Poitou, Pais d'Aunis et Saintonge*, 5 February 1719.

Carton 2, Art.5, Section 7, §4, *Mémoire de Mrs. les proprietaires des salins de Pecais*, 1742.

Carton 1, Art.4, Section 2, §4, *Mémoire sur la carte générale [...] du Bas Poitou*, 15 March 1702; ibid., Art.5, Section 7, §1, Carton 1, *Rapport sur le dessèchement du Bas Artois*, 13 agosto 1791; ibid., §3, Carton 1, *Mémoire pour le dessèchement à faire des prairies depuis Landrecy jusqu'à Castillon*, 1693.

Carton 1, Art.5, Section 7, §3, *Mémoire au sujet des marais de la rivière de Somme*, par M***, Lieutenant de Roi de la ville de ***, date of publication unknown.

Bibliothèque du Génie (Vincennes),

Ms.183 (4^ 133), *Mémoire qui accompagne la carte de l'isle de Ré pour expliquer l'estendue des digues* (date of publication unknown); see also ibid., *Mémoire géographique de Masse sur partie du Bas Poitou, Pays d'Aunis et Saintonge*, 1715) and *Mémoire sur la carte des costes du bas Poictou, et partie du Pays d'Aunis & Bretagne*, 28 March 1704.

ENPC

Ms. 2584, *Précis historique sur les moëres*, Dunkerque, 24 janvier 1791, par Duclos.

Ms. 2634, *Mémoire sur le projet de canal pour le faire servir au dessèchement des marais d'Arles*, Beaucaire 25 January 1826.

Select Bibliography

Abel, W., *Agrarkrisen und Agrarkonjunktur. Eine Geschichte der Land- und Ernährungswirtschaft Mitteleuropas seit dem hohen Mittelalter*, Hamburg, 1966 (English translation *Agricultural Fluctuations in Europe from the Thirteenth to the Twentieth Centuries*, New York, 1980).
———. *Geschichte der deutschen Landwirtschaft*, Stuttgart, 1967.
Agostinetti, Giacomo, *Cento e dieci ricordi che formano il buon fattor di villa*, Venice, 1704.
Agricola (Georg Bauer), *De re metallica libri XII*, [1550], Wiesbaden 2003.
Agricoltura e sviluppo del capitalismo, edited by the Istituto Gramsci, Rome, 1970.
Allen, R.C., *Enclosure and the Yeoman*, Oxford, 1992.
Altieri Biagi, M.L. and Basile, B. (eds), *Gli scienziati del Seicento,* Milan, 1980, 2 vols.
Ambrosoli, M., *The Wild and the Sown. Botany and Agriculture in Western Europe: 1350–1850* (Turin 1992), Cambridge, 1997.
Angladette, A., *Le riz*, Paris, 1967.
Arnaldi, G. and Pastore Stocchi, M. (eds), *Storia della cultura veneta. Dal primo Quattrocento al Concilio di Trento*, 3/I and II, Vicenza, 1980.
———. *Storia della cultura veneta. Il Seicento*, 4/I, 1983.
———. *Storia della cultura veneta. Dalla controriforma alla fine della Repubblica. Il Settecento*, 5/I and II, 1985–86.
Aubriot, O. and Jolly, G. (eds), *Histoire d'une eau partagée. Provence, Alpes Pyrénées*, Aix-en-Provence, 2002.
Aymard, M., *Venise, Raguse et le commerce du blé pendant la seconde moitié du XVIᵉ siècle*, Paris, 1966.
———. 'Per una storia della produzione agricola in età moderna', in *Quaderni Storici*, 25 (1974), pp. 264–77.
———. 'La transizione dal feudalesimo al capitalismo', in *Storia d'Italia. Annali 1, Dal feudalesimo al capitalismo*, R. Romano and C. Vivanti (eds), Turin, 1978, pp. 1131–92.
———. (ed.), *Dutch Capitalism and World Capitalism*, Cambridge, 1982.
———. 'L'Europe des nourritures végétales. Une nouvelle visite aux prisons de longue durée', in *Alimentazione e nutrizione, secc.XIII–XVIII* (28th Settimana di Studio, Prato 1996), S. Cavaciocchi (ed.), Florence, 1997, pp. 91–112.
Baars C., *De geschiedenis van de landbouw in de Beijerlanden*, Wageningen, 1973.
———. 'Andries Vierlingh', in *Civiele Techniek*, 37 (1982), pp. 15–19.
———. 'Landaanwinning door Nederlanders in Frankrijk en Italië', *Civiele Techniek*, 38 (1983), n. 5, pp. 15–20.
Baehrel R., *Une croissance. La basse Provence rurale de la fin du XVIᵉ siècle à 1789*, I, Paris, 1988, 2 vols.
Baldini U., 'La scuola galileiana', in *Storia d'Italia. Annali 3*, G. Micheli (ed.), Turin, 1980, pp. 383–463
———. 'L'attività scientifica nel primo Settecento', in *Storia d'Italia. Annali 3*, G. Micheli (ed.), Turin, 1980, pp. 467–545.

277

_____. *Saggi sulla cultura della Compagnia di Gesù (secoli XVI–XVIII)*, Padua, 2000.

Barentsen, W., 'De zeedijk van zijn ontstaan tot het jaar 1730', in *Orgaan van de Vereniging van Waterstaatkundige Ambtenaren van de Rijkswaterstaat*, 45 (1961), n. 9, pp. 195–205 and 46 (1961), n. 1, pp. 1–16.

Barpo, Giovanbattista, *Le delitie e i frutti dell'agricoltura*, Venice, 1634.

Barsanti, D. and Rombai, L. (eds), *Scienziati idraulici e territorialisti nella Toscana dei Medici e dei Lorena*, Florence, 1994.

Béaur, G., *Histoire agraire de la France au XVIIIe siècle*, Paris, 2000.

Beekman, A.A., *Nederland als polderland*, Zutphen, 1932.

_____. *Het Dijk- en Waterschapsrecht in Nederland voor 1795*, 's-Gravenhage, 1907.

Beggio, G., *I mulini natanti sull'Adige*, Florence, 1969.

Bélidor, Bernard Forêst de, *Architecture hydraulique, ou l'art de conduire, d'élever et de menager les eaux pour les differents besoins de la vie*, Paris, 1737, 2 vols.

Bellone, E., *Il mondo di carta. Ricerche sulla seconda rivoluzione scientifica*, Milan, 1976.

Beltrami, D., *La penetrazione economica dei veneziani in Terraferma: forze di lavoro e proprietà fondiaria nelle campagne venete dei secoli XVII e XVIII*, Venice-Rome, 1961.

_____. *Saggio di storia dell'agricoltura nella Repubblica di Venezia durante l'età moderna*, Venice-Rome, 1955.

Bennassar, B., 'L'Europe des campagnes', in *Histoire économique et sociale du monde*, P. Léon and B. Bennassar (eds), I, Paris, 1977, pp. 449–92.

Berengo, M., 'Africo Clementi, agronomo padovano del Cinquecento', in *Miscellanea Augusto Campana*, I, Padua, 1981, pp. 27–69.

_____. 'Introduzione' to Camillo Tarello, *Ricordo di agricoltura*, Turin, 1975, pp. vii–xlv.

_____. *L'agricoltura veneta dalla caduta della Repubblica all'unità*, Milan, 1963.

Berkel, Klaas van, *In het voetspoor van Stevin. Geschiedenis van de natuurwetenschap in Nederland, 1580–1940*, Amsterdam, 1985.

Bernard, Pons-Joseph, *Nouveaux principes d'hydraulique appliqués à tous les objets, particulièrement aux rivières*, Paris, 1787.

Bertelli, Carlo Antonio, *Discorso sopra l'origine delle atterrazioni della laguna veneta antica, e moderna*, Venice, 1676.

Berthold, R., 'Wachstumsprobleme der landwirtschaftlichen Nutzfläche im Spätfeudalismus (zirka 1500 bis 1800)', in *Jahrbuch für Wirtschaftsgeschichte* (1964, Teil II/III), pp. 5–23.

Bertrand, M.J., *De l'eau relativement à l'économie rustique, ou traité de l'irrigation des prés*, Lyon, 1764.

Berveglieri, R., *Inventori stranieri a Venezia (1474–1788). Importazione di tecnologia e circolazione di tecnici artigiani inventori. Repertorio*, Venice, 1995.

_____. 'Tecnologia idraulica olandese in Italia nel secolo XVII: Cornelius Janszoon Meijer a Venezia (gennaio-aprile 1675)', in *Studi Veneziani*, n.s., 10 (1985), pp. 81–97.

Bessoni, Iacobi, *Theatrum instrumentorum et machinarum*, Lugduni, 1578.

Bethemont, J., *De l'eau et des hommes. Essai géographique sur l'utilisation des eaux continentales*, Paris, 1977.

Beutler, C., 'Un chapitre de la sensibilité collective: la littérature agricole en Europe au XVIe siècle', in *Annales E.S.C.*, 28 (1973), pp. 1091–1122.

Bevilacqua, P., 'Le rivoluzioni dell'acqua. Irrigazione e trasformazioni dell'agricoltura tra Sette e Novecento', in *Storia dell'agricoltura italiana. Spazi e paesaggi*, P. Bevilacqua (ed.), I, Venice, 1989, pp. 275–313.

————. *Venezia e le acque. Una metafora planetaria*, Rome, 1995.

Bevilacqua, P. and Rossi-Doria, M. (eds), *Le bonifiche in Italia dal '700 a oggi*, Bari, 1984.

Bigatti, G. (ed.), *Uomini e acque. Il territorio lodigiano tra passato e presente*, Lodi, 2000.

Billaud, J.-P., *Le Marais Poitevin. Rencontres de la terre et de l'eau*, Paris, 1984.

Biswas, A.K., *History of Hydrology*, Amsterdam, 1970.

Bloch, M., 'Pour une histoire comparée des sociétés européennes' (1928), in *Mélanges Historiques*, Préface de Charles-Edmond Perrin, Paris, 1963, pp. 16 40.

Blok, D.P. and Prevenier, W. (eds), *Algemene geschiedenis der Nederlanden*, VIII, Haarlem, 1979.

————. *Algemene Geschiedenis der Nederlanden*, VII, Haarlem, 1980.

Boerio, G., *Dizionario del dialetto veneziano*, Venice, 1856.

Bolens, L., *Les méthodes culturelles au Moyen Age d'après les traités d'agronomie andalous: traditions et techniques*, Genève, 1974.

Bonardo, G.M., *Le ricchezze dell'agricoltura*, Venice, 1590.

Bonifica e programmazione nel Veneto, edited by the Unione regionale veneta dell'associazione nazionale delle bonifiche, delle irrigazioni e dei miglioramenti fondiari, Venice, 1974.

Borelli, G., *Un patriziato della Terraferma veneta tra XVII e XVIII secolo. Ricerche sulla nobiltà veronese*, Milan, 1974.

————. 'Per una tipologia della proprietà fondiaria della villa tra XVII e XVIII secolo', in *La villa nel Veronese*, G.F. Viviani (ed.), Verona, 1975, pp. 141–72.

————. (ed.), *Una città e il suo fiume. Verona e l'Adige*, Verona, 1977, 2 vols.

————. (ed.), *Uomini e civiltà agraria in territorio veronese*, Verona, 1982, 2 vols.

Bourde, A., *Agronomie et agronomes en France au XVIIIe siècle*, Paris, 1967, 3 vols.

Braudel, F., *La Méditerranée et le monde méditerranéen à l'époque de Philippe II*, Paris, 1966, 2 vols.

Braudel, F., *Civilisation matérielle, économie et capitalisme, XVe–XVIIIe siècle, I. Les structures du quotidien: le possible et l'impossible*, Paris, 1979 (English translation: *Civilization and Capitalism: 15th–18th Century, 1. The Structures of Every Day Life. The Limits of the Possible*, London, 1988).

————. *Civilisation matérielle, économie et capitalisme, XVe–XVIIIe siècle, III. Le temps du monde*, Paris, 1979 (English translation: *Civilization and Capitalism: 15th–18th century, 3. The Perspective of the World*, Berkeley, 1992).

Braudel, F. and Labrousse, E. (eds), *Histoire économique et sociale de la France, 1660–1789. Des derniers temps de l'âge seigneurial aux préludes de l'âge industriel*, II, Paris, 1970.

Bray, F., 'Agriculture', in *Science and Civilisation in China*, J. Needham (ed.), 6/II. Cambridge, 1984.

Bresc, H., 'Les jardins de Palerme (1290–1460)', *Mélanges de l'Ecole Française de Rome, Moyen Age-Temps Modernes*, 84 (1972), pp. 55–127.

Broc, N., *La géographie des philosophes. Géographes et voyageurs français au XVIIIe siècle*, Paris, 1975.

Brusatin, M., *Venezia nel Settecento: stato, architettura, territorio*, Turin, 1980.

Bruschetti, G., *Storia dei progetti e delle opere per l'irrigazione del Milanese*, Lugano, 1834.

Buffon, Nadualt de, *Des subversions fertilisantes comprenant les travaux de colmatage, limonage et irrigations d'hiver*, Paris, 1867.

Buonora, P., *La Valle Umbra. Genesi e trasformazione di un sistema idraulico (secoli XVI–XIX)*, Ancona (Proposte e Ricerche, 17), 1994.

Burke, P., *Venice and Amsterdam*, London, 1974.

Busch, B. and Foerster, L. (eds), *Wasser* (Schriftenreihe Forum 9, Elemente des Naturhaushalts, 1), Cologne, 2000.

Bussato, Marco, *Giardino di agricoltura*, Venice, 1599.

Caizzi, B., *Aspetti economici e sociali delle bonifiche nelle Venezie*, Padua, 1937

Campos, E., *I consorzi di bonifica nella repubblica veneta*, Padua, 1937.

Caporali, G., Emo De Rhao, M. and Zecchini, F., *Brenta vecchia, nova, novissima*, Venice, 1980.

Carmignani, Filippo (ed.), *Nuova raccolta d'autori italiani che trattano del moto delle acque*, Parma, 1766–68, 7 vols.

Cazzola, F., 'Fiumi e lagune: le acque interne nella vita regionale', in *Cultura popolare nell'Emilia-Romagna. I mestieri della terra e delle acque*, C. Poni (ed.) III, Milan, 1979, pp. 168–213.

⸻. 'Le bonifiche nella valle padana. Un profilo', in *Rivista di Storia dell'Agricoltura*, 27 (1987), n. 2, pp. 37–66.

⸻ and Olivieri, A., *Uomini, terra e acque. Politica e cultura idraulica nel Polesine tra '400 e '600*, Rovigo, 1990.

Ceredi, Giovanni, *Tre discorsi sopra il modo d'alzar acque da' luoghi bassi*, Parma, 1567.

Cessi, R. and Spada, N. (eds), *Antichi scrittori d'idraulica veneta. La difesa idraulica della laguna veneta nel secolo XVI. Relazioni dei periti*, III, Venice, 1952.

Chambers, J.D. and Mingay, G.E., *The Agricultural Revolution 1750–1880*, London, 1966.

Chi Ch'ao-Ting, *Key Economic Areas in Chinese History as Revealed in the Development of Public Works for Water-control* [1936], New York, 1970.

Chittolini, G., 'Alle origini delle "grandi aziende" della bassa lombarda', in *Quaderni Storici*, 14 (1979), n. 39, pp. 828–37.

Cipolla, C.M., *Before the Industrial Revolution. European Society and Economy*, London, 1993.

Ciriacono, S., 'Trattati di agricoltura, di idraulica e di bonifica', in *Trattati di prospettiva, architettura militare, idraulica e altre discipline*, V. Fontana (ed.), Venice, 1985, pp. 45–60.

⸻. 'Le bonifiche venete alla caduta della Repubblica e al tempo di Pietro Paleocapa', in *Ingegneri e politica nell'Italia dell'800: Pietro Paleocapa*, Venice, 1990, pp. 317–40.

⸻. 'The Venetian Economy and its Place in the World Economy of the 17th and 18th Centuries. A Comparison with the Low Countries', in Nitz (ed.), *The Early Modern World-system in Geographical Perspective*, 1993, pp. 120–35.

⸻. 'Land Reclamation in Early Modern Europe. Dutch Windmills, Private Enterprises and State Intervention', in *Review. Fernand Braudel Center*, 18 (1995), n. 2, pp. 281–304.

————. (ed.), *Land Drainage and Irrigation* (Studies in the History of Civil Engineering, vol. 3), Aldershot (Hampshire), 1998.

————. (ed.), *Eau et développement dans l'Europe moderne*, Paris, 2004.

Clark, G., 'Productivity Growth without Change in European Agriculture before 1850', in *Journal of Economic History*, 47 (1987), pp. 419–32.

Clementi, Africo, *Trattato dell'agricoltura*, Venice, 1572.

Clout, H.D. (ed.), *Themes in the Historical Geography of France*, London, 1977.

Coi, G., *Ragionamento intorno ai fiumi del Veronese, Polesine e Padovano*, Padua, 1777.

Cools, R.H.A., *Strijd om den grond in het lage Nederland. Het proces van bedijking, inpoldering en droogmaking sinds de vroegste tijden*, Rotterdam, 1948.

Coppola, G., 'L'agricoltura dell'irriguo milanese nel secolo XVI', in *Contributi dell'Istituto di storia economica e sociale. Aspetti di vita agricola lombarda (secoli XVI–XIX)*, Milan, 1973.

————. *Il mais nell'economia agricola lombarda*, Bologna, 1979.

Corazzol, G.L., *Fitti e livelli a grano*, Milan, 1979.

————. *Livelli stipulati a Venezia nel 1591. Studio storico*, Pisa, 1986.

Corbin, A., *Le miasme et la jonquille. L'odorat et l'imaginaire social XVIIIe–XIXe siècles*. Paris, 1982.

Cornaro, Alvise and Sabbadino, Cristoforo, *Antichi scrittori d'idraulica veneta. Scritture sopra la laguna*, II, part II, R. Cessi (ed.), Venice, 1941.

Cornaro, Marco (1412–1464), *Antichi scrittori d'idraulica veneta. Scritture sulla laguna*, I, G. Pavanello (ed.), Venice, 1919.

Corni, G., *Stato assoluto e società agraria in Prussia nell'età di Federico II*, Bologna, 1982.

Cosgrove, D. and Petts, G. (eds), *Water, Engineering, and Landscape: Water Control and Landscape Transformation in the Modern Period*, London, 1990.

Costantini, M., *L'acqua di Venezia. L'approvvigionamento idrico della Serenissima*, Venice, 1984.

Costantino, Cesare, *De notevoli et utilissimi ammaestramenti dell'agricoltura*, Venice, 1592.

Crosby, A., *The Columbian Exchange. Biological and Cultural Consequences of 1492* (foreword by Otto von Mering), Westport CT, 1972.

Crouzet-Pavan, E., *'Sopra le acque salse'. Espaces, pouvoir et société à la fin du Moyen Age*, Rome, 1992, 2 vols.

———— and Maire-Vigueur, J.-C. (eds), *Le contrôle des eaux en Europe occidentale, XIIe–XVIe siècles*, Proceedings Eleventh International Economic History Congress, Section B2, Milan, 1994.

Da Mosto, A., *L'archivio di Stato di Venezia*, Rome, 1937, 2 vols.

Darby, H.C., *The Changing Fenland*, Cambridge, 1983.

————. *The Draining of the Fens*, Cambridge, 1956.

Davis, J.C., *A Venetian Family and its Fortune: 1500–1900. The Donà and the Conservation of their Wealth*, Philadelphia, 1975.

De Dienne, Edouard, *Histoire du dessèchement des lacs et marais en France avant 1789*, Paris, 1891.

De Maddalena, A., 'Il mondo rurale italiano nel Cinque e nel Seicento. Rassegna di studi recenti', in *Rivista Storica Italiana*, 76 (1964), pp. 349–426.

————. 'Rural Europe 1500–1750', in *The Fontana Economic History of Europe. The Sixteenth and Seventeenth Centuries*, C.M. Cipolla (ed.), Glasgow, 1974, pp. 273–353.

Dekker, C., *Zuid-Beveland. De historische geografie en de instellingen van een Zeeuws eiland in de Middeleeuwen*, Assen, 1971.

Delort, R. and Walter, F., *Histoire de l'environnement européen*, Préface de Jacques Le Goff, Paris, 2001.

Derex, J.-M., *La gestion de l'eau et des zones humides en Brie de la fin de l'Ancien Régime à la fin du XIXe siècle*, Préface de Andrée Corvol-Dessert, Paris, 2001.

Dion, R., *Le Val de Loire. Etude de géographie régionale*, Marseille, 1978.

Dooley, B., 'Social Control and the Italian Universities, from Renaissance to Illuminismo', in *Journal of Modern History*, 61 (1989), pp. 205–39.

Doorman, G., *Patents for Inventions in the Netherlands during the 16th, 17th and 18th Centuries*, The Hague, 1942.

Downing, T.E. and McGuire, G. (eds), *Irrigation's Impact on Society*. Tucson, Anthropological Papers of University of Arizona, n. 25, 1974.

Dugas, R., *Histoire de la mécanique*, Neuchatel, 1950.

Ewbank, T., *A Descriptive and Historical Account of Hydraulic and Other Machines for Rising Water*, New York, 1972.

Fabroni, A., *Vitae italorum doctrina excellentium qui saeculi XVII et XVIII floruerunt*, Pisis, 1779, 20 vols.

Faccini, L., 'I lavoratori della risaia fra '700 e '800. Condizioni di vita, alimentazione, malattie', in *Studi Storici*, 15 (1974), pp. 545–88.

————. *L'economia risicola lombarda dagli inizi del XVIII secolo all'unità*, Milan, 1976.

————. *Uomini e lavoro in risaia. Il dibattito sulla risicoltura nel '700 e nell'800*, Milan, 1976.

Falcone, Giuseppe, *La nuova, vaga, et dilettevole villa*, Venice, 1612.

Ferrone, V., *Scienza, natura, religione. Mondo newtoniano e cultura italiana nel primo Settecento*, Naples, 1982.

Filiasi, J., *Memorie storiche de' veneti primi e secondi*, Padua, 1811, 2 vols.

Finzi, R. *Monsignore al suo fattore. La "Istruzione di agricoltura" di Innocenzo Malvasia*, Bologna, 1979.

————. 'Stato regionale e inconcepibilità del mercato nazionale in Italia nell'età della transizione europea al capitalismo', in *Storia d'Italia. Annali 1*, Romano, R. and Vivanti, C. (eds), Turin, 1978, pp. 511–74.

Fischer, O., *Das Wasserwesen an der schleswig-holsteinischen Nordseeküste. Sonderprobleme und Einzel-fragen des Küstenraumes*, Berlin, 1955.

————. *Das Wasserwesen an der schleswig-holsteinischen Nordseeküste. Eiderstedt*, Berlin, 1956.

Flinn, M. (ed.), *Proceedings of the Seventh International Economic History Congress*, I, Edinburgh, 1978.

Fockema Andreae, S.J., 'Waterschaps-organisatie in Nederland en in den Vreemde', in *Mededelingen der Koninklijke Nederlandse Akademie van Wetenschappen*, 14 (1951), pp. 309–30.

————. 'Het Watergerecht van Valencia', in *Mededelingen der Koninklijke Nederlandse Akademie van Wetenschappen, afd. Letterkunde*, deel 23, 1960, n. 14, pp. 385–401.

Forbes, R.J., 'Hydraulic Engineering', in *The Principal Works of Simon Stevin. The Works on Engineering*, R.J. Forbes (ed.), Amsterdam, 1966, vol. v, pp. 67–81.

Foster, R., 'Obstacles to Agricultural Growth in Eighteenth-Century France', in *American Historical Review*, 75 (1970), pp. 1600–15.

Fournier, P., *Eaux claires, eaux troubles dans le Comtat Venaissin (XVIIe-XVIIIe siècles)*, Perpignan, 1999.

Franz, G., *Geschichte des deutschen Bauernstandes*, Stuttgart, 1970.

Gallo, Agostino, *Le vinti giornate dell'agricoltura et de' piaceri della villa*, Venice, 1569.

Gambi, L., *Una geografia per la storia*, Turin, 1973.

Garavaglia, J.C., 'Atlixco: l'eau, les hommes et la terre dans une vallée mexicaine (15e–17e siècles)', in *Annales. Histoire, Sciences Sociales*, 50 (1995), pp. 1309–49.

Georgelin, J., *Venise au siècle des lumières*, Paris, 1978.

Giacomelli, A., 'Le aree chiave della bonifica bolognese', in *Problemi d'acque a Bologna*, Bologna, 1983, pp. 123–72.

Gille, B., *Les ingénieurs de la Renaissance*, Paris, 1964.

Gillispie, C.C., *Dictionary of Scientific Biography*, New York 1974, 16 vols.

———. *Science and Polity in France at the End of the Old Regime*, Princeton, 1980.

Glick, T.F., *Irrigation and Society in Medieval Valencia*, Cambridge (Mass.), 1970.

———. *Irrigation and Hydraulic Technology. Medieval Spain and its Legacy*. Aldershot (Hampshire), 1996.

Gloria, A., *Della agricoltura nel Padovano*, Padua, 1855, 2 vols.

Gottschalk, M.K.E., *Stormvloeden en rivieroverstromingen in Nederland*, Assen, 1971–77, 3 vols.

Goubert, P., *Beauvais et le Beauvaisis de 1600 à 1730*, Paris, 1960, 2 vols.

Goubert, J.-P., *The Conquest of Water: the Advent of Health in the Industrial Age*, Cambridge, 1989.

Grantham, G., 'The Diffusion of the New Husbandry in Northern France', in *Journal of Economic History*, 38 (1978), pp. 311–37.

Grillo, S., *Venezia. Le difese a mare*, Venice, 1989.

Grinovero, C., *Ricerche sull'economia dell'irrigazione. Risultati economici delle irrigazioni nel Veneto*, II, Rome-Milan, 1933.

Guarducci, A. (ed.), *Agricoltura e trasformazione dell'ambiente, secoli XIII–XVIII* (11th Settimana di studio, Prato), Florence, 1984.

Guicciardini, Ludovico, *Descrittione di tutti i Paesi Bassi, altrimenti detti Germania inferiore*, Anversa, 1567.

Guillerme, A., *Les temps de l'eau. La cité, l'eau et les techniques*, Seyssel, 1983.

Gullino, G. , 'Le dottrine degli agronomi e i loro influssi sulla pratica agricola', in *Storia della cultura veneta. Il Settecento*, Arnaldi and Pastore Stocchi eds, 5/II, 1986, pp. 379–410.

Hahn, R., *The Anatomy of a Scientific Institution. The Paris Academy of Sciences, 1666–1803*, Berkeley, 1971.

Haitsma Mulier, E.O.G., *The Myth of Venice and Dutch Republican Thought in the Seventeenth Century*, Assen, 1980

Harris, L.E., *The Two Netherlanders, Humphrey Bradley and Cornelis Drebbel*, Leiden, 1961.

———. *Vermuyden and the Fens*, London, 1953.

Haussmann, G., 'Il suolo d'Italia nella storia', in *Storia d'Italia. 1, I caratteri originali*, Romano and Vivanti (eds), pp. 63–131.

Herrera, Gabriel Alonso (de), *Libro di agricoltura utilissimo, tratto da diversi autori, novamente venuto a luce*, Venice, 1558.

Higounet, C., *Les allemands en Europe centrale et orientale au Moyen Âge*, Paris, 1989.

Hill, C., *Reformation to Industrial Revolution. A Social and Economic History of Britain, 1530–1780*, London, 1969.

Hoogewerff, G.J., *Bescheiden in Italië*, III, 's-Gravenhage, 1917.

Hunt, R.C. and Hunt, E., in 'Canal Irrigation and Local Social Organization',
   Current Anthropology, 17 (1976), n. 3, pp. 389–411.
Ibn-al-Awwäm, Le livre de l'agriculture, Paris, 1866–67, 2 vols.
Isenburg, T., Acque e stato. Energia, bonifiche, irrigazione in Italia fra 1930 e
   1950, Milan, 1981.
Israel, J., Dutch Primacy in World Trade, 1585–1740, Oxford, 1989.
Jacquart, J., 'La productivité agricole dans la France du Nord aux XVIᵉ et XVIIᵉ
   siècles', in Troisième conférence internationale d'histoire économique. Production
   et productivité agricole, Section II (Munich 1965), Paris, 1969, II, pp. 65–74.
'Jeux et enjeux de l'eau au XVIIᵉ siècle' (Journée d'étude, Maintenon 26
   Octobre 2002), in XVIIᵉ siècle, 55 (2003), n. 221, pp. 585–714.
Jodogne, P. (ed.), Proceedings of the Colloquium on Lodovico Guicciardini,
   Florence 1521–Anvers 1589, Leuven, 1991.
Jones, E.L. and Woolf, S.J., 'The Historical Role of Agrarian Change in
   Economic Development. Introduction' to Agrarian Change and Economic
   Development, Jones and Woolf (eds), London, 1969, pp. 1–21.
Kaup, M., 'Die Urbarmachung des Oderbruchs. Umwelthistorische
   Annäherung an ein bekanntes Thema', in Umweltgeschichte – Methoden,
   Themen, Potentiale, G. Bayerl, N. Fuchsloch and T. Meyer (eds), Münster,
   1994, pp. 111–33.
Kerridge, E., The Agricultural Revolution, London, 1967.
Keunen, G.H., 'Waterbeheersing en de ontwikkeling van de bemalingstechniek
   in West-Nederland. De historische ontwikkeling van poldermolens en
   gemalen tot heden', in Bijdragen en Mededelingen betreffende de geschiedenis
   der Nederlanden, 103 (1988), n. 4, pp. 571–606.
Klasen, J., Vergleichende Landschaftskunde der englischen Marschen, Wiesbaden-
   Köln, 1967.
Korthals Altes, J., Polderland in Engeland, Den Haag, 1924.
_____. Sir Cornelius Vermuyden, London, 1925.
_____. Polderland in Italië, Den Haag, 1928.
Kula, W., Les mesures et les hommes (texte établi et revu par K. Pomian et J.
   Revel), Paris, 1984.
_____. Problemi e metodi di storia economica, Milan, 1972.
La Maillardière, Charles François Lefèvre, Traité d'économie politique,
   embrassant toutes ses branches, ou les intérêts de la population, de l'agriculture,
   des arts, du commerce, Place of publication unknown, 1782.
Lambert A.M., The Making of the Dutch Landscape. An Historical Geography of
   the Netherlands, London-New York, 1971.
Lazzarini, A., Fra terra e acqua. L'azienda risicola di una famiglia veneziana nel
   delta del Po, Rome.
Le Roy Ladurie, E., Les paysans de Languedoc, Paris, 1966, 2 vols.
_____. 'L'historiographie rurale en France', in Marc Bloch aujourd'hui.
   Histoire comparée et sciences sociales, Atsma, H. and Burguière, A. (eds),
   Paris, 1989, pp. 223–52.
_____. Histoire humaine et comparée du climat. Canicules et glaciers,
   XIIIᵉ–XVIIIᵉ, Paris, 2004.
Leeghwater, Jan Adriaensz., Haarlemmermeer boek, Amsterdam, [1641] 1710⁷.
_____. Een kleyne Chronycke en de Voorbereydinge van de Afkomste ende't
   vergrooten van de dorpen van Graft en de Ryp, Amsterdam, 1654.
Lemeunier, G. and Pérez Picazo, M.T. (eds), Agua y modo de producción,
   Présentation de P. Vilar, Barcelona, 1990.

Léon, P. (ed.), *Histoire économique et sociale du monde,* Paris, 1977, vols. I and II.

Léon, P. and Carrière, C., 'L'appel des marchés', in *Histoire économique et sociale de la France, 1660–1789,* II, F. Braudel and E. Labrousse (eds), Paris, 1970, pp. 161–215.

Linden, H. van der, *De Cope. Bijdrage tot de rechtsgeschiedenis van de openlegging van de Hollands-Utrechtse laagvlakte,* Assen, 1956.

––––––. 'L'influence de l'eau sur les institutions rurales hollandaises', in *Agricoltura e trasformazione dell'ambiente, secoli XIII–XVIII* (11th Settimana di Studio, Prato 1979), Florence, 1984, pp. 665–82.

Lindlay, K., *Fenland Riots and the English Revolution,* Cambridge, 1982.

Lombardini, E., *Dell'origine e del progresso della scienza idraulica nel Milanese ed in altre parti d 'Italia,* Milan, 1872.

Lombardini, G., *Pane e denaro a Bassano tra il 1501 e il 1799,* Vicenza, 1963.

Lugaresi, L., 'La bonificazione Bentivoglio nella traspadana ferrarese (1609–1614)', in *Archivio Veneto,* 126 (1986), pp. 5–50.

Macías Hernández, A.M., 'Les Îles Canaries, 1480–1525. Irrigation et première colonisation atlantique: le domaine de l'eau', in *Eau et développement,* Ciriacono (ed.), 2004, pp. 37–48.

MacFarlane, A., *The Origin of English Individualism: the Family, Property and Social Transition.* Oxford, 1978.

Maffioli, C.S., *Out of Galileo: the Science of Waters 1628–1718,* Rotterdam, 1994.

Maffioli, C.S. and Palm, L.C. (eds), *Italian Scientists in the Low Countries in the XVIIth and XVIIIth centuries,* Amsterdam, 1989.

Mainardi, Daniele, *Della coltivazione del riso e della coltura dei prati e degli arativi,* Padua, 1792.

Malanima, P., *I piedi di legno. Una macchina alle origini dell'industria medievale,* Milan, 1988.

Malavasi, S., *Giovanni Maria Bonardo. Agronomo polesano del Cinquecento,* Venice, 1988.

Marini, Andrea, *Antichi scrittori d'idraulica veneta. Discorsi,* IV, A. Segarizzi (ed.), Venice, 1923.

Marsigli, Iacopo (ed.), *Nuova raccolta d'autori italiani, che trattano del moto delle acque,* Bologna, 1821–26, 10 vols.

Martini, A., *Manuale di metrologia,* Turin, 1883.

––––––. *Manuale di ragguaglio fra le misure e pesi veronesi ed il sistema metrico decimale e viceversa,* Verona, 1871.

Marzolo, F., 'L'idraulica veneta e l'apporto dell' Università di Padova nelle discipline idrauliche', in *Il diritto dell'uomo al sapere e al libero uso di esso,* G. Ferro, and S. Policardi, (eds), Padua, 1954.

Marzolo, F. and Ghetti, G., *Fiumi, lagune e bonifiche venete: guida bibliografica,* Padua, 1949.

––––––. *Appendice di aggiornamento,* Venice, 1963.

Massé, P., 'Le dessèchement des marais du Bas-Médoc', in *Revue Historique de Bordeaux,* nouvelle série, 6 (1957), pp. 25–38.

Mayhew, A., *Rural Settlement and Farming in Germany,* London, 1973.

McCloskey, D.N., 'The Enclosure of Open Fields: Preface to a Study of its Impact on the Efficiency of English Agriculture in the Eighteenth Century', in *Journal of Economic History,* 32 (1972), pp. 15–35.

Menegazzo, E. 'Alvise Cornaro: un veneziano del Cinquecento nella Terraferma padovana', in *Storia della cultura veneta,* Arnaldi and Pastore Stocchi (eds,) 3/II, 1980, pp. 513–38.

Messedaglia, L., *Per la storia dell'agricoltura e dell'alimentazione*, Piacenza, 1932.
_____. *Per la storia delle nostre piante alimentari. Il riso*, in 'Rivista di Storia delle Scienze Mediche e Naturali', 29 (1938), fasc. I–IV, pp. 17–27.
Meuvret J., *Le problème des subsistances à l'époque Louis XIV. I, La production des céréales dans la France du XVIIᵉ et du XVIIIᵉ siècle, Texte*, Préface by P. Goubert, Paris, 1977.
_____. *Le problème des subsistances à l'époque Louis XIV. II, La production des céréales et la société rurale. Texte et Notes*, Préface by G. Postel-Vinay, Paris, 1987, 2 vols.
Meyer, J., *La noblesse bretonne au XVIIIᵉ siècle*, Paris, 1966.
Micheli, G. (ed.), *Storia d'Italia. Annali 3, Scienza e tecnica nella cultura e nella società dal Rinascimento a oggi*, Turin, 1980.
Mitchell, W.P., 'The Hydraulic Hypothesis. A Reappraisal', in *Current Anthropology*, 14 (1973), n. 5, pp. 532–34.
Mokyr, J., *The Lever of Riches: Technological Creativity and Economic Progress*, New York and London, 1990.
Monkhouse, F.J., *A Regional Geography of Western Europe*, London, 1976.
Morineau, M., *Les faux-semblants d'un démarrage économique: agriculture et démographie en France au XVIIIᵉ siécle*, Paris, 1971.
Mostra storica della laguna veneta (Venice, 11 July to 27 September 1970), edited by the Ministero dell'interno. Direzione generale degli archivi, Venice, 1970.
Mozzi, U., *I magistrati veneti alle acque e alle bonifiche*, Bologna, 1927.
Musset, A., *De l'eau vive à l'eau morte. Enjeux techniques et culturels dans la vallée de Mexico (XVIᵉ–XIXᵉ siècle)*. Paris, 1991.
Needham, J. (ed.) (with the collaboration of Ling Wang and Gwei-Djen Lu), *Science and Civilisation in China. Physics and Physical Technology*, 4/III, Cambridge, 1971.
Nitz, H.-J. (ed.), *The Early Modern World-System in Geographical Perspective* (Conference Acts, Reinhausen/Göttingen, 4–8 April 1990), Stuttgart, 1993.
_____. (ed.), *The Medieval and Early-modern Rural Landscape of Europe under the Impact of the Commercial Economy*, Göttingen, 1987.
O'Brien, P. and Keyder, C., *Economic Growth in Britain and France (1780–1914): Two Paths to the Twentieth Century*, London, 1978.
Ostrom, E., *Governing the Commons: the Evolution of Institutions for Collective Action*, Cambridge, 1990.
Overton, M., *Agricultural Revolution in England. The Transformation of the Agrarian Economy, 1500–1850*, Cambridge, 1998.
Palerm, Á., *Obras hidráulicas prehispánicas en el sistema lacustre del Valle de México*, México City, 1973.
Palissy, Bernard, *Discours admirables de la nature des eaux et fontaines* (Paris 1580), Paris, 1777.
Pallotti, V., 'Domenico Guglielmini sopraintendente alle acque', in *Problemi d'acque a Bologna*, Bologna, 1983, pp. 9–62.
Pegrari, M. (ed.), *Agostino Gallo nella cultura del Cinquecento*, Brescia, 1989.
Pellizzato, M. and Scattolin M. (eds), *Materiali per una bibliografia sulla laguna e sul golfo di Venezia*, Chioggia, 1982.
Pierenkemper, T. (ed.), *Landwirtschaft und industrielle Entwicklung*, Stuttgart, 1989.
Pitteri, M., *Segar le acque*, Treviso, 1984.
Poni, C., *Gli aratri e l'economia agraria nel Bolognese dal XVII al XIX secolo*, Bologna, 1963.

_____. 'Aratri e sistemazioni idrauliche nella storia dell'agricoltura bolognese', in *Studi Storici*, 5 (1964), pp. 633–74.

_____. 'Alcuni problemi di storia della mezzadria nei secoli XIV–XVII', in *Agricoltura e sviluppo del capitalismo*, Rome, 1970, pp. 456–66.

_____. 'Un privilegio d'agricoltura. Camillo Tarello e il Senato di Venezia', in *Rivista Storica Italiana*, 72 (1970), pp. 592–610.

_____. 'All'origine del sistema di fabbrica: tecnologia e organizzazione produttiva dei mulini da seta nell'Italia settentrionale (secoli XVII–XVIII)', in *Rivista Storica Italiana*, 88 (1976), pp. 444–97.

_____. *Fossi e cavedagne benedicon le campagne*, Bologna, 1982.

Porta, Io. Baptista, *Villae libri XII*, Francofurti, 1592.

Pounds, N.J.G. *An Historical Geography of Europe, 1500–1840*, Cambridge, 1979.

Problemi d'acque a Bologna (Conference Acts, Istituto per la storia di Bologna, 10–11 October 1981), Bologna, 1983.

Pullan, B., edited with an introduction by, *Crisis and Change in the Venetian Economy in the 16th and 17th Centuries*, London, 1968.

_____. 'Wage-Earners and the Venetian Economy, 1550–1630', in *Crisis and Change in the Venetian Economy in the 16th and 17th Centuries*, London, 1968, pp. 146–74.

Radkau, J., *Natur und Macht. Eine Weltgeschichte der Umwelt*, München, 2000.

Rapp, R.T., *Industry and Economic Decline in Seventeenth-Century Venice*, Cambridge (Mass.), 1976.

Ravensdale, J.R., *Liable to Floods. Village Landscape on the Edge of the Fens, AD 450–1850*, Cambridge, 1974.

Reuss, M. (Guest editor), *Water Technology in the Netherlands*, Special issue of *Technology and Culture*, 43 (2002), n. 3.

Ringelmann M., *Essai sur l'histoire du génie rural*, Paris, 1905, 4 vols.

Roche, D., 'Le temps de l'eau rare du Moyen Âge à l'époque moderne', in *Annales E.S.C.*, 39 (1984), pp. 383–99.

Rojas Rabiela, T. et al., *Nuevas noticias sobre las obras hidraulicas prehispanicas y coloniales en el Valle de Mexico*. México, 1974.

Romani, M., *L'agricoltura in Lombardia dal periodo delle riforme al 1859. Struttura, organizzazione sociale e tecnica*, Milan, 1957.

Romano, R., *Tra due crisi: l'Italia del Rinascimento*, Turin, 1971.

_____. 'L'Italia nella crisi del secolo XVII', in *Agricoltura e sviluppo del capitalismo*, Rome, 1970, pp. 467–82.

Romano, R. and Vivanti, C. (eds), *Storia d'Italia. 1, I caratteri originali*, Turin, 1972.

_____. *Storia d'Italia. I documenti*, 5/I, Turin, 1973.

_____. *Storia d'Italia. Annali 1, Dal feudalesimo al capitalismo*, Turin, 1978.

Rompiasio, G. , *Metodo in pratica di sommario, o sia compilazione delle leggi, terminazioni, ed ordini appartenenti agl'Ill.mi ed Ecc.mi Collegio e Magistrato alle acque* (Venice 1733), G. Caniato (ed.), Venice, 1988.

Rosenthal, J.-L., 'The Development of Irrigation in Provence, 1700–1860: the French Revolution and Economic Growth', in *The Journal of Economic History*, 50 (1990), pp. 615–38.

_____. *The Fruits of Revolution: Property Rights, Litigation and French Agriculture, 1700–1860*, Cambridge (Mass.), 1991.

Rouse, H. and Ince, S., *History of Hydraulics* (Iowa Institute of Hydraulic Research), Iowa City (IA), 1957–80.

Rozier, Jean-Baptiste François, *Cours complet d'agriculture théorique, pratique, économique, et de médecine rurale et vétérinaire*, Paris, 1781–1805, 12 vols.

Sabbadino, Cristoforo, *Antichi scrittori d'idraulica veneta. Discorsi sopra la laguna,* II, part I, R. Cessi (ed.), Venice, 1930.

Sacco, Bernardo, *De italicarum rerum varietate et elegantia libri X,* Papiae, 1565.

Scarborough, V.L. and Isaac, B.L. (eds), *Economic Aspects of Water Management in the Pre-Hispanic World,* Research in Economic Anthropology, Supplement 7, London, 1993.

Schama, S., *Landscape and Memory,* New York, 1995.

Schultz, E., *Waterbeheersing van de Nederlandse droogmakerijen,* Lelystad, 1992.

Sella, D., *Italy in the Seventeenth Century,* London, 1997.

———. *Commerci e industrie a Venezia nel secolo XVII,* Venice-Rome, 1961.

Serena, A., *Il canale della Brentella e le nuove opere di presa e di derivazione nel quinto secolo dagli inizi,* Treviso, 1929.

———. *Fra Giocondo e il canale della Brentella,* Treviso 1907.

Sereni, E., *Storia del paesaggio agrario italiano,* Bari, 1976 (English translation *History of the Italian Agricultural Landscape,* Princeton, 1997).

Serpieri, A., *La bonifica nella storia e nella dottrina,* Bologna, 1957.

Serres, Olivier de, *Le théâtre d'agriculture, et mesnage des champs* [1600], Paris, 1804–05, 2 vols.

Sigaut, F., *L'agriculture et le feu. Rôle et place du feu dans les techniques de préparation du champ de l'ancienne agriculture européenne,* Paris, 1975.

Sinclair, Sir John, *L'agriculture pratique et raisonnée,* Paris, 1825.

Slicher van Bath, B.H., *The Agrarian History of Western Europe, A.D. 500–1850,* translated from the Dutch by O. Ordish, London 1966.

———. 'La productivité agricole. Les problèmes fondamentaux de la société pré-industrielle en Europe occidentale', in *Troisième conférence internationale d'histoire économique. Production et productivité agricole, Section II* (Munich 1965), Paris, 1969, II, pp. 23–30.

Smith, C.T., *An Historical Geography of Western Europe before 1800* (revised version), London, 1978.

Smith, N., *Man and Water: a History of Hydro-Technology,* London, 1975.

Soppelsa, M.L., 'Le scienze teoriche e sperimentali', in *Storia della cultura veneta., Il Settecento,* Arnaldi and Pastore Stocchi (eds,) 5/II, 1986, pp. 271–345.

Sorcinelli, P., *Storia sociale dell'acqua: riti e culture,* Milan, 1998.

Spufford, M., *Contrasting Communities. English Villagers in the Sixteenth and Seventeenth Centuries,* Cambridge, 1974.

Stefano, Carlo (Charles Estienne), *Agricoltura nuova, et casa di villa,* Venice, 1591.

Stella, A. 'Bonifiche benedettine e precapitalismo veneto tra Cinque e Seicento', in *S. Benedetto e otto secoli (XII–XIX) di vita monastica nel Padovano,* Padua, 1980, pp. 171–93.

Steward, J. (ed.), *Irrigation Civilizations: a Comparative Study. A Symposium on Method and Result in Cross-cultural Regularities,* Westport (Conn.), 1981

Stol, T., *Wassend Water, Dalend Land: geschiedenis van Nederland en het water,* Utrecht, 1993.

Stratico, Simone, *Raccolta di proposizioni d'idrostatica, d'idraulica e d'applicazione di esse alla dottrina de' fiumi, alle costruzioni sopra i loro alvei,* Padua, 1773.

Tagliaferri, A. (ed.), *Relazioni dei rettori veneti. La Patria del Friuli (Luogotenenza di Udine),* I, Milan, 1973.

———. *Relazioni dei rettori veneti in Terraferma, Podestaria e Capitanato di Belluno – Podestaria e Capitanato di Feltre,* II, 1975.

————. *Relazioni dei rettori veneti in Terraferma. Podestaria e Capitanato di Treviso,* III, 1975.

————. *Relazioni dei rettori veneti. Podestaria e Capitanato di Verona,* IX, 1977.

————. *Relazioni dei rettori veneti. Podestaria e Capitanato di Brescia,* XI, 1978.

————. *Relazioni dei rettori veneti. Podestaria e Capitanato di Bergamo,* XII, 1978.

————. *Relazioni dei rettori veneti. Podestaria e Capitanato di Crema – Provveditorati di Orzinuovi e Asola,* XIII, 1979.

Tatti, Giovanni, *Della agricoltura libri cinque,* Venice, 1561.

Tentori, Cristoforo, *Della legislazione veneziana sulla preservazione della laguna,* Venice, 1792.

Thirsk, J. (ed.), *The Agrarian History of England and Wales, 1640–1750. Regional Farming Systems,* V/1, Cambridge, 1984.

————. *The Agrarian History of England and Wales, 1640–1750. Agrarian Change,* V/2, Cambridge, 1985.

————. *The Agrarian History of England and Wales, 1750–1850,* VI, Cambridge, 1989.

Thurkow, A.J., 'De droogmakerij van Bleiswijk en Hillegersberg, een opmerkelijke onderneming', in *Holland,* 22 (1990), pp. 35–44.

————. 'The Draining of the Lakes in the Netherlands (18th–19th Centuries)', in *Eau et développement,* Ciriacono (ed.), pp. 103–16.

Tiepolo, M.F. (ed.), *Laguna, lidi, fiumi. Cinque secoli di gestione delle acque* (Mostra documentaria, Venice, 10 June to 2 October 1983), Venice, 1983.

Tipaldo, Emilio de, *Biografia degli Italiani illustri nelle scienze, lettere ed arti del secolo 18., e de' contemporanei,* Venice, 1834–45, 10 vols.

Trevisan, Bernardo, *Della laguna di Venezia,* Venice, 1718.

Tucci, U., 'L'Ungheria e gli approvvigionamenti veneziani di bovini nel Cinquecento', in *Rapporti veneto-ungheresi all'epoca del Rinascimento,* Budapest 1975, pp. 153–71.

Ulmen, G.L. (ed.), *Society and History. Essays in Honour of Karl August Wittfogel,* The Hague, 1978.

Vacani di Forteolivo, C., *Della laguna di Venezia e dei fiumi delle attigue province,* Florence, 1867.

Veen, J. van, 'Inpoldering in vroegere eeuwen door Nederlanders in het buitenland', in *De Ingenieur,* 1939 (22), pp. 215–19.

————. *Dredge, Drain, Reclaim. The Art of a Nation,* The Hague, 1948.

Ven, G.P. van de (ed.), *Man-made Lowlands: History of Water Management and Land Reclamation in the Netherlands,* Utrecht, 1993.

Ventura, A., 'Considerazioni sull'agricoltura veneta e sull'accumulazione originaria del capitale nei secoli XVI e XVII', in *Agricoltura e sviluppo del capitalismo,* Rome, 1970, pp. 519–60.

Veranzio, Fausto, *Machinae novae,* U. Forti (ed.), Milan, 1968.

Vergani, R., *Brentella. Problemi d'acque nell'alta pianura trevigiana dei secoli XV e XVI,* Treviso, 2001.

Verhulst, A., *Précis d'histoire rurale de la Belgique,* Bruxelles, 1990.

Verhulst, A. and Augustyn, B., 'Deich- und Dammbau', in *Lexikon des Mittelalters,* III, München-Zürich, 1986, pp. 640–48.

Vidal de la Blache, P., *Principes de géographie humaine,* Paris, 1922.

Vidal-Naquet, P.A., *Les ruisseaux, le canal et la mer,* Paris, 1993.

Vierlingh, Andries, *Tractaat van Dijckagie,* edited and introduced by J. De Hullu and A.G. Verhouven, 's-Gravenhage, 1920 (reprint, Rotterdam, 1970).

Vilar, P., *La Catalogne dans l'Espagne moderne,* Paris, 1962, 2 vols.

Vivanti, C., *Le campagne del Mantovano nell'età delle riforme*, Milan, 1959.

Viviani, G.F. (ed.), *La villa nel Veronese*, Verona, 1975.

Vries, Jan de, *The Dutch Rural Economy in the Golden Age, 1500–1700*, New Haven and London, 1974.

———. *Barges and Capitalism: Passenger Transportation in the Dutch Economy, 1632–1839* (A.A.G. Bijdragen, 21), Wageningen, 1978.

Vries, Johan de, *De economische achteruitgang der Republiek in de achttiende eeuw*, Amsterdam, 1968.

Wagret, P., *Les polders*, Paris, 1959.

Wallerstein, I., *The Modern World-System. Mercantilism and the Consolidation of the European World-Economy, 1600–1750*, II, New York and London, 1980.

Wee, H. van der, *The Rise and Decline of Urban Industries in Italy and in the Low Countries*, Leuven, 1988.

Weston, Richard, *Verhandeling over de landbouw in Vlaanderen en Brabant 1644–1645* (1650), P. Lindemans (ed.), Brugge, 1950.

Weulersse, G., *Le mouvement physiocratique en France (de 1756 à 1770)* (1910), La Haye-Paris, 1968, 2 vols.

Wittfogel, K.A., *Oriental Despotism. A Comparative Study of Total Power*, New Haven, 1957.

———. 'The Hydraulic Approach to Pre-Spanish Mesoamerica', in *Chronology and Irrigation*, F. Johnson (ed.), Austin and London, 1972, pp. 59–80.

Woolf, S., 'Venice and the Terraferma: Problems of the Change from Commercial to Landed Activities', in *Crisis and Change*, B. Pullan (ed.), pp. 175–203.

Worster, D., *Rivers of Empire: Water, Aridity, and Growth of the American West*, New York, 1985.

Woude, A.M. van der, *Het Noorderkwartier* (AAG Bijdragen, 16), Wageningen, 1972, 3 vols.

Woude, A.M. van der and Vries, Jan de, *The First Modern Economy: Success, Failure, and Perseverance of the Dutch Economy, 1500–1815* (Amsterdam 1995), Cambridge, 1997.

Zalin, G., 'Economia agraria e insediamento di villa tra Medioevo e Rinascimento', in *La villa nel Veronese*, G.F. Viviani (ed.), Verona, 1975, pp. 51–86.

Zanden, J.L. van, *The Rise and Decline of Holland's Economy. Merchant Capitalism and the Labour Market*, Manchester, 1993.

Zaninelli, S., *Una grande azienda agricola della pianura irrigua lombarda nei secoli XVIII e XIX*, Milan, 1964.

Zeeuw, J.W. de, 'Peat and the Dutch Golden Age', in *AAG Bijdragen*, 21 (1978), pp. 3–27.

Zendrini, Bernardino, *Leggi e fenomeni, regolazioni ed usi delle acque correnti*, Venice, 1741.

——— . *Memorie storiche dello stato antico e moderno delle lagune di Venezia e d fiumi che restarono divertiti per la conservazione delle medesime*, Padua, 1811, 2 vols.

Zonca, Vittorio, *Novo teatro di machine et edificii per varie e sicure operationi*, Padua, 1621.

Zucchini, M., *L'agricoltura ferrarese attraverso i secoli. Lineamenti storici*, Rome, 1967.

Zunica, M., (ed.), *Il delta del Po. Terra e gente al di là dei monti di sabbia*, Milan, 1984.

✎ Index

€ 74.85

€ 45.- €10,-

Btmo6   H